Human Communication Theory

THE HISTORY OF A PARADIGM

Human Communication Theory

THE HISTORY OF A PARADIGM

NANCY L. HARPER

Associate Professor, University of Iowa

Series Editor: Brent D. Ruben,
Rutgers University

HAYDEN BOOK COMPANY, INC.
Rochelle Park, New Jersey

Dedication

To John Waite Bowers, who practices equity in all things except in love where he is extravagant; whose honesty is always leavened by humor; and who thinks never of forever, but always of tomorrow.

P90
H3345

Library of Congress Cataloging in Publication Data

Harper, Nancy L
    Human communication theory.

    Bibliography: p.
    Includes index.
        1. Communication—Philosophy—History.   I. Title.
P90.H3345   001.5′1   79-19851
ISBN 0-8104-6091-2

Printed in the United States of America

2   3   4   5   6   7   8   9   PRINTING

82 83 84 85 86 87   YEAR

Preface

This book is about rhetoric, logic, grammar, poetics, eloquence, belles lettres, and elocution; it is about theories of human communication. It is not about public speaking, interpersonal interaction, individual decision making, creative and expository writing, dramatic performance, photography, film, radio, television, or interactive computers, the products of human communication; yet it is about all of these also. It is a systematic account of the results of twenty-five centuries of study of the products of human communication, study which led scholars to develop generalizations about what communication is, how it works, why it works "better" in some instances than in others, how it can be taught, and what its functions are.

The basic assumption of all these scholars has been that communication is fundamental to every human activity. It is the primary thinking tool. It is the primary socializing tool. It is the process by which humans come to know, believe, and act. As Isocrates explained in the fourth century B. C., "There is no institution devised by man which the power of speech has not helped us to establish." Furthermore, he says, it is through our ability to communicate that we "contend against others on matters which are open to dispute and seek light for ourselves on things which are unknown; for the same arguments which we use in persuading others when we speak in public, we employ also when we deliberate in our own thoughts" (*Antidosis*, 254–255). Many centuries later, in 1967, Berger and Luckmann make similar observations. They explain that the entire structure of everyday reality is created out of our "continually interacting and communicating with others" (*The Social Construction of Reality*, p. 23), that "The most important vehicle of reality-maintenance is conversation" (p. 152), and that language is the basis of personal cognition and awareness, of "identity" (p. 132). In short, theorists throughout history have pointed out that it is through our ability to communicate, to assign meaning to verbal and nonverbal signs, that we individually and collectively create and order our reality.

This book traces the development of our understanding of human communication. It is written for those who teach or plan to teach others "to communicate better." It is also written for students and researchers, for individuals who are looking for analytic tools that will help them better understand how novels work, or why one movie outsells another, or how it is that some people in organizations are more influential, more powerful, than others, or in what sense contemporary communication theory is "neo-Aristotelian," or "sociological," or whatever. More generally, the book is written for anyone whose interest is in the differences and similarities among historical conceptions of communication and in the implications of these for the present and the future.

Based on a reconceptualization of the ancient Greek and Roman paradigm (the "five canons of rhetoric"), the book systematically analyzes theories of human communication from approximately 500 B. C. to the twentieth century. Chapter 1 defines communication and the parts of the paradigm, and identifies contemporary concerns within each part. Chapters 2–5 are analyses of classical, medieval and Renaissance, and modern communication theory in terms of the paradigm. Chapter 6 is an analysis of the invariant concerns in human communication theory. The results of the historical analyses are summarized and their significance examined in light of recent developments in communication research.

The book is the result of many years of thinking and research and of "communication" with a large number of people, both living and dead. Most of these people are acknowledged, in one way or another, in the text. Some, however, deserve special recognition.

De Quincey says that there is a "secret magic lurking in the peculiar life, velocities, and contagious ardour of conversation," an "electric kindling of life" which cannot be found in books or private study. Through conversation, he says, we not only refine our ideas, but we discover ideas we had not previously conceived (*Conversation*, p. 268). I have been singularly blessed with conversational partners throughout my preparation of this book. Among those who not only allowed me to "talk it," sometimes incessantly, a number actively encouraged conversation and provoked me to new enthusiasm and commitment as well as to new ideas.

Special thanks go to John Waite Bowers, who should have became exhausted with the book, but didn't. Larry Martin not only discussed my findings with me, but spurred me to new industriousness by asking me daily "How many pages?" James J. Bradac asked the crucial questions and helped me to keep things in perspective. Linda Lederman allowed me to "pollute" afternoons off at the swimming pool and set an example by finishing her book while actively teaching and pursuing her doctorate. Brent D. Ruben provided the initial provocation for the book and hounded me about it until I left Rutgers. Then he managed to continue the pressure by telephone and letter. Donovan J. Ochs read the manuscript, chapter by chapter, as I wrote it. His criticisms were always thorough and insightful. He read the last chapters under excessive time pressure. Part of Chapters 4 and 5 he read under the most harrowing circumstances known to contemporary man or woman—while flying on a commercial airline in a thunderstorm. I could not tell which comments were made in the air and which were made on the ground. Most important, Donovan always told me to "keep smiling," and he occasionally pursuaded me to leave my typewriter and spend a day boating and picnicking at Coralville Reservoir.

A number of others contributed to this book in more or less direct ways. My mother and father, Joe and Willa Brown, taught me how to think. John C. Lehman, of Emporia State University, gave me my first introduction to "rhetoric" and led me, as a reluctant undergraduate, into Aristotle. Alfred Haefner, professor of classics at Wartburg College, taught me some Greek to go with my less Latin and, in the course of numerous digressions during our tutoring sessions, renewed my philosophia. John M. Wiemann read the original prospectus and wrote on the cover, "Rhetoric never tasted so good." Donald C. Bryant, Douglas Ehninger, and Samuel L. Becker demonstrated scholarship to me. The University of Iowa expected me to do research and provided an atmosphere in which I could. It also supported me with a research grant in summer 1977 and research assistants over three semesters. Jay Swartz helped me collect materials for Chapters 4 and 5. Peter Gross checked quotations for accuracy and took on the boring task of counting words to determine where permissions to quote were required. Loretta Anania proofread the galleys. Also, special thanks to Bob Jones and Carol Schrage who did much of the typing.

NANCY L. HARPER

Contents

Human Communication Theory

THE HISTORY OF A PARADIGM

Chapter 1

The Paradigm

Introduction

Human communication theory has a long and, for the most part, illustrious history. The earliest recorded theories of human communication are those of Plato and Aristotle in the fifth century B.C. Following them, such major thinkers as Cicero, Augustine, Erasmus, Ramus, Bacon, Descartes, Locke, Priestley, De Quincey, J.S. Mill, John Dewey, and Kenneth Burke have contributed major treatises on the subject.[1] In the contemporary academic world, human communication is a major field of study and an area of concern to many disciplines in the social sciences and the liberal arts as well as to many professional fields.

In spite of, or perhaps because of, the volume of research being conducted on human communication processes in diverse areas of study, many communication scholars have noted a lack of unity in the theoretical development of the discipline. Increasingly in the last ten years, communication scholars have begun publishing monographs calling for, or proposing, an integrative framework for human communication theory.[2]

The ultimate justification for this book is its potential contribution to the contemporary search for a unified framework of this sort. Its goal is to discover and trace the development of, and nature of, the invariant concerns in recorded theories of human communication. Its function is to "look backward into the future," in the belief that we can better see where we are and where we are going if we know where we have been.

---

[1] See the Appendix, "A Historical Chronology of Authors and Works," for a more complete listing.

[2] See, for instance, C. David Mortensen, *Communication: The Study of Human Interaction* (New York: McGraw-Hill, 1972), pp. 21–26; Samuel L. Becker, "What Rhetoric (Communication Theory) Is Appropriate for Contemporary Speech Communication?," a paper presented at the University of Minnesota Spring Symposium on Speech Communication, 1968; and Charles R. Berger, "The Covering Law Perspective as a Theoretical Basis for the Study of Human Communication," *Communication Quarterly* (Winter 1977), pp. 7–18.

Purpose and Scope

More specifically, since this book plans to synthesize some twenty-five centuries of thinking and writing about human communication, it may be viewed as a chronicle of the development of human communication theory from the time of its inception in ancient Sicily to the beginning of the twentieth century. It is not a history of specialized applications, i.e., journalism, broadcasting, film, advertising, theatre, linguistics, English, speech, information processing, literature, symbolic interaction, public opinion, human relations, sociology of knowledge, group dynamics, etc. It is a history of thought. It is not an analysis of communicating, but a synthesis of thinking about communication. It is not about how people talk to each other; rather it is about how people have talked about talk.

The basic premise of this history is that the five-part paradigm first developed by early Greek and Roman theorists provides an integrative and heuristic framework for tracing the development of communication theory through the centuries. Thus, the bulk of the book focuses on the treatment of the parts of the paradigm in the works of major theorists. This focus is realized through analysis of three major historical periods: the classical period (500 B.C.–400 A.D.), the medieval and Renaissance periods (400–1600), and the modern period (1600–1900).

This introductory chapter outlines the basic parameters of the paradigm in terms of contemporary thought. Later chapters analyze the nature of communication theory in each of the periods. Emphasis is placed on the cultural and educational needs that give rise to particular variations in the basic conceptions of human communication, but the primary focus is on the treatment of each part of the paradigm. The concluding chapter summarizes the concerns and concepts that have been central to human communication theory since its inception and that will continue to be central to its future development.

Basic Definitions

The paradigm to be used throughout is shown graphically in Fig. 1.1. It includes five fundamental processes, each of which is equally important to understanding human communication both as an act and as a scholarly discipline.

As an act, human communication is the process of "message making." A message may be purely mental; it may take the form of internal conclusions, thoughts, etc. It may also be physical, being operationalized in sounds, pictures, gestures, print, etc., to be transmitted to others. Human beings make messages *from* the persons, objects, and events around them; they receive information and understand it. Human beings also make messages *about* the persons, objects, and events around them; they send information and use it to accomplish goals. As a model of the

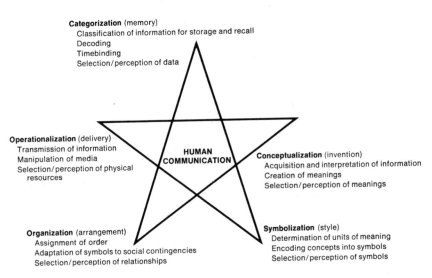

Categorization (memory)
  Classification of information for storage and recall
  Decoding
  Timebinding
  Selection/perception of data

Operationalization (delivery)
  Transmission of information
  Manipulation of media
  Selection/perception of physical
    resources

HUMAN COMMUNICATION

Conceptualization (invention)
  Acquisition and interpretation of information
  Creation of meanings
  Selection/perception of meanings

Organization (arrangement)
  Assignment of order
  Adaptation of symbols to social contingencies
  Selection/perception of relationships

Symbolization (style)
  Determination of units of meaning
  Encoding concepts into symbols
  Selection/perception of symbols

Fig. 1.1   A Model of the Paradigm

communication act, the paradigm can be understood as follows: An individual, whether a sender or a receiver, (1) perceives data—phenomena—which he or she classifies and stores for future use (*categorizes*), (2) assigns meaning to the data in light of some present concern (*conceptualizes*), (3) represents the meaning in symbols (*symbolizes*), (4) adapts the symbols to social contingencies (*organizes*), and (5) embodies the message in some physical form (*operationalizes*). Whether the goal of the act is to understand, to influence, to console, to share, etc., the process remains fundamentally the same. It is not altered by the end result of the act, whether a conversation, a book, a television show, or a social movement.

As a model of the discipline of human communication, the paradigm specifies the areas for research and theory construction. Scholarly attention should focus on (1) categorization, the process of perception, storage, and recall of data, (2) conceptualization, the nature of knowledge and the processes of information acquisition and interpretation, (3) symbolization, the nature of symbols and the processes of meaning-making, (4) organization, the nature of ordering and the processes of relationship, and (5) operationalization, the nature of media, the nature of information transmission, and the processes of symbolic interaction.

Analysis of the Paradigm

Human communication is fundamentally an activity, a process. Therefore, the paradigm must be understood holistically. The star-shaped arrangement of the model in Fig. 1.1 is meant to symbolize the interactive and simultaneous relationship of the five parts. The connecting lines are meant to indicate further the mutual interdependence of the parts. The five parts are shown separately, however, for though symbolization and operationalization, for example, are interdependent, they are not the same phenomena. Symbols are embodied in physical forms (operationalizations), and form affects the decoding of symbols (a categorization process), but symbols, forms, and interpretations are distinguishable aspects of messages. It is impossible to conceptualize data (make sense of it) without organizing it in terms of social contingencies, e.g., a purpose. The area in the middle of the star diagram represents the total integration of the parts. The points of the star indicate the distinctiveness of each of the parts.

Because of the distinctiveness of each of the parts, it is possible to treat them in an ordered sequence. Because of their interaction, however, the order chosen must vary with the purpose of a given analysis. For instance, if the paradigm is to be used as a model of the act of message sending, it makes sense to begin with categorizing, because the data available to a potential sender—the experience stored and classified in his or her mind—is the raw material out of which he or she creates meaning. The second step might be conceptualizing. Here the sender, given a purpose, analyzes and names the various problems, goals, and possibilities. The third step might be symbolizing, the cognitive representation of ideas in appropriate symbols. The fourth might be organizing the symbols into some time order, and the fifth, operationalizing the message in some transmittable form.

If, on the other hand, the paradigm is to be used as a model of message receiving, the process might begin with operationalization, because it is the physical form of the message with which the receiver first interacts. The next step might be categorization, for, having perceived the physical message, the receiver then classifies it as containing certain kinds of information or as being of a particular type or class, e.g., as relevant/irrelevant, as a novel or a poem, etc. The third step might be organization: The message "arrives" in some order and in some context. The fourth might be symbolizing: Messages are made up of collections of symbols to which meanings must be assigned. Finally, we might move on to conceptualization, the interpretation of the message, the receiver's construction of its total meaning in light of his or her categorization processes, habits, and abilities to decode, process, classify, and store information.

The preferable alternative to either of these approaches would be to consider the parts of the paradigm simultaneously rather than in a necessarily arbitrary order. Given the constraints of the print medium and of human psychology, however, such an approach is impossible. Thus, the subsequent discussion of the parts of the paradigm will follow an order based on the process of message sending. Within the discussion of each part, however, attention will also be given to the process of message receiving and to the priorities of theory and research.

Categorization

Categorization is the process of perceiving, storing, and recalling data. Historically, categorization has most often been discussed in terms of sensing, learning, and memory. Perception of data is the fundamental process. Through our senses—sight, hearing, touch, etc.—we perceive objects and events in "reality." Through education and experience, we learn to pay attention to some of these sensations and to ignore others. Those that we notice, we store, and, when a situation arises that makes them relevant, we remember them. The transformation of data into information—that is, the process of assigning meaning or value to stored data—is the conceptualization process.

In terms of message sending, then, categorization immediately precedes conceptualization. Given a particular communication situation, the sender's selection and interpretation of data depend upon his or her classification systems. Certain data stored in the mind are recalled in light of the perceived demands of the situation. Additional information is sought and interpreted in light of the information already stored and of the classifications available to the sender. Whorf's notion of language as classification of reality is consistent with this concept of categorization.[3] What the sender sees as relevant depends upon the symbol system he or she uses to classify and store data. As general semanticists such as Hayakawa point out, we see what we expect to see.[4] In the same manner, the receiver's conceptualization, his or her interpretation of a message, depends partly upon the categorization process. Like the sender, the receiver sees, or hears, what he or she expects to see or hear in accordance with past experiences with symbols and messages.

Again, from the sender's point of view, categorization precedes not only conceptualization but also operationalization. The sender's categorical schemes, methods of storing and recalling information, have important effects upon selection and use of media; that is, choice of medium depends upon categorization of purpose, content, and audience. From the receiver's point of view, expectations about the appropriateness of medium to message affect the ability to perceive the meaning intended by the sender. A televised situation comedy, for instance, is an unlikely vehicle for instructions about how to grow tomatoes, and any attempt to use it in such a manner is unlikely to be perceived as serious.

[3] Benjamin Lee Whorf, *Language, Thought, and Reality: Selected Writings* (Cambridge: Massachusetts Institute of Technology Press, 1956).
[4] S.I. Hayakawa, *Language in Thought and Action*, 2nd ed. (New York: Harcourt, Brace, & World, 1964).

Korzybski's definition of human beings as "timebinders" provides a useful perspective for looking at the role of categorization in the overall communication process.[5] It is our ability to classify, store, and selectively recall information that allows us to construct and maintain our reality. Because we can remember, because we think that one thing is like or unlike another in specifiable ways, we can order our world and share that world with others. Thus, the ability to categorize is fundamental to the human communication process.

Conceptualization

Conceptualization is the acquisition and interpretation of information. It is the process by which an individual assigns meaning to data in light of some present concern. Historically, conceptualization has been discussed in terms of the *discovery* of pertinent information, or research, and in terms of the *creation* of information, or management and use. Generically, we might say that conceptualization can be thought of as both an objective and subjective process.

Essentially, conceptualization is the process Berger and Luckmann characterize as "the social construction of reality."[6] They stress the dialectical nature of the relationship between the objective and subjective world. The basic process is subjective; human beings are the producers of their world. They invent it through their ability to communicate, that is, to interact symbolically. However, human beings are also the product of their world. Through communication, people reify their own subjective creations so that those creations become, in effect, objective realities. Thus, the relationship between "my world" and "our world" is dialectical. Historically, theories of conceptualization have posited much the same relationship between the tasks of discovering objective realities and creating subjective realities, for to conceive of objects or events is not only to perceive them but to interpret them. Human beings not only *sense* their world, they also *make sense* of it.

Acquiring and interpreting information relevant to the goals of the communicator are prerequisite to constructing a message to be sent to others. Acquisition and interpretation are dialectically related in that the information that the communicator defines as relevant depends upon an interpretation of the potential audience, the available information on the subject, the self, and the interrelationships among these factors. The sender must know *self*—goals and capabilities, *audience*—goals and susceptibilities, beliefs, values, and attitudes, and the *cultural milieu*—including the kinds of arguments and evidence that are generally accepted in the

[5] Alfred Korzybski, *Science and Sanity* (Lakeville: The International Non-Aristotelian Library Publishing Co., 1958).
[6] Peter L. Berger and Thomas Luckmann, *The Social Construction of Reality: A Treatise in the Sociology of Knowledge* (Garden City, New York: Doubleday, 1966).

particular society with which the sender is dealing and the cultural rules of appropriateness. Thus, information acquisition is never merely a process of discovering what exists, but always a matter of interpreting "objective" data in terms of the subjective information-processing abilities of the communicator.

Looked at from the point of view of the receiver, the process of conceptualization remains essentially the same. Senders, in the process of deciding what to say, are also receivers; they "audience" previous messages of other communicators. These messages are sources of data to be purposefully acquired and interpreted. Conceptualization in terms of receiving messages, then, is not essentially different. Potential message-senders begin first by audiencing the messages of others. Their receivers audience their message in the same way. Both the potential message-senders and the receivers will construct their own messages (patterns of meanings) out of the messages sent by others. Thus, whether the goal of an individual is to send or receive a message, the process of conceptualization is essentially one of creating meanings out of data.

In research and theory, conceptualization is studied from two basic points of view, analogous to Berger and Luckmann's distinction between subjective and objective sources of reality. In the first, often called *intrapersonal* communication theory, we find the following kinds of topics: predispositions, frames of reference, personal constructs, social schemas, creativity, psychological orientations, consistency, self-perception, cognitive processing, problem-naming, etc. In the second, often called *interpersonal* or social communication, we find problem-solving, decision-making, information acquisition, co-orientation, person perception, audience analysis, social psychology, symbolic interaction, credibility, proof, motivation, etc.

Symbolization

Symbolization is the cognitive representation of meanings in symbols. Historically, it has been viewed primarily as the selection of appropriate words, or *style*. Symbolization, however, includes all symbolic behavior. Nor only words, but actions, such as marches or sit-ins, and contextual clues, such as clothing or furnishings, may have symbolic implications, may potentially elicit meanings. And any symbolic behavior or objects that have suasive potential can be purposively selected to function as symbols. Thus, the symbolization process from the perspective of message-sending may include any and all artifacts or phenomena that can be consciously manipulated to achieve a goal. The basic symbolic unit of a newspaper editorial may be the word, of a film may be the shot, of a social movement may be hairstyle or clothing, of an office may be furniture, and so on.

Whatever the units, the meanings arrived at in the conceptualization process can be elicited in others only through symbolic interaction. The selection of appropriate symbols is a decision that the communicator must make in light of prior decisions about self, available information, and potential audience.

However, the symbolization process is more than the simple act of selecting appropriate symbols. Given that communication is a basic human process, that human beings are constantly metabolizing information,[7] or that humans "cannot not communicate,"[8] symbolization is constantly occurring. We are constantly observing, interpreting, and reacting to our world in symbolic ways—that is, we are constantly receiving and sending messages. Take, for example, the experience of going to visit another person in his or her office. The overall message of the office may be that the inhabitant is busy, important, and cannot be bothered with trivialities. This may be the connotation, or implication, of such items (not generally thought of as symbols) as a clock, a desk and desk chair, a visitor's chair, and a clutter of papers. The clock may suggest the importance of time in the interaction. If it faces the occupant of the office and cannot be seen by the visitor, it may suggest that the occupant is, in effect, "clocking" the time that he or she is "giving up." The isolation of the occupant behind the desk in a chair may be an assertion of dominance of the interaction. The provision of an uncomfortable chair for the visitor may further emphasize the temporariness of the visitor's presence and the one-up/one-down or controller/petitioner relationship. The clutter of papers on the desk top may reinforce the idea that the occupant has more important things to do and is only temporarily suspending this work in order to attend to the visitor.[9]

The occupant of the office may have purposely designed it in order to send such message or may be unaware that it does so. In either case, the visitor is free to create such a message if he or she so chooses.

Thus, the symbolization process is one of assigning meanings to symbols, from either the point of view of the sender or the receiver of messages. For the sender, it is a matter of attempting to predict the receiver's most likely responses to a given symbol; for the receiver, it is a matter of attempting to understand the sender's predictions and intentions.

Communication scholars categorize symbols in terms of dimensions such as *denotation* (literal meaning) and *connotation* (affective meaning) and distinguish between *form* (context or genre) and *content* (meaning). The symbolization process is discussed in terms of *syntactics* (the relation-

---

[7] For discussion of this concept, see George A. Miller, *Language and Communication* (New York: McGraw-Hill, 1962).

[8] For discussion of this concept, see Paul Watzlawick, Janet Helmick Beavin, and Donald Jackson, *Pragmatics of Human Communication* (New York: W. W. Norton & Co., 1967).

[9] The symbolism of offices is discussed in Michael Korda, "Office Power—You Are Where You Sit," *New York Magazine* (January 1975), pp. 36–44.

ships among symbols), *semantics* (the relationships among symbols and meanings), and *pragmatics* (the relationships among symbols, meanings, and behaviors). However, the major emphasis in the communicative study of symbolization has most commonly been on pragmatics, on the function of symbols in light of the nature of meanings, receivers, senders, and occasions. Technical and artistic considerations have generally been viewed as secondary, as merely instrumental, to the pragmatics of symbols in use.

Organization

Organization is the adaptation of symbols to social contingencies. It is the study of the nature of ordering and relationship. Historically, organization has been viewed as the process of arranging information in time and/or space in light of the functional relationships among salient variables, including persons, symbols, statements, events, or places.

In organizing a message to be sent to others, we usually say that, whether it is an editorial, a novel, a speech, a film, or whatever, it must have an introduction, a body, and a conclusion, and that these parts must have significantly different content and placement. We also tend to categorize message organization in terms of primacy vs. recency effects, deductive vs. inductive patterns of development, two-sidedness vs. one-sidedness, and in terms of the ordering of evidence, examples, emotional and logical appeals, etc. Issues such as these must be taken into account and resolved in the design of a message, either consciously or unconsciously.

On a more basic level, the ordering of the contents of a message depends on the needs of, and relationships among, the participants in the communicative interaction, on the statements to be made and the relationships between them, and on the context of the interaction. Thus, the organization of the "same" message necessarily varies, depending upon who is involved, and where, and why. The sender who, in organizing a message, takes into account appeals, sidedness, patterns of development, etc., but ignores such human factors as time, situation, and relationship, has failed in the most fundamental part of the organization phase, having failed to adapt the message to social contingencies.

From the receivers' point of view, a well-organized message, one that conforms to their expectations in its construction, is easier to follow. Furthermore, as Burke explains, form is in itself an important message, informing the receiver that the sender is properly socialized, conscientious, knowledgeable, and concerned about the auditors.[10] And, perhaps even more important, form has a special aesthetic effect over and above specific content; it may not only reassure an audience but may be a source of pleasure in itself.

---

[10] See Kenneth Burke, *Philosophy of Literary Form* (New York: Vintage Books, 1957).

In communication theory and research, organization is discussed in terms of interpersonal concepts such as situational geography, communication networks, interaction patterns, heterophily and homophily, etc. Organization also receives attention in terms of public, or societal, concepts such as hierarchies, bureaucracy, diffusion patterns, information networks, reference groups, cultural norms, genres, etc.

Operationalization

Operationalization is the embodiment of a message in some physical form. It is the mediated transmission of information, the process of symbolic interaction. Historically, operationalization theory has focused on the selection, use, and impact of media.

The physical form that a message takes is, of course, extremely important to the sender's categorization, conceptualization, symbolization, and organization of the content. A film and a novel are different "things." As we know, some concepts that are easily expressed in words are resistent to visual expression. For instance, a novelist can easily tell us that "George sat for three hours not thinking about anything at all." Though a film maker can use conventional techniques to show time passing, visual representations of time are necessarily more ambiguous than verbal ones. More significant, it is virtually impossible to express "not thinking" visually. Form, in other words, does affect content.

In terms of message receivers, the physical appearance of the message is their first clue to the meaning intended by the sender. For instance, an opening shot of a crowd of people, bright colors, and rapid movements creates different expectations from an opening shot of a grey, cloudy, and "empty" landscape. Of course, the individual communicator, whether sender or receiver, views the physical message in light of prior experiences with such forms (categorization processes) and experiences with meanings, symbols, and relationships relevant to the message.

In terms of communication theory and research, the human body and voice have traditionally been primary concerns in operationalization theory. Nonverbal communication has generally been viewed as the impact of form upon content. Thus, a communicator may "say one thing" in words and quite another in facial expression. In print messages, similar conflict is possible. For instance, advertisements in the form of a "personal" letter, which say "you are our dear and good friend" but are addressed to "occupant," are universally regarded as incongruous. The proliferation of electronic media has led to a growing concern about the "message" of the medium. For instance, many critics believe that television violence is socially dysfunctional, because they fear that the impact of visual messages (the police "have to" beat up the "bad guys" in order to get a confession) may be stronger than the impact of the conceptual message that violence (robbing a liquor store and shooting the owner) never pays. Certainly, they point out, the visual and conceptual messages conflict. Many television programs, in fact, seem to "teach" that violence works when all else fails, or even that violence is so effective that "all else" is a waste of time and effort.

Finally, we might note that the academic departmentalization of communication studies into such categories as speech, journalism, mass media, theatre, broadcasting, film, etc., is evidence of the general belief that operationalization is a key factor in both the act and the study of human communication.

An Illustration of the Paradigm

Human communication is a complex process. The above exposition of the process in terms of the parts of the paradigm is necessarily incomplete. The next five chapters should begin to fill the gaps. Before turning to the history of the paradigm, however, an extended example of the workings of the paradigm in a "real life" situation may serve to clarify some basic ideas.

Normally, a discussion of "How I wrote this book" is reserved for the preface. In this case, however, I believe that it might more usefully be included at this point to illustrate the functioning of the paradigm as a whole.

This book is a human communication about human communication. As I worked on it, I was constantly struck by the reflexiveness of it. In rough chronological order, this is what I believe happened.

Like most messages, this book is a response to a situation. In large part, it grew out of a series of violations of my categorization system, a system developed over thirty years of experience. In terms of the conception of this project, however, the most significant of those was my two years of graduate study at the University of Iowa. In my graduate program I "learned" about the field of human communication.[11] From Donald Bryant and Donovan Ochs I learned that it was an ancient discipline, and that the Greeks and Romans called it "rhetoric," whereas the medieval and Renaissance scholars called it "eloquence." From Douglas Ehninger I learned that modern theorists revised it significantly and began to call it "communication," though they still sometimes called it rhetoric, or eloquence, or even composition and belles lettres. I also learned that a group of contemporary scholars still used the term "rhetoric" to describe their field of study, though others used the term "communication." From Sam Becker and John Bowers I learned that communication research was the study, usually using experimental

[11] Due to my personal categorization system, of course, what I "learned" may not have been what I was "taught."

methods, of theories garnered from "rhetorical" theory. From Jim Bradac I learned that interpersonal and small group communication had a "rhetoric," and from Dudley Andrew I learned that visual media did also.

When I graduated, I felt that I "belonged" to an orderly and ancient discipline. Then I got my first job. I began reading introductory communication textbooks. The more I read, the more I realized that my categorization of the field differed in a systematic way from that of a number of other scholars. For example, in the first chapter of Mortensen's *Communication*, I read the following:

> Since the so-called science of human communication cuts through so many fields, it cannot, in a strict sense, claim to be a single discipline at all. It is rather, as Schramm . . . indicated, an extraordinarily active crossroads of research and theory, a focal point of the social sciences that Lasswell . . . called the "very center of contemporary intellectual concern."[12]

I was, of course, more than willing to view communication as a "central" concern, but I found it difficult to adjust to the idea that it was not a "discipline."

In conversations with my colleagues, I discovered similar differences. When some of them talked about "old" communication theory, I learned that they meant the theories of Lewin and Schramm.[13] "Old" meant thirty or forty years ago. To me, "old" meant twenty-five hundred years ago. One day, as Brent Ruben, Dave Davidson, Louie Bender, and I were constructing a model to be used in one of our courses, I observed that what we had done was to reinvent the classical "five canons" model. My observation was met with blank stares.

In short, after a number of similar experiences, I conceived of the need for a book which would concisely summarize the origins of human communication theory and provide a consistent framework for defining the discipline.

Given this basic conception, I began to search for relevant data. My categorization of the field led me to certain authors, e.g., Aristotle, Cicero, Bacon, and Campbell, and to certain scholars who had done research on the history of rhetoric and communication. Somewhere along the way, I conceived of my focus as theoretic rather than operational; therefore, I was able to rule out histories of public address, journalism, and for the most part, histories of literary criticism. I constructed bibliographies, read a number of specialized histories of particular

[12] C. David Mortensen, *Communication: The Study of Human Interaction* (New York: McGraw-Hill, 1972).
[13] For examples of Kurt Lewin's approach, see Dorwin Cartwright and Alvin Zander, *Group Dynamics: Research and Theory* (New York: Harper and Row, 1953); for Wilbur Schramm's, see Wilbur Lang Schramm, *Communication in Modern Society: Fifteen Studies of the Mass Media* (Urbana: University of Illinois Press, 1948).

theorists and periods as well as more generalized statements on the field of communication and its intellectual roots. And, of course, I reviewed my graduate study notes (to my amazement at all that I had once known!).

As I conceptualized and categorized, searched and researched, and made notes, I was constantly thinking about symbolization and organization. Terminology (use of symbols) was a problem. The terms "communication," "rhetoric," "eloquence," "discourse," "oratory," etc., were all used to symbolize the "same thing" on occasion, but not always. Also, I had to keep in mind my contemporary audience and their symbolization, their concepts for these terms. In reference to organization, I had formed a general commitment to chronological order, and I knew that in operationalizing I would need an introduction and conclusion. But I needed something more specific to help me decide what to say and where to say it.

I talked to many people about my ideas and my organizational problems. Gerry Miller suggested an organization based on epistemological movements. Linda Lederman suggested a sender/receiver/message organization. I thought about a "major theorists" or a cultural and educational "revolutions" organization. My categorization system led me to review previous research for answers. There were precedents in the literature for all of these and more. What kept recurring, however, was the conceptual model my colleagues and I were using in our survey course. As I discussed "information acquisition" with my students, I found myself telling them about "artistic and inartistic inventional theory" as developed by classical theorists. Eventually, as should now be obvious, I settled on the paradigm shown in Fig. 1.1 as the central organizing framework. Epistemology, process models, major theorists, and cultural and educational trends became secondary and tertiary organizational factors.

Over the three years I worked on this project, I continually revised and refined my initial decisions. My categorization system changed from time to time. For instance, some theorists that I had assumed would be "major" because they had written books with "rhetoric" in the title turned out to be less relevant than others who symbolized their subjects in titles like *Metalogicon* or *Lectures on Criticism*. I regularly, in the early stages, reconceptualized. For instance, one day as I was writing the intitial draft of this chapter, I realized that I had been thinking of the project as a "history of communication theory," but I suddenly understood that it was "really" a history of *the paradigm*. From then on, I was able to improve the efficiency of my research; my reading and notetaking, my conceptualizing and categorizing, became much more productive, for I knew more clearly what to look for. As I prepared to write each chapter, I began operationalizing my conceptions of the parts of the paradigm. For instance, as I read each major work, I took notes in six categories— nature and province of communication theory, categorization, conceptualization, symbolization, organization, and operationalization. If I found something important that I could not "fit" into one of these categories, I made a temporary category for it. Eventually I was either able to find a place for it or to decide that it was not relevant.

In symbolizing my ideas, I was constantly striving to overcome the problem of terminology. I began, of course, by defining ancient concepts and drawing equivalances between and among symbols. I also tried to construct sentences in ways that I hoped would reveal the contemporary implications of archaic-sounding terms. As I operationalized at my typewriter or with a pen and yellow pad, I strove to "remember" my purposes. I wrote myself notes like "That's all very interesting, Harper, but what does it have to do with symbolization?!" Or, "All you have to do is STATE IT and PROVE IT. Be calm, dummy!" I constantly struggled with the problem of representing dynamic processes in a static medium. Operationalization interfered with conceptualization and symbolization. It also interfered with organization. I was plagued by the awareness that what I would say ten pages later would help explain what I was saying "now," but that *something* had to come first; I could not say everything at once.

In the final stages, I wrote from my notes. I gathered all the notes on, for instance, symbolization in modern theory. I made notes on my notes. I labeled and relabeled each quotation or paraphrase. I classified "like" quotations in order to discover an organizational pattern. I made "figures" to guide myself and my eventual reader. I often felt like a beginning journalism student doing one of those "scrambled outline" exercises. I frequently had to return to the original sources to make sure that my interpretations of particular quotations fit with the context from which they were taken. Sometimes they did not, and I had to reconceptualize a major section. Often I found that I had twice as many pages of notes as I needed in order to explain a concept. Every time I discarded a page of notes I was aware that I was throwing away material gathered at great expense of time and energy. It was like discarding a piece of my life. It was throwing away *my* words, *my* thoughts, *my* classifications, *my* writing, *my* ordering.

As I wrote, I was also conscious of a number of physical constraints. It seemed to me that, conceptually, I could have written forty or fifty pages on some days. But operationally, the typewriter, and my fingers, could go only so fast.[14] And after seven or eight hours of sitting, the body rebels. A human being also must sleep a certain number of hours out of

[14] At one point, my frustration led me to try dictation. It was a miserable failure. I believe that this is because (1) I am a child of the print age, and (2) the ideas with which I was working were too complex to be organized and symbolized in an oral medium. I had to be able to see the words on paper in order to know if they would work. Also, my ultimate goal was a *book*. To operationalize a print product orally is as inappropriate, to me, as to "write" a painting.

every twenty-four. Whenever I was actively writing, I dreamed my manuscript nearly every night; I not only conceptualized, I operationalized; I wrote hundreds of pages. But the next day I again confronted reality. I was never able to write more than twenty pages in a day. Most days I was lucky to complete ten. Some days, those when I was beginning to write a new chapter, for instance, I would find that ten hours of work resulted in only four pages of finished manuscript. Then, of course, there were those days when I "realized" that I had lost my way, that the fifty-two pages I had accumulated were no good. They had to be thrown away. I had to start over. I felt betrayed. I felt as though the words I had written had taken control and carried me away through some mysterious power of their own. I developed a new conception of the phrase "to struggle with words."

In a sense, it was in the operationalization that I ultimately conceptualized. Fortunately, at this stage, I did not "talk" only to myself. From time to time, my friends would ask how I was doing or where I was in my work. One day, as I discussed Erasmus' notion of "copia" with Larry Martin, I suddenly became aware that it was an early version of Bradac's "lexical diversity" research and I "knew" better what I wanted to say about it. Another day, I expressed my fascination with Campbell's "wish-fulfillment" theory of persuasion to John Bowers. That led us into a conversation about subjective-expected-utility theory which helped me to clarify my written explanation. In a letter to John Wiemann I mentioned that I had discovered a number of references to social conversation in Aristotle, Augustine, Bacon, De Quincey, *et al.* In the process of explaining to him why I thought he might find them interesting (that is, in the process of operationalizing), I clarified my own understanding (my conceptualization). Such occurrences were so frequent that I cannot begin to cite them all. Certainly I "learned" something nearly every day from the courses I was teaching.

Conclusion

This example illustrates some of the complexity of human communication. It also illustrates the interrelationships among the parts of the paradigm. Categorization, conceptualization, symbolization, organization, and operationalization are processes that take place throughout the process of framing and implementing a message. One does not "end" when another "begins." As I write, I think. As I think, I write, and so on, and so on.

The "success" of the ultimate outcome, of course, is relative. This particular endeavor has been successful because it is finished, and I like it. Whether it will have impact on anyone else, or be useful to someone, only anyone and someone can know.

Chapter 2

The Classical Period

The classical period of human communication theory spanned some 900 years, from approximately 500 B.C. to approximately 400 A.D. It began with the rise of democracy in ancient Greece, was extended and refined through the years of the Roman empire, and came to a close with the rise of Christianity in the fifth century A.D. The period can be characterized as consisting of three general phases: (1) initial awareness of communication as an area of scientific study, (2) development of the paradigm, and (3) adaptation and decline of the paradigm.

Phase 1: Initial Awareness

Initial awarness of communication as a potential discipline occurred in early Sicily. Although there is considerable evidence of man's interest in the nature of communication prior to the fifth century B.C. (as in the *Old Testament*, the Babylonian epic *Gilgamesh*, the Egyptian *Precepts of Kagemni and Ptah-Hotep*, Homer's *Iliad*), we have no records of any systematic study of the communication process before then.[1]

According to later theorists, especially Cicero and Aristotle, human communication theory was "invented" by Corax of Syracuse. In the fifth century B.C. the citizens of Syracuse deposed their tyrannical government and established democratic rule. After the revolution, the courts were deluged with suits for the return of confiscated property. Tradition credits Corax with writing an "Art of Rhetoric" designed to instruct citizens in the legal communication skills necessary for the conduct of these suits.[2]

[1] See D. A. G. Hinks, "Tisias and Corax and the Invention of Rhetoric," *Classical Quarterly* (1940), pp. 169-178; George A. Kennedy, "The Earliest Rhetorical Handbooks," *American Journal of Philology* (1959), pp. 169–178; Stanley Wilcox, "The Scope of Early Rhetorical Instruction," *Harvard Studies in Classical Philology* (1942), pp. 121–155, and Douglas Ehninger, "History of Rhetoric and Public Address," in *Introduction to the Field of Speech*, ed. by Ronald F. Reid (Glenview, Illinois: Scott, Foresman and Co., 1965), pp. 164–183.

[2] See Plato, *Phaedrus*, 266C–267B.

Corax's student, Tisias, is thought to have introduced his teacher's theories to Athens in approximately 428 B.C.[3] The initial reaction to the Corax/Tisias theory was apparently intense and widespread. Within a very short time there appeared a number of teachers of "rhetoric" who found a ready supply of pupils, and the major philosophers began to examine, and publish treatises on, this new discipline.

As with most significant innovations in human history, the study of communication as a science came into existence as a practical response to social exigencies. Initially, the impetus was the legal entanglement resulting from the overthrow of the tyrants in Syracuse. The later proliferation of communication study throughout Greece was in response to the demands of the Greek social structure, which was oral, democratic, and communal.

In ancient Greece, business, government, law, education, and entertainment all primarily involved oral communication. As George Kennedy explains:

> Greek society relied on oral expression. Although literacy was clearly extensive in fifth- and fourth-century Athens, even then reading and writing, whether on stone, bronze, clay, wood, wax, or papyrus, was difficult and unnatural. Both the mechanics of ancient civilization and its primary expression remained oral. The political system . . . operated through the direct speech of the citizens. . . . The judicial system was similarly oral. . . . There were written business contracts, but they were negotiated and enforced by face-to-face argument. . . . There were no newspapers, magazines, handbills, or circulars; information was spread orally. Entertainment was provided only to a limited extent by reading; informal conversation, the legitimate stage, or the sound of the human voice in some form constituted the commonest form of diversion.[4]

Thus, the social structure of the society demanded oral skills in a variety of communicative situations.

The Greek legal system required that each citizen be his own lawyer. For many years, the Athenian could not hire a professional to speak for him in court. Each Athenian jury consisted of several hundred persons, and the citizen, whether the accuser or the accused, had to use his ability as a public speaker to persuade a majority of the jury to believe in his side of the case.[5] Because lawsuits were common in Athens, legal speaking became the central concern of early communication instruction.

[3] See Donald C. Bryant, ed., *Ancient Greek and Roman Rhetoricians: A Biographical Dictionary* (Columbia, Missouri: Artcraft Press, 1968).
[4] George Kennedy, *The Art of Persuasion in Greece* (Princeton: Princeton University Press, 1963), pp. 3–4.

Corax and Tisias' theory focused on the demands of courtroom speaking. They defined "rhetoric" (the Greek word for human communication theory) as the "craft of persuasion." The theory centered on techniques for arguing from probability, i.e., establishing the most probable conclusions—given no conclusive evidence to prove either guilt or innocence—in light of what we know of typical human behavior. The argument that a person charged with theft is probably guilty if he has once been convicted of theft is an argument from probability. In addition to this central notion, which remains at the core of later classical theory, the Corax/Tisas doctrine specified the three parts of a public speech: introduction, proof or refutation, and conclusion. Because their "Art of Rhetoric" no longer survives, and we have only the reports of later theorists to go on, we do not know what other topics it may have included.[6]

Soon after Tisias' introduction of the idea that public speaking could be taught as an art, a number of rhetoric instructors began to refine the basic theory taught in the "Art of Rhetoric." These instructors, called *sophists,* were usually traveling teachers. Protagoras (485–415 B.C.) was one of the earliest. He created debating exercises that eventually became a standard part of communication instruction. Focusing on legal speaking, he believed that a skilled communicator could almost always defeat an unskilled opponent whatever the "real" merits of his position. He was accused by the philosophers of teaching the art of "making the weaker appear the better case." His often quoted "Man is the measure of all things" undoubtedly contributed to his disrepute among philosophers like Socrates and Plato, who believed in the existence of objective truth. Protagoras' conception of truth and reality as social construction (an early symbolic interactionist point of view) was in direct conflict with academic "science." As we will see, however, it was Protagoras' view that ultimately became central to classical human communication theory (especially, as will be discussed later, in the works of Aristotle and Cicero).

A second area of Athenian culture that contributed to the rapid proliferation of human communication theory was the democratic political system. Citizens were expected to participate personally in government. Leaders, would-be leaders, and special interest groups were required to present their ideas publicly, and orally. Since decisions were made by a majority vote of the citizenry, the individual who could communicate most effectively with the most people was the one who was most likely to become politically powerful.[7] The early sophists quickly realized the need for, and potential profit to be gained from, instruction in political speaking.

[5] M. J. Cary and J. J. Haarhoff, *LIfe and Thought in the Greek and Roman World* (London: Methuen and Co., Ltd., 1940).
[6] Bryant, pp. 30–31.

Antiphon (448–411 B.C.) was one of the first sophists to extend the concept of "rhetoric" to include political as well as legal communication. He opened a school of communication in which he taught both judicial and legislative speaking. He also taught stylistic techniques, such as the use of the periodic sentence (a construction in which the central point is expressed at the end of the sentence) and of antithesis, and is credited with creating a standard organizational format made up of an introduction, background statement, presentation of facts, presentation of argument, proof and evidence, and a conclusion. He used debating exercises to instruct students in the practice of speaking but went beyond the practical to develop a broader conception of rhetoric as a technical discipline. He was also a successful logographer (professional speech writer) and is traditionally credited with having begun that profession.[8]

A third aspect of Athenian society requiring public communication skills was the ceremonial gathering. As a communal society, Athens was characterized by frequent public ceremonies. Celebrations of holidays and special events, public funerals for heroes, etc., all called for speeches to characterize the event appropriately. The oral reading of fiction or poetry or the recitation of ancient stories was a common entertainment at social gatherings. The sophists early realized that these kinds of events called for communication skills similar to, but different from, legal and political events. The most famous, or infamous, of the sophists made ceremonial communication the center of his instruction.

Gorgias of Leontini arrived in Athens from Sicily in 427 B.C., and within four years he had established a school of rhetoric and a national reputation. He was most celebrated, and attacked, for his emphasis on ornamental language; he is quoted in later works as having claimed that "poetry is prose with meter."[9] In terms of human communication theory, his contribution lies primarily in his extension of rhetorical theory to include ceremonial (literary) as well as legal and political communication. As we will see, he represented to the philosophers the worst of sophistic rhetoric. His personal view of communication as an art of verbal display was repugnant to those who believed that the discipline, if it were to become a reputable area of learning, must be concerned with more "serious" matters.

These early teachers established the first boundaries of human communication theory. From their teaching it became apparent that successful human communication was more than a simple knack or an inherent ability. As Aristotle, the first true theorist among the classical writers, explained in the first paragraph of his *Rhetoric*:

---

[7] Cary and Haarhoff, p. 29.
[8] Bryant, p. 4.
[9] James J. Murphy, ed., *A Synoptic History of Classical Rhetoric* (New York: Random House, 1972), p. 10.

To a certain extent all men attempt to discuss statements and to maintain them, to defend themselves and to attack others. Ordinary people do this either at random or through practice and from acquired habit. Both ways being possible, the subject can plainly be handled systematically, for it is possible to inquire the reason why some speakers succeed through practice and others spontaneously; and every one will at once agree that such an inquiry is the function of a science (1345a 3–11).[10]

Before the beginning of the second phase in classical human communication theory—the development of a paradigm—the basic outlines of this science were established. Preparadigmatic theory focused on public speaking; oral communication was a given and remained so throughout the period. Plato has Gorgias say of human communication theory, "Its whole activity and efficacy is by means of speech" (*Gorgias,* 450E).[11] Though the major theorists did deal, briefly, with written communication, the primary mode of operationalization was oral, unmediated, and public. Furthermore, classical communication theory was situation-bound. On the basis of their observations of the needs of their culture, the sophists developed a taxonomy for later theoretical development that comprised the demands of legal (forensic), political (deliberative), and ceremonial (epideictic) communication situations. They also established the basic agreement that human communication theory must include attention to symbolization (style) and organization (arrangement) as well as operationalization (oral delivery) and categorization (memory). Their development of the concept of argument became an important part of conceptualization theory later in the period. The lack of unity in the sophistic conception of rhetoric—no one sophist seemed to deal with all of the issues relevant to a complete theory—and the extremely prescriptive nature of their instruction led to criticism from the philosophers and, eventually, to the development of the full classical paradigm.

Phase II: Development of the Paradigm

Two figures stand out as bridges between the first stirrings of interest in communication as a science and the development of that science. One, Plato, was an academic philosopher. The other, Isocrates, was

---

[10] Aristotle, *Rhetoric and Poetics,* translated by W. Rhys Roberts (New York: Random House, The Modern Library, 1954). Most of the subsequent references to this work in the text are to this translation. On occasion I have used my own translation from the Greek text in the Loeb Classical Library Edition.

[11] Plato, *Gorgias,* translated by Benjamin Jowett, in *The Dialogues of Plato* (Chicago: Great Books of the Western World, Encyclopaedia Britannica, Inc., 1952). All subsequent references to Plato's works in the text are to this edition.

generally viewed as a sophist, although he expended a great deal of energy attempting to defend his standing as a philosopher.

Plato (427–347 B.C.) was a pupil of Socrates (470–399 B.C.) and makes Socrates the speaker in his dialogues on human communication theory. Plato was a serious critic of Athenian social life. He was especially convinced that Greek democracy had resulted in public rejection of the ideals of truth and justice. Though he served as a statesman for a brief period during his middle age, he spent most of his life in philosophic contemplation. His primary influence was through his teaching in a grove known as "Academus." This "academy" eventually became a formal school that lasted from the fifth century B.C. until the Roman Emperor Justinian closed it in 529 A.D.—a span of nearly 900 years. [12]

By the time Plato began writing, "rhetoric" had become an integral part of Greek academic life. As H. I. Marrou points out in his *A History of Education in Antiquity*, "Rhetoric [was] the specific object of Greek education and the highest Greek culture." Furthermore, he says that rhetoric was "the queen of subjects" and "higher education meant taking lessons from the rhetor." [13] By the time Plato began his career, schools of rhetoric had begun to compete successfully with schools of philosophy, and the general citizenry were more aware of, and more attracted to, rhetorical than to philosophical teachings. Thus, as a philospher, social critic, and educator, Plato inevitably found himself in conflict with the sophists. His most severe attack on sophistic rhetoric is in the dialogue *Gorgias*.

In this dialogue, Plato has Socrates, the ultimate philosopher, hold a dialectic on the nature of "rhetoric" with Gorgias, the ultimate sophist. Predictably, Gorgias is shown to be something of a charlatan. Plato has Gorgias define rhetoric as:

> [T]he ability to persuade with speeches either judges in the law courts or statesmen in the council chamber or the commons in the Assembly or an audience at any other meeting that may be held on public affairs. And I tell you that by virtue of this power you will have the doctor as your slave, and the trainer as your slave; your money-getter will turn out to be making money not for himself but for another—in fact for you, who are able to speak and persuade the multitude (450 A).

Having drawn this definition from Gorgias, Plato (through Socrates) goes on to conclude that rhetoric is not a science but merely a knack (like cooking), that it depends not upon knowledge of right and

---

[12] Murphy, 1972, pp. 15–18.
[13] H. I. Marrou, *A History of Education in Antiquity* (New York: New American Library, 1956), pp. 267–268.

wrong but upon knowledge of human weaknesses to achieve its goals. Worst of all, according to Plato, teachers of rhetoric claim to impart virtue to their students through instruction in this "art of contention."

In the years following the writing of the *Gorgias*, however, Plato continued to think about the nature of human communication and eventually published the dialogue *Phaedrus*, which is an outline for a scientific, or "philosophic," theory of human communication. This outline forms the basis of Aristotle's later, fully developed, science of human communication. Plato claims that rhetoric, to become a scientific body of knowledge, must include a study of knowledge (conceptualization), a study of the nature of words (symbolization), a study of the nature of human beings and their ways of approaching life (categorization), a study of the nature of order (organization), and a study of the instruments by which human beings are affected (operationalization). Finally, he adds that a science of communication requres its practitioners to have a high moral purpose acceptable to God.

Plato adds that if there is to be a science of communication, it must be concerned not only with public speaking but with human communication in general. In *Phaedrus* he has Socrates say:

> Is not rhetoric, taken generally, a universal art of enchanting the mind by arguments; which is practised not only in courts and public assemblies, but *in private houses also*, having to do with *all matters*, great as well as small, good and bad alike (261; emphases mine).

Plato's most famous student, Aristotle, makes a similar statement in his *Rhetoric*:

> The use of persuasive speech is to lead to decisions. (When we know a thing, and have decided about it, there is no further use in speaking about it.) This is so *even if one is addressing a single person* and urging him to do or not to do something, as when we scold a man for his conduct or try to change his views: the single person is as much your 'judge' as if he were one of many; we may say, without qualification, that any one is your judge whom you have to persuade (1391b 7–13; emphases mine).

Another early Greek thinker who influenced the development of a paradigm for the study of human communication was Isocrates (436–338 B.C.). Popularly known as a sophist, Isocrates was a pupil of Socrates, like Plato, but also studied under Protagoras and Gorgias. Referred to by later writers as "The Old Man Eloquent," and as the "Father of Eloquence," Isocrates was most well-known for his school of rhetoric from which, according to Cicero, the major statesmen "came forth like the true chieftains from the Trojan horse" (*De Oratore* II. 94).[14] Isocrates claimed that

---

[14] Cicero, *De Oratore*, translated by H. Rackham (Loeb Classical Library, Cambridge. Harvard University Press, 1949). All subsequent text references are to this translation.

he taught "political philosophy," but, according to his contemporaries as well as later reporters, and based on the evidence of his surviving works, the foundation of his instruction was "rhetoric." Isocrates' dislike for the term "sophist" and his disassociation of himself from that term was not without foundation. The rhetoric he taught was more in line with the guidelines laid down in Plato's *Phaedrus* than with the practices of Gorgias, et. al. He viewed human communication as the *sine qua non* of social organization. In *Antidosis* (254) he writes, "There is no institution devised by man which the power of speech has not helped us to establish."[15] Though the primary focus of his instruction was on public political speaking, he, like Plato, thought of rhetoric as potentially a general science of human communication:

> With this faculty [the power of communication] we both contend against others on matters which are open to dispute and seek light for ourselves on things which are unknown; for *the same arguments which we use in persuading others when we speak in public, we employ also when we deliberate in our own thoughts;* and while we call eloquent those who are able to speak before a crowd, we regard as sage those who most skillfully debate their problems in their own minds (255; emphasis mine).

Isocrates clearly thought of training in communication as training for life: "People can become better and worthier if they conceive an ambition to speak well, if they become possessed of the desire to be able to persuade their hearers, [and] the power to speak well and think right will reward the man who approaches the art of discourse with love of wisdom and love of honor" (274–280).

Unlike the early sophists, who taught lists of commonplace arguments, Isocrates insisted that conceptualization depends upon a thorough education in history, politics, law, music, etc. Rather than drilling his students in "catch phrases" and similar stylistic tricks, Isocrates required them to develop skill in symbolization through extensive reading, writing, and careful revision of their own compositions. He required training in music for developing a feeling for rhythm and formal organization. He believed that reading great works of literature and discussing the ideas found there developed skill in categorization. Practice (through class exercises) and observation of the outstanding leaders of the present and the past, he believed, developed not only the student's skill in operationalization but also his moral sense. In sum, Isocrates conceived of rhetoric as a general theory of human behavior and the highest human

---

[15] Isocrates, *Antidosis*, translated by Larue Van Hook (Loeb Classical Library, Cambridge. Harvard University Press, 1944). All subsequent references in the text are to this translation.

culture. His influence was felt throughout the classical period not only in the conduct of public life—his students were among the greatest statesmen—but also in the treatises of the major communication theorists, Aristotle and Cicero.

Rhetoric, in the initial phase of the classical period, was thought of primarily as a technical skill. It consisted of a set of prescriptions for delivering public speeches in the courts, legislative assemblies, and other public gatherings. It consisted of rules for gathering materials, organizing them into messages, and delivering them orally to large groups of people. Under the scrutiny of thinkers and teachers like Plato and Isocrates, however, rhetoric began to emerge as a general science of human communication.

It was Aristotle (384–322 B.C.), Plato's student and a contemporary of Isocrates, who first gathered the scattered bits and pieces of theory and prescription into a unified theory of human communication. Aristotle studied with Plato until the latter's death in 348 B.C. He then spent twelve years teaching, first at the court of Hermias in Assos and later at the court of Philip of Macedon. He returned to Athens in 335 B.C. where he set up a school in the grove of the Lyceum. According to tradition, "in the mornings he lectured on philosophy and on the logic and methodologies of the sciences, in the afternoons on ethics, politics, and rhetoric" (Bryant, ed., 1968, pp. 15–16). Aristotle published treatises on all of these subjects. In terms of the history of human communication theory, however, the most significant work is his *Rhetoric*, which shows his familiarity with the teachings of the sophists and of course with Plato and in which he manages to combine the best of both approaches, achieving in the process a blend of both the philosophic and the pragmatic.

The *Rhetoric* is arranged in three parts. Books I and II are primarily devoted to conceptualization theory—what Aristotle called "invention." His major criticism of earlier thinking about communication is that it overlooked this most important aspect of the process. In Book I he examines the general nature of human communication theory, defining it as a science concerned with understanding human thought and action through analysis of language behavior. Its central concern, he says, should be with the "modes of proof," with how human beings arrive at conclusions, how they maintain them, and how they interact with others who have arrived at conclusions of their own (*Rhetoric*, 1354a 3–14). In Book I he also gives his definition of human communication theory *qua* theory. He defines it as the "science of observing in any given case the available means of persuasion" (1355b 26). In other words, it is concerned with the study of instrumental behavior, with methods of studying how people influence one another in various contexts. He also sets forth his theory of conceptualization (see Fig. 2.1), in which categorization is viewed as a subprocess. Book I, then, deals with methods of acquiring information in light of the categorization systems of the potential auditor(s). Book II continues to develop conceptualization and categorization theory but the emphasis shifts from the auditor to the speaker and the content of messages. Book III focuses on the processes of symbolization, organization, and operationalization (which Aristotle labels "style," "arrangement," and "delivery"). These more pragmatic aspects of the study of communication processes were of less interest to Aristotle—less susceptible, he thought, to theorizing—and thus he devotes much less space to them.

In addition to the *Rhetoric*, Aristotle published several treatises dealing with subjects related to communication. Most of these are referred to in the *Rhetoric* and their relevance explicated. The following are of special interest to communication scholars: *On Poetics* (an analysis of imaginative communication), the *Organon* (a collection of treatises analyzing the processes of reasoning), *On Memory and Reminiscence* (an analysis of categorization), the *Nicomachean Ethics* (an analysis of the goals of human behavior), and the *Politics* (an analysis of the nature of human organization).

Aristotle's *Rhetoric* established human communication theory as a respectable academic discipline. It also established the boundaries of the full classical paradigm.

We do not know exactly how, or when, or by whom, the paradigm was "invented." We only know that it was sometime between the publication of the *Rhetoric* and the first century B.C. No major treatises survive from this two-hundred-year period, and later writers tell us little about what may have been occurring. We do know that the most important academic activity took place at Alexandria, the site of the largest library in the ancient world. Tradition tells us that it was a center for scholarship that included many buildings in which were housed several hundred thousand book rolls. The Alexandrian scholars reportedly "edited a standard version of Homer's *Iliad*, wrote commentaries . . . on existing treatises in a variety of subjects, and . . . [collected] a definitive set of Aristotle's works."[16] They also developed a standard list of the ten most important Greek orators.

We also know that the early Roman treatises on human communication reveal few major new developments, that they are primarily summaries of the works of the sophists and of Plato, Isocrates, and Aristotle. Furthermore, we know that rhetoric continued to be a dominant subject in the educational system,[17] and that the early Roman rhetorics treat the paradigm as a given. They assume that the reader knows of it and that it is the standard way of defining the field. From all these facts, we can only assume that educators of the first and second century B.C. developed the

---

[16] Murphy, 1972, p. 77.
[17] Marrou, pp. 267–282.

paradigm from their understanding of the works of the early Greeks and that the Alexandrian scholars perpetuated it through their codification systems.

Although Aristotle never explicitly sets forth the full paradigm, it is implicit in the overall organization of the *Rhetoric*. In Book III, which is devoted primarily to the communication act, he lists four of the five dimensions of the paradigm as the "points" to be studied by the communicator: "the means of producing persuasion (invention)," "style, or language, to be used," "proper arrangement of the various parts of the speech," and "the proper method of delivery" (1403b 5–21). Memory, the fifth dimension, Aristotle treats explicitly only in a separate treatise, *On Memory and Reminiscence*. Given that Aristotle was the most influential of the early Greeks, his *Rhetoric* is a likely source of the later universal acceptance of the paradigm.

The early Romans first treated the paradigm as a model of the communication act. The earliest extant Roman rhetoric, the anonymous *Rhetorica Ad Herrenium* (c. 100 B.C.), presents the dimensions as steps in the practice of communicating. These were commonly referred to as the "five canons" (also as the "five arts" or the "five faculties") of rhetoric. The first step was *invention*, the process of deciding what to say. Second was *style*, selecting the appropriate words with which to say it. Third was *arrangement*, organizing the message into parts. Fourth was *memory*, storing the matter, style, and arrangement in the mind. Fifth was *delivery*, disseminating the message. Although the *Ad Herrenium* is a very prescriptive textbook, rather than a theoretical treatise, this use of the paradigm as a model was common in Roman writings. In fact, the longevity of the paradigm can probably be attributed in part to its dual function as model for the practice of, and framework for the study of, human communication.

The classical theorists were, for the most part, both theoreticians and professional communicators, and the impetus for the development of communication as a discipline was a pragmatic one. Thus, classical theory is characteristically pragmatic. The distinction between theory and practice was maintained in the language ("rhetoric" was the theory and "oratory" was the practice) of the discipline, but the two were not infrequently merged so fully that it was difficult to determine which was being referred to. (We obviously have the same problem in the contemporary period with our terms "communication" and "communicating.")

In spite of this potential source of confusion, the major classical theorists treated the "five canons" not only as a model but as a theoretic paradigm. Thus, *invention* was defined as the study of the nature of knowledge, of the methods of information acquisition and interpretation. *Style* was the study of the nature of language. *Arrangement* was the study of the processes of ordering and relationship. *Memory* was the study of the processes of information storage and recall—theoretically an integral part of the investion process. And *delivery* was the study of the nature of information transportation systems—theoretically closely related to style and arrangment.

The major elaboration of the paradigm must be credited to Cicero. In fact, it is commonly referred to as "Ciceronian." Marcus Tullius (Tully) Cicero (106–43 B.C.) is known as a major figure in the history of philosophy, law, literature, and politics as well as of human communication. He was a practicing lawyer from 81 B.C. until his death. He was a prominent statesman and rose to the position of Consul in 63 B.C. In 44 B.C., after the assassination of Caesar, he was a leader of republicanism and the major opponent of Antony . He died a political martyr in 43 B.C. when he was executed for his opposition to Antony.

He enjoyed a reputation as Rome's greatest orator and in the history of oratory is ranked with Demosthenes as the world's most outstanding speaker. Many of his speeches were published and survive to testify to his skill. He wrote several treatises on literature and philosophy as well as on rhetoric. His earliest treatise on communication is *De Inventione* (86 B.C.), a highly prescriptive textbook written when he was only twenty years old. It sets forth the standard rules for the invention, arrangement, and style of messages. Cicero later repudiated the work as not representative of his mature thinking on the subject, but it remains useful to historians as an example of the prescriptive tradition in classical rhetoric, and it was a major source for medieval and renaissance scholars.

Cicero's major work on human communication theory is *De Oratore* (55 B.C.) which examines the full classical paradigm from a primarily theoretic point of view. He includes most of the precepts of the traditional schools of rhetoric and examines them in light of his experience as a professional communicator, but, like Aristotle, he goes beyond description to explanation and investigation of rhetoric as a general theory of human communication. *De Oratore* contains the best of Cicero's thinking on the subject. His later works add some depth to the ideas presented in *De Oratore* but do not include any totally new developments. *Topica* (44 B.C.). is a more technical treatise on the topical approach to conceptualization (invention). *Brutus* (46 B.C.) is a history of Roman oratory and gives depth to Cicero's concept of operationalization. *Orator* (46 B.C.) includes more detail on the technicalities of language. *Partitiones Oratoriae* (54 B.C.) presents a summary of Ciceronian rhetoric. Written presumably as a study guide for his son, it covers the major tenets and divisions of classical theory in a straightforward, terse, nontheoretic manner.[18]

In *De Oratore*, Cicero divides human knowledge into three branches: the "mysteries of nature," the "subtleties of dialectic," and

---

[18] See Bryant, pp. 27–28, and Donovan Ochs, "Cicero's Rhetorical Theory" in Murphy, *A Synoptic History of Classical Rhetoric*, pp. 90–92.

"human life and conduct." The first two he says are the province of the philosophers, but the third "has ever been the orator's province" (*De Oratore*, I. xv. 68). Thus, Cicero concludes, communication is a science concerned with people and their interactions. In scope, he says:

> [I]t embraces the origin and operation and development of all things, all the virtues and duties, all the natural principles governing the morals and minds and life of mankind, and also determines their customs and laws and rights, and controls the government of the state (*De Oratore*, III. xx. 76).

Cicero's conception of the nature of human communication is directly traceable to Isocrates, who conceived of it as *the* significant activity of humankind. As H. I. Marrou puts it:

> [I]n the eyes of the ancients, eloquence [skillful communication] had a truly human value transcending any practical applications that might develop as a result of historical circumstances; it was the one means for handing on everything that made man man; the whole cultural heritage that distinguished civilized men from barbarians.[19]

Communication was the ultimate science to Cicero not only because it was fundamental to his notion of the nature of human beings, but also because it was the means by which cultural reality was created. As he explains in *De Oratore*, the subject matter of human communication theory includes:

> [A]ll things relating to the intercourse of fellow-citizens and ways of mankind, or concerned with everyday life, the political systems, our own corporate society, the common sentiments of humanity, natural inclinations and morals (II. xvi. 68).

Thus, through his ability to communicate, the human being creates organized societies with socially accepted concepts of right and wrong, maintains those societies, and passes them on to future generations.

Like his intellectual ancestors, Isocrates, Plato, and Aristotle, Cicero conceived of the functions of communication as including much more than simple persuasion. He lists warning, teaching, comforting, and encouraging as important uses (*De Oratore*, II. xv. 68).

Cicero's conception of human communication as an activity and as a subject of study includes the whole of what in our own period is known as the social sciences. He uses the five canons as the organizing paradigm

[19] Marrou, p. 270.

for his discussion of the boundaries of human communication theory, defining the ultimate communicator as one "who, whatever the topic that crops up to be unfolded in discourse, will speak thereon with *knowledge, method, charm,* and *retentive memory,* combining these qualifications with a certain *distinction of bearing*" (*De Oratore,* I. xv. 64; emphases mine).

In other words, mastery of the field of communication requires that the scholar/practitioner be skilled in all areas of human knowledge (he lists social organization, politics, psychology, morals and ethics, law, history, philosophy, mathematics, music, and geometry as basics). Knowledge is acquired from skill in *invention.* Method requires understanding of the nature of organizing and results from skill in *arrangement.* Charm comes from skill in the use of symbolic forms, from *style.* Retentive *memory* is developed through years of disciplined study, and distinction of bearing (*delivery*) from observation, practice, and physical exercise.

Cicero's works represent the peak of classical human communication theory. "Rhetoric" began as a set of precepts for the presentation of public, usually legal, speeches. It consisted of set formulae for constructing and delivering messages designed to outmaneuver an opponent. The focus was on arousing the emotions of the audience through graphic description. Rhetoric was not a science, but a trade with a set of teachable "tricks." Throughout the classical period, textbooks continued to be written that took this point of view.

Within a brief span after its initial introduction into Athens, however, "rhetoric" also began to be conceived of as a scientific discipline. Plato's criticism of sophistic prescriptivism gave impetus to the development. His outline of a philosophical rhetoric set the goal. Isocrates' high moral and ethical demands set the tone. And Aristotle's philosophical analysis of the nature of human interaction set the boundaries. In Aristotle and Cicero we see the extension of the concept of rhetoric to include all of human interaction, not just public speaking. In the works of these major theorists, rhetoric became a theory of symbolic behavior. The public communication situation remained prototypical, but both major theorists clearly understood the pervasiveness of communication at all levels of human interaction. Instrumentality remained a significant part of the defining nature of their theory, but both Aristotle and Plato recognized the importance of functions other than immediate goal satisfaction. Finally, both realized the futility of attempting to prescribe practice without a theoretical framework as well as the emptiness of theory without reference to practice. Thus, the best of classical theory was ultimately operational.

After the death of Cicero there were few new developments in human communication theory. Only one name stands out as an important contributor to Roman theory. M. Fabius Quintilian (35–95 A.D.)

was holder of the first endowed chair of rhetoric in the Roman Empire. Known primarily for his distinction as an educator, Quintilian is important to the history of human communication theory primarily as a synthesizer of some five hundred years of thought. His *Institutes of Oratory* (approx. 93 A.D.) is a summary of the collective thinking on human communication from Plato and Isocrates to Cicero.[20] This work, consisting of twelve books, was of enormous influence throughout the medieval and Renaissance period, and, for the centuries during which Aristotle's *Rhetoric* was lost to scholars, served as a primary source for early Greek theory. The *Institutes* is a treatise on communication education, covering the training of the "citizen-orator" from birth to retirement.

In his preface, Quintilian describes the contents of the books:

> My first book will be concerned with the education preliminary to the duties of the teacher of rhetoric. My second will deal with the rudiments of the schools of rhetoric and with problems connected with the essence of rhetoric itself. The next five will be concerned with Invention (in which I include Arrangement). The four following will be assigned to Elocution [style], under which head I include Memory and Delivery. Finally there will be one book in which our complete orator will be delineated; as far as my feeble powers permit, I shall discuss his character, the rules which should guide him in undertaking, studying and pleading cases, the style of his eloquence, the time at which he should cease to plead cases and the studies to which he should devote himself after such cessation (i. Preface 21–22).[21]

Thus, the *Institutes of Oratory* represents a complete statement of the nature of rhetoric and its function in the everyday life of the citizen of the classical world. It offers little that is new or startling but provides a fitting climax to the second phase of classical human communication theory—the development of the basic paradigm.

After Quintilian, as we shall see, theorizing came to a virtual standstill. Treatises from the last three hundred years of the classical period reveal a concern with *maintaining* the Aristotelian/Ciceronian paradigm rather than with *developing* it. Before turning to the history of the decline, however, we must detail the nature of theory within each part of the paradigm.

Conceptualization

The classical period is rich in theories of conceptualization. Conceptualization was treated under the heading of "invention," meaning the process of "finding out" what could be said about a particular subject.

---

[20] Bryant, 1968, pp. 90–91.

[21] Quintilian, *Institutiones Oratoriae*, translated by H. E. Butler (Loeb Classical Library, Cambridge: Harvard University Press, 1922). All subsequent references in the text are to this translation.

The Greek and Romans developed a complex taxonomy of the process, which is summarized in Fig. 2.1.

Fig. 2.1   Classical Taxonomy of Conceptualization

I. Inartistic—discovered materials; data; research
   A. Laws
   B. Statements of Witnesses
   C. Contracts
   D. Statements made under torture
   E. Oaths
II. Artistic—Created materials; modes of proof
   A. The "Commons"—Sources of probable arguments relevant to all situations and subjects
      1. The possible and impossible
      2. Past fact
      3. Future fact
      4. The greater and lesser
   B. Special Topics—Sources of arguments relevant to special situations and subjects (see Fig. 2.3)
      1. Deliberative situations
      2. Forensic situations
      3. Epideictic situations
   C. Generic Modes of Proof—For all situations and subjects, each may be achieved through use of the commons and the special topics
      1. Ethos
      2. Pathos
      3. Logos
         a. Example
         b. Enthymeme
            (1) From signs and probabilities (some of the latter take the form of maxims)
            (2) From the formal topics (see Fig. 2.4 for 28 species)

Conceptualization is that branch of human communication theory concerned with the acquisition of knowledge. Theorists such as Cicero saw it as closely related to philosophy. In *De Oratore,* Cicero explains that the communicator must:

> fully comprehend the matter he speaks about. . . . [He] will not be able to achieve what he wants by his words unless he has gained profound insight into the characters of men, and the whole range of human nature, and those motives whereby our souls are spurred on or turned back. And all this is to be the special province of philosophers, nor will the orator, if he take my advice resist their claim; but when he has granted their knowledge of those things . . . still he will assert his own claim to the oratorical treatment of them (I. xi. 48; xii. 53–54).

This statement is reminiscent of Plato's *Phaedrus:*

> He who is to be a rhetorician must know the various forms of soul
> . . . various classes of speeches. . . . [why] men of a certain sort are
> easily persuaded by speeches of a certain sort for a certain reason to
> actions or beliefs of a certain sort, and men of another sort cannot
> be so persuaded . . . when he has acquired all this, and has added
> thereto a knowledge of the times for speaking and for keeping
> silence, and has also distinguished the favorable occasions . . . and
> all the classes of speech . . . then, will his art be fully and com-
> pletely finished (268C).

Though most of the surviving treatises contain some treatment of
the necessity for, and methods of, acquiring and interpreting data, classical conceptual theory is almost wholly Aristotelian in its particulars. The
above quotation from the *Phaedrus* is a general outline of the content of
Aristotle's *Rhetoric*, which is devoted primarily to the topic of knowledge
acquisition. Aristotle's definition of human communication theory as
"the science of discovering, in any given case, the available means of
persuasion" (1355b 26) subordinates all other aspects of human communication theory to the processes of conceptualization. Aristotle says
that earlier treatises on human communication "have constructed but a
small portion" of the subject. They have concentrated on nonessentials,
such as the arousing of emotions, and ignored the process of discovering
the available means of persuasion, which process is the heart of the
discipline (1354a 15–16).

Kinds of Conceptualization   To Aristotle, neither Plato's injunc-
tions to know the "truth" of human nature nor the sophists' prescriptions
for arousing emotions were sufficient to explain the process of acquiring
and utilizing information to achieve specific communicational goals. He
therefore offered a taxonomy of the process, which eventually became a
staple part of conceptual theory. He posits two genre of conceptualization: (1) artistic, and (2) inartistic. He defines these as follows:

> By the latter I mean such things as are not supplied by the com-
> municator but are there at the outset—witnesses, evidence . . .
> written contracts, and so on. By the former I mean such as we can
> ourselves construct by means of the principles of rhetoric. The one
> kind has merely to be used, the other has to be invented (1355b
> 36–1356a).

The inartistic mode of conceptualization corresponds to what we
now call *research*—the collection of factual data, like statistics,
statements of authorities, laws, etc. This mode of conceptualization Aristotle considered inferior in persuasive potential to the artistic mode. His

point was that artifactual evidence is impotent until it is combined with interpretive evidence, or arguments, which define the significance of the data in relation to the goals and values of those involved in the decision-making process.

The ultimate function of communication, according to Aristotle, is to "aid in the making of decisions" (1377b 21) in those areas in which there is no necessary "truth":

> Most of the things about which we make decisions, and into which therefore we inquire, present us with alternative possibilities. For it is about our actions that we deliberate and inquire, and all our actions have a contingent nature; hardly any of them are determined by necessity (1357a 25).

Thus, the ineffectiveness of inartistic data is inherent in the nature of the most common subjects about which people communicate. The artistic modes are obviously more important, for these are what ultimately enable one interpretation of the data, one "truth," to triumph over another. A public confronted with two or more conflicting assessments of the effects of fictional violence on young children chooses between them not on the basis of "research" but on the basis of which side presents its research in the most compelling manner.

Artistic Sources of Material   Aristotle distinguishes three basic sources of artistic materials: (1) the commons, (2) the special topics, (3) the modes of proof.

The notion of "topics" played an important part in classical conceptual theory. The Greek word for topics is *topoi*, which translates as "places" where arguments can be found. The "places" were, of course, metaphorical and referred to categories of ideas, beliefs, and values which could serve as a basis for arguments. The topics were thus analytic guides. The commons, though not literally topics, were part of the topical system and served as guides to subject analysis; the special topics served as guides to situational analysis.

The Commons   The commons represent a sociology of knowledge approach to information acquisition and utilization. Working from his basic premise that communication theory must be concerned with socially accepted concepts of "truth," Aristotle developed a set of four generic assertions representative of current conceptions of reality. These, he claimed, were the general lines of argument applicable in all communication situations—"the commons." He argued that anyone who had occasion to speak on any subject to any audience would use these lines of argument and would find them to be socially compelling (1393a 12–15).

Aristotle called the first common "the possible and impossible." He explains that it works from the belief that "if it is possible for one of a pair of contraries to be or happen, then it is possible for the other." He gives a series of examples of the lines of arguments growing out of this topic:

> [I]f of two similar things one is possible, so is the other. . . . if the harder of two things is possible, so is the easier. . . . if the beginning of a thing can occur, so can the end; for nothing impossible occurs or begins to occur. . . . if that which is posterior in essence or in order of generation can come into being, so can that which is prior: thus if a man can come into being, so can a boy. . . . anything is possible the first step in whose production depends on men or things which we can compel or persuade to produce it, by our greater strength, our control of them, or our friendship with them (1939a 7–27).

The second common is "past fact." It posits that

> if the less likely of two things has occurred, the more likely must have occurred also . . . if one thing that usually follows another has happened, then that other thing has happened . . . for instance . . . if a man had the power and the wish to do a thing he has done it; for every one does do whatever he intends to do whenever he can do it, there being nothing to stop him. . . . Of all these sequences some are inevitable and some merely usual. The arguments for the *non*-occurrence of anything can obviously be found by considering the opposites of those that have been mentioned (1392b 14–35).

The third common, which works similarly, is "future fact." Thus, "a thing will be done if there is both the power and the wish to do it . . . if the means to an end have occurred, then the end is likely to occur; thus, if there is a foundation, there will be a house" (1393a 1–10).

Finally, the fourth common yields arguments about the "greatness and smallness of things." Aristotle explains, "The 'great' is that which surpasses the normal, the 'small' is that which is surpassed by the normal; and so with 'many' and 'few.' " Further, this topic leads to ordering of classes: "If the largest member of one class surpasses the largest member of another, then the one class surpasses the other; and if one class surpasses another, then the largest member of the one surpasses the largest member of the other. Thus, if the tallest man is taller than the tallest woman, then men in general are taller than women [and] conversely" (1363b 5–25).

The commons constituted a general problem-naming scheme. The classical theorists did not consider them "logical" in the technical sense. Aristotle claims that his list grew out of empirical observation of everyday argumentation. The commons are thus psycho-logical—that is, they function as logically compelling deduction, or as warrants for belief, though they do not meet the criteria of philosophical implication. His point is that, because of the principle of probability, there is some universality in the kinds of arguments human beings consider reasonable, whatever the subject under consideration. Thus, Aristotle claims, any communicator—whether his subject is war and peace, a work of art, or criminal law—will use the commons and should consider them carefully in his initial analysis of his subject.

Special topics   The second major source of materials for conceptualizing consists of the special topics. Aristotle conceived of these as growing out of (1) the specific subject to be discussed, and (2) the nature of the occasion. He says:

> Whether our argument concerns public affairs or some other subject, we must know some, if not all, of the facts about the subject on which we are to speak and argue. Otherwise we can have no materials out of which to construct arguments. I mean, for instance, how could we advise the Athenians whether they should go to war or not, if we did not know their strength, whether it was naval or military (1396a 5–10).

One of the primary values of human communication theory, according to Aristotle, was that it provided a method for discovering the information necessary to make decisions on human affairs. The special topics were an analytic scheme for discovering the relevant information about a particular subject given a specific kind of occasion.

Aristotle posits three general kinds of occasions within which communication may occur (see Fig. 2.2). These correspond to the three areas

---

Fig. 2.2   Genres of Communication Situations

I. Deliberative (political)
  A. Divisions—Exhortation and dehortation
  B. Time—Future
  C. Ends—Expediency and inexpediency
II. Forensic (legal)
  A. Divisions—Accusation and defense
  B. Time—Past
  C. Ends—Justice and injustice
III. Epideictic (ceremonial)
  A. Divisions—Praise and blame
  B. Time—Present
  C. Ends—Honor and dishonor

of public life in which the citizens of Athens, and of the later Roman republic, were most frequently involved—politics, law, and public ceremony. He specifies the exigencies, constraints, and purposes appropriate to each genre. For the first two genres he also lists "special topics" about which the communicator ought to be knowledgeable (see Fig. 2.3).

Fig. 2.3   Special Topics Growing out of Communication Situations

I. Deliberative (when deciding on the expediency of a proposed course of action)
  A.   Ways and means (e.g., financial and material resources)
  B.   War and peace (e.g., military strength, past performance)
  C.   National defense (e.g., strategic points, strengths and weaknesses)
  D.   Imports and exports (e.g., areas of self-sufficiency and dependence)
  E.   Legislation (e.g., nature of laws, forms of constitutions, history of the country)
II. Forensic (when deciding on the justice of an action)
  A.   Wrongdoing—Motives, perpetrations, victims
  B.   Law—Special (written statutes) and general (social conceptions of right and wrong)
  C.   Causes of human action
    1.   Involuntary—Chance, nature, compulsion
    2.   Voluntary—Habit, reasoning, anger, appetite
III. Epideictic (when deciding on the "goodness" of an action, event, object, or person)
  A.   Virtue (e.g., justice, courage, temperance, magnificence, magnanimity, liberality, gentleness, prudence, wisdom)
  B.   Vice (the opposites of the virtues)

The first of these is the *deliberative* situation, of which political decision-making is the prototype. Deliberative situations are those in which the problem is to decide on a course of action appropriate to future goals. Policy decisions are the outcome of deliberative situations. The communicator's task is to establish goals and to distinguish between means in terms of expediency and inexpediency. Deliberative communication, then, is characterized by exhortation of one set of means and ends and dehortation of other sets.

The second kind of situation is the *forensic,* of which the judicial system is an example. Forensic situations are those in which the problem is too characterize a past event accurately. Judgments are the outcome of forensic situations. The communicator's task is to classify the event as either right or wrong, just or injust. Forensic communication, then, is characterized by accusation and defense.

The third genre of situation is the *epideictic,* or ceremonial. Religious and patriotic occasions, state funerals, national successes or failures all call for spokespersons who can place events in a context. Thus epideictic situations are those in which the problem is to explain the present.

Appreciation is the outcome of an epideictic situation. The communicator's task is to classify the event in terms of the prevailing concepts of honor and dishonor, virtue and vice. Epideictic communication, then, is characterized by praise and blame.

Modes of Proof   The third major source of materials for conceptualizing is the modes of proof. Aristotle begins his *Rhetoric* by saying that "all men attempt to discuss statements and to maintain them, to defend themselves and to attack others. Ordinary people do this either at random or through practice and from acquired habit . . . [but] it is possible to inquire the reason why some speakers succeed" (1354a 3–10). This sort of inquiry, he says, is the function of science. Rhetoric, he says, is potentially a science of communication, but earlier treatises "have constructed but a small portion" of the subject; they have ignored the "modes of persuasion [which] are the only true constitutents of the art: everything else is merely accessory" (1354a 12–13). The modes of persuasion, also referred to as "modes of proof," are the three constitutents of the communication act that influence the receivers' judgment.

The first of these is *ethos*, the receiver's perception of the character of the speaker. Every major classical theorist recognized the importance of this mode of artistic proof. Isocrates says,

> [T]he man who wishes to persuade people will . . . apply himself above all to establish a most honorable name among his fellow-citizens; for who does not know that words carry greater conviction when spoken by men of good repute . . . and that the argument which is made by a man's life is of more weight than that furnished by words? (*Antidosis*, 285).

Cicero argues, in *De Oratore*, that one of the most important factors in successful persuasion "is for the characters, principles, conduct and course of life [of the communicator] to be approved . . ." (II. xliii. 182).

Aristotle's conception of ethos differed from those of his contemporaries in that he was more concerned with the audience's perception of the communicator as a result of his message. Reputation, like laws, witnesses, etc., is inartistic, a given fact which the communicator must use. What was important to Aristotle was the artistic creation of personal credibility (1356a 4–12). He says:

> There are three things which inspire confidence in the orator's own character—the three, namely, that induce us to believe a thing apart from any proof of it: good sense, good moral character, and goodwill. False statements and bad advice are due to one or more of the following three causes. Men either form a false opinion through want of good sense; or they form a true opinion, but because of their

moral badness do not say what they really think; or finally, they are both sensible and upright, but not well disposed to their hearers, and may fail in consequence to recommend what they know to be the best course (1378a 6–13).

Following this introduction, Aristotle devotes eighteen chapters to discussion of the cues that will lead auditors to perceive the speaker as credible. Given his belief that interpretation, rather than data, is the most important means of influence, Aristotle considered these cues among the most important knowledge to be gained from the study of human communication. His explication of the sources of credibility constitutes a social psychology of early Greek society.

The second mode of artistic proof is *pathos*, or emotional proof. *Pathos* is often translated as "emotional proof," but a more accurate synonym would be "empathetic" proof. As Aristotle explains, an involved communicator "always makes his audience feel *with* him" (1408a 24; emphasis mine). According to Cicero, whose *De Oratore* draws heavily on the *Rhetoric*,

> [It] is impossible for the listener to feel indignation, hatred or ill-will, to be terrified of anything, or reduced to tears of compassion unless all those emotions . . . are visibly stamped or rather branded on the advocate himself (II. xliii. 182).

Apparently, pathos was the major mode discussed in treatises preceding Aristotle, for he opens the *Rhetoric* with an attack on writers who concentrate on the methods of arousing emotional responses. He writes that appeals *to* the emotions warp the judgment, preventing the auditor from making the best decision: "It is not right to pervert the judge [the receiver] by moving him to anger or envy or pity—one might as well warp a carpenter's rule before using it" (1354a 25). Aristotle's point is not that emotional appeals are morally or ethically wrong, but that they may lead to a lack of control in the communication situation. Once the receiver's anger, envy, or pity, etc., has been aroused, it may be impossible for him, or for the source, to channel those emotions toward any desirable judgment or action. Thus, Aristotle condemned the earlier theorists whose predominant concern was with prescriptive rules for emotional appeals.

However, Aristotle did understand that emotions play a part in any decision-making process. Therefore, he urged that the communicator know and understand the emotions, what they are, how they affect people, and which objects tend to be associated with which emotions. With this knowledge he is then able to exercise some control, through choice of words, examples, metaphor, etc., over his own emotional responses and therefore over those of his auditors. Aristotle's question was not "how can the speaker arouse emotions" but rather "how can the inevitable emotional response to a message be controlled and channeled?" Aristotle urged that the speaker know not only how to generate *fear*, for instance, but how to recognize a fear reaction as well as a fear-inducing stimulus, and how to recognize situations in which fear is functional, dysfunctional, or, perhaps, irrelevant. In other words, Aristotle's theory of *pathos* was based on a thorough understanding of societal beliefs, attitudes, values, and of the socially accepted concept of motives.

Aristotle's third major source of artistic was *logos*. Logos is usually interpreted as "logical proof," but a more accurate translation would be "proof through the words of the message." Though Aristotle is generally recognized as the first great logician, and though he considered logic, or reason, as human beings' greatest asset, he understood that we do not make decisions in accordance with the rules of strict logical deduction. For this reason he went to great lengths to distinguish between logical and rhetorical deduction. Logic deduces through syllogisms; the human decision-maker deduces through enthymemes. To Aristotle this difference was crucial, for people, he believed, make decisions based on their perceptions of what is "best" for them, not on the basis of the linguistic validity of the available arguments. In any overtly persuasive situations, the success of an attempt to influence is contingent upon the audience's perception of the communicator and the situation as much as, if not more than, upon the "logic" of the arguments. Human communication theory, as conceived by Aristotle, is concerned with understanding how people select the appropriate action from among alternative possibilities, none of which are logically "necessary" or valid independent of the people involved in the decision.[22]

Given this basic understanding, then what is *logos* as an artistic mode of proof? Essentially, it is the arrangement of relevant bits of information into linguistic forms that are similar in appearance to logical inference and logical deduction. The names Aristotle gives to these forms are *example* and *enthymeme*. The example gains its potency in large part from its resemblance to scientific inference. It is the discovery of actions or events in the past, or the creation of fictional events, which seem to parallel the events being considered in the present or future. Aristotle explains the example in the following manner:

> Let us say, for example, that in asking for a bodyguard, Dionysius is plotting to make himself tyrant. This can be said, for Pisistratus before him was hatching a plot when he asked for a bodyguard and, upon receiving one, promptly set up a tyranny. Likewise Theagenes

---

[22] For a more detailed discussion, see Nancy L. Harper, "An Analytical Description of Aristotle's Enthymeme," *Central States Speech Journal* (Winter 1973), pp. 304–309.

of Megara. And all other tyrants known serve as an example of Dionysius, though we do not yet know his reason for asking for a bodyguard. All these instances are included in the one generalization: that one who is plotting a tyranny asks for a bodyguard. We have now described the sources of those means of persuasion which are popularly supposed to be demonstrative (1357b 26–1358a 2).[23]

Hence, in terms of conceptualization theory, one of the major sources of ideas for the communicator is parallel cases from the past. Further, one of the most effective modes of persuasion is the citation of those cases in relation to current problem-solving.

More important for Aristotle was the second form of *logos*, the enthymeme. The enthymeme relates to example as deduction relates to induction. Having observed a number of instances, a general conclusion—a pattern of invariances—emerges. This conclusion may then become a premise for deductive argumentation. The example quoted above illustrates Aristotle's awareness of the fact that induction, or example, is the source of enthymemes. In the case of that example, for instance, the general conclusion is that a man who asks for a bodyguard is plotting to make himself a tyrant. Such a statement may become an accepted "truth" in a particular society and once it has, it is then available for use in enthymemes. Thus, the observation of a particular fact—Dionysius is asking for a bodyguard—when tied to the generally accepted truth about the meaning of such an action leads to the "reasonable" conclusion that Dionysius is plotting a tyranny. An enthymeme, then, looks like a syllogism (a logical deductive form invented by Aristotle: If A entails B, and B entails C, *then* A entails C). It differs in that it draws specific conclusions about individual events from the observation of a particular instance of a general rule. Its impact does not lie in its logical validity as form, but in the acceptability of its premises as probable truth. In other words, it depends upon the strength of the audience's belief in the generalization (asking for a bodyguard is a sign of a tyranny plot) and their belief that this current case is similar to previous cases. The "truth" of an enthymematic conclusion can only be determined through empirical test. In terms of specific communication events, however, truth is *granted* by the audience.[24] That, is, enthymematic conclusions are true only to the extent that relevant individuals *agree* to their truth.

Aristotle explains that the substance of enthymemes is provided by signs and probabilities and by the formal topics. A sign is an observation of a particular datum, e.g., "Socrates is feverish." A probability is a

---

[23] Translation from Harper, p. 308.
[24] The role of the audience is emphasized in Lloyd F. Bitzer, "Aristotle's Enthymeme Revisited," *Quarterly Journal of Speech* (1959), pp. 399–408.

generalization about the meaning of the sign, e.g., "People who have fevers are usually ill." The conjunction of a sign and interpretation of the probable meaning of that sign leads to an inference, or enthymeme. In this case, the inference is "Socrates is ill" (*Rhetoric*, 1357b 15).

In order to use enthymematic proof, the communicator must thoroughly investigate his subject, searching for data (signs) and acceptable generalizations about the relationship between the pieces of data. Aristotle lists twenty-eight kinds of relationships which may exist. These kinds of relationships constitute the "formal topics" (see Fig. 2.4). The communicator is expected to analyze his subject in terms of these topics, e.g., in terms of past parallel cases, antecedents and consequences, relevant motives, etc. (*Rhetoric*, 1397a 6–1400b 32). Full investigation of these topics provides the communicator with the substance of potential arguments, or enthymemes. He eventually decides which ones to use in particular cases on the basis of further conceptualization.

Fig. 2.4 Formal Topics (Relationships That Can Exist Between "Pieces" of Information; Sources for Enthymemes)

1. Considering the opposite of the thing in question
2. Considering some modification of the key word
3. Considering the correlative ideas
4. Considering the *a fortiori*
5. Considering time relationships
6. Applying to the opposition what they have charged against you
7. Defining your terms
8. Explaining the various senses of key words
9. Making logical divisions
10. Making logical inductions from past parallels
11. Examining precedents
12. Investigating the parts of the subject
13. Analyzing the good and bad consequences
14. Contrasting opposites (divarication)
15. Contrasting implicit and explicit values
16. Discovering rational correspondences
17. Discovering common antecedents
18. Comparing past and present criteria for decisions
19. Comparing real and possible motives
20. Considering inducements and deterrents
21. Comparing the credible and incredible
22. Analyzing contradictions
23. Examining alternative explanations
24. Deducing the effect from the cause
25. Examining alternative means to an end
26. Comparing the consistency of past and future actions
27. Comparing probabilities
28. Analyzing the meaning of names

In summary, the ancient Greeks and Romans created a complex system for understanding the process of acquiring and interpreting information. The system demanded a thorough analysis of the subject, the audience, and the occasion. The focus was on the creation of "meaning," which was viewed as created by the researcher and dependent upon the context of the communication event. For both Aristotle and Cicero, conceptualization was the fundamental process in human communication. The classical theorists in general saw conceptualization as closely tied to categorization (or "memory" as they called it). The communicator's first source of information is the knowledge stored in his mind. This knowledge, and the new information added in each information search, are the determining factors in later decisions about appropriate symbolization, organization, and operationalization strategies.

Categorization

Classical writers treated the process of categorization primarily as a matter of memory. To the more prescriptive writers, memory meant simply "memorizing." The author of the *Ad Herrenium* calls memory the "treasure-house of the ideas supplied by Invention . . . the guardian of all the parts of rhetoric" (III. xi. 19).[25] To the more theoretical writers it meant stored knowledge—information acquired, classified, and available to be used whenever the individual required it. The prior discussion of conceptualization schemes illustrates the classical approach to knowledge: the emphasis was on classifying knowledge in such a way that it could be systematically retrieved according to the demands of the situation. Most communication situations in the classical world were, as explained earlier, oral, unmediated, and public; thus, the communicator frequently had to be his own library and his own computer.

Traditionally, human communication theorists have had little to say about the categorization process. Aristotle never mentions it explicitly in the *Rhetoric*. Plato mentions it only in passing, in his comparison of the relative merits of written as opposed to oral messages. In the *Phaedrus* he has Socrates say that writing "is an aid not to memory but to reminiscence." Further, he explains:

> I cannot help feeling, Phaedrus, that writing is unfortunately like painting; for the creations of the painter have the attitude of life, and yet if you ask them a question they preserve a solemn silence. And the same may be said of [written] speeches. You would imagine that they had intelligence, but if you want to know anything and put a question to one of them, the speaker always gives one unvary-

25 *Rhetorica ad Herennium*, translated by Harry Caplan (Loeb Classical Library, Cambridge: Harvard University Press, 1939). All subsequent references in the text are to this translation.

ing answer. And when they have been once written down they are tumbled about anywhere among those who may or may not understand them, and know not to whom they should reply, to whom not: and, if they are maltreated or abused, they have no parent to protect them; and they cannot protect or defend themselves (275).

Cicero gives only slightly more attention to the process. In *De Oratore* he presents a brief summary of the "science of mnemonics," which he says was invented by Simonedes of Ceos. According to Cicero, Simonedes attended a dinner at the home of a man named Scopas. During the meal, Simonedes was called out of the house to take a message, and while he was gone the roof of the building caved in, crushing Scopas and his guests. When the bodies were excavated, they were unrecognizable and the relatives were unable to identify them for burial. Simonedes then came to the rescue, identifying the bodies from his memory of the positions they had been sitting in around the table. This experience led him to the discovery that "the best aid to clearness of memory consists of orderly arrangement" (II. lxxxvi. 354). Cicero then proceeds to explain the rules for memorizing developed out of Simonedes' discovery (see Fig. 2.5).

The prescriptive writers treated memory as a step in the process of message-sending. Once the communicator had invented the material, selected an appropriate style and order of arrangement, the next step was to commit all of this to memory. The most common system of memorizing consisted of imagining "backgrounds" or "scenes," such as the interior of a house, within which the ideas of the message were represented by "images." The author of the *Ad Herrenium* explains it as follows:

Fig. 2.5   Classical Taxonomy of Categorization

I. Natural Memory—Sense experiences that impress themselves in the mind; an inherent ability of human beings
II. Artificial Memory—Learned system for classifying and storing information
   A. General—Socially learned classifications of reality
   B. Specific—Methods of memorizing
      1. Backgrounds—Scenes arranged in a series
         a. Permanent
         b. About 30 feet apart
         c. Each fifth one marked
         d. Taken from unpopulated areas
         e. Each distinct and of moderate size
      2. Images—Likeness of the subject
         A. General representation of a line of thought
         b. Specific representations of words
         c. Should be novel and active

Those who know the letters of the alphabet can thereby write out what is dictated to them and read aloud what they have written. Likewise, those who have learned mnemonics can get in backgrounds what they have heard, and from these backgrounds deliver it by memory. For the backgrounds are very much like wax tablets or papyrus, the images like the letters, the arrangement and disposition of the images like the script, and the delivery is like the reading (III. xvii. 30).

The author goes on to explain that backgrounds should be carefully selected, for they remain permanently in the mind. They should be arranged in a permanent series, about thirty feet apart; each fifth one should be marked by a special sign; they should be taken from unpopulated areas; and each should be distinct and of moderate size.

Images vary with the message. They are likenesses—figures, marks, or portraits—of the object and may be either representative of a general line of thought or of particular words. He advises against using images to represent each word of the message. He explains that the Greeks developed lists of images to correspond to particular words and that some writers favor that approach. The problem with it, he says, is that there are too many words and if we invent images for each of them, the backgrounds will become too crowded. Furthermore, specifying particular images for particular words takes away from the creativity of the communicator; since different people perceive things differently, one person's image may not be suitable for another, and, he explains, the science of mnemonics is a general method, not a specific prescription.

Images, he continues, should be active, engaged in movement, and novel, exceptional in appearance, comic, strange, etc. He explains:

Now nature herself teaches us what we should do. When we see in everyday life things that are petty, ordinary, and banal, we generally fail to remember them, because the mind is not being stirred by anything novel or marvelous. But if we see or hear something exceptionally base, dishonorable, extraordinary, great, unbelievable, or laughable, that we are likely to remember a long time (III. xxii. 35).

Cicero points out in his summary of this method that it is like painting pictures in our mind:

[T]he most complete pictures are formed in our minds of the things that have been conveyed to them and imprinted on them by the senses, [and] the keenest of all our senses is the sense of sight (II. lxxxvii. 357).

In summary, the Greek and Roman teachers of rhetoric viewed the categorization process primarily in terms of memorization. They developed and taught systematic memory exercises. The theorists, on the other hand, rarely dealt with the subject explicitly. Cicero, like Aristotle, viewed categorization as fundamental to conceptualization and discussed it primarily in terms of the store of general and specific knowledge the communicator must have ready at his disposal. For both the major classical theorists, human communication theory was a system of general culture, and categorization of information was an inextricable part of the fundamental conceptualization process.

Symbolization

The process of symbolizing was of great importance to the classical theorists. To some, especially Quintilian and Longinus, the later Romans, it was the central aspect of human communication theory. To others, like Aristotle, it was subordinate to, even a part of, conceptualization. In spite of varying emphases, however, a taxonomy developed that in its general outline was widely subscribed to (see Fig. 2.6).

Fig. 2.6   Classical Taxonomy of Symbolization

I. Functions
   A.   To instruct—Create ethos (understanding)
   B.   To please—Create logos (conviction)
   C.   To persuade—Create pathos (empathy)
II. Levels
   A.   Plain—Natural, conversational
   B.   Middle—Metaphorical, philosophical
   C.   Vigorous—Ornate, copious, sublime
III. Criteria
   A.   Accuracy—Clarity, correctness
   B.   Aesthetics—Lively, graphic, novel, emotive
   C.   Propriety—Appropriateness to audience, place, time, speaker, and subject

---

Aristotle devotes most of the third, and briefest, chapter of the *Rhetoric* to symbolization (which the classical theorists called "style"). He opens with a brief disclaimer: "The arts of language cannot help having a small but real importance, whatever it is we have to expound to others: the way in which a thing is said does affect its intelligibility" (1403b 8–12). Cicero makes a similar statement in *Orator:* "Although a word has no force apart from the thing, yet the same thing is often either approved or rejected according as it is expressed in one way or another" (XX,

69).[26] Both Aristotle and Cicero clearly regarded the selection and use of symbols as instrumental to the accomplishment of the communicator's goals. Aristotle explains that the first question for a communicator is "how persuasion can be produced from the facts themselves. The second is how to set these facts out in language" (1403b 18–20).

Cicero goes further, tying the functions of communication directly to the levels of style:

> The man of eloquence . . . will be one who is able to speak . . . so as *to prove, to please* and *to sway or persuade.* To prove is the first necessity, to please is to charm, to sway is victory. . . . For these three functions of the orator there are three styles, *the plain style* for proof, *the middle style* for pleasure, *the vigorous style* for persuasion; and in this last is summed up the entire virtue of the orator (*Orator,* XX. 69–XXIX. 101; emphases mine).

Thus, the pragmatics of influence were primary in classical conceptions of the symbolization process.

Cicero's three levels of style are distinguished, first, in light of the goals of communicating: to instruct, to please, and to persuade; second, they are distinguished in terms of Aristotle's three modes of proof. The plain style achieves its ends through ethos. Because it is restrained, natural, clear, and factual, it enhances the credibility of the speaker. The middle style is philosophical, uses many figures and commonplaces, thereby convincing and pleasing the audience with intricate reasoning and achieving its ends primarily through logos. The vigorous style is "magnificent, opulent, stately, and ornate"; it overwhelms the audience, stirring them beyond understanding and commitment to action. The vigorous style, then, achieves its ends primarily through pathos. Cicero warns that the communicator must master all three styles: for proof alone leads only to general agreement; pleasure alone leads only to appreciation; and emotional involvement alone leads to floundering and confusion (II, liii, 215). Of the third style, Cicero says that the vigorous speaker who

> does not temper his abundance with the other two styles . . . is much to be despised. For the plain orator is esteemed wise because he speaks clearly and adroitly; the one who employs the middle style is charming; but the copious speaker, if he has nothing else, seems to be scarcely sane (*Orator,* XX. 69–XXIX. 101).

A later Roman treatise, *On the Sublime* (c. 200 A.D.), further

---

[26] Cicero, *Orator,* translated by H. M. Hubbell (Loeb Classical Library, Cambridge: Harvard University Press, 1939). All subsequent references in the text are to this translation.

amplifies the notion of vigorous style.[27] The author calls his ultimate level of style "sublimity." Sublimity, he explains, occurs only in brief passages and phrases. He considers persuasion too tame a word to describe the effect of the sublime:

> [I]t is not to persuasion but to ecstasy that passages of extraordinary genius carry the hearer: now the marvelous, with its power to amaze, is always and necessarily stronger than that which seeks to persuade and to please: to be persuaded rests usually with ourselves; genius brings force sovereign and irresistible to bear upon every hearer, and takes its stand high above him. Again, skill in invention and power of orderly arrangement are not seen from one passage nor from two, but emerge with effort out of the whole context; sublimity, we know, brought out at the happy moment, parts all the matter this way and that, and like a lightning flash, reveals, at a stroke and in its entirety, the power of the orator.[28]

Though his language is more extreme than Cicero's, the anonymous author's conception of the special impact of the most powerful style is in keeping with the general attitude of classical theorists: Most communicators, most times, must be satisfied to prove their case and hope to please their auditors. To overwhelm, to be sublime, is a goal achieved only occasionally and briefly.

Criteria for Symbolization   Cicero's three levels also parallel the three basic criteria for good style: (1) Accuracy was the primary criterion and achieved through mastery of the plain style. (2) Aesthetic expression was the second criterion and was mastered along with the middle style. (3) Propriety was the third criterion and was considered of the most importance in the vigorous style. Each criterion, of course, was relevant to all three styles, for most communicative situations call for the speaker to prove, *and* to please, *and* to persuade. Thus all messages should be characterized by accuracy, aesthetic expression, and propriety.

In the *Rhetoric*, Aristotle avers that "The foundation of good style is correctness of language" (1407a 18) and that "Style to be good must be clear" (1404b 1). Quintilian says, "For my own part, I regard clearness as the first essential of good style. . . ." (*Inst. Or.*, VIII). Cicero, of course, considered the mastery of plain style (whose primary characteristic is clarity) as the first necessity for a communicator.

---

[27] At one time the author was believed to be Longinus, but authorities no longer credit him with this work.
[28] *On the Sublime*, translated by G. M. A. Grube (Loeb Classical Library, Cambirdge: Harvard University Press, 1899). All subsequent references in the text are to this translation.

Given this baseline, however, the classical theorists were more in-trigued by the other two characteristics. Accuracy (clarity and correct-ness in the use of language) was seen as necessary but not sufficient. Accuracy establishes the communicator's ethos, makes it possible to in-struct the hearer, but it does not, in itself, move the hearer toward action.

The aesthetics of expression, were, for most theorists, the keys to motivation. Audiences, the Greeks and Romans believed, were most likely to be pleased, and thereby moved, by messages that were lively, graphic, novel, and emotive. Figurative language was commonly seen as the source of these attributes.

Aristotle devotes special attention to the nature of "metaphor,"in which category he includes almost all figurative language. Metaphor, he says, has a special power to involve the receiver of the message both cognitively and emotionally:

> *Liveliness* is specially conveyed by metaphor, and by the further power of surprising the hearer; because the hearer expected some-thing different, his acquisition of the new idea impresses him all the more. His mind seems to say, 'Yes, to be sure; I never thought of that' (1412a 17–21).

He goes on to explain how metaphorical language works:

> [W]e all naturally find it agreeable to get hold of new ideas easily: words express ideas, and therefore those words are the most agree-able that enable us to get hold of new ideas. Now strange words simply puzzle us; ordinary words convey only what we know already; it is from metaphor that we can best get hold of something fresh. . . . The simile . . . is a metaphor, differing from it only in the way it is put; and just because it is longer it is less attractive. Besides, it does not say outright that "this" *is* "that," and therefore the hearer is less interested in the idea. We see then that both speech and reasoning are lively in proportion as they make us seize a new idea promptly. . . . People are . . . much taken . . . only by those [arguments] which convey their information to us as soon as we hear them, provided we had not the information already; or which the mind only just fails to keep up with (1410b 10–25).

The later Roman treatise on symbolization, *On the Sublime*, supports Aristotle's analysis of the nature of the impact of metaphor:

> That is really great which gives much food for fresh reflection; which it is hard, nay impossible, to resist; of which the memory is strong and indelible (II).

Novelty and liveliness, then, are major characteristics of messages of great impact, those which critics call "sublime" or "vigorous." In addition to these characteristics, however, the message must be memorable. Aristotle claims that this characteristic is another function of metaphor. Metaphor is "graphic," that is, it makes the hearers *see*. Aristotle defines the ability to be graphic as the ability to "set the scene before our eyes" so that we can *see* the relationships between things (1410b27-1412a11). In fact, he says, "the style of oratory addressed to public assemblies is really just like scene-painting" (1414a7). He lists several other figures that work like metaphor to give liveliness, novelty, and graphic visualization: epigrams, riddles, verbal jokes, proverbs, and hyperboles.

Having understood the nature and characteristics of these aesthetic features of language, Aristotle warns the communicator that they must not be overused. Ornament, he claims, is for poetry where the goal is pleasure. In prose, since pleasure is instrumental to persuasion,

> [the writer] must disguise his art and give the impression of speaking naturally and not artificially. Naturalness is persuasive, artificiality is the contrary; for our hearers are prejudiced and think we have some design against them, as if we were mixing their wines for them (1404b 18–22).

Aristotle's philosophical treatment of the nature of figurative language contrasts with the more prescriptive approach of later Romans like Quintilian.

Quintilian's exhaustive analysis of tropes and figures in *The Institutes of Oratory* is based on his study of the treatises of the early Greek sophists and grows out of his many years as a teacher of rhetoric. Though his prescriptions contribute little to the theory of communication, his analysis of figurative language is important in its considerable impact on later theorists, especially those of the Renaissance who, like Quintilian, considered symbolization as almost the whole of communication theory. His influence is apparent in the distinction between the two genres of figurative language, tropes and figures (also sometimes called figures of thought and figures of speech). Also influential was his listing of the various tropes and figures with examples from classical literature.

Quintilian identifies several kinds of "tropes," e.g., metaphor, simile, synecdoche, and metonymy. He defines the trope as "the artistic alteration of a word or phrase from its proper meaning to another. . . . the changes involved concern not merely individual words, but also our thoughts and the structure of our sentences" (VIII. v. 35–vi. 29). Any time a speaker gives his language "a conformation other than the obvious and ordinary" he is using a figure. Figures of thought are those expressions which show an unusual combination of conceptions which do not mean quite what they say, e.g., the rhetorical question. Figures of speech are those based on unusual combinations of "words, diction, expression, language," e.g., parallelism and antithesis.

The importance of tropes, according to Quintilian, is that they "move the feelings, give special distinction to things and place them vividly before the eye." Figures are important for they

> lend credibility to our arguments and steal their way secretly into the minds of the judges [audience]. . . . Further, there is no more effective method of exciting the emotions. . . . But, above all, figures serve to commend what we say to those that hear us, whether we seek to win approval for our character . . . or to win favor for the cause . . . to relieve monotony by variation of our language, or to indicate our meaning in the safest or most seemly way (IX. il. 25).

In this last statement we can see again the classical theorists' emphasis upon the pragmatics of symbolization. Even the criterion of aesthetic expression was justified in light of the Aristotelian modes of proof.

The third classical criterion was propriety, or appropriateness, of the language to the place, time, audience, subject, and speaker. In *Orator*, Cicero claims that propriety is the ultimate criterion of symbolization:

> [T]he orator must have an eye to propriety not only in thought but in language. For the same style and the same thoughts must not be used in portraying every condition in life, or every rank, position or age, and in fact a similar distinction must be made in respect of *place, time,* and *audience.* The universal rule, in oratory as in life, is to consider propriety. This depends on the subject under discussion, and on the character of both the speaker and the audience (XX. 69–XXIX. 101; emphases mine).

In the *Rhetoric*, Aristotle emphasizes the importance of audience analysis in determining propriety. He devotes seven chapters to an analysis of the conditions, ranks, and positions of society as part of the knowledge necessary for selecting appropriate symbolization strategies. He segments audiences according to two primary dimensions: "ages" and "fortunes." There are three ages: youth, prime, and old age. His description of youth forms the basis of the analysis:

> [The] Young . . . have strong passions, and tend to gratify them indiscriminately. Of the bodily desires, it is the sexual by which they are most swayed and in which they show absence of self-control. They are changeable and fickle in their desires, which are violent while they last, but quickly over. . . . While they love honor, they love victory still more; for youth is eager for superiority

over others, and victory is one form of this. They love both more
than they love money. . . . They look at the good side rather than
the bad, not having yet witnessed many instances of wicked-
ness. . . . Their lives are mainly spent not in memory but in ex-
pectation. . . . They are shy, accepting the rules of society in
which they have been trained, and not yet believing in any other
standard. . . . their lives are regulated more by moral feeling than
by reasoning. . . . they love too much and hate too much. . . .
They think they know everything, and are always quite sure about
this. . . . They are ready to pity others, because they think every
one an honest man, or anyhow better than he is (1389a 2–1389b
10).

Old age leads to opposite characteristics: older people are cynical,
stingy with money, self-centered, utilitarian, prefer memory over hope,
expect the worst, are ruled by reasoning rather than passion, etc. People
in the prime of life "have a character between that of the young and that
of the old, free from the extremes of either" (1390a 27–30).

Aristotle further segments audiences in respect to "fortunes" and
spends four chapters analyzing the influence of *birth* (rank), degree of
wealth, and degree of *power* on human character, for symbolization
strategies necessarily differ in accordance with fortune as well as age.

Also important to determining propriety or appropriateness is the
emotional state of the audience. Cicero advises the communicator to
prepare his message only after checking the audience's "thoughts, judgments, anticipations and wishes and the direction in which they seem
likely to be led away most easily by eloquence" (*De Oratore*, II. xli. 186).

Aristotle goes further by providing a typology of emotions and advising the communicator to know (1) the states of mind in which a particular emotion is felt, (2) the people towards whom it is felt, and (3) the
grounds on which it is felt (1378a 24–26). He states that the communicator must be aware of the nature, objects, and causes of the emotions, for "emotions are all those feelings that so change men as to affect
their judgments," and the science of making "good judgments" is the
function of human communication theory. Both sender and receiver are
affected by human emotions. He devotes eleven chapters to analyzing
them, carefully describing and functionally defining nine types: (1) anger
and calmness, (2) friendship and enmity, (3) fear and confidence, (4)
shame and shamelessness, (5) kindness and unkindness, (6) pity, (7)
indignation, (8) envy, and (9) emulation (1378a 20–1388b 30).

The classical taxonomies of place, time, and subject have been
outlined in the preceding discussion of conceptualization. In the classical
scheme, if the communicator had carefully analyzed these dimensions
during the conceptualization phase, then he merely had to review these

earlier decisions (categorizations) before selecting the appropriate symbols for the message.

Organization

Organization is that part of human communication theory concerned with order and relationship. Greek and Roman rhetoric texts focused heavily on the ordering of messages, a topic they discussed under the heading of "arrangement" or "disposition." This part of the classical conception of organization was highly prescriptive, consisting of complex series of rules. The more philosophical treatises, however, paid little attention to arranging messages, focusing more on the relationships among the persons, and among the persons and the symbols, involved in the interaction.

Classical organizational theory can be discussed under two headings, the first of which is prescriptive and message-centered, the second of which is functional and person-centered (see Fig. 2.7).

The Prescriptive Approach   Cicero's rhetoric text, *De Inventione*, written when he was twenty years old, presents the typical precepts of message organization. As a student, Cicero was taught that "arrangement" was the second part of rhetoric ("invention" was the first part), and that arrangment consisted of the proper distribution of the materials gathered during the conceptualization phase. He was also taught that there are six divisions to a message, each having a distinct and necessary function. His divisions and definitions are typical of classical thought:

[1] An exordium is a passage that brings the mind of the auditor into a proper condition to receive the rest of the speech by making him well-disposed, attentive, and receptive (I, 20–27).[29]

(Cicero divides exordia into two parts, the *introduction* and the *insinuation*. The introduction sets forth the scope of the subject; the insinuation discredits opposing views on the subject and is only necessary with hostile audiences.)

[2] The narrative is an exposition of events that have occurred or are alleged to have occurred. There are three kinds. One type contains only the case and the rationale for the dispute; a second type consists of a digression that is made for the purpose of attacking somebody or of amusing the audience. . . . The third kind is unconnected with the issue but is given for amusement and, at the same time, for valuable information.

[29] Cicero, *De Inventione*, translated by H. M. Hubbell (Loeb Classical Library, Cambridge: Harvard University Press, 1949). All subsequent references in the text are to this translation.

Fig. 2.7 Classical Taxonomies of Organization

I. Prescriptive: Arranging the message into parts
   A. Exordium—Introduction
   B. Narration—Exposition of salient facts
   C. Partition—Statement of method
   D. Confirmation—Presentation of arguments and proofs
   E. Refutation—Anticipation of counter arguments and proofs
   F. Peroration—Conclusion
II. Functional: The final selection, ordering, and proportioning of concepts
   A. Definition—Analysis of the subject
   B. Division—Analysis of the subject in a context
       1. Epideictic
           a. Introduction—Praise or censure, advice, personal appeal
           b. Statement—Intermittent narration, facts interspersed with interpretation
           c. Argument—Establishing that acts were noble and useful, or vice versa
           d. Epilogue—Making audience well-disposed to you and ill-disposed to the opposition, magnifying or minimizing leading facts, exciting required emotion, refreshing audience's memory
       2. Forensic
           a. Introduction—Foretaste of theme
           b. Statement—Clear statement of facts (logos), of character (ethos), of effects (pathos)
           c. Argument—Establishing whether the act was committed (*an sit*), whether it did harm and how much (*quid sit*), whether it was justified (*quale sit*); enthymeme most suitable form
           d. Epilogue—Same as for Epideictic
       3. Deliberative
           a. Introduction—Personal appeal, statement of significance, exciting or dispelling prejudice
           b. Statement—Current situation, past comparable situations, hypothetic future results
           c. Argument—Establishing whether proposal is practicable, just, important; example most suitable form, also maxims
           d. Epilogue—Same as for epideictic
   C. Proportion—Analysis of the sender/receiver relationship
       1. Teacher/student
       2. Performer/judge
       3. Leader/follower

[3] The partition makes the entire speech clear and lucid. It has two general forms: One indicates where we agree with our opponents and what is still left in dispute; the second is a preview of the remainder of our argument.

[4] The confirmation is that part of a narration that, by marshaling

arguments, lends force, authority, and support to our case (I, 27–35).

(Under confirmation, Cicero discusses the nature, sources, and kinds of argument. Most of what he has to say here is a brief summary of Aristotelian conceptualization theory. He discusses the idea of probability, the uses of the topics, and the two genres of argument, example (which he calls analogy) and enthymeme. Having explained the confirmation, he goes on to the next part of the message.)

[5] The refutation is that part of an oration in which arguments are used to disprove or weaken the confirmation and proof in our opponent's speech. Every argument is refuted in one of these ways: either one or more of its assumptions is not granted, or, if the assumptions are granted, it is denied that a conclusion follows from them, or the form of the argument is shown to be fallacious, or a strong argument is met by one equally strong or stronger.

[6] The peroration completes the speech and has three parts: the resumé of what has been discussed throughout the speech, the arousing of animosity against your opponent, and, finally the arousing of sympathy for your own client (I, 78–100).

Having set forth the six parts of a message in summary form, Cicero proceeds to more detailed prescriptions for the content of the parts. In this treatise, he treats rhetoric as primarily a theory of legal communication. Though he cites the three-fold Aristotelian divisions (deliberative, forensic, and epideictic), he conceives of these as genera of arguments rather than of occasions. His examples and precepts clearly deal with situations involving conflict. Furthermore, Cicero's treatment of organization is almost wholly message-centered. He deals with the issues of emotional and logical appeals, of two-sided vs. one-sided messages, of primacy and recency effects, and the ordering of evidence and arguments, but has little to say about the rationale for his system of message organization. In his later works, this emphasis disappears, and his treatment of organization follows the functional, humanistic pattern set b; Plato and Aristotle. The earlier Ciceronian approach remains an important aspect of classical theory, however, for it is this approach that most influenced later teachers and practitioners.

The Functional Approach   The functional relationships between the sender and receiver were the focus of theoretical classical treatises on human communication. We can isolate three conceptions of this relationship in the works of Plato, Aristotle, and Cicero. The most basic is the teacher/student relationship in which the purpose is instruction, and the setting, philosophical or epideictic. The second, and most commonly cited, is the performer/judge relationship, in which the purpose is persuasion and the setting, forensic. Next in priority is the leader/follower relationship, in which the purpose is advising and the setting, deliberative or political. To many theorists, this was the more humanly important of the possible relationships, but socially it was less common than the forensic.

Plato's dialogues are primarily concerned with the teacher/student relationship. Thus, he saw communication theory as the source of principles useful in imparting "truth" to learners or in teaching citizens to make "wise" decisions. He conceived of organization as the final selection, ordering, and proportioning of the "truths" arrived at in conceptualization. Organizing a message requires three kinds of skills that can be learned from human communication theory: definition, division, and proportioning (or audience analysis).

Definition   In the *Phaedrus*, he describes the first as skill in "perceiving and bringing together in one idea the scattered particulars, that one may make clear by definition the particular thing which he wishes to explain . . ." (262C). Definition, then, is an analogic process. It depends upon the ability to, as Plato's student Aristotle explains, "perceive resemblances even in things far apart" (1412a 11). Aristotle's discussion of metaphor, discussed earlier, centers on the ability to see, and communicate, resemblances.

Division   Plato goes on to say that once ideas have been made clear by definition, they can then be divided; once we know the similarities, we can perceive the differences. Furthermore, once we know the whole, we can know the parts. The second skill in organizing is "that of dividing things again by classes, where the natural joints are, and not trying to break any part, after the manner of a bad carver" (262C).

Plato's premise is that all ideas have "true" or natural divisions and that the problem in organizing is to discover and use them. Furthermore, messages themselves have natural divisions regardless of the specific subject. He has Socrates explain this to Phaedrus, as follows:

> [E]very discourse must be organized, like a living being, with a body of its own, as it were, so as not to be headless or footless, but to have a middle and members, composed in fitting relation to each other and to the whole (261C).

Thus, in addition to the natural divisions of the subject, the communicator is constrained by the natural divisions of messages; messages must have beginnings, middles, and ends.

Aristotle posits a third constraint on division. Plato was essentially concerned only with the teacher/learner, or epideictic, context. Thus, he sees the contextual restraints as consisting of an obligation to "truth." Aristotle was interested in communication in all contexts and therefore presents a broader treatment. As usual, his approach is a compromise between sophistic prescription and Platonic philosophy; he realizes some precepts are necessary, but he also realizes that all precepts demand theoretical justification and have exceptions. Unlike the sophists, he presents generic explanations; unlike the philosophers, he presents specific applications. Opening his discussion of arrangement, he says:

> A speech has two parts. You must state your case, and you must prove it. . . . The current division is absurd. For "narration" surely is part of a forensic speech only: how in a political speech or a speech of display can there be "narration" in the technical sense? or a reply to a forensic opponent? or an epilogue in closely reasoned speeches? Again, introduction, comparison of conflicting arguments, and recapitulation are only found in political speeches when there is a struggle between two policies. They may occur then; so may even accusation and defense, often enough; but they form no essential part of a political speech. Even forensic speeches do not always need epilogues; not, for instance, a short speech, nor one in which the facts are easy to remember, the effect of an epilogue being always a reduction in the apparent length. It follows, then, that the only necessary parts of a speech are the Statement and the Argument. These are the essential features of a speech; and it cannot in any case have more than Introduction, Statement, Argument, and Epilogue (*Rhetoric*, 1414a 30–1414b 9).

Having asserted that organization depends upon the specific context, Aristotle goes on to discuss the four possible divisions of a message in light of his three-part typology of occasions—epideictic, forensic, and deliberative. In general, he says, the introduction functions "to show what the aim of the speech is" and to establish ethos (1415a 22–40). Whether or not these functions are necessary and the manner in which they are attempted are matters that depend upon the specific situation. Likewise, the statement is a recital of the relevant facts (inartistic proofs), the argument is proof of the speaker's interpretation of the facts (logos), and the epilogue is a summary and final prioritizing of the facts and interpretation (pathos).

Given this general understanding of the functions of the possible divisions of a message, Aristotle then discusses in more detail the differences in the appropriate content of each division within each of the three general contexts. This discussion is summarized in Fig. 2.7. The discussion is unified by Aristotle's consistent concern for appropriate use of the modes of proof—logos, ethos, and pathos—given the constraints of the context. Thus, Aristotle's treatment of the topic of division goes beyond

Plato's in that Aristotle provides an analytic scheme which the speaker can use to make decisions about the appropriate ordering of his materials, but he does not provide the hard and fast rules favored by the sophists. The later Romans, Cicero and Quintilian, followed the Aristotelian approach in spirit, though they tended to be somewhat more prescriptive.

Proportioning   Like Aristotle, Plato criticizes the complex theories of organization then being taught by sophists such as Gorgias. From his remarks we can conclude that the sophistic approach was essentially the same as the six-part Ciceronian system discussed above. But Aristotle's criticism focused on the context-free nature of the system, while Plato's criticism is that the sophistic precepts do not require definition before division and that they do not take into account the hearers of the message. For both Plato and Aristotle, audience analysis is the third necessity. Plato compares the sophistic approach to that of a deaf and blind person:

> [S]urely he who pursues any study scientifically ought not to be comparable to a blind or a deaf man, but evidently the man whose rhetorical teaching is a real art will explain accurately the nature of that to which his words are to be addressed, and that is the soul. . . . anyone . . . who seriously teaches the art of rhetoric, will first describe the soul with perfect accuracy . . . (*Phaedrus*, 269C).

Thus, the last necessary skill in organizing is proportioning, or prioritizing, the materials of the message in light of the nature of the audience to whom it is to be addressed.

Aristotle's analysis of social roles, presented above in the discussion of symbolization strategies, is an operationalization of Plato's injunction to know the "souls" to whom one wishes to speak. Aristotle segments audiences on the bases of age (young, middle-aged, and old) and of position (social rank, wealth, and power). As we have seen above, he further segments them on the basis of the occasion, or context, within which one communicates. In addition to these taxonomies of audience segmentation, the classical theorists also concerned themselves with the general nature of the relationships between senders and receiver.

In the *Gorgias*, Plato bitterly attacks sophistic communication theory for its "warped" view of the relationship between speakers and audiences. He has Socrates tell Gorgias that his brand of instruction turns out hucksters and con artists, that it trains speakers in the arts of flattery and deceptive packaging. He defines sophistic rhetoric by analogy: "as self-adornment is to gymnastic, so is Sophistry to legislation [wise decision-making]; and as cookery is to medicine, so is [Sophistic] rhetoric to justice [true instruction]" (447A–465E). Sophistic rhetoric,

Socrates says, teaches the speaker to be a good "cook," that is to pretend to know what foods are best for the body and to prepare these foods in attractive, appetizing compositions. Philosophical rhetoric, on the other hand, would teach the speaker to be a "doctor," to know what foods are best and to prescribe them regardless of packaging. He then compares the popular audience to a group of schoolboys who are more susceptible to "cookery" than to "medicine," but whose lives can be ruined if they succumb to form without regard to substance (Gorgias, 455E).

In the later dialogue, the Phaedrus, Plato further develops his notion of a philosophic rhetoric. Here he admits that while speakers can flatter and mislead audiences more successfully if they are trained in communication theory, they can also instruct and guide more successfully if they have these skills. Plato assumed that public audiences were highly susceptible and easily swayed and and that the only defense against "wrong" instruction was equally skilled "right" instruction. He personifies Rhetoric as saying:

I do not compel anyone to learn to speak without knowing the truth, but if my advice is of any value, he learns that first and then acquires me. So what I claim is this, that without my help the knowledge of the truth does not give the art of persuasion (260C).

Aristotle's treatment of the general nature of the relationship between speakers and audiences is less idealistic, though somewhat reminiscent of Plato's. In the Rhetoric, he too criticizes those who attempt to flatter audiences and to wrap their emotions. However, he does not stop with a simple appeal to "truth" and "justice." Instead, he claims that intelligent, competent, sincere speakers have more chance of success, for the public's judgment of the man has much to do with their reaction to his message. Of the speaker he says, "his character may almost be called the most effective means of persuasion he possesses" (1356a 12). Furthermore, he says, the truth of a speaker's character and his message, generally outs:

[T]hings that are true and things that are just have a natural tendency to prevail over their opposites, so that if the decision of the judges [audience members] are not what they ought to be, the defeat must be due to the speakers themselves . . . (1355a 21–23).

The view of audience implied in this statement is very different from Plato's gullible "schoolboys" image. Aristotle's audiences are "judges"; they are capable of accurately perceiving the character of a speaker and of evaluating his message. If the audience does not come to a "correct" judgment, then it is probably because of poor communication skills on the part of the speaker, not because the speaker is so skilled that he has twisted their minds. According to Aristotle, the usefulness of human communication theory and instruction in communication skills is that knowledge in itself will never be sufficient to convince a popular audience:

> [B]efore some audiences not even the possession of the exactest knowledge will make it easy for what we say to produce conviction. For argument based on knowledge implies instruction and there are people whom one cannot instruct. Here, then, we must use, as our modes of persuasion and argument, notions possessed by everybody, as we observed in the *Topics* when dealing with the way to handle a popular audience (1355a 24–28).

We have already discussed Aristotle's system of audience analysis, of how to discover the notions possessed by everybody, and of the "topics." The important point here is that Aristotle, and most of the other classical theorists, saw the general relationship between the speaker and his audience as complex and multidimensional. They were willing to make a few basic generalizations about kinds of audiences and occasions and relationships between kinds of speakers and kinds of audiences. Most of them, however, were not willing to go beyond providing a fundamental analytical system.

Operationalization

Verbally, the classical theorists assign great importance to operationalization (which they called "action" or "delivery"). Most, however, have little to say about it once they have granted its significance. Plato ignores it; Aristotle dismisses the topic in about 300 words; Cicero devotes no more than four or five pages to it. Apparently, even the sophists had little to say about it. This somewhat paradoxical state of affairs is probably traceable to the fact that, since most communication events were face-to-face and unmediated, the primary physical resources for the dissemination of information were the voice and body, and most theorists seemed to view use of the voice and body as more amenable to prescription than to theory. However, in spite of the scarcity of treatment, there does seem to be agreement among the classicists on some basic generalizations (see Fig. 2.8).

Aristotle says that delivery is "a thing that affects the success of a speech greatly; but hitherto the subject has been much neglected" (1403b 20). He explains that there are two reasons that no systematic theory has emerged. One is that the subject is not inherently worthy; the other is that delivery is a natural ability which can be improved by practice but probably is not amenable to being taught. The few who have tried to deal with it, he says, have come up with prescriptions more appropriate to "poetics," especially theatrical performance, than to practical communi-

---

Fig. 2.8   Classical Taxonomy on Operationalization

I. Appropriate Management of Voice Qualities
  A.   Volume
  B.   Stability
  C.   Flexibility
    1.   Conversational tone—Relaxed
      a.   Dignified—Impressive, restrained
      b.   Explicative—Calm
      c.   Narrative—Suspenseful
      d.   Facetious—Comedic
    2.   Tone of debate—Energetic
      a.   Sustained—Full-voiced and accelerated
      b.   Broken—Punctuated with short intermittent pauses
    3.   Tone of amplification—Rousing, emotional
      a.   Hortatory—Indignant
      b.   Pathetic—Pitying
II. Appropriate Management of the Body
  A.   Inconspicuous—Natural
  B.   Varied
  C.   Suitable to ideas, emotions, and context

---

cation. Still, he says that a practical theory could, and should, be devised, for operationalization is of practical importance:

> [D]elivery is—very properly—not regarded as an elevated subject of inquiry. Still, the whole business of rhetoric being concerned with appearances, we must pay attention to the subject of delivery, unworthy though it is, because we cannot do without it. The right thing in speaking really is that we should be satisfied not to annoy our hearers, without trying to delight them: we ought in fairness to fight our case with no help beyond the bare facts: nothing, therefore, should matter except the proof of those facts. Still, as has been already said, other things affect the result considerably, owing to the defects of our hearers. . . . the way in which a thing is said does affect its intelligibility (1404a 1–10).

Cicero, in De Oratore, says that delivery is "the most dominant factor in oratory" (III. lvi. 213). He too regrets that the subject has not been sufficiently dealt with in communication theory, that it "has been abandoned by the orators, who are the players that act real life, and has been taken over by the actors, who only mimic reality" (III. lvi. 214). He goes on to assert that the nonverbal factors, voice tone and body movement, must be consonant with the verbal in order for the speaker to be perceived as credible:

For nature has assigned to every emotion a particular look and tone of voice and bearing of its own; and the whole of a person's frame and every look on his face and utterance of his voice are like the strings of a harp, and sound according as they are struck by each successive emotion (III. lvii. 216).

These nonverbal accompaniments of the emotions, then, are natural and expected; to not exhibit them is to seem unnatural and therefore not trustworthy. To illustrate his point, Cicero provides a brief list of common classes of emotions and a description of the tones of voice that most often seem to accompany them. For each of the six classes of emotions he identifies, Cicero provides not only a brief description but also a phrase or two of poetry which he believes illustrates that particular emotion:

> [F]or anger—shrill, hasty, with short clauses, compassion and sorrow, wavering, full, halting, in a mournful key . . . fear, low and hesitating and despondent . . . energy, intense, vehement, eager with a sort of impressive urgency . . . joy, gushing, smooth, tender, cheerful and gay . . . dejection, heavy . . . drawn out in a single articulation and note (III. lviii. 217–lix. 220).

In addition to these paralinguistic accompaniments, emotions also are expressed in gestures:

> But all these emotions must be accompanied by gesture—not this stagy gesture reproducing the words but one conveying the general situation and idea not by mimicry but by hints (III. lix. 220).

For gestures, Cicero provides little description, seeming to agree with Aristotle that gesture should be natural, calling no attention to itself. Theatrical body movements or absence of any body movement are both unnatural and will inhibit the speaker's credibility. "For," Cicero says, "by action the body talks, so it is all the more necessary to make it agree with the thought" (III. lix. 223).

The most important part of body talk, according to Cicero, is the face, especially the eyes:

> But everything depends on the countenance, while the countenance itself is entirely dominated by the eyes. . . . For delivery is wholly the concern of the feelings, and these are mirrored by the face and expressed by the eyes; for this is the only part of the body capable of producing as many indications and variations as there are emotions, and there is nobody who can produce the same effect with the eyes shut (III. lix. 221).

Cicero has no prescriptions for the proper use of the body other than to observe the natural concurrence of movement and emotion and to maintain the body through exercise and nutrition.

He concludes his discussion of operationalization with a final observation of the function and scope of nonverbal communication:

> [I]t is delivery that has most effect on the ignorant and the mob and lastly on barbarians; for words influence nobody but the person allied to the speaker by sharing the same language, and clever ideas frequently outfly the understanding of people who are not clever, whereas delivery which gives the emotion of the mind expression influences everybody (III. lix. 223).

Thus, the classical theorists recommended that anyone who would be a public communicator understand the significance of appropriate use of media, in their case, voice and body. Convinced of the futility of written instruction about delivery, they made few prescriptions. Instead, they recommended that the communicator study music to improve voice control, gymnastics and wrestling to improve body control, and theatrical and private conversation to improve understanding of the concurrence of emotions with tone of voice, gesture, and facial expression.

Though the theorists tended to stop with this very general advice, classical educators apparently felt the need for more specific instruction, and there were textbooks written to fill this need. Typical of the prescriptive classical approach is the anonymous *Rhetorica Ad Herrenium*. This early Roman text attempts to provide specific precepts on every aspect of public communication, including delivery. The author's treatment foreshadows the detailed, technical approach of the English elocutionary movement of the eighteenth century and is therefore worthy of some attention (see summary in Fig. 2.8). It is not unusual in its general outline. He opens with a typical statement of the importance of delivery:

> Many have said that the faculty of greatest use to the speaker and the most valuable for persuasion is Delivery. For my part, I should not readily say that any one of the five faculties is the most important; that an exceptionally great usefulness resides in the delivery I should boldly affirm. For skillful inventions, elegant style, the artistic arrangement of the parts comprising the case, and the careful memory of all these will be of no more value without delivery, than delivery alone and independent of these (III. xi. 19).

He then divides the topic into management of voice and of body. He distinguishes three characteristics of voice quality: volume, stability, and flexibility. The first two, he says, are primarily gifts of nature which can be improved by practice, but the last can be learned from study. From this point, his treatment diverges from the norm somewhat, in that he further divides flexibility into three tones—conversational, debate, and amplification—which are discussed and analyzed in detail. Having prescribed the appropriate tones of voice for each of these, he then goes on to correlate the tones with specific body movements:

1. For the Dignified Conversational Tone, the speaker must stay in position when he speaks, lightly moving his right hand, his countenance expressing an emotion corresponding to the sentiments of the subject. . . .

2. For the Explicative Conversational Tone, we shall incline the body forward a little from the shoulders, since it is natural to bring the face as close as possible to our hearers when we wish to prove a point and arouse them vigorously.

3. For the Narrative Conversational Tone, the same physical movement as . . . for the Dignified. . . .

4. For the Facetious Conversational Tone, we should by our countenance express a certain gaiety, without changing gestures.

5. For the Sustained Tone of Debate, we shall use a quick gesture of the arm, a mobile countenance, and a keen glance.

6. For the Broken Tone of Debate, one must extend the arm very quickly, walk up and down, occasionally stamp the right foot, and adopt a keen and fixed look.

7. For the Hortatory Tone of Amplification, it will be appropriate to use a somewhat slower and more deliberate gesticulation, but otherwise to follow the procedure for the Sutained Tone of Debate.

8. For the Pathetic Tone of Amplification, one ought to slap one's thigh and beat one's head, and sometimes to use a calm and uniform gesticulation and a sad and disturbed expression (III. xv. 26–28).

The author is not totally unaware of the limited potential of his prescriptions. In concluding his treatment of the subject of delivery, he says:

I am not unaware how great a task I have undertaken in trying to express physical movements in words and portray vocal intonations in writing. True, I was not confident that it was possible to treat these matters adequately in writing. Yet neither did I suppose that, if such a treatment were impossible, it would follow that what I have done here would be useless, for it has been my purpose merely to suggest what ought to be done. The rest I shall leave to practice. This, nevertheless, one must remember: good delivery ensures that what the orator is saying seems to come from his heart (III. xxiv. 40).

Thus, even the most prescriptive of the classical treatments focuses in on the effects of operationalization in maintaining credibility and ensuring appropriate emotional response. In general, the classical writers agreed that the criteria of operationalization should be that it be natural, varied (depending upon relevant emotions), and appropriate to the ideas, the speaker, the audience, and the context.

Phase III: Adaptation and Decline

Classical human communication theory reached a peak of development in the first century B.C. with Ciceronian rhetoric. The five-part paradigm was broadly conceived and generally accepted. Rhetoric had become the most important discipline in Roman education. Academic training at Rome consisted of three levels: elementary—training in grammar, middle—training in literature, and advanced—training in rhetoric. The educational system was adapted from the Greek system, and, as Marrou puts it, "Hellenistic culture was above all things a rhetorical culture."[30] Ironically, however, having reached a peak of social and academic respectability, rhetoric in the last half of the first century B.C. ceased to be a dynamic, developing theoretical discipline. After the death of Cicero, there were no new classical theorists. Rhetoric became the province of professional educators—a subject to be taught rather than a science to be explored.

Caplan attributes this state of affairs primarily to the fall of the republic and the rise of dictatorial government. After the death of Caesar, Antony became a virtual dictator of Rome. He was succeeded by Emperor Augustus Octavian, who ruled from 30 B.C. to 14 A.D. Following Octavian, a series of dictatorial Emperors ruled Rome until its fall in 410 A.D. Under these reigns, the social conditions that had nourished the development of human communication theory in the ancient world ceased to exist.[31] The oral, democratic, communal society of Athens and early Rome gave way to the written, authoritarian, mass society of the Roman Empire. As Prentice Meador explains,

Conditions in the new Empire were inimical to creative oratory [the practice of public communication]: the length of speeches, number of advocates, and duration of court trials were reduced; orators ran

[30] Marrou, p. 269.
[31] Caplan, "Introduction," in *Rhetorica ad Herrenium.*

the risk of crossing the Emperor in every speech they gave; the dynamic issues of the past were, for the most part, absent; the power of the monarchy steadily encroached on the self-governing bodies. The problem of reconciling the organizational requirements of empire and self-government based on free interchange of ideas proved too difficult for Rome. The result was a general loss of those habits of self-government that had been nurtured in the earlier city-states. In short, the social and political conditions productive of creative rhetoric no longer marked the Roman world.[32]

Public speaking had been the prototypical communication situation for early human communication theory. Three areas of life especially demanded rhetorical skills: law, politics, and entertainment. In the new Roman Empire the first two ceased to be arenas for public participation.

Property rights, the administration of the colonies, the intricacies of trade became the primary legal questions to be dealt with in the courts of the Roman Empire. The practice of law became a profession. Legal technicians, who could interpret the complex details of written law to the satisfaction of the ruling class began to replace orators who could persuade large audiences of the justice of their case. The relatively small community of first-century B.C. Rome gave way to the metropolis of the first century A.D. Roman citizens lived in every part of the known world. As Murphy explains, "This widely distributed population demanded standardization of several kinds of institutions—schools, armies, and also laws. Standardization in turn increased the emphasis placed upon the written documents that were records of the laws."[33] Forensic speaking, which had been the backbone of rhetorical theory since Corax and Tisias, thus ceased to be a major outlet. The second type of speaking, deliberative, also became almost nonexistent. The senate became a rubber stamp for the Emperor. Secret police infiltrated the general population, eager to stamp out "sedition" even in the private sector. Serious deliberative discussion of the sort taught by Isocrates and practiced by Cicero became virtually impossible.

The only sphere of public communication left to the orator was epideictic, or ceremonial. The "speech to entertain" became the dominant form for the first time in the history of human communication theory. In terms of the theoretical paradigm, symbolization and operationalization began to be emphasized while the other three processes were either ignored or reduced to mechanical formulas. Display, rather than decision-making, became the dominant function of communication.

[32] Prentice A. Meador, Jr., "Quintilian and the *Institutio Oratoria*," in Murphy, ed., A *Synoptic History of Classical Rhetoric*, p. 152.
[33] Murphy, p. 178.

Traveling lecturers drew large crowds to their performances. Students in the schools of rhetoric presented public demonstrations of their skill in declamation. The focus was on technique—ornamental language, complex argument, and dramatic gesture. As Cary and Haarhoff explain:

> With the fall of the republic the scope of oratory was so far reduced that its study, though carried on with unabated zeal, was no longer directed to practical ends, but became an academic exercise. The rhetoricians abandoned Cicero's ideal of wide knowledge, sound morality, and practical experience, and endeavoured to disguise the lack of content in their speeches by the pyrotechnics of *sententiae* or pointed sayings. It is true that the greatest of the teachers of oratory, Quintilian (c. 35–100), endeavoured to revert to the sounder traditions of republican times. . . . But he failed to carry his contemporaries with him.[34]

One of the first critics of human communication practice, Seneca (55 B.C.–38 A.D.), noted these trends early in the first century A.D. He charged that rhetorical training no longer focused on the serious questions of everyday life. Seneca published two works, the *Controversiae* and the *Suasoriae*. These were collections of excerpts from school exercises used to teach communication skills. Controversiae were legal, and suasoriae were political, declamations. Originally, declamations were designed to allow the student to practice and develop skill in dealing with questions and topics relevant to "real world" concerns. By the middle of the first century A.D., however, when Seneca's collections were published, declamation had become a fanciful, unrealisitic exercise in ingenuity. Topics often involved dragons carrying off beautiful young maidens or impossibly tangled legal situations involving complex kinship and inheritance issues. The fictiousness of the exercises led Seneca to claim that rhetorical training had become an end in itself rather than preparation for life.[35]

One of the first historians of human communication, Tacitus (55–120 A.D.), made similar observations in his *Dialogue Concerning Oratory*. The major speakers in the dialogue are Maternus, an orator who has retired from law to write poetry, and Aper, a practicing orator. A major theme in the discussion is the decline in quality of oratory since the early days of the Roman Republic. The decline is attributed to the loss of democratic government, lax morality, and inferior rhetorical instruction.[36]

[34] Cary and Haarhoff, p. 270.
[35] Seneca the Elder, *Suasoirae*, translated by W. A. Edward (Cambridge: The University Press, 1928); see also Bryant, pp. 92–93.
[36] Tacitus, *Dialogues on Oratory: The Complete Works of Tacitus*, translated by A. J. Church and W. J. Brodribb (New York: The Modern Library, 1942).

Needless to say, lack of opportunity for serious public communication because of political repression and poor quality instruction in the schools were not independent events. Given that the main outlet for the practice of communication was public entertainment, it is not surprising that instruction focused on stylistic ornamentation and operational virtuosity rather than on systematic analysis of the topic, audience, and situation. Other treatises on communication which survive from the end of the classical period for the most part tend to support the charges of Seneca and Tacitus.

One of the most important was Hermogenes' textbook, the *Progymnasmata* (second century A.D.). The book includes five chapters: Elementary Exercises (grammar), On Status (a technical term for the analysis of the central issue in legal cases), On Invention, On Qualities of Style, and On the Pattern for Rhetorical Effectiveness. As the titles of the chapters indicate, Hermongenes dealt with the full classical paradigm, but his emphasis was on the consummatory rather than instrumental functions of communication. He elevates style and delivery to major importance and treats memory, arrangement, and invention in terms of the mechanical formulae of the ancient sophists. In spite of this imbalance, the *Progymnasmata* is one of the few later Roman treatises to deal with all the constituents of classical rhetoric, and it was a major influence not only in the later Roman schools but also in the schools of the medieval and Renaissance periods.[37] Hermogenes' work led to another, by Aphthonius (fifth century A.D.). Aphthonius' *Progymnasmata* included fourteen exercises—similar to those of Hermogenes—in the composition of fables, proverbs, commonplaces, and vituperations. Aphthonius' textbook also remained popular in the schools from the fifth through the seventeenth century.[38]

Given the emphasis upon composition and the focus on symbolization characteristic of the late classical period, it is not surprising that grammatical theory began to compete with rhetorical. The first textbooks on grammar appeared around 350 A.D. Donatus, a grammar instructor in Rome, wrote two manuals, *Ars Minor* (an exposition of the eight parts of speech) and *Ars Major* (a treatment of the figures of speech) which remained standard textbooks for nearly twelve hundred years. Throughout the medieval and renaissance period, rhetorical and grammatical theory were so interwoven in the area of symbolization that it was difficult to distinguish the two. By the end of the fourth century, grammarians and rhetoricians had compiled a taxonomy of some 200 different figures of speech and thought—called "schemes and tropes." In the *Institutes*, Quintilian had warned that grammarians seemed to have "appropriated what does not belong to them" (II. 1). He foresaw the

[37] See Bryant, pp. 56–57.
[38] See Bryant, p. 5.

possibility that the study of grammar might replace the study of rhetoric. As it turned out, he was not far wrong. The study of the technicalities of language, however, did not replace rhetoric, it became almost the whole of rhetoric. In other words, rhetoric ceased to be a general theory of communication and became a theory of symbolization and operationalization.

In short, we can say that the classical period of human communication theory began with a focus on speaking skills and ended with a focus on speaking and writing skills. In between was a whole theory of the processes of human interaction. Once the complete classical paradigm was developed, it never completely died out; but it was distorted to the point that at the beginning of the medieval period "rhetoric" was no longer viewed as a major and respected academic discipline. Plato's criticisms of "sophistic" rhetoric in the *Gorgias* are as applicable to the rhetorical literature of the end of the period as they were to that of the beginning. In fact, among historians of communication theory, the last 300 years of the classical period are known as the "Second Sophistic."

The medieval and Renaissance period in the history of human communication theory thus begins, conceptually, back at the beginning.

Chapter 3

The Medieval
and Renaissance Period

From the declining centuries of the classical period, we move into the Middle Ages and the Renaissance. Trends appearing at the end of the classical period (during the Second Sohisitic) accelerate in the early medieval period (approximately 400 to 1000 A.D.) and continue to influence the development of human communication theory throughout the late medieval period and the Renaissance (approximately 1000 to 1600 A.D.), that is, until the beginning of the modern period. The orderliness and sense of progressive theory building that had been characteristic of the classical period give way to disorder and confusion as scholars attempt to adapt classical theory to a very different social world. The content of medieval and Renaissance human communication theory, though maintaining a surface resemblance to that of the classical, seems by comparison superficial and academic rather than philosophical and pragmatic. Many contemporary scholars have characterized the period as being essentially "scholastic," in the worst sense of that term.

As we have seen, the final centuries of the classical period were characterized by stagnation and decay in political, social, and scholarly spheres. Cary and Haarhoff explain:

In the later years of the second century the Roman world was showing signs of becoming hard-set. New land was no longer being brought into cultivation, and in the absence of fresh technical inventions economic production achieved no further growth. In art and literature new ideas were no longer finding expression. This arrest of progress . . . had not yet passed over into the stage of actual decay, and need not have done so, if the Roman Empire had continued to enjoy political stability.[1]

---

[1] M. Cary and T. J. Haarhoff, *Life and Thought in the Greek and Roman World* (London: Methuen and Co., Ltd., 1940), pp. 88–89.

The Empire, however, did not maintain political stability. In the third century, a series of revolutions led by the Roman army resulted in military anarchy. Civil wars abounded. Emperors were installed and deposed with startling rapidity. Invasions of the Empire by Germanic tribes, Goths, and Franks further disrupted the political, social, and, of course, academic life of Rome. In spite of the efforts of leaders like Diocletian and Constantine, the orderly, unified world of the classical period was irreparably disrupted. By the fourth century, national government had virtually disappeared. A class of major landholders had emerged and begun to develop the feudal system of quasi-independent states. The Christian clergy, thanks primarily to the support of Constantine, had become a politically powerful bureaucracy.[2] In the fifth century, the last emperor was deposed and the Roman Empire in the West clearly came to an end.[3] It was replaced by what might most accurately be characterized as "Monolithic Christian Feudalism." It was "monolithic" in the sense that by the end of the fourth century A.D., the Christian Church was established as the most pervasive and powerful institution in the Western world. Its bureaucracy was in place. "Religion" meant Christianity. Although the landholders were all-powerful dictators, maintaining absolute control over every aspect of their subjects' lives, they in turn were subject to the laws, practices, and principles of the Roman Catholic Church. Politics, law, and ceremony revolved around the Church. All questions were utilmately religious questions.[4] The effects of this social revolution on human communication theory were extensive.

Probably the most far-reaching of these was the repudiation of the classical rhetorical tradition. In our discussion of the classical period, it seemed appropriate to use the terms "rhetoric" and "human communication theory" as virtually synonymous. Rhetoric was *the* discipline of communication. Its paradigm was clearly established and widely subscribed to. With the advent of Christianity, however, rhetoric ceased to be a vital, developing discipline. Christian leaders saw the rhetorical tradition as a threat to their most fundamental beliefs. Classical human communication theory was predicated upon "probability," the premise that in human affairs "the truth" is unknowable, that human realities are socially constructed. Christianity, however, was predicated upon "fact," the premise that absolute truth is knowable through divine revelation. The problem for the Christian communicator is not to "persuade" himself and others of likelihoods, but to discover for himself and instruct others in "the will of God." Thus, Christian leaders condemned the study of the "pagan" art of rhetoric. The effect of their condemnation was the fragmentation of the classical paradigm and the virtual disap-

---

[2] Cary and Haarhoff, pp. 89–90.
[3] Eileen Power, *Medieval People* (London: Methuen and Co., Ltd., 1963), p. 11.
[4] Paul Abelson, *The Seven Liberal Arts* (New York, Thesis, Columbia University, 1906), p. 8.

pearance of the concept of human communication as a unified discipline. Ultimately, this led to nearly one thousand years of stagnation of communication theory.

Human communication did not, however, cease to be studied and written about during the medieval and Renaissance periods. In terms of pragmatics, there were two major genres of communicative acts, letter writing and preaching, which claimed the attention of scholars. Both were classified as "rhetorical" activities, and most of the machinery of classical rhetoric was adapted to the need for instruction in them. For instance, official letters were generally treated as deliberative or forensic "oratory," and writers were instructed to pay close attention to the use of proof, especially example and enthymeme. Familiar letters were treated as a species of epideictic oratory, and writers were instructed in the use of figures of speech for embellishment. Likewise, sermons could be classified as dealing primarily with expedience and inexpedience, justice and injustice, or praise and blame.

Letter writing was an activity central to both secular and religious order. Compared to the relatively close-knit social world of the classical period, the medieval world was widely dispersed. Rather than one center of power and culture, there were hundreds. The secular world was made up of relatively independent feudal kingdoms. The church bureaucracy was spread throughout the Western world. Both the feudal kingdoms and the church organization required means for communicating across distances, and both required complicated machinery for record keeping. Letter writing thus became an important activity for political, legal, and social reasons. Letters were used to request or dispense political decrees, privileges, and commissions, legal mandates, dispensations and contracts, and also to maintain personal relationships. Murphy quotes a typical medieval form letter for announcing the establishment of a ruler/subject relationship:

> It is right that those who have promised us unbroken faith should be rewarded by our aid and protection. Now since our faithful subject (name) with the will of God has come to our palace with his arms and has there sworn in our hands to keep his trust and fidelity to us, therefore we decree and command by this present writing that henceforth the said (name) is to be numbered among our *antrustiones* (i.e., dependents). If anyone shall presume to slay him, let him know that he shall have to pay 600 solidi as a wergeld for him.[5]

This letter clearly demonstrates the dual informing/recording functions of the letter in medieval life as well as the political, legal, and social func-

[5] James Murphy, *Rhetoric in the Middle Ages: A History of Rhetorical Theory from Saint Augustine to the Renaissance* (Berkeley: University of California Press, 1974), p. 20.

tions. The fact that it is a form letter, one of dozens of forms for every purpose preserved in collections, further indicates the importance of letters as governmental and legal records.

Letter writing was taught in medieval schools, and eventually, in the early Renaissance, a body of practical manuals and theoretic literature evolved, the *ars dictaminis*.

If letter writing was the primary genre of written communication, preaching was the primary genre of formal oral communication. As with letter writing, preaching was taught in the schools, but, with the exception of Augustine's *On Christian Doctrine* (426 A.D.), formal theories began to emerge only in the eleventh century. From then until the end of the Renaissance, however, hundreds of practical manuals and treatises, known as *artes praedicandi*, appeared. As with the *ars dictaminis*, *artes praedicandi* employed much of the terminology and classification system of classical rhetorics.

The primary focus in these manuals was on organization and categorization. Their purpose was to assist the preacher in ordering, and recalling, the substance of his sermon. Many also provided help in symbolization through the methods of "copia," or amplification. Much of classical conceptualization theory was also preserved in the use of the topics as organizational devices. Instruction in operationalization, though scanty, was based on the precepts for the use of voice and body in the *Rhetorica ad Herrenium* and was taught in conjunction with levels of style (grand, middle, plain) and the functions of oratory (to persuade, please, and instruct).

In terms of practice, a third activity, the medieval "miracle play," may have contributed somewhat to the continuation of interest in formal communication. As with letter writing and preaching, there was little theorizing connected with acting before the later Renaissance. The few treatises that appeared before the fourteenth century tended to focus on the content and staging of plays. In the later Renaissance, however, acting began to be a more central concern. As we will see, in the early modern period, the boundaries between theatre and "real life" became gradually less distinct in communication literature. The seventeenth- and eighteenth-century manuals on "elocution," or artistic oral delivery, assumed that an actor and an "orator" were engaged in overlapping professions and thus needed essentially the same training. For instance, in Heywood's *Apology for Actors* (1612), we find that an "excellent actor" is characterized as an "orator" who "charms our attention." In line with a tradition going back to ancient treatises on pantomime, acting is clearly regarded as a "rhetorical" activity. Heywood says that an actor must master the five rhetorical arts, especially the second part of delivery, bodily action:

> In the *Rhetorica ad Herrenium*, Cicero [sic] requires five things in an orator—invention, disposition, elocution [style], memory, and

pronuntiation; yet all are imperfect without . . . action, for be his invention never so fluent and exquisite, his disposition and order never so composed and formall, his eloquence and elaborate phrases never so materiall and pithy, his memory never so firme and reten- tive, his pronuntiation never so musicall and plausive, yet without a comely and elegant gesture, a gratious and bewitching kinde of action, a naturall and familiar motion of the head, the hand, the body, and a moderate and fit countenance sutable to all the rest, I hold all the rest as nothing.[6]

Though, as this excerpt reveals, drama was generally viewed as a branch of formal public communication, the medieval and early Renais- sance scholars apparently did not view it as worthy, in the same sense as letter writing and preaching, of either practical instruction or theoretic inquiry. (The excerpt also reveals the preoccupation with "dramatic delivery" that flowered in the seventeenth and eighteenth century elocutionary movement—see Chap. 4.)

Thus, it was the manuals on letter writing and preaching that served to keep much of the content of classical theory alive; however, these tended to be prescriptive and atheoretic. Their focus on the everyday concerns of the bureaucrat and the preacher contributed little to the advancement of human communication theory. Also, in contrast to the classical period, there was no single, respected discipline that could serve as a focus for theoretic synthesis. The classical paradigm of "pagan rhetoric" did not completely disappear from scholarship, but its parts were, for the most part, treated as "steps" to follow in writing and speaking. The theoretic content was divided among four different disci- plines: theology, grammar, rhetoric, and dialectic. Metaphorically, we might view classical human communication theory as a large jigsaw puz- zle. The early medieval scholars did not destroy this puzzle; they merely scattered the pieces. In a sense, the history of the period, then, is the story of a continuing struggle to put the pieces back together in some meaningful pattern; it is the story of an assortment of theories in search of a discipline.

In tracing this "struggle," we will examine (1) the medieval and Renaissance taxonomy of knowledge, with special emphasis on the de- valuation of human communication as a theoretic study, (2) the disper- sion of the parts of the paradigm into a number of specialized studies, e.g., public speaking, letter writing, preaching, literary analysis, scholas- tic logic, and (3) the specific treatment of each part of the paradigm in the scholarship of the period.

[6] Quoted in A. M. Nagler, A Source Book in Theatrical History (New York: Dover Publications, Inc., 1952), p. 124.

The Medieval and Renaissance
Taxonomy of Knowledge

The ascendance of Christianity and of the Christian Church in the medieval period led to significant revisions in the educational curriculum inherited from the Greeks and Romans. At the height of the classical period, education in Greece consisted of four elementary subjects: grammar, gymnastics, music, and drawing. There were two secondary subjects, arithmetic and geometry, and one higher subject, rhetoric, which, as we have seen, included philosophy, ethics, politics, etc. Education for the Greek citizen continued into his early thirties. Early Roman adaptations of this system consisted primarily of shortening the number of years devoted to education and emphasizing the practical over the theoretic. In the last years of the classical period, the Second Sophistic, the educational time span was further reduced, theoretic studies nearly eliminated, and the number of subjects limited to seven.[7]

In the medieval period, these trends continued, but with additional modifications. What is most relevant here is that medieval culture was theological rather than rhetorical; thus the communication disciplines were reduced to the most elementary of technical studies. Also, education began to be the privilege primarily of those who chose careers in the Church. Schools belonged to monasteries, and monks served as the "professors." One result of this development was that, until about the eleventh century, illiteracy was more the rule than the exception. In tenth-century Europe, not only the general population but most kings and princes were unable to read or write.[8] Even with the rise of the universities in the early Renaissance, illiteracy remained widespread. The universities were Church-dominated and tended to be equivalent to our high schools in terms of the ages of the students and the level of study in areas other than theology. Nontheological, popular education did not begin to flourish until the beginning of the modern period.[9]

The general taxonomy of knowledge developed within this system had important implications for medieval and Renaissance conceptions of human communication theory. By the end of the fourth century, education—and by extension, all knowledge—was divided into two classes: divine and secular. Divine knowledge meant theology; more specifically, it meant understanding the precepts of "the holy scriptures." Secular knowledge meant "the seven liberal arts."

The liberal arts were divided into two subclasses. The first, the *trivium* (also called the "language arts," the "arts of discourse," or the

---

[7] Abelson, pp. 1–3.

[8] Murphy, *Rhetoric in the Middle Ages*, p. 197.

[9] For a more detailed discussion, see volume I of Hastings Rashdall, *The Universities of Europe in the Middle Ages*, new edition, edited by F. M. Powicke and A. B. Emden, three volumes (Oxford: Claredon Press, 1936).

"rational arts"), included three disciplines—grammar, rhetoric, and dialectic. The second class, the *quadrivium* (also called the "mathematical arts," the "sciences," or "philosophy"), included four disciplines—arithmetic, music, geometry, and astronomy.[10] The acceptance of this taxonomy was apparently universal and absolute. Not until the late Renaissance did scholars begin even to question the usefulness and comprehensiveness of this scheme. As late as the mid-sixteenth century, it continued to be the standard taxonomy for defining knowledge. Thomas Wilson, in his *Arte of Logike*, summarizes this tradition in a brief poem:

> *Grammar* doeth teach to utter wordes:
> To speake both apt and plaine.
> *Logike* by Arte, settes forthe the truthe,
> And doeth tell what is vaine.
> *Rhetorike* at large paintes well the cause,
> And makes that seem right gaie
> Which *Logike* spake but at a word
> And taught us by the waie.
> *Musike* with tunes, delites the eare:
> And makes us thinke it heaven.
> *Arithmetike* by nomres can make
> Reckenynges to be even.
> *Geometrie* thynges thicke and broade,
> Measures by line and square:
> *Astronomie* by starres doeth tell;
> Of foule and eke of faire.[11]

Thus, for more than one thousand years, theology or divine knowledge and the seven liberal arts or secular knowledge formed the controlling scholarly paradigm.

Divine Learning: Theology

A primary effect of this taxonomy was the replacement of the classical rhetorical tradition with a theological one. In fact, much of what was originally included in rhetoric was transferred, with some fundamental revisions, to theology. Although they repudiated the rhetorical tradition as pagan, the early medieval theorists were heavily influenced by classical

---

[10] We do not know exactly when the concept of the seven liberal arts was formalized or by whom the phrase was coined. The earliest authoritative treatment that survives is *The Marriage of Philology [Grammar] and Mercury [Rhetoric]* (c. 330) by Martianus Capella. Most scholars believe the work to be derivative rather than original, but its existence established the emergence of the seven liberal arts taxonomy in the late third or early fourth century. See Abelson, *The Seven Liberal Arts*, pp. 6–7.

[11] G. W. Mair, ed., "Introduction," in Thomas Wilson, *Arte of Rhetorique* (Oxford: Clarendon Press, 1909), p. xx.

scholarship. In the classical taxonomy, the highest good was "eloquence," and the highest study was rhetoric. In the medieval taxonomy, the highest good became "sacred eloquence," and the highest study, "divine communication."

The major (some would say "only") medieval theorist, Augustine (354–430 A.D.), makes this transference from rhetoric to theology explicit both in his career and in his writing. Augustine was born in Tagaste, Africa, where, in 373, he began a career as a teacher of grammar. After a year as a *grammaticus*, he left Tagaste to go to Carthage, where he established himself as a rhetorician. In 384, he accepted the municipal chair of rhetoric at Milan.

After only two years in this post, Augustine converted to Christianity, retired from his chair, and began preparing to enter the Catholic Church. In 388, he sold his property and entered a monastery, planning to devote his life to study and writing. During this period, he published several philosophical dialogues on Christian doctrine and practice and rejected his former study of the "pagan" philosophy of rhetoric. In 391, despite his preference for the monastic life, he was ordained into the priesthood, and five years later he was appointed Bishop of Hippo.[12] In these positions, first as priest and later as Bishop, he became an extremely influential preacher, teacher, and theologian. This career led to many requests for advice and interpretation of Christian precepts, and these probably prompted him to continue writing and publishing theological and philosophical treatises.

In terms of human communication theory, Augustine's most important work is *On Christian Doctrine* (397–426). In this treatise he summarizes the best of classical human communication theory, applying it to the interpretation of the Bible and other theological writing and to preaching. In the preface, he explains that the purpose of his work is to teach rules for "interpretation," for "earnest students of the word, that they may profit not only from reading the works of others who have laid open the secrets of the sacred writings, but also from themselves opening such secrets to others."[13] As Augustine defines "interpretation," we discover that his topic is communication, that is, the processes of understanding messages, of making meanings of persons, objects, and events (receiving), and of using messsges, of making meanings about persons, objects, and events (sending): "There are two things on which all interpretation of scripture depends: the mode of ascertaining the proper meaning, and the mode of making known the meaning when it is ascertained" (I. 1). Furthermore, Augustine defines the central aspect of

[12] See J. F. Shaw, trans., "Intrpduction," in Augustine, *On Christian Doctrine*, in *Great Books of the Western World*, vol. 18 (Chicago: Encyclopaedia Britannica, Inc., 1952).
[13] Augustine, *On Christian Doctrine*, J. F. shaw, trans., p. 621. All subsequent references within the text are to this translation.

interpretation as what we would call "symbolic interaction," that is, the human use of symbols (which he calls "signs"). As he explains: "All instruction is either about things or about signs; but things are learnt by means of signs" (I. 2). Thus, knowledge can be acquired only through human interpretation of symbolic representation, through human communication.

Though *On Christian Doctrine* is ostensibly a theological treatise, its primary focus is on the communication process. Augustine is not interpreting Christianity so much as teaching others how to interpret it for themselves and for others. He thus sets precedents for those scholars who followed him. First, he takes the teachings of Plato, Aristotle, and Cicero, purges them of their "heretical" premises, and makes them fundamental to all learning and thus a part of the domain of theology. In Book I, he discusses the categorization process, the basic perception of "things," or phenomena. In Book II, he concentrates on conceptualization, the interpretation of "signs of things" in accordance with the precepts of Christianity. Though he introduces his theory of signs in this book, it is in Book III that he turns explicitly to symbolization. In Book II, signs are treated in terms of information acquisition; in Book III, in terms of clarity and ambiguity of signification. Book IV focuses explicitly on operationalization and includes much of the more technical aspects of organization and symbolization theory from classical rhetoric, especially as presented by Cicero. Thus Augustine legitimizes much of classical rhetorical theory by making it basic to Christian learning.

Later Christian scholars made the subjugation of rhetoric to theology more explicit. For instance, "The Venerable Bede," writing in the late seventh and early eighth centuries, sets out to show that divine literature is the original and superior source of secular knowledge.

Bede is primarily known as the author of the first history of England, *An Ecclesiastical History of the English People*. His other works include more than thirty books on theology, grammar, history, and science, as well as a collection of sermons. In 701, Bede published a very influential treatise, *Concerning Figures and Tropes*, the purpose of which was to prove that "Holy Writ [the Bible] surpasses all other writings not merely in authority because it is divine, or in usefulness because it leads to eternal life, but also for its age and artistic composition. . . ."[14] Bede's method is "to demonstrate by means of examples collected from Holy Writ that teachers of secular eloquence in any age have not been able to furnish us with any of these figures and tropes which did not appear first in Holy Writ" (*Figures and Tropes*, p. 237).

Bede's source for the eighteen figures and thirteen tropes he iden-

[14] Gussie Hecht Tannenhaus, "Bede's De Schemetibus et tropis—A Translation," *Quarterly Journal of Speech* (October 1962), 237. All subsequent references within the text are to this translation.

tifies is the Roman handbook, the *Rhetorica ad Herrenium*. His approach is unique only in the fact that his examples come from the Bible rather than from classical literature.

Later in the medieval and Renaissance periods, when the predominance of theological studies was so firmly established that scholars no longer felt the need to take such a defensive posture toward secular subjects, Biblical and classical examples and allusions tend to appear side by side. For instance, one of the most influential treatises on human communication, Alcuin's *Dialogue of Alciun and Charlemagne Concerning Rhetoric and the Virutes* (794), includes a discussion of the Christian virtues—prudence, justice, temperance, and courage—as part of the subject matter of rhetoric. John of Salisbury's *Metalogicon* (1159) relies on biblical examples, such as the virgin birth, to illustrate Aristotelian concepts of syllogistic argumentation. Thomas Wilson, in his *Arte of Rhetorique* (1553), uses many examples from sermons and preaching to illustrate good and bad rhetorical practice. By the time Wilson was writing, of course, the Renaissance and its secular learning and the Reformation, the revolt against the Catholic Church, were in full swing. However, even though the monolithic control of scholarship eventually weakened, religion remained a dominant force in communication theory, education, and practice.

A second precedent set by Augustine's *On Christian Doctrine* is the explicit study of preaching as a legitimate activity for theological scholarship. This had the initial effect of further subjugating secular to theological learning. The long-term effect was that late medieval and early Renaissance scholars produced a massive body of literature on the "art of preaching." Though of little theoretic value, these manuals assured the continued interest in human communication as an activity worthy of study. Furthermore, they preserved much of the content of classical rhetorical theory, for Augustine explicitly approved the use of classical rhetoric as a foundation for this study:

> Now, the art of rhetoric being available for the enforcing either of truth or falsehood, who will dare to say that truth in the person of its defenders is to take its stand unarmed against falsehood? For example, that those who are trying to persuade men of what is false are to know how to introduce their subject, so as to put the hearer into a friendly, or attentive, or teachable frame of mind, while the defenders of the truth shall be ignorant of that art? That the former are to tell their falsehoods briefly, clearly, and plausibly, while the latter shall tell the truth in such a way that it is tedious to listen to, hard to understand, and, in fine, not easy to believe it? That the former are to oppose the truth and defend falsehood with sophistical arguments, while the latter shall be unable either to defend what is true, or to refute what is false? That the former, while imbuing the minds of their hearers with erroneous opinions, are by their power

of speech to awe, to melt, to enliven, and to rouse them, while the latter shall in defence of the truth be sluggish, and frigid, and somnolent? Who is such a fool as to think this wisdom? Since, then, the faculty of eloquence is available for both sides, and is of very great service in the enforcing either of wrong or right, why do not good men study to engage it on the side of truth, when bad men use it to obtain the triumph of wicked and worthless causes, and to further injustice and error? (*Chris. Doc.*, IV. 2).

Thus, due to Augustine's influence, rhetoric ceased to be a forbidden subject for the Christian scholar, as did the other secular arts. However, Augustine's legitimation of the study of rhetoric did not restore the subject to its original role in scholarship. Augustine clearly subjugates rhetoric, and all secular learning, to theology; the skills one may develop from the study of secular arts are thought of as aids to the study of religion. For instance, he urges the study of grammar, for the scriptures are full of grammatical figures, i. e., metaphor, allegory, etc., and the Christian communicator should learn how to recognize and interpret them (*Chris. Doc.*, II. 29). Dialectic also is useful, for this art, "which deals with inferences, and definitions, and divisions, is of the greatest assistance in the discovery of meaning" (II. 37).

Secular Learning: The Seven Liberal Arts

Augustine's tone throughout *On Christian Doctrine* is highly reminiscent of Cicero's in *De Oratore*. He urges broad general learning; he is philosophical rather than prescriptive. However, while Cicero's objective was the description of the ideal citizen, an "orator," Augustine's is the description of an ideal Christian, a scholar-priest. Writers of the next few centuries, heavily influenced by Augustine, tended to overlook the broad theoretic thrust of his work, reducing it to a narrow, and narrowing, prescriptiveness. For instance, while Augustine lists more than a dozen educational subjects which the Christian communicator should study, later writers tended to narrow this list to the prescribed seven liberal arts. While Augustine had urged continued and integrated study of both secular and theological subjects, later writers tended to view the secular as elementary and preparatory to the theological. Thus a rigid curriculum developed.

An eighth century treatise, *Elements of Philosophy* (attributed to "The Venerable Bede"), summarizes this view:

> The order of learning is as follows. Since *eloquentia* is the instrument of all teaching, they are instructed in it first. Its three parts are correct writing and correct delivery of what is written; proof of what is to be proved, which *dialectica* teaches; figures of words and sentences, which *rhetorica* hands down. Therefore we are to be initiated in *grammatica*, then in *dialectica*, afterward in *rhetorica*.

Equipped with these arms, we should approach the study of philosophy. Here the order is first the quadrivium, and in this first *arithmetica*, second *musica*, third *geometria*, fourth *astronomia*, then holy writ, so that through knowledge of what is created we arrive at knowledge of the Creator (emphases by translator).[15]

Thus is broad general learning reduced to seven "steps" to the study of theology. Thus also the communication disciplines, the arts of the trivium, are made the basic, but most elementary, subjects.

The Trivium   The reduction of human communication from the most advanced to the most elementary of subjects necessarily led to simplistic and technical conceptions. The division of the discipline into three school subjects furthered this trend and led to a great deal of confusion over the contents of each "art." Parts of the classical paradigm were given to each of the three arts, but whether conceptualization, for instance, "belonged" to dialectic or to rhetoric was a topic of constant debate. On the other hand, scholars often seemed to accept that one part of the paradigm could belong to more than one art but could not agree on how to distribute the contents of that part. For instance, both grammar and rhetoric were obviously concerned with symbolization, but medieval scholars debated for centuries about which "figures of speech" belonged to grammatical and which to rhetorical symbolization.

A major source, and thus exemplar, of these technical, simplistic, and confusing conceptions of the trivium was Cassiodorus Senator (480–575). Cassiodorus was an influential statesman and scholar in sixth century Italy. From 503 to 539 he held a series of important political positions; then, at sixty, he retired from political activity and devoted himself to Christian scholarship. He established two monasteries, collected important classical and theological manuscripts, taught the monks to copy and preserve them, and published scriptural commentaries.

In terms of the history of human communication theory, Cassiodorus' most important work is *An Introduction to Divine and Human Readings* (c. 555). The title indicates Cassiodorus' acceptance of the traditional medieval taxonomy. The first half of the book is a summary of Christian theology and a guide to the writings of major Christian theologians. The second half is a summary of each of the seven liberal arts. In the Preface, Cassiodorus explains that his purpose is to outline the Christian approach to learning. He says that the book is meant to serve "in the place of a teacher," to guide those eager for learning, and to show how "the unbroken line of the Divine scriptures and the compendious knowledge of secular letters might with the Lord's beneficence be re-

[15] Quoted in C. S. Baldwin, *Medieval Rhetoric and Poetic* (New York: Macmillan Co., 1928), pp. 128–9.

lated. . . ."[16] Cassiodorus clearly subjugates secular to religious studies. He urges initial study of the tenets of religion, followed by general study of the liberal arts and by in-depth study of theology. Then, as he says, "Happy indeed the soul which . . . through critical searching has learned the paths of knowledge and . . . is filled with divine communication" (I. 2).

The order by which one progresses is the same as that recommended in *Elements of Philosophy*—trivium, quadrivium, scripture. Cassiodorus, however, is clearly fearful of the possible effects of secular learning. On Augustine's authority, he claims that secular knowledge must be "restored to sacred literature and taught in connection with it" (I. xxvii. 1), and he warns his readers repeatedly of the dangers of getting sidetracked.

Having set forth his plan for religious education, and having cautioned his readers about the dangers of "human" learning, Cassiodorus turns to his summaries of the seven liberal arts. His treatment of the arts of the trivium is an excellent example of medieval and early Renaissance tendencies to preserve the terminology and form, the "dry husks,"[17] of classical theory while discarding the substance. The summaries also re-

---

Fig. 3.1   Taxonomy of Grammar from Cassiodorus' *Introduction to Divine and Human Readings*

I. Province—Poetry and prose, oral and written messages
II. Purpose—The creation of faultless prose and verse; to please through skill in finished speech and blameless writing
III. Parts
    A.   The spoken word—Vibration of air perceptible to hearing
    B.   The letters of the alphabet—The smallest part of a word
    C.   The syllable—A single unit of a word, a group of letters or a vowel
    D.   Feet—Proper reckoning of syllables and quantity
    E.   Accentuation—Proper pronunciation
    I.   Punctuation and proper phrasing—Well-regulated pausing
    G.   The eight parts of speech—Noun, pronoun, verb, adverb, participle, conjunction, preposition, interjection
    H.   Figures of Speech—Transformations of words or thoughts; ninety-eight in number
    I.   Etymologies—Origins of words
    J.   Orthography—Composing

---

[16] Cassiodorus, *An Introduction to Divine and Human Readings*, Leslie Weber Jones, trans. (New York: Columbia University Press, 1946), p. 67. All subsequent references within the text are to this translation.
[17] Luke M. Reinsma, "Rhetoric in England: The Age of Aelfric, 970–1020," *Communication Monographs* (1977), p. 400.

veal the confusing and overlapping nature of typical conceptions of the three arts.

Cassiodorus begins with grammar (see Fig. 3.1), which he calls "the source and foundation of liberal studies" (Preface, Book II). He defines grammar as "skill in the art of cultivated speech—skill acquired from famous writers of poetry and prose; its function is the creation of faultless prose and verse; its end is to please through skill in finished speech and blameless writing" (II. ii. 1). Thus grammar includes the study of fiction as well as nonfiction, prose as well as poetry, and includes both oral and written communication. The subject matter of grammar, he says, is "the spoken word, the letter, the syllable, feet, accentuation, punctuation and proper phrasing, the eight parts of speech . . . figures of speech [of which there are ninety-eight kinds], etymologies, and orthography" (II. i. 2). As we can see from this list, medieval grammar included a mixture of what we would call grammar plus materials from poetics, composition, linguistics, typography, and speech. It's essential content, however, was symbolization.

After grammar, Cassiodorus turns to rhetoric (see Fig. 3.2), which, he says, is an extensive and rich discipline that "has been amply treated by many illustrative writers." The word *rhetoric*, he explains, means "skill in making a set speech . . . [it] is expertness in discourse on civil questions" (II. ii. 1). He goes on to add Quintilian's definition of the practitioner, the orator, as "a good man skilled in speaking." The function of an orator, he explains, is to persuade (or come as near that goal as possible). The orator's topics are fairness and goodness. Following this terse introduction, Cassiodorus gives a brief summary of the "five parts" of rhetoric: "invention, arrangement, proper expression, memorization, delivery" (II. ii. 2). These are treated solely as steps to be followed in preparing and delivering a speech. Cassiodorus seems to have no knowledge of the broader implications of the paradigm. The remainder of the section on rhetoric is a dry recitation of the contents of rhetoric. He includes the three classical genres (demonstrative, deliberative, and judicial), which he calls "kinds of rhetorical cases," summarizes the complicated technical apparatus for analysis of legal cases (stasis), the five-part Roman classification of kinds of legal cases, the six parts of an oration, the use of syllogism, enthymeme, and induction in argumentation, and urges the development of strong memory and proper delivery through practice.

Cassiodorus' conception of rhetoric, like that of most medieval scholars, is based on the minor technical Roman treatises, especially Cicero's youthful *De Inventione* and the anonymous *Rhetorica ad Herrenium* (believed at the time to be Cicero's). Aristotle's *Rhetoric* was lost to the medieval world and not recovered until the late thirteenth century. Cicero's *De Oratore* was not recovered until the early fifteenth century, and only portions of Quintilian's *Institutes* were available before

Fig. 3.2   Taxonomy of Rhetoric from Cassiodorus' *Introduction to Divine and Human Readings*

  I. Province—Public speaking; discourse on questions which fall within the range of common understanding; affecting persuasion in civil matters

 II. Parts

        Invention—Devising arguments that are true or that resemble true arguments to make a case appear credible

     B. Arrangement—Excellent distribution in regular order of the arguments devised

     C. Proper expression—Adaptation of suitable words to the arguments

     D. Memorization—Lasting comprehension by the mind of the arguments and the language

     E. Delivery—Harmonious adjustment of voice and gesture in keeping with the dignity of the arguments and the language

III. Kinds of Cases

     A. Demonstrative—For praising and blaming

     B. Deliberative—For persuading and dissuading

     C. Judicial—For accusing or defending

        1. Honorable

        2. Paradoxical

        3. Insignificant

        4. Uncertain

        5. Obscure

 IV. Status (or Position)—Central issue in a case

     A. Rational

        1. Conjectural

        2. Definitional

        3. Qualitative

        4. Transference

     B. Legal

        1. Letter and spirit

        2. Contradictory laws

        3. Ambiguous laws

        4. Precedent

        5. Legal definition

  V. Parts of a Speech

     A. Exordium

     B. Narration

     C. Partition

     D. Direct argument

     E. Refutation

     F. Conclusion

 VI. Kinds of Arguments

     A. Induction—Proposition, inference, conclusion

     B. Rhetorical syllogism (categorical and hypothetical belong to dialectic)

        1. Epichireme—Three to five parts; "complete"

        2. Enthymeme—Two parts; "incomplete"

           (a) Five kinds—Conclusive, demonstrative, sentitious, comparative, collective the late fifteenth century. Even though some philosophical and theoretic works were available, the medieval scholars tended to seek out the technical and narrow. For instance, Plato's statements on rhetoric were either ignored or reduced in scope. Even Augustine's sophisticated analysis of rhetoric seems to have been largely unused in spite of the fact that he was one of the most influential writers of the period. Cassidorus, for instance, though he quotes Augustine as having labeled rhetoric as a "science," makes no reference to the use of classical rhetorical theory in preaching. In fact, Cassiodorus is typical of the period in that he makes no effort to show the relevance of his heavily forensics-oriented, public speaking-centered summary to any aspect of medieval life.

Given that Cassiodorus' treatment is prototypically medieval, it is not at all surprising that rhetoric, which had once been the highest study of the educated person, became in the Middle Ages a subject for school children. Furthermore, it is not surprising that the medieval scholars made no major advances in human communication theory, for the discipline which could have provided a focus for such development was reduced to a small set of prescriptive rules for an activity of no immediate relevance to a feudal society—the delivery of set speeches on civil questions.

Cassiodorus' treatment of the final member of the communication arts, dialectic (see Fig. 3.3), is even more technical than his treatment of rhetoric. He begins by claiming that dialectic was invented by Aristotle; he does not, however, seem personally familiar with Aristotle's major work on the subject, the *Topics*. Instead he relies on Roman commentaries and summaries from the Second Sophistic.

Cassiodorus opens his discussion by distinguishing between rhetoric and dialectic—a favorite exercise of medieval scholars. The basic distinction is an analogy that appears in nearly every medieval and Renaissance treatise on either subject: rhetoric is to dialectic as the "open hand" is to the "closed fist." He goes on to explain that dialectic is characterized by compression of arguments, brevity of language, and subtle reasoning and is most often practiced by small groups of learned communicators (the paradigm for dialectic was Plato's "transcriptions" of Socrates' dialogues). Rhetoric, on the other hand, is characterized by expanded arguments, copious language, and eloquence and is employed in the public forum with "the great mass" (II. iii. 2). The great classical orators, Demonsthenes and Cicero, exemplified rhetoric.

According to Cassiodorus, the content of dialectic is what is usually referred to as "scholastic logic" or the "logical topics" of classical conceptualization theory. These topics were a major concern of medieval and early Renaissance scholars.·Cassiodorus lists five predicables, ten categories (also called predicaments), seven classes of interpretation, fifteen kinds of definition, and a number of artistic and inartistic commonplaces. The classification system for these "topics," and the numbers

Fig. 3.3   The Topics of Dialectic from Cassiodorus' *Introduction to Divine and Human Readings*

I. The Five Predicables—Attributes of phenomena
   A. Genus
   B. Species
   C. Difference
   D. Property
   E. Accident
II. The Ten Categories (or Predicaments)—Classes of verbal symbols (what a name can tell us)
   A. Substance
   B. Quantity
   C. Relation
   D. Quality
   E. Action
   F. Passivity
   G. Place
   H. Time
   I. Position
   J. Possession
III. Classes of Interpretation—Ways of saying
   A. Noun
   B. Verb
   C. Clause
   D. Declaration
   E. Affirmation
   F. Negation
   G. Contradiction
IV. Definitions—Ways of determining sigification
   A. Essential
   B. Notional
   C. Qualitative
   D. Descriptive
   E. Substitutional
   F. Distinguishing
   G. Metaphorical
   H. By negation of the opposite
   I. By use of image
   J. By example
   K. By what is lacking
   L. By praise
   M. By proportion
   N. By relation
   O. By cause
V. Commonplaces—sources of arguments
   A. Inherent—From the whole, the parts, or etymology
   B. Affected—Created by communicator
      1. Cognate words
      2. Genus
      3. Species

Fig. 3.3   The Topics of Dialectic (Cont'd)

    4. Likeness
    5. Difference
    6. Opposites
    7. Analogy
    8. Antecedents
    9. Consequents
   10. Contradictions
   11. Causes
   12. Effects
   13. Comparisons
VI. Extrinsic Sources of Argument—From persons, nature, circumstances (talent, wealth, age, luck, art, experience, necessity, concourse of events), from ancestors, from torments

---

and names of subdivisions within them varied greatly throughout the period. Often certain of them are included in rhetoric while other are classified in dialectic. Cassiodorus, however, does not make clear distinctions. He simply notes that certain of the topics "furnish arguments alike to orators, dialecticians, poets, and lawyers; but when they treat a particular point they have to do with orators, poets, and lawyers, and when they treat a general question they clearly concern dialecticians" (II. iii. 17).

Having completed his outline of dialectic, Cassiodorus moves without transition to arithmetic. He makes no attempt to bind the discussion of the three arts of the trivium into a coherent whole. Though his discussion of them reveals commonalities and overlaps, he clearly does not view them as subdivisions of a single discipline.

Cassiodorus' *Divine and Human Readings* was one of the most influential of the early medieval encyclopedias. More than any other single work it explains why human communication ceased to be a vital and developing discipline in the medieval and Renaissance period. We have seen that monolithic Christian feudalism replaced rhetorical humanism. Thus rhetoric, or classical human communication theory, was categorized along with all other "secular" subjects as preliminary to the advanced study of Christian theology. The content of classical theory was distributed among the three arts of the trivium and reduced in complexity as befitted an elementary school subject. The more philosophic and theoretic content of classical theory was dispersed throughout a variety of works on theology, preaching, letterwriting, style, logic, etc.

The Dispersion of The Paradigm

The classical paradigm did not cease to exist in the scholarship of the medieval and Renaissance period. As we have seen, Cassiodorus preserves it by defining it as the "five parts of rhetoric." Throughout the period, every treatise with the word "rhetoric" in the title lists the parts of the paradigm. Those that used the paradigm as an organizing framework have been called "Ciceronian Rhetorics."

Ciceronian Rhetorics

In 794, Alcuin writes, "There are five parts of the art of rhetoric: Invention, Arrangement, Style, Memory, Delivery."[18] Thomas Wilson organizes his *Arte of Rhetorique* (1553) around the "five things to be considered in an orator." He lists: "invention of the matter, disposition of the same, elocution, memorie, utterance" (*Rhet.*, p. 6).

Alcuin uses the five parts as a paradigm for a theory of administration, focusing heavily on the technical, forensic apparatus of conceptualization. His primary sources are Cicero's *De Inventione* (87 B.C.) and the *Ars Rhetorica* of Julius Victor, a fourth century summary of *De Oratore* and *Orator*. Much of Victor's work consists of verbatim statements from Cicero. Alcuin in turn incorporates these statements almost word for word in his *Rhetoric* (Howell, "Introduction," p. 68). Thus Alciun's work is highly derivative, adding little that is new but introducing at least the technical outlines of classical theory into eighth century scholarship.

Alcuin's *Rhetoric* opens with Charlemagne's request that he be taught "the precepts of the art of rhetoric." Charlemagne says:

> I remember you once said that the strength of this art lay wholly in dealing with public questions. As you very well know, in the course of the duties of government and the cares of State, we are constantly wont to be busy with questions of this kind; and it seems absurd not to know the rules of an art when the necessity of using it confronts us daily (*Rhet.*, p. 68).

Alcuin responds to this request by presenting a series of definitions and divisions. In a statement which closely echoes Isocrates' defense of the study of rhetoric cited in Chap. 2,[19] he explains that rhetoric is the source of civilization:

> For there was once a time, as it is said, when mankind wandered here and there over the plains very much as do wild beasts, and men did nothing through the reasoning power of the mind, but everything by sheer brute strength. The duty of revering God and of respecting humanity was not yet heeded; and Passion, that blind

[18] Alcuin, *The Rhetoric of Alcuin and Charlemagne*, ed. and trans. by W. S. Howell (Princeton University Press, 1941), p. 71. All subsequent references within the text are to this translation.
[19] This "defense" was apparently a commonplace in classical rhetorics, for nearly every theorist at least mentions these ideas in his introductory comments.

and rash tyrant, wasted the strength of men's bodies in the mad pursuit of his own satisfactions. At that time a man undeniably great and wise indeed discovered what latent genius—how great a capacity for the highest things—was in the human soul if only some one could draw it forth, and by nurturing perfect it; and by force of reason he collected men into one place from being scattered as they were over the plains, and hidden in dwellings in the forests; and he assembled them together, and led them into each useful and honorable pursuit; they, at first protesting against the strangeness of it, yet finally with eagerness listening because of his reason and eloquence, were made gentle and mild from being savage and brutal. And it seems to me, my Lord King, that a mute wisdom, or a wisdom endowed but weakly with the gift of speech, would not have been able suddenly to turn men against their previous habits, and bring them to the diverse pursuits of civilized life (*Rhet.*, p. 69).

Having explained the origin of rhetoric, Alcuin goes on to give more specific definitions. He defines rhetoric as "fluency of discourse," explaining that its end is "the art of speaking well" in public affairs. Public affairs, he says, include the three classical genres of communication or "three kinds of questions": demonstrative (praise of a person), deliberative (persuasion and dissuasion), and judicial (accusation and defense).

Alcuin's primary emphasis is on the technical aspects of legal argumentation, i. e., determining the central issue, selecting a line of reasoning, interpreting written laws, etc. For the most part, his *Rhetoric* is a nontheoretic restatement of the content of Roman rhetorical handbooks. It differs from these primarily in the references to Christian doctrine, the inclusion of preaching as a rhetorical activity, and a somewhat limited conception of the province of rhetoric. Alcuin's definition, for instance, is much more narrow than those of the major classical theorists. Rather than dealing with "whatever topics come up for discussion," Alcuin's rhetoric is limited to "public" questions. He accepts the typical medieval concept of dialectic as the art of private, learned discourse or "Disputation." Rhetoric is viewed as the art of public communication, speaking or writing on "hypotheses" (specific questions such as "Should Nancy marry John?"), while dialectic is the art of speaking and writing on "theses" (general questions such as "Should women marry?"). In other words, Alcuin's overall approach is similar, in its basic outline, to Cassiodorus'. Alcuin is, however, more detailed and does make some effort to present the study of human communication as a practical activity relevant to important aspects of medieval life.

Thomas Wilson presents a much more philosophic and theoretic analysis of communication in his *Rhetorique*. His approach is also more pragmatic than Alcuin's. He uses the paradigm as a framework for the criticism of legal, political, and religious discourse as practiced in the sixteenth century. His primary concern is simplicity, clarity, and directness, believing that the rules of rhetoric should aid human beings in understanding each other and in arriving at satisfactory decisions. For instance, in his discussion of organization, he condemns current practices of the clergy because: "They begin as much from the matter as it is betwixt Dover and Barwick, whereat some take pity and many for weariness can scant abide their beginning so long ere they speak anything to the purpose" (*Rhet.*, p. 105).[20]

Wilson justifies the study of rhetoric in the traditional manner—speech is the civilizer of mankind, the ability to communicate is the source of all human organization, etc. He defines rhetoric as one of the liberal arts, as "an Arte to set forth by utterance of words, matter at large, or (as *Cicero* doth say) it is a learned . . . declaration of the mind, in the handling of any cause, called in contention, that may through reason largely be discussed" (*Rhet.*, p. 1). Thus Wilson opens the province of rhetoric to include whatever specific questions human beings might discuss. He accepts that general questions are the province of dialectic, but explains that all specific questions must be dealt with in the context of the more general one, and therefore the rhetorician must also be a dialectician (*Rhet.*, p. 2).

Having outlined the province of his subject, Wilson gives a quick preview of the components of the art. These include all the subjects of classical theory. For instance, the "ends" are to teach, to delight, and to persuade; the genres are demonstrative, deliberative, and judicial; the parts of an oration are the traditional seven. More important, however, than Wilson's inclusion of the traditional lore is his adaptation of it to the needs of his audience. He organizes the *Rhetorique* around the five classical canons and faithfully presents the contents of each part, but his examples and recommendations are based on the everyday life of his readers. Thus, rather than a dry recital of ancient knowledge, the *Arte of Rhetorique* is a vital guide to communication as a common human activity.

Practical Manuals

The Ciceronian rhetorics, as we have seen, maintained the classical taxonomy of communicative acts—deliberative, forensic, and epideictic. These were treated in standard ways: as oral communication in the senate, the courtroom, and in public ceremonies. This view of the taxonomy, however, was of little immediate relevance to medieval and Renaissance society. As we have seen, the major genres of communication acts were letter writing and preaching. Though both genres were

---

[20] I have modernized much of Wilson's spelling, although Mair does not.

treated as "rhetoric," the practical demands for instruction led to some specialized applications of rhetorical theory.

Letter writing   The large body of manuals that evolved on this subject were known as *ars dictaminis*. A key concern in the manuals was security. Since letters served as legal records, it was important to guard against forgeries. Special operationalizations, such as the use of code, personal handwriting, and official seals, were strongly advised for security purposes. For kings and church officers, however, security stemmed primarily from skill in symbolization and organization. Most hired scholars as "dictators," official letter-writers. (Since most European kings up to about the tenth century were illiterate, this was more than a security device; it was a necessity.) The dictator was not just a secretary; he composed and wrote all the official as well as the personal correspondence. Cassiodorus, for instance, served as dictator to the sixth century Italian king, Theodoric. His letters have been preserved in *Variae*, a collection viewed as a major literary work and widely used as a source of models for instruction in letter writing. Cassiodorus composed for the king a description of his duties and included it in *Variae*:

> [The dictator] has to learn our inmost thoughts, that he may utter them to our subjects. . . . He has to be always ready for a sudden call, and must exercise the wonderful powers which, as Cicero has pointed out, are inherent in the art of an orator. . . . He has to speak the king's words in the king's own presence . . . with suitable embellishments (Quoted in Murphy, p. 197).

Thus, we see that letter writing clearly classified as a rhetorical activity. "Suitable embellishments" and intimate knowledge of the king and his political and social relationships were key security devices. Embellishments came from the use of "rhetorical colores," or figures of speech from classical symbolization theory. Figures were a primary topic in medieval and renaissance communication theory and scholarly writing was characterized by an abundant use of them. Cassiodorus asserts that there are at least ninety-eight different figures recognizable to the educated person. Obviously, the highly "colored" style of the scholar was difficult to imitate.

In addition to skill in symbolization, security depended upon organizational skill. Letter writing was taught in the context of complex formal social relationships. Early *ars dictaminis* consisted primarily of precepts for appropriate forms of address in the salutation and closing. C. Julius Victor's *Ars Rhetorica*, a fourth century summary of Cicero's *De Oratore*, includes an appendix on letter writing. Victor defines the letter as a form of conversation and claims that the relationships between the correspondents is the key variable. He proposes three kinds of relationships

which determine the selection of appropriate forms of address: superior/
inferior, equals, inferior/superior. For each he suggests an appropriate
tone.

By the eleventh century, when the full-scale *ars dictaminis* made its
appearance, this rather simple taxonomy had been greatly complicated.
The *Dictaminum Radii* (1087) of Alberic of Monte Cassino and his student, John of Gaeta, for instance, provides a detailed analysis of the
kinds and degrees of relationship that may exist between a writer and
reader. This work brings classical organizational and conceptualization
theory together by recommending the use of the classical topics of
epideictic oratory (for praise of a person) as categories for analyzing these
relationships; these include comparative age, birth (status), wealth, position, etc. Alberic and John, like Victor and the scholars who followed,
emphasize salutations and closing. If the form and tone violated the
received rules of appropriateness for letters between persons of a given
relationship, it was suspect and might be successfully challenged in a
court of law.

Thus the feudal government system, the church bureaucracy, and
the decentralization of society led to an emphasis on letters as records of
events, relationships, and agreements, and eventually to the development of a new theoretical genre, the *ars dictaminis*. Instruction in this
activity guaranteed continued interest in the pragmatics of human communication and the preservation, though in fragmented form, of the
classical paradigm.

Preaching   Like the manuals on letter writing, the *artes
praedicandi* contributed to the maintenance of much of the content of
classical communication theory. All five parts of the paradigm receive
attention, though they are often confounded.

Categorization, organization, and conceptualization, for instance,
were often inextricably intertwined. Theories of sermon composition
illustrate this phenomenon. The earliest and simplest aid to composition
was the homily form. Based on Augustine's precept of close analysis of
scriptural text, the homily was conceived and organized around a series of
scriptures, each of which was interpreted for the audience. With the
scriptures before him, the preacher's only problem was remembering his
interpretations. Even this ceased to be a problem, however, with the
introduction of the notion of "the four senses of interpretation." The
preacher was advised to explain each text systematically in terms of each
"sense." A *Book about the Way a Sermon Ought to Be Given*, written by the
Benedictine monk, Guibert (c. 1084), explains:

> There are four ways in interpreting Scriptures; on them as though
> on so many scrolls, each sacred page is rolled. The first is *history*,
> which speaks of actual events as they occurred; the second is *alleg-
> ory*, in which one thing stands for something else; the third is

tropology, or moral instruction, which treats of the ordering and arranging of one's life; and the last is *ascetics*,[21] or spiritual en-lightenment, through which we who are about to treat of heavenly and lofty topics are led to a higher way of life. For example, the word Jerusalem: historically it represents a specific city; in allegory it represents the holy Church; tropologically, or morally, it is the soul of every faithful man who longs for the vision of eternal peace; and ascetically it refers to the life of the heavenly citizens, who already see the God of Gods, revealed in all his glory in Sion (emphases mine).[22]

Given this concept of "senses," the preacher's conceptual, categori-zational, and organizational problems were, if not solved, at least virtu-ally eliminated. The four senses continued to be important devices throughout the period. Eventually, however, an even greater variety of such techniques were explicated in the manuals. Caplan lists twenty of the common methods of interpreting and expanding upon scriptures contained in these manuals (see Fig. 3.4).[23] These were based on the classical topics of conceptualization but were thought of as methods of expression rather than as methods of discovery. Thus, they served the function of copia in symbolization as well as assisting organization and memory.

Specialized Treatises

Another body of literature contributing to the preservation, and fragmentation, of the paradigm was a number of detailed theoretic treatises on one or two of the parts. Bede, for instance, preserves much of the classical theory of symbolization in his eighth-century treatise, *Fig-ures and Tropes*. Erasmus, in *On Copia of Words and Ideas* (1512), elevates symbolization to the level of a discipline by defining human communica-tion as the art of introducing lexical diversity into written messages. He defines "copia" as the art of saying (and thus of conceiving of) "the same thing" in a variety of different ways. Within the context of symboliza-tion, he includes much of the content of the other four parts of the paradigm. For instance, he treats the essential aspects of classical concep-tualization theory as "The Eleventh Method" of varying. Artistic and

---

[21] In later theory, the first sense became known as "literal" and the last as "anagogical," meaning "from the point of view of heavenly things."

[22] Guibert de Nogent, "A Book about the Way a Sermon Ought to Be Given," trans., Joseph M. Miller in Joseph M. Miller, Michael H. Prosser, and Thomas W. Benson, *Readings in Medieval Rhetoric* (Bloomington: Indiana University Press, 1973), pp. 170–171.

[23] Harry Caplan, "Classical Rhetoric and the Mediaeval Theory of Preaching," in Raymond F. Howes, ed., *Historical Studies of Rhetoric and Rhetoricians* (Ithaca, New York: Cornell University Press, 1961), pp. 83–84.

Fig. 3.4   Methods of expansion in Medieval and Renaissance *Artes Praedicandi**

1. Concordance of authorities, Biblical, patristic, philosophic
2. Questioning and discussion of words and terms
3. Discussion of the properties of things
4. Analogies and natural truths
5. Ratiocination and argument from simile, example, greater and lesser, opposites
6. Comparison, a play upon adjectives or verbs
7. Similitudes
8. Explication of hidden terminology
9. Multiplication of synonyms
10. Dialectical topics—Species and genera, whole and parts, the "categories"
11. Explication of scriptural metaphors
12. Cause and effect
13. Anecdotes
14. Observation of the end or purpose of a thing
15. Definition of a word
16. Interpretation of Hebrew names
17. Etymology of a word
18. Parts of speech
19. Figures of speech, "rhetorical colors"
20. Four senses of interpretation

* From Caplan, in Howes, *Historical Studies*, pp. 83–84.

inartistic sources of materials, the classical topics, commonplaces, example, and enthymeme, etc., are all treated as methods of "enriching" a basic message.[24]

Agricola, a fifteenth century scholar, contributed to the preservation of the paradigm in a similar manner, though his emphasis is on conceptualization rather than on symbolization. In his *Dialectical Invention* (c. 1450), Agricola seems to be trying to unite the various theories of human communication under one discipline, dialectic. He claims that dialectic includes "all discourse whatsoever," and that its function is "to discover what will produce belief and to arrange what is discovered."[25] Thus Agricola's dialectic has the same province as Aristotle's rhetoric.

Agricola does not, however, conceive of dialectic as a complete theory of human communication. He accepts the medieval taxonomy of

[24] Erasmus, *De Copia Verborum ac Rerum*, trans. Donald B. King and H. David Rix (Milwaukee: Marquette University Press, 1963), pp. 66–97.
[25] Translated and quoted in James Richard McNally, "An Appraisal of Rudolf Agricola's *De Inventione Dialectica Libri Tres* as a Philosophy of Artistic Discourse" (University of Iowa: Unpublished Ph. D. Dissertation, 1966), p. 65. All subsequent references within the text are to this translation.

the liberal arts and divides the parts of the paradigm among the members of the trivium. He defines the "universe of knowledge" as consisting of three parts: speculative, rational, and practical. The second of these deals, he says, with "the ordering of discourse and speech" and consists of three arts—grammar, rhetoric, and dialectic:

> Three observations are to be followed in speaking: that what the speaker intends to be understood; that the hearer be eager to listen; and that probability and credibility characterize what is said. The first is taught by *grammar*, which discusses the way to speak correctly and clearly; the second by *rhetoric*, which discovers ornateness and culture of language and all the blandishments used to capture the hearer. And what remains, it seems, *dialectic* furnishes: speaking probably on any subject which is introduced into language (McNally, trans., pp. 58–59; emphases mine).

The main body of *Dialectical Invention* is a detailed analysis of the medieval and Renaissance system of topics. Thus, although his definition implies that dialectic is concerned with the broad range of human communication, Agricola rules out theoretic (speculative) and pragmatic (practical) concerns, divides symbolization between grammar and rhetoric, ignores categorization and all but the "logical" aspects of conceptualization theory, and, though he includes organization ("judgment") in dialectic, treats it in no more than a few paragraphs. Like Cassiodorus, he preserves the "dry husks" of topical conceptualization theory (which he rearranges into one comprehensive set of classifications). Though Agricola's treatment is considerably more detailed, it contributed little to the development of a complete theory of human communication.

In terms of the treatment of the paradigm, the trend throughout the medieval and Renaissance period was to deal with the parts separately in the context of the three liberal arts of the trivium. Even those, like Alcuin and Wilson, who used the full paradigm as an organizing framework, viewed it as steps in speech making or as a list of the basic competencies required for "rhetorical," as opposed to "grammatical" or "dialectical," communication. Though there were tentative movements in the direction of synthesis, the medieval taxonomy inhibited their realization. Aside from Augustine, only two scholars, John of Salisbury (c. 1115–1180) and Francis Bacon (1561–1626), had any significant success in overcoming this taxonomy, and neither was particularly influential on the concept of communication held by their contemporaries, although, as we shall see, their efforts did bear fruit in the reconstruction of human communication as a single discipline in the modern period.

In the last century of the Renaissance, the popular "solution" to the overlapping and confusing conception of the communication arts as presented by Cassiodorus was further division and fragmentation. Peter Ramus (Pierre de la Ramee) was the primary author of this solution. Ramus (1515–1572) came to the attention of the scholarly world by attacking the prevailing system of philosophy being taught in the universities. This philosophy was commonly labeled as Aristotelian, but Ramus claimed that it was based on inauthentic works. Furthermore, he claimed that Aristotle's authentic writings were confused and redundant and that he could, through the application of three of Aristotle's own "laws," purge Aristotelianism and make it simple and clear. Ramus' three laws were based on Agricola's interpretation of Aristotle's *Posterior Analytics*. The first, the Law of Truth, proposes that "any statement employed as a principle in any art or science must be universally true"; there must be no exceptions. The second, the Law of Justice, proposes that there must be no redundancy in statements employed as principles in a discipline. The third, the Law of Wisdom, states that principles must be arranged from the most general to the most specific.[26]

The application of these laws led Ramus to develop a taxonomy that divided the arts and sciences into nonoverlapping, noninteractive bundles. Ramus thus saw knowledge as a set of neat, easily outlined disciplines. He defines each of the arts in parallel but distinctive terms: rhetoric is "the art of speaking well"; dialectic is "the art of disputing well"; grammar is "the art of composing well'; mathematics is "the art of computing well"; religion is "the art of living well," etc. Each of the arts is then divided into two parts, then each part is divided into two other parts, and so on. Figure 3.5 illustrates the typical Ramistic vision of the nature of academic disciplines.

In terms of human communication theory, Ramus and his many

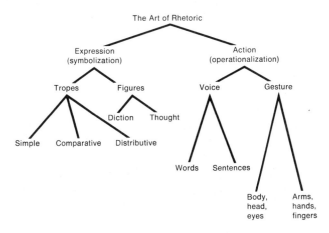

Fig. 3.5   Schemata of Ramistic Rhetoric

[26] Howell, 1951, p. 9.

followers are primarily important because of their definitions and taxonomies of rhetoric and dialectic. Though Ramism is atheoretic, it had tremendous impact on scholars in the late sixteenth and early seventeenth centuries, for it summarized a trend that began in the early medieval period; and it served to clear up, at least temporarily, a number of questions that had plagued scholars and educators for centuries. Figures of speech, for instance, were defined as belonging exclusively to rhetoric. The two parts of grammar were defined as etymology and syntax, technical studies related to rhetoric and dialectic only in a preliminary manner. The "topics" were assigned exclusively to dialectic. In brief, rhetoric was given custody of two parts of the classical paradigm, symbolization (style or expression) and operationalization (delivery or action). Dialectic was given custody of conceptualization (invention) and organization (judgment or arrangement). Categorization is treated not as a process of its own but is mixed in with organization. This is not surprising, given the emphasis in this period on written communication. The classical concept of categorization was a mental one; it focused on memory processes. The medieval and Renaissance concept was a visual one; it focused on categorization as filing systems, as written outlines, as library catalogues, and as handbooks of examples, arguments, and ideas.

The judgment of Walter Ong, the foremost authority on Ramus and Ramism, is that Ramus was an opportunist, an intellectual entrepeneur. His impact upon the sixteenth and seventeenth centuries was significant not because of his theoretic brilliance, but because of his ability to reduce complex subjects into simplistic formulas easily teachable to young students. Ramus and his followers wrote treatises on all the subjects of the seven liberal arts as well as on medicine and religion. These were eagerly picked up by elementary educators, and entire generations learned about scholarship in a Ramistic framework. Ong reports that between 1550 and 1650 there were some 1100 separate printings of works by Ramus and his collaborator, Omer Talon (1510–1562).[27] In addition to these works, there were dozens of Ramistic treatises on rhetoric and dialectic. The best known of these are by Antoine Foclin (1555), Charles Butler (1598, 1629), Dudley Fenner (1584), and Abraham Fraunce (1588).

Thus, a number of scholars contributed to the dispersion of the paradigm. Early in the period, the content of human communication theory was distributed among four competing disciplines: theology, rhetoric, dialectic, and grammar. Later in the period, the manuals on letter writing and preaching and the treatises by scholars such as Bede, Erasmus, and Agricola tended to emphasize one or two aspects of human communication while de-emphasizing others. The parts of the paradigm most commonly emphasized were symbolization, organization, and the

[27] Walter Ong, I. S. J., *Ramus and the Decay of Dialogue* (Cambridge: Harvard University Press, 1958), p. 9.

topical system of conceptualization. Seldom were these treated in theoretic terms. The common approach was categorical, academic, and technical. These trends toward fragmentation—competing disciplines, emphasis on parts of the paradigm rather than the whole, and technical or scholastic treatment—come to a culmination in the Ramistic taxonomy of the arts. Ramus's solution to the problem of how to adapt classical scholarship to the medieval and Renaissance world is an outgrowth of centuries of debate and confusion.

Comprehensive Treatises

Though the body of literature culminating in Ramism is fragmenting in its essential tendency, it did serve to maintain the study of human communication, and it preserved the content of the classical paradigm. It also led some theorists to seek a nonfragmenting "solution" to the problem of putting the classical "puzzle" back together. These theorists, in contrast to the rhetoricians and the Ramists, attempted to rise above the prevailing taxonomy and provide a perspective for combining the scattered parts of the paradigm into a coherent whole.

We have seen that Augustine, in spite of his general acceptance of the medieval taxonomy, treats all five processes in his fourth-century treatise, On Christian Doctrine (397–426). Some seven hundred years later, John of Salisbury incorporates the full paradigm into a theory of human reasoning in the Metalogicon (1159). John's objective in this work is to write a unified theory of "eloquence," which is his general term for the arts of the trivium. More specifically, his purpose is to combine the principles of grammar, rhetoric, and dialectic into one philosophic discipline. He calls this discipline "logic," which he defines as "the science of verbal expression and reasoning."[28] He admits that some writers have used this term in a more restricted sense to mean the rules of argumentative reasoning but says that his concept includes all "verbal intercommunication" (I. 1). One of the problems with current scholarship, he says, is that there is no agreement on how to talk about this phenomenon. In fact, he complains, "There are practically as many sets of terminology as there are branches of learning, and often authors differ as much in their use of language as they do in physical appearance" (I. 4).

Having explained his general purposes, John goes on to present the standard introductory justifications for the study of human communication. The first is that study can improve native ability, and skill in communication is a primary path to success:

> If a man is superior to other living beings in dignity because of his powers of speech and reason, what is more universally efficacious

[28] John of Salisbury, Metalogicon, Daniel McGarry, trans. (Berkeley: University of California Press, 1955), I. 10. All subsequent references within the text are to this translation.

and more likely to win distinction than to surpass one's fellows, who possess the same human nature, and are members of the same human race, in those sole respects wherein man surpasses other beings? (I. 7).

John expands this justification by defining "logic" as the combination of eloquence and wisdom:

> Just as eloquence, unlightened by reason, is rash and blind, so wisdom, without the power of expression, is feeble and maimed. Speechless wisdom may sometimes increase one's personal satisfaction, but it rarely and only slightly contributes to the welfare of human society. Reason, the mother, nurse, and guardian of knowledge, as well as of virtue, frequently conceives from speech, and by this same means bears more abundant and richer fruit. Reason would remain utterly barren, or at least would fail to yield a plenteous harvest, if the faculty of speech did not bring to light its feeble conception, and communicate the perceptions of the prudent exercise of the human mind. Indeed, it is this delightful and fruitful copulation of reason and speech which has given birth to so many outstanding cities, has made friends and allies of so many kingdoms, and has unified and knit together in bonds of love so many peoples (I. 1).

Although this beginning sounds very traditional, the *Metalogicon* is far from a traditional recount of Ciceronian rhetoric. John's sources include the names of almost every important theorist, both secular and theological from 500 B.C. to his own time. His primary source is Aristotle. John was the first scholar of his time to have access to the whole of Aristotle's *Organon* (his works on logic). In addition, however, John draws on Plato, Cicero, Quintilian, Augustine, Alcuin, Bede, Cassiodorus, and a host of writers on history, natural science, and literature.[29]

John does not use the classical paradigm explicitly in his exposition, though he does deal with all five processes. His emphasis, like Aristotle's, is on conceptualization, the process by which human beings acquire "knowledge." The use of language, the ordering of perceptions, etc., are all discussed in terms of this central process. His terminology, not surprisingly, is a mixture of classical and medieval. He accepts the standard terminology and definitions of the parts of the trivium, yet he takes the very classical view that "eloquence" requires a combination of all the knowledge contained in these three separate arts.

---

[29] McGarry, "Introduction," pp. xxiii–xxiv.

The last major theorist of the medieval and Renaissance period, Francis Bacon, also transcends the divisiveness of the trivium taxonomy. In two works, *Of the Proficience and Advancement of Learning: Divine and Humane* (1605) and *Novum Organum: Aphorisms Concerning the Interpretation of Nature and the Kingdom of Man* (1620), Bacon surveys the state of scholarship from the ancient Greeks to the beginning of the seventeenth century. His purpose is to assess "progress" to date, pointing out successes and failures, and to provide guidelines for future development. In this context he proposes a new taxonomy, which he calls "the arts intellectual," and in which he includes the substance of the three liberal arts of the trivium. This taxonomy is a revised version of the classical paradigm:

> The arts intellectual are four in number; divided according to the ends whereunto they are referred: for man's labour is to invent that which is sought or propounded; or to judge that which is invented; or to retain that which is judged; or to deliver over that which is retained. So as the arts must be four: art of inquiry or invention [conceptualization]; art of examination or judgement [organization]; art of custody or memory [categorization]; and art of elocution or tradition [operationalization and symbolization]. (*Adv. Learn.*, II. xii. 3)[30]

Having set forth his paradigm, Bacon critiques historical developments in each area. He summarizes the various conceptions scholars have of each, pointing out that the present state of knowledge is for the most part deficient, having progressed little since the ancient Greeks and Romans:

> For out of twenty-five centuries, with which the memory and learning of man are conversant, scarcely six can be set apart and selected as fertile in science and favorable to its progress. For there are deserts and wastes in times as in countries, and we can only reckon up three revolutions and epochs of philosophy. 1. The Greek. 2. The Roman. 3. Our own, that is, the philosophy of the western nations of Europe (*Nov. Org.*, I. 78).

The first cause of this lack of progress, then, is that so few centuries have been favorable times for science. The second cause, Bacon says, is that in the early medieval period theology replaced science as the focal point of scholarship:

> It is well known that after the Christian religion had been acknowl-

[30] Francis Bacon, *Advancement of Learning, Novum Organum,* and *New Atlantis,* in *Great Books of the Western World,* vol. 30 (Chicago: Encyclopaedia Britannica, 1952), p. 56. All subsequent references to Bacon's works within the text are to this edition.

edged, and arrived at maturity, by far the best wits were busied upon theology, where the highest rewards offered themselves . . . (Nov. Org., I. 79).

Those who were not engaged solely in religious activity, Bacon says, produced "scholastic philosophy" which "ground down the sciences by their numerous treatises, more than they increased their weight" (Nov. Org., I. 78).

The more fundamental reason for the lack of advancement, however, has to do with what Bacon sees as the inherent human tendency to "construct" reality rather than discover it. This tendency results in what Bacon calls "Idols." Idols are to nature, he says, as sophisms are to logic; they look very much the same, but one is valid or true and the other is distorted. He identifies four sets of idols. First, the "idols of the tribe." These result from people's tendency to project themselves on reality, to take their senses as the measure of nature. The second, the "idols of the den," result from socialization: each individual distorts nature because of his own special experiences—with education, with reference groups, etc. The third, the "idols of the market," result from the nature of language, which is abstractive, static, and socially invented. The names we have for things "force" our understanding of them and prevent us from accurately perceiving them. Finally, the "idols of the theatre" result from theories, systems of philosophy, and ideologies. These are often more consistent, elegant, and pleasurable than real life, and thus we tend to ignore evidence which disconfirms our pet beliefs (Nov. Org., I. 39-70).

Bacon finds each of the intellectual arts deficient in at least some respects because of the influence of these idols. For instance, popular conceptualization theory is insufficient for the discovery of new knowledge because it is bound by scholastic logic—the topics system—which presupposes what can be found, thus preventing the investigator from finding things he did not expect to see. It is, he says, a theory of remembering rather than of inventing.

Bacon serves as an important transitional figure to the modern period because of his systematic critique of the medieval and Renaissance treatment of the parts of the paradigm and because of his "solution" to the lack of advancement in learning during the period. This solution is empirical experimentation:

All the better interpretations of nature are worked out by instances, and fit and apt experiments, where the senses only judge the experiment, the experiment of nature and of the thing itself (Nov. Org., I. 50).

Though Bacon's redefinition of the paradigm did not win immediate and widespread acceptance, it did signal a new age in intellectual history and was an important influence on the thinking of the major communication theorists of the modern period.

Treatment of the Paradigm

With the overview of the period and of the general fate of the paradigm in mind, we can now turn to an examination of medieval and Renaissance theory in terms of the content of each part of the paradigm. The classical taxonomies presented in Chap. 2 will serve as an organizing framework for this analysis.

Categorization

Categorization is that branch of human communication concerned with the perception, storage, and recall of data. Emphasis in medieval and Renaissance treatments of categorization was on the storage of data for future use, that is, the development of "right" attitudes, beliefs, and values through education. The ability to recall stored data was discussed primarily in terms of memory devices, especially in relation to the needs of the Christian preacher. Treatment of perception as the basis of knowledge acquisition and generation appeared only after theorists began to turn from theological preoccupations, with their attendant conceptions of "the scriptures" as the source of truth and reality, and began to be concerned with "science," the advance of secular knowledge (see Fig. 3.6). Medieval and Renaissance scholars' treatments of storage and recall

---

Fig. 3.6   Categorization in Medieval and Renaissance Theory

I. Storage of Data for Future Use ("Learning")
   A. Specific knowledge of subject matter
   B. General knowledge of "things" and "signs of things"
   C. Use of written records
      1. Canonical scriptures
      2. Commentaries
      3. Commonplace books
      4. Letters
II. Recall of Stored Data
   A. General familiarity acquired through practice
   B. Artificial memory systems
      1. Classical system of backgrounds and images (see Fig. 2.5)
      2. Methods of amplification (see Fig. 3.4)
         a. Concordance with authorities
         b. Definitions of words and terms, etc.
III. Perception of Data
   A. Recognition—Sense perception, sensation
   B. Remembrance—Storage, recall, prenotion
   C. Imagination—Emblem, imagaic representation, preconception

correspond generally to classical "artificial memory" systems, and the treatment of perception is an elaboration of the classical notion of "natural memory."

Categorization as Storage   The first book of Augustine's *On Christian Doctrine* deals specifically with storage of data for future use. The focus is on providing guidelines for the Christian who wishes to develop "full understanding" or wisdom. Prerequisites for obtaining wisdom are (1) a store of specific knowledge of Christian doctrine, and (2) a store of general knowledge about "things" and "signs of things." These guidelines are intended not only for the preacher, but for all people who desire to be "educated." The ultimate goal of education, for Augustine and for most medieval scholars, is, or course, to enable the individual to lead a good Christian life. Thus, the first requisite for becoming "wise" is to learn the fundamental principles of doctrine.

Augustine lists six steps that lead to wisdom. The first two are prerequisites for data acquisition, or knowledge, which is the third step, and the last three are requirements for accurate classification of data. In other words, first come "right attitudes," then categorization. The first step is a desire to learn: the individual must be "led by the *fear* of God to seek the knowledge of His will, what He commands us to desire and what to avoid" (II. 7). Second, he must be subdued by piety, and third, he must acquire basic data, knowledge of scriptures. He must read the canonical books, especially "those that are received by all the Catholic Churches . . . [and] such as have the sanction of the greater number of those of greater authority" (II. 8). The data contained in these books is then to be stored in the mind for future interpretation and use. As Augustine explains:

> [T]he first rule to be observed is . . . to know these books, if not yet with the understanding, still to read them so as to commit them to memory. . . . [so that] we may proceed to open up and investigate the obscure passages, and in doing so draw examples from the plainer expressions to throw light upon the more obscure, and use the evidence of passages about which there is no doubt to remove all hesitation in regard to the doubtful passages. And in this matter memory counts for a great deal (II. 9).

He goes on to explain that this stored data provides protection as well as serving as a basis for eventual understanding, for the learner can then read other books "with greater safety when built up in the belief of the truth" (II. 8).

Having gone through the first three steps, the Christian communicator must then (4) be righteous in his life, (5) love himself, God, his neighbor, and his enemy, and (6) be pure in his pursuit of truth.

These last three steps to wisdom will enable him to accurately categorize the data he has stored in his search for "full understanding." In other words, once the classification system has been established, all future data can be "accurately" categorized. As we have seen, later Christian scholars, like Cassiodorus and Bede, build their precepts for education on this premise. They recommend initial study of Christian ideology followed by study of the seven liberal arts as a basis for the higher study of theology.

Augustine takes a somewhat more theoretic position on the acquisition of general, or secular, knowledge. He claims, "all instruction is either about things or about signs; but things are learnt by means of signs" (I. 2).

Augustine classifies things as being of two sorts, those created by God and those created by human beings. Things created by God include the basic truths of Christianity (i. e., faith, love, and charity) and the laws of nature. Augustine explains that in order to communicate, to ascertain the meaning of messages made by others (as in reading the scriptures) or to make meanings known to others (as in preaching), knowledge of things is a necessity. Much of the complicated imagery of the Bible, for instance, is based on "the nature of animals, or minerals, or plants," of numbers, of diurnal and annual revolutions, etc. (II. 16). Accurate interpretation and categorization of many scriptures depends first upon reference to the Christian truths—if an interpretation is inconsistent with "the law of love," it is obviously inaccurate— and second upon reference to the laws of nature. Other scriptural imagery may be based on things created by human beings, such as music and musical instruments. Thus Augustine urges the study of such subjects as history, natural science, medicine, agriculture, navigation, dancing, wrestling, architecture, pottery, music, languages, mathematics, and astronomy (II. 16–30). In other words, like Cicero, his primary classical source, Augustine believes a broad general education is fundamental to the skilled communicator. It provides him with a store of data that can be accessed when the need arises.

This knowledge of things is fundamental, but, Augustine points out, knowledge is obtained by interpreting signs. Thus knowledge of signs, symbolization processes, is even more fundamental. Signs, he explains, are of two sorts: natural and conventional (today we would call the first "signs" and the second "symbols"). Augustine defines a "sign" as a thing which "causes something else to come into the mind as a consequence of itself: as . . . when we hear the voice of a living man, we think of the feeling in his mind" (II. 1). A natural sign is one created by God. These include such things as smoke (indicative of fire), animal footprints, the expressions on people's faces: "the countenance of an angry or sorrowful man indicates the feeling in his mind, independently of his will" (II. 1). In contrast, conventional signs are created by human beings and are thus arbitrary and intentional. They are "those which living beings mutually exchange for the purpose of showing, as well as they can, the feelings of their minds, or their perceptions, or their thoughts" (II. 2). In the class of conventional signs Augustine includes sounds (such as bugles), gestures (nods), clothing (military uniforms), scents (incense), etc. "And all these signs are as it were a kind of visible words. . . . yet all these signs are very few in number compared with words. For among men words have obtained far and away the chief place as a means of indicating the thoughts of the mind" (II. 3). Conventional signs exist for only one reason, "the desire of drawing forth and conveying into another's mind what the giver of the sign has in his own mind" (II. 2).

This emphasis on signs, especially words, and more especially written words, as repositories of information reveals an important difference between classical and medieval concepts of categorization. Plato, from the point of view of an oral culture, attacked writing as an inadequate medium for learning or instructing. Writing, he said, "is an aid not to memory, but to reminiscence." More important, documents cannot respond to questions. They can be read by those who lack the ability or background to understand them and who therefore misinterpret their meanings. Written documents can neither explain nor justify themselves (Phaedrus, 275). In the feudal Christian social order of the early medieval period, these criticisms became irrelevant. The classical theorists were primarily concerned with the pursuit of knowledge. The medieval theorists were primarily concerned with the preservation of knowledge. To the classical theorists, truth existed in people. To the medieval theorists, truth existed in God, but could only be discovered through "signs," especially the words of documents such as "the holy writ." A central problem for the medieval Christian was accurate interpretation of the truths contained in these documents. As Augustine points out, the primary function of communicating is disseminating truth, and writing is essential to that function since it preserves truth and makes it physically apparent: "because words pass away as soon as they strike the air and last no longer than their sound, men have by means of letters formed signs of words. Thus the sounds of the voice are made visible to the eye" (II. 4). The visible sign, then, can be carefully studied to determine exactly "the thought and will of those by whom it was written" (II. 5) and is less likely to be corrupted by faulty memory or insertion of personal bias. Furthermore, one set of written words can be easily compared with another as an additional check on the accuracy of interpretation.

The presumption that truth exists in documents is reflected in the "collecting and categorizing" activity of medieval scholars. Monks devoted a major part of their energies to finding, copying, and preserving manuscripts. Cassiodorus established two monasteries devoted to this purpose. His Divine and Human Readings is a guide, or directory, for accessing knowledge stored in books. Most of the scholarship of the medieval period consists of summaries, reviews, and commentaries.

This concept of categorization as the storage of knowledge in documents continues throughout the period. (In a sense, one might say that medieval libraries did more to preserve the classical heritage than did medieval scholars.) In the early Renaissance, scholars continued to search in books for "truths." The revival of classical learning brought about by the recovery of Aristotle's *Rhetoric* in the late thirteenth century, and of Cicero's *De Oratore* and the missing books of Quintilian's *Institutes of Oratory* in the late fifteenth century, led to a new series of commentaries and summaries explaining these "new" discoveries. The Renaissance conception of "copia" led to the phenomenon of commonplace books. Erasmus explains that copia, the theory of varying, consists of having a store of ideas and words that can be retrieved at will. Having this store does not necessarily lead to verbosity. Who, he asks, "could speak more tersely than he who has ready at hand an extensive array of words and figures from which he can immediately select what is most suitable for conciseness?" (*On Copia*, p. 15). For the most part, however, the goal of copia was amplification. In Chap. 33, Erasmus illustrates the method of varying with figures of speech by writing two hundred different versions of one sentence and one hundred fifty versions of another. The theory of copia, then, consists of the various devices of amplification, such as the figures of speech and the "topics" of dialectic and rhetoric. We have seen how these methods were recommended highly for Christian preachers in the *artes praedicandi*.

Skill in copia is developed by skill in storing data, by collecting sayings, maxims, examples, witty phrases, etc., in "commonplace" books. In *The Advancement of Learning*, Francis Bacon defines categorization as "retaining of knowledge in either writing or in memory," and he recommends that the would-be communicator keep a notebook with him at all times to immediately jot down worthwhile thoughts or expressions (II. xv. 1). For those who did not wish to collect their own "commonplaces," there were innumerable collections available. In the sixteenth and seventeenth centuries, there were literally hundreds of commonplace books on the market. Richard Rainolde's *The Foundation of Rhetorike* (1563), for instance, adapts Aphthonius' *Progymnasmata* (a fourth-century Greek collection of "topics") to meet the needs of sixteenth-century Europe. Another very popular collection, Textor's *Epitheta* (late fifteenth century), lists epithets for almost any subject, e. g., 95 for death, 163 for love, 113 for Apollo, etc.[31]

Thus we can see that the rise of Christianity in the early medieval world significantly increased the importance of the categorization process, especially in terms of data storage as a prerequisite to conceptualization. The importance of "the scriptures" led to an emphasis on writing as

---

[31] Walter J. Ong, S. J., *Rhetoric, Romance, and Technology* (Ithaca: Cornell University Press, 1971), p. 43.

data storage. The role of official letters in establishing, maintaining, and enforcing political, legal, and social contracts reinforced this emphasis.

Categorization as Recall   The earliest recorded treatment of categorization was in terms of memory, or recall of previously stored data. The classical writers were primarily interested in recall in terms of oral, nonmediated communication. In the medieval and Renaissance period, this concern is relevant primarily to Christian preachers and, to some extent, to lawyers. Equally important to oral recall, however, was written recall—that is, the use of notes or manuscripts in preaching and other public address.

Oral recall in classical theory was treated as a natural ability which could be (1) improved through practice, and (2) assisted by artificial systems. Medieval and Renaissance scholarship continued this tradition. Augustine advises the Christian preacher to "practice himself in writing, or dictating, and at last also in speaking the opinions he has formed on grounds of piety and faith" (IV. 3). In the course of this practice he will become more certain of what to say and how to say it. Further, the preacher should "retain in memory the words of the scriptures . . . [and] the confirming testimony of great men" (II. 5), so that he can draw on them for proof and illustration. Quotations of this sort have the added advantage of adding "eloquence" to the sermon and thereby securing attention and providing pleasure for the audience.

Medieval and Renaissance "rhetorics" consistently define oral recall, memory, as the fourth part of rhetoric. Cassiodorus calls it "a lasting comprehension by the mind of the arguments and the language" (*Divine and Human Readings*, II. ii. 2). Alcuin, in his *Rhetoric*, defines it as "an unalterable mental recollection of subject matter and words formed in the course of invention" (*Rhet.*, p. 71). He also quotes Cicero's definition from *De Inventione* that calls memory the "storehouse of all our experiences" and "the treasury of our thoughts and reflections" (p. 137). In answer to the question, how can memory be improved, Alcuin recommends "exercise in memorizing, practice in writing, and application to studious activity" (p. 137). He further recommends living a "healthy" life, especially avoiding drunkenness, which weakens the mind.

In addition to practice, medieval and Renaissance theorists often added a brief description of the artificial system of backgouunds and images. In his *Arte of Rhetorique*, Thomas Wilson relies on Cicero for his treatment of categorization. Wilson defines memory as a faculty which "contains things received, calls to mind things past, and renews afresh things forgotten" (*Rhet.*, p. 209). For the improvement of this faculty he recommends practice but also recommends the classical system of associating words and ideas to symbolic images that are then arranged in an orderly fashion within a series of backgrounds stored in the mind (e. g., in the rooms of an imaginary house).

In spite of the consistent inclusion of oral recall in medieval and Renaissance rhetorics, memory, during this period, has often been referred to as "the lost canon." References to it are many but treatment of it is brief and usually superficial. The shift from orality to writing made "memorizing" nearly obsolete. Accuracy became more important in recall, and writing was seen as the most accurate means of recording information. Even in the references to oral situations, we see theorists including practice in writing as an aid to memory. Preachers were generally taught to write their sermons; some read them to the audience; most spoke from detailed notes. Augustine even urges the preacher who has difficulty in composing sermons to use the sermons of others: "If such men take what has been written with wisdom and eloquence by others, and commit it to memory, and deliver it to the people, they cannot be blamed, supposing they do it without deception" (IV. 29). A person who must do this, Augustine says, may be a good preacher, if his delivery is good, though never, of course, a good teacher, for he cannot design messages and adapt them to the particular needs of his congregation. Still, it is better for people to hear wise and eloquent words than dull and boring ones. (Many collections of sermons were available for those who needed them, and sample sermons were often included in Renaissance manuals on preaching.)

Though the major emphasis in the *artes praedicandi* was on devices useful for the preacher's recall, an almost equal emphasis was placed on the memory of the receiver because of the importance of transmitting Christian ideology. The first century Roman rhetorical handbook, *Rhetorica ad Herrenium*, was a major source for the organizational theory of the manuals. The anonymous author of that handbook justified the traditional method of organizing speeches in five parts on the basis that by this method the speaker can more easily remember what he wants to say, *and* "the hearer can perceive and remember the distribution of the parts in the whole cause and also in each particular argument" (II. xvii. 27). Two typical thirteenth-century manuals that use this taxonomy of organization, Alexander of Ashby's *On the Mode of Preaching* and Thomas of Salisbury's *Summa de Arte Praedicandi*, justify its use as an aid to the audience's memory rather than to the preacher's.[32] Augustine, though he urges no particular system, likewise reminds the preacher that his "first and chief aim" is to present material in such a way that his hearers will "understand" it, that is, categorize it for recall (IV. 8).

Other memory devices used by preachers have been explained earlier. The four senses of interpretation served this purpose as did the methods of amplification (the classical topics of conceptualization).

Categorization as Perception   The third approach to categorization

[32] See Murphy, *Rhetoric in the Middle Ages*, pp. 312–325.

grows in part out of the late medieval emphasis on dialectic, or logic, as the primary communication discipline and in part out of the renewed interest in "science" in the Renaissance. In this approach, perception is treated as the fundamental process in logical reasoning, and logic is viewed as the method by which sciences are "invented." For theorists such as John of Salisbury and Francis Bacon, perception of data is prior to either storage or recall. These three processes are, in turn, viewed as preconceptual, that is, human beings first sense, second store, third recall, and fourth conceptualize—imaginatively order their perceptions.

In his Metalogicon, John of Salisbury presents a taxonomy of conceptualization based on categorization. His concern is with the process through which human beings create scientific knowledge. Quoting from Aristotle's Posterior Analytics (II. 19, 100a, 3ff), he says: "Sense perception is a prerequisite for memory; the memory of frequently repeated sense perceptions results in experimental proof; experimental proofs provide the materials for a science or an art" (IV. 8). He goes on to say, "many experimental proofs [result] in a rule, and many rules in an art, which provides scientific skill" (IV. 12).

John views the processes of categorization and conceptualization as a single "faculty" or power: "the same power at one time senses, at another remembers, at another imagines, at still another discriminates as it investigates, and finally comprehends by the [intuitive] understanding what it investigates" (IV. 9; emphases mine; insertion by translator). From John's discussion of these activities, however, it becomes clear that sensing and remembering are categorization processes, whereas imagination is preconceptual, and discrimination and comprehension are conceptualization processes.

The first step in perception is sensing. Ultimately, John says, sensation "constitutes the basis for all the arts" (IV. 8). Quoting Aristotle, he defines sensation, initial sense perception, as "an innate power that discriminates things," an awareness of "being affected by action" (IV. 9). It is not, however, passive. Sensing is an activity; people select things to perceive. The basis for this selection process is not spelled out, but from John's discussion of logical reasoning in general, we can assume that it is learned. As people perceive and make sense of their world, they develop an ability to attend to some things and ignore others.

Bacon, whose taxonomy of categorization closely parallels John's, makes this selectivity explicit. In his analysis of the "idols and false notions" that prevent theoretic development of the sciences, he focuses on sense perception (Nov. Org., I. 38). The fundamental notions are the "idols of the tribe [which] are inherent in human nature and the very tribe or race of man; for man's sense is falsely asserted to be the standard of things; on the contrary, all the perceptions both of the senses and the mind bear reference to man and not to the universe" (Nov. Org., I. 39). Thus human beings project themselves on reality. They invent order and qualities. They create propositions and then search for evidence to support them, ignoring contrary perceptions. In sensing, they are most excited by striking images, what is present rather than what is past or future. They tend to believe what fits best with their hopes, prides, superstitions. They rely primarily on their sense of sight, ignoring what is not visible. Bacon concludes that "by far the greatest impediment and aberration of the human understanding proceeds from the dullness, incompetency, and errors of the senses" (Nov. Org., I. 40–50). This does not mean, however, that sense perception cannot be used to order and classify reality: "All the better interpretations of nature are worked out by instances, and fit and apt experiments, where the senses only judge the experiment" (Nov. Org., I. 50). Thus, experimental induction, Bacon's preferred method of conceptualization, must rely on sense perception as does John's logical conceptualization, but whereas the object of perception for one is "nature in the raw," for the other it is experimental manipulation of nature through human intervention. Bacon thus anticipates theory of the modern period in his more detailed analysis of how people sense and order their world.

In The Advancement of Learning, Bacon defines categorization (which he calls "custody") as the third intellectual art. Categorization is defined as the "retaining of knowledge in either writing or memory" (Adv. Learn., II. xv. 1). As we have seen, Bacon recommends the study of grammar and the collection of commonplaces for retaining in writing, that is, for storage and recall of specific information. The second part of categorization, memory, Bacon says has no well-developed theory. He then presents a two-part analysis upon which a theory could be based. The first step is essentially a combination of John's first two. John says that after initial sensing, the second step in categorization is memory: "As it perceives things, our soul stores up their images within itself, and in the process of retaining and often recalling them . . . builds up for itself a sort of treasury of the memory" (IV. 9). Bacon calls his first step "prenotion." On the basis of past experiences and perceptions, individuals form gross classifications for things, i. e., words, relationships, etc. These are prenotions, John's "treasury of stored sensation." In terms of the communication process, prenotion prevents randomness and "directs us to seek in a narrow compass, that is, somewhat that hath congruity with our place of memory" (Adv. Learn., II. xv. 3). These "places" get established, of course, through the inherent time-binding tendency of the human "tribe." In contrast, John seems to assume that each individual begins life with a "clean slate" upon which sense perceptions are impressed and recorded.

In spite of these differences in their view of initial perception, Bacon and John agree on their treatment of the next phase. John calls this "imagination." With the addition of imagination, remembering becomes a creative process: As the mind "mentally revolves the images of

. . . things, there arises imagination, which proceeds beyond the [mere] recollection of previous perceptions, to fashion, by its own [creative] activity, other representations similar to these" (IV. 9; insertions by translator). Imagination, John says, is "the offspring of sensation," which is "nourished and fostered by memory" (IV. 10). In other words, with imagination, categorizations can become conceptualizations. (John's next two steps make this potential real and are therefore treated in the next section under conceptualization.) What John calls "imagination," Bacon calls the development of an "emblem." It is the creation of "images sensible, which strike the memory more; out of which axioms may be drawn" (Adv. Learn., II. xv. 3). In other words, a wide variety of perceptions combine to form a prenotion. These notions are then imaginatively drawn together in striking emblems from which hypotheses can be abstracted. John makes the same point, saying that the importance of this process is that it allows us to conceive of things in their absence, to see relationships among things which we originally perceived as unrelated, and to conceive of outcomes which have not yet occurred. In other words, John explains, perception, storage, and imaginative recall result in "opinions" about patterns of events—Bacon's "hypotheses" (IV. 12). The accuracy of these opinions is a function of the conceptualization process, and both Bacon and John suggest verification methods. In brief, for Bacon the method is experimental induction; for John, it is logical reasoning and faith.

In summary, categorization became a dominant concern in medieval and Renaissance scholarship. The "triumph" of Christianity led to an increased emphasis on "right learning" and on written messages as repositories of truth and reality. The "revival of learning" in the twelfth through the seventeenth centuries added another body of "right learning," knowledge of the books and category systems of the ancient Greeks and Romans in addition to Christian doctrine. This focus on ancient knowledge led to a recognition of the degree to which scholars of the period, especially those of the "Dark Ages," had neglected nontheological knowledge, "science." Categorization then became an important process in relearning the fundamentals of scientific inquiry. Oddly enough, this emphasis on categorization was both destructive and constructive in its effects on the study of human communication. On the one hand, it led to an almost total neglect of conceptualization. This neglect is reflected in the theoretic stagnation of not only human communication but of all the secular disciplines. On the other hand, this same tendency led theorists of the Renaissance to revive classical theory and thus preserved the paradigm and made it possible for theorists in the modern period to revitalize human communication as a theoretic discipline.

Conceptualization

Conceptualization is that branch of human communication theory concerned with the nature of knowledge and the processes of information acquisition and interpretation. In terms of the communicative act, it is the process by which an individual assigns meaning to data in light of some present concern.

To the Greek and Roman theorists, conceptualization was the focal point in human communication theory. Communication was viewed as the process of "inventing" ways of comprehending and ordering reality. Theorists such as Plato, Aristotle, and Cicero thus devoted much of their intellectual energy to the development of a theoretic taxonomy of the conceptualization process. The result was a complex analytic scheme for acquiring and interpreting information relevant to the variety of subjects, situations, and persons involved in communication events. How any particular phenomenon could be conceived on any particular occasion was viewed as a matter of choice, as an opportunity for creative decision-making.

As we have seen, much of what had been viewed as the province of conceptualization in classical theory became the province of categorization in medieval and Renaissance scholarship. In a phrase, *invention becomes revelation*. Christianity posited not a socially constructed but a divinely created world. Medieval and Renaissance scholars thus began to treat conceptualization primarily as a matter of assessing previously learned material in a formulary manner. Meanings were not viewed as created in the categorization process but as learned.

Much of the taxonomy of classical conceptualization theory was retained in medieval and Renaissance scholarship, but it was treated primarily as a classification system (see Fig. 3.7). As we have seen, the topical system of analysis began to be thought of as an information storage, rather than as an information generating, system. Ethos, pathos, and logos, the classical modes of proof, began to be thought of as "appeals" added to the message rather than as methods of conceiving a message. (This notion of the modes of proof has remained dominant into the twentieth century.) In Aristotle's terminology, they began to be treated

---

Fig. 3.7   Conceptualization in Medieval and Renaissance Theory

I. Inartistic—Formulaic recall
   A. The classical topics
      1. Commonplace formulas for forensic, deliberative, and epideictic "oratory"
      2. Positions of argument—fact, name, quality, procedure
   B. The modes of proof
      1. Ethos—Appeal to personality
      2. Pathos—Appeal to emotion
      3. Logos—Appeal to logic
II. Artistic—"Imaginative" ordering of perception
   A. Discrimination—Judgment of hypotheses
   B. Prudence—Testing of hypotheses
   C. Knowledge—Acceptance of hypotheses, belief or faith

as "inartistic" sources of material, as something which existed and only had to be used, rather than as "artistic" creations of the communicator.

The "Topics" of Conceptualization   In his critique of the history of scholarship, Bacon summarizes this development. He explains that conceptualization (which he calls the art of inquiry or invention), as it has been treated by most scholars, "is not properly an invention: for to invent is to discover that we know not, and not to recover or resummon that which we already know" (*Adv. Learn.*, II. xiii. 6). He goes on to summarize the dominant medieval and Renaissance approach:

> [T]he use of this invention is no other but, out of the knowledge whereof our mind is already possessed, to draw forth or call before us that which may be pertinent to the purpose which we take into our consideration. So as to speak truly it is no invention, but a remembrance or suggestion, with an application, . . . Nevertheless, because we do account it a chase as well of deer in an enclosed park as in a forest at large, and that it hath already obtained the name, let it be called invention: so as it be perceived and discerned, that the scope and end of this invention is readiness and present use of our knowledge, and not addition or amplification thereof (*Adv. Learn.*, II. xiii. 6).

We will follow Bacon and call medieval and Renaissance "invention" conceptualization. Though it differs in degree from the classical and contemporary, it is still, as Alcuin puts it, "the devising of subject matter" (*Rhet.*, p. 71).

The major content area of medieval and Renaissance conceptualization was the classical topics. Scholars condensed the "commons," the "special topics" relevant to the three classical genres, and the "formal topics" growing out of the subject to be discussed into one mass of "sources for arguments." Each scholar had his own system of classifying this mass of "topics" (or "places" or "commonplaces," as they were often termed), but the systems became almost hopelessly confused. One scholar's inartistic topics became another's artistic topics. Some used the same topic in several different categories. In general, there was some agreement on the nature of the difference between dialectical and rhetorical topics, though classification systems never fully agreed.

Bacon explains this general difference by saying that the topical approach to conceptualization has two theoretic components. The first comes from dialectic. He calls this "preparation," that is, the lore of "places" or previously thought-out arguments that can be applied to particular cases whenever the need arises. The communicator, having thoroughly analyzed a general question, a thesis such as "The cost of war usually exceeds the rewards," has only to apply the argument when confronted with the specific question, an hypothesis such as "Should the Athenians go to war with the Carthaginians in the present case." The second component of this approach to conceptualization Bacon calls "suggestion," the use of the "topics of invention." The topics are "marks, or places, which may excite our mind to return and produce such knowledge as it hath formerly collected to the end we may make use thereof" (*Adv. Learn.*, II. xiii. 9). Dialectical "places" are the general prenotions; rhetorical topics are the specific "suggestion" in regard to the special subject, persons, and circumstances of the case.

Wilson identifies the places of dialectic (logique) as "definition, causes, parts, effects, things adjoining, and contraries" (*Rhet.*, p. 23). Cassiodorus labels some of these as categories, some as commonplaces, and others as predicables. Agricola includes them all, plus a number of others, as the "places" of dialectical invention (see Fig. 3.8).

Fig. 3.8   Agricola's "places" of dialectical invention[*]

I. Intrinsic	12. Ends
A. Intrasubstantial	13. Effects
1. Definition	14. Intentions
2. Genus	B. Circumstances
3. Species	15. Place
4. Property	16. Time
5. Whole	17. Possessions
6. Parts	C. Accidents
7. Conjugates	18. Contingencies
B. Extrasubstantial	19. Pronouncements
8. Adjacents	20. Name
9. Acts	21. Likenesses
10. Subjects	22. Comparisons
II. Extrinsic	D. Repugnancies
A. Cognates	23. Opposites
11. Agents	24. Differences

[*] From McNally, 1966, p. 103

Following the precedent of Aristotle, the places of rhetoric were usually presented as the topics of deliberative, forensic (judicial), and epideictic (demonstrative) oratory. For epideictic situations, for instance, the topics for "praise of a person" included the birth and infancy, the childhood, adolescense, adulthood, old age, and manner of death, or the virtues of mind, body, and fortune (Wilson, *Rhet.*, p. 12). Topics for "praise of a deed" included its honesty, difficulty, who did it, what it was, and where, when, why, and how it was done (Wilson, *Rhet.*, p. 17).

One of the primary topical systems was the four positions of argument (or "status" or "stasis") used for analyzing legal cases. Alcuin lists the same four standard positions as Cassiodorus and others. Alcuin defines a position as "the place where the question stands as a result of the preliminary disagreement between parties" and identifies disagreements of fact, name, quality, and procedure (*Rhet.*, p. 73). In the development of a case, the communicator first decides on the status of the dispute and then proceeds to build a case taking into account the person, the nature of the deed, the time, place, manner of the deed, and the motive and ability of the accused (Alcuin, *Rhet.*, p. 73).

Erasmus brings together nearly all the materials of classical conceptualization theory (rhetorical and dialectical topics, the commons, the three genres of communicative acts, and argument from example and enthymeme) as the "eleventh method" of copia:

> The eleventh method of enriching depends on the copious accumulation of proofs and arguments. . . . Some proofs, moreover, are technical . . . i. e., "artificial"; some are nontechnical. . . . Arguments of the latter kind are derived chiefly from precedents, from rumors, from evidence taken under torture, from documents, from an oath, from witnesses. Those of the former class are taken chiefly from the signs . . . [and] some are taken from arguments (for Quintilian distinguishes these from signs), some of which are credible, others highly probable, others not inconsistent. For the most part these are derived from circumstances, which are indeed twofold in nature, pertaining to persons or things. The personal are entirely of this sort: Family, race, country, sex, age, education, physical appearance, fortune, rank, natural disposition, desires, inclinations, previous acts and sayings, passion, wisdom, name. Circumstance of things are these: cause, place, time, occasion, antecedents of the affair, collateral circumstances, consequences, opportunity, instrument, method (*On Copia*, pp. 66–67).

Erasmus continues, under the heading of "commonplaces," to say that arguments generally are derived from definition, description, and etymology. Topics he lists are "class, species, peculiarity, differences, partition, division . . . contraries, contradictions, consequences . . . relatives, causes, events; from comparison, which is threefold, the greater, the lesser, the equal; from derived forms and whatever others there are" (p. 67). In addition to these places, the communicator looking for arguments should look for *exempla*, examples, which are the most powerful forms of proof. These can be used as similes, *dissimilia*, or contraries, and example forms such as proverbs and analogies "hold first place, whether you advise, or exhort, or praise, or attack, in short, whether you desire to produce belief, to move, or to entertain" (pp. 67–68). Thus are the complexities of classical conceptualization theory reduced to methods of enriching and embellishing messages.

In concluding his critique of the topical approach to conceptualization, Bacon admits that it may, to some extent, be useful in the discovery as well as the recovery of knowledge. He quotes Plato (*Meno*, 80) as saying that anyone who seeks for knowledge must have a general notion of what it is and where to look for it. Thus the topics, which serve to remind us of what we already know, can also "direct our inquiry," can help us to know "what questions to ask" or "what points to search and revolve" (*Adv. Learn.*, II. xii. 9–10). He concludes that in some cases searching out the topics may lead to discovery of new knowledge.

For the most part, however, the medieval and Renaissance scholars viewed "invention" as a method of finding material with which to improve the appearance of the message. Cassiodorus says, "Invention is the devising of arguments which are true or which resemble true arguments to make the case appear credible" (*Divine and Human Readings*, II. 2). Alcuin defines it as the "devising of subject matter either true or apparently true, which makes a case convincing" (*Rhet.*, p. 71). Wilson describes it as "finding out of apt matter, . . . searching out of things true, or things likely, the which may reasonably set forth a matter, and make it appear probable" (*Rhet.*, p. 6).

The Modes of Proof   The classical modes of proof tend to be treated in much the same manner as topical arguments, as something to be added to messages to make them more effective.

Ethos is typically defined both as the auditor's perception of the communicator as the result of the message and as the credibility or reputation of the source prior to his presentation. The latter conception, which Aristotle defines as "inartistic," is of primary importance to Christian scholars. Quintilian's definition of the "orator" as a "good man speaking well" was one of the most often quoted phrases in medieval and Renaissance communication literature. Augustine claims that "the life of the speaker will count for more in securing the hearer's compliance" than will any degree of skill in communication techniques (*Chris. Doc.*, IV. 59). John of Salisbury cites Cicero, saying, "It is a well-known fact that 'Eloquence without wisdom is futile' " (*Met.*, II. 9), and he also claims that, "An erroneous life is more pernicious than faulty speech" (IV. 22). In Alain de Lille's *On the Preacher's Art* (1199?), three types of preaching are identified—by word, by writing, and by deed.[33]

Rhetoric and letter-writing manuals tend to discuss the modes of proof in terms of the functions of the parts of an oration. In the *Dictaminum Radii*, Alberic and John say that the salutation and introduction of the letter serve to establish the intent and credibility of the writer. Alcuin says that the sender must establish his ethos early in the message:

But above all it should never be forgotten that an Introduction

---

[33] Murphy, *Rhetoric in the Middle Ages*, p. 308.

ought to bespeak the utmost purpose and seriousness—in a word, every trait of honesty—and ought never to have parade and a self-conscious beauty. Display and manufactured elegance produce in the listener a suspicion that the style is counterfeit, and this misgiving diminishes his confidence in the speech and limits the influence of the speaker (*Rhet.*, p. 101).

Alcuin lists four "places" for arguments establishing ethos: "A friendly disposition toward the speaker is created by topics drawn from four localities—from considerations respecting ourselves, our adversaries, the person of the judges [audience], and the nature of the dispute" (*Rhet.*, p. 97). Thus the speaker can use arguments to build his own ethos as well as to denigrate the ethos of his opponents.

The primary source of ethos in medieval and Renaissance scholarship was thought to be the communicator's life, his personality and habits, his activities and accomplishments prior to his attempt to communicate with a particular audience. Within the communication act, ethical "appeals" could be made by direct or indirect reference to these credentials, by recalling his experience, by comparing his credentials to those of his opponents, or by demonstrating his broad knowledge of his subject as in quoting passages of scriptures from memory.

Pathos in the medieval and Renaissance period ceases to be defined as the creation of empathy, feeling *with* another, and becomes "emotional appeal." It is normally discussed in terms of arousing pleasure or of "moving to action." Augustine says that it is necessary to please readers or listeners in order to keep their attention and impress ideas in their minds. Using an analogy between eating and learning, he says, "the very food without which it is impossible to live must be flavored to meet the tastes of the majority" (*Chris. Doc.*, IV. 11). On the other hand, he says that the Christian communicator may often find that other emotions, such as grief, fear, or anger, are more likely to produce belief and lead to action. Augustine tells of his own experience in attempting to dissuade the citizens of Caesaria from initiating a civil war. He says, "I strove with all the vehemence of speech that I could command; . . . it was not, however, when I heard their applause, but when I saw their tears, that I thought I had produced an effect" (IV. 24). He concludes with the general observation that often people "show the effect made on them by the powerful eloquence of a wise man, not by clamorous applause so much as by groans, sometimes even by tears, finally by change of life" (IV. 24).

As with ethos, most of the medieval and Renaissance writers who discuss pathos do so in terms of the functions of parts of the message. The Ciceronian dictum that the introduction should make the hearer or reader "attentive, docile, and well-disposed" is widely quoted in manuals on preaching, letter writing, and rhetoric. In letter writing theory, the introduction to the letter was generally conceived of as having two parts. First, the greeting or salutation, and second, the *benevolentiae captatio*, the securing of the reader's good will through appeal to his emotions. In letters, emotional appeal was generally thought to be a function of the "colores," the figures of speech, and the primary appeal was to pleasure. Figures were similarly treated in preaching manuals, though preachers were more frequently interested in arousing other emotions, such as indignation, fear, or shame. For these purposes, *exempla*, e. g., brief stories of persons who sinned and suffered just punishment, parables, analogies, etc., were often recommended.

In rhetoric manuals, which usually focused on legal communication, the less pleasant emotions were also given emphasis. Alcuin, for instance, sees pathos as a major function of the conclusion as well as of the introduction. He says that the introduction should arouse sympathy for the proponent whereas the conclusion should arouse antipathy for the opponent. For arousing sympathy, he suggests graphically, but modestly, describing the reputation of the client, using prayer, flattering the hearers on their good sense and honesty, and emphasizing the novelty and/or importance of the case they are about to hear (*Rhet.*, pp. 97–99). For the conclusion, where arousing antipathy is the goal, Alcuin lists ten possible approaches, for instance, maligning the opponent's reputation and graphically describing the commission and consequences of the crime. The object here, and in all uses of emotional appeal, is "to make the judge [audience member] consider the crime in relation to himself and his loved ones" and to make him see and feel emotions which will lead to the conclusion desired by the communicator (*Rhet.*, pp. 125–126).

Though pathos is a subject much mentioned in medieval and Renaissance documents, there is little attempt to build a theory of emotional response. Even in Wilson's *Rhetorique*, where "moving the feelings of the listener" is described as of major importance to the preacher and the lawyer as well as in everyday intercourse, we find helpful hints rather than theoretic explanation. It was not until the advent of the belletristic movement in the eighteenth century that pathos (defined as "sympathy") again became an object of theorizing.

In classical theory, *logos* was defined as "proof through the words of the message" and was discussed in terms of enthymeme and example. In the medieval and Renaissance periods, logos begins to be thought of as "logical appeal" and is dealt with primarily in terms of the topical system discussed earlier. Some attention is given to enthymeme, which is defined not as a psychological counterpart to the logical syllogism but as an "incomplete syllogism" and is discussed, as in Cassiodorus' summary of dialectic, in terms of the various moods and forms a syllogism may take. Other writers also devote some time to the epichireme, which is a five-part rather than three-part syllogism. Sophisms also come in for some attention. They are treated as untruthful and logically invalid syllogistic arguments.

For the most part, these discussions are technical and nonpragmatic. Augustine, however, does make the important classical distinction between logical validity and empirical truth: "The truth of a statement stands on its own merits; the validity of an inference depends on the statement or the admission of the man with whom one is arguing" (*Chris. Doc.*, II. 33). Thus, logical validity is linguistic; it depends upon making connections between premises and conclusions. Truth is verifiable by reference to empirical reality (or to Christian doctrine). This distinction becomes crucial in the modern period when theorists revolted against "scholastic logic" in favor of empirical observation.

In discussing sophisms, Augustine prefigures another important development in the modern period—the use of logical argument to induce "dissonance" and thus change of attitude:

> For there are many of what are called *sophisms*, inferences in reasoning that are false, and yet so close an imitation of the true as to deceive not only dull people but clever men too. . . . There are also valid processes of reasoning which lead to false conclusions, by following out to its logical consequences the error of the man with whom one is arguing; and these conclusions are sometimes drawn by a good and learned man, with the object of making the person from whose error these consequences result, feel ashamed of them, and of thus leading him to give up his error, when he finds that if he wishes to retain his old opinion, he must of necessity also hold other opinions which he condemns (*Chris. Doc.*, II. 31).

Augustine is thus one of the few medieval scholars to make any practical or theoretic statements under the heading of logos. Two later theorists, however, take "logic" as the starting point for a theoretic approach to conceptualization.

Imaginative Conceptualization   Both John of Salisbury and Francis Bacon attempt to reconstruct the "science" of human communication as a theory of how people come to know, believe, and act. Both argue that conceptualization is the result of imaginative ordering of sense perceptions. People perceive (1) data (sense reality), and (2) remember and store it in their minds, thus forming a "prenotion," or concept. Through the ordering of these prenotions in "the imagination," they (3) form what John calls "opinions" and what Bacon calls "hypotheses."

The fourth step in John's taxonomy, discrimination, is the application of judgment to opinions. This judgment results in "prudence" which John says, "according to Cicero, is a virtue of the conscious soul, a virtue whose object is the investigation, perception, and skillful utilization of the truth" (IV. 12). John provides no methodology for discrimination, or development of prudence, other than the precept that it requires full cognizance of all relevant sensations and images, past, present, and future. The only criterion he provides is that opinions be tested to determine whether they represent "things to be as they really are" (IV. 11). This is the final goal of the categorization process, truth, or scientific knowledge. John personifies the final step, saying, "When it has ascertained the truth, prudence develops into a form of scientific knowledge" (IV. 12).

This final perception, knowledge, John says, may be more or less certain. The "opinion that after the night has run its course, the sun will return" is very reliable. In contrast, "Since human affairs are transitory, only rarely can we be sure that our opinion about them is correct" (IV. 13). Between these two extremes is "faith," the "opinion" upon which religion is based. Though we cannot be quite certain about many things, it is necessary for us to behave as though we were. Faith is "most necessary in human affairs, as well as in religion. Without faith, no contracts could be concluded, nor could any business be transacted" (IV. 13). Finally, John says, his theory of conceptualization is a theory of perception based upon perception and therefore subject to no external test. We must accept it on faith.

Bacon, of course, anticipating the development of "empirical logic" in the modern period, describes the final step in conceptualization as the experimental testing of hypotheses. The essential problem with traditional conceptualization theory, he says, is that it leads to John's predicament—a theory of perception based on perception subject to no external verification. Conceptualization based on formal logic draws conclusions from received axioms and from inadequate observation of particulars. Both logical induction and deduction result, he says, not in conclusions, but in "conjectures" (Adv. Learn., II. xiii. 2–3). Both are based on language and "consist of propositions, and propositions of words, and words are but the current tokens or marks of popular notions of things" (Adv. Learn., II. xiii. 4). These popular notions cannot possibly lead to better understanding of the nature of things, for they are abstractions. It is no wonder, Bacon says, that many ancient philosophers believed that human knowledge was limited to "appearances and probabilities," given this approach to conceptualization.

Symbolization

Symbolization is the study of the nature of symbols in human interaction. From the point of view of the sender, it is the selection of symbols to represent and elicit meanings; for the receiver, it is the process of assigning meaning to symbols. The classical approach to symbolization was highly integrated and focused on the pragmatics of symbols in use.

Though medieval and Renaissance scholars retained the terminology and general content of the classical taxonomy, for the most part their treatment focused on syntactics and semantics (see Fig. 3.9). A number of scholars, for instance, wrote detailed treatises analyzing the complexities of various figures of speech. In addition to Bede's *Figures and Tropes* (701), and Erasmus' *On Copia* (1512) there were such works as Alberic's *Flowers of Rhetoric* (1087), Sherry's *A Treatise of Schemes and Tropes* (1550), and Peacham's *Garden of Eloquence* (1557). The focus in these kinds of treatises was on figures as technical, linguistic structures, as "colors," or ornaments to be added onto messages with little or no regard for purpose or effect beyond the aesthetic.

Fig. 3.9   Symbolization in Medieval and Renaissance Theory

I. Classical Approaches—Pragmatics (use of symbols for instruction, pleasing, and persuading)
   A.   Three levels of style—Subdued, temperate, majestic
   B.   Three criteria of style—Accuracy, aesthetics, propriety
II. Technical Approaches—Syntactics and semantics (language as form and/or adornment of thought)
   A.   Formulary analysis of audiences
   B.   Linguistic structure of figurative language
   C.   Interpretation of ambiguous language
       1.   Literal interpretation through knowledge of grammar and linguistics, context, and comparison of texts
       2.   Figurative interpretation through broad general education; focused study of grammar, logic, and rhetoric

---

Semantics was a major concern of writers such as Augustine, Alcuin, John of Salisbury, Wilson, and Bacon as well as of the authors of letter writing and preaching manuals. Here the focus was on language as a source of misunderstanding. While classical theorists viewed language as inherently creative and interactive, medieval and Reanaissance writers more often saw it as a subject for technical study, as a method of beautifying thought, and as an obstacle to "reasonable" (as opposed to "emotional") decision-making and to "accurate" perception of reality.

The Classical Approach   It is in their discussions of message sending that the medieval and Renaissance scholars are most "classical." The classical system consisted of the integration of the three levels of style with the three basic functions of communication. These were further tied to the three modes of proof and criteria of effectiveness (see Fig. 2.6). Augustine, though essentially a semanticist, did more than any other single theorist to maintain this integrated pragmatic approach.

Augustine's focus in Book IV of *On Christian Doctrine* is on the use of symbols ("signs") in message sending, on "the mode of making meanings known." His goal is to provide guidance for Christian teachers. All Christians, he says, must teach:

> It is the duty, then, of the interpreter and teacher of Holy Scripture, the defender of the true faith and the opponent of error, both to teach what is right and to refute what is wrong, and in the performance of this task to conciliate the hostile, to rouse the careless, and to tell the ignorant both what is occurring at present and what is probable in the future (IV. 4).

Understanding of the use of "signs" is vital to this function, for "all things are learnt by means of signs" (I. 2).

Teaching, Augustine says, is first a matter of having knowledge (acquired in categorization and conceptualization) and, second, a matter of "eloquence," skill in the use of language. Instruction cannot be accomplished by putting information "in any shape no matter what"; how a thing is said determines in part how it will be reacted to. He quotes Cicero (*Orator*, 21) as having given the most succinct definition of skill in symbolization:

> [Cicero] embraced the whole in one sentence thus: "He, then, shall be eloquent, who can say little things in a subdued style, in order to give instruction, moderate things in a temperate style, in order to give pleasure, and great things in a majestic style, in order to sway the mind" (IV. 17).

In some particular cases, Augustine says, the communicator may concentrate on only one of these levels:

> If the hearers need *teaching*, the matter treated of must be made fully known by means of narrative. On the other hand, to clear up points that are doubtful requires *reasoning* and the exhibition of proofs. If, however, the hearers require to be roused rather than instructed, in order that they may be diligent to what they already know, and to bring their feelings into harmony with the truths they admit, greater vigour of speech is needed. Here entreaties and reproaches, exhortations and upbraidings, and all the other means of *rousing the emotions* are necessary (Emphases mine; IV. 4).

In the long run, however, Augustine claims that all three goals are necessary and all three styles must be mastered. Once the hearer or reader has been clearly informed or taught, he "must be pleased in order to secure his attention" (IV. 12). Further, "it is possible that a man may be taught and delighted and yet not give his consent. And what will be the use of gaining the first two ends if we fail in the third?" (IV. 12).

An additional justification for mastering all three styles is the kinds of questions that must be discussed. The plain style is required "when knotty questions turn up for solution [and] accuracy of distinction is required" (IV. 23). The middle style is to be used "whenever praise or blame is to be given" (IV. 23). The vigorous or majestic style is to be used only sparingly and then only when a course of action is urged as when the goal is "to break down hardness," to lead people "to do what they ought to do but were unwilling to do" (IV. 24). Thus, for the sender, Augustine concludes that the ultimate goal of "eloquent" symbolization is pragmatic; symbols are instrumental to behavior.

Other theorists make similar statements. Wilson, for instance, defines the three "ends of rhetorique" as a series of interlocking steps. First, *to teach*, the "orator must labor to tell his tale, that the hearers may well know what he means." Clarity is not enough, however; the sender must also *delight* his receivers, "for except men find delight, they will not long abide." The third step, "when these two are done," is *to persuade*, "to move the affections of his hearers in such wise that they shall be forced to yield unto his saying" (*Rhet.*, pp. 2–4).

The three criteria for symbolization in classical theory were accuracy, aesthetics, and propriety. Medieval and Renaissance scholars, for the most part, employ the same criteria. Erasmus says, "above all, care must be taken that speech be appropriate, be Latin, be elegant, be correct" (*On Copia*, p. 18). Wilson lists "plainness, aptness, composition [grammatcial construction], and exornation [use of figures and colors]" (*Rhet.*, p. 169). John of Salisbury urges reference to the rules of grammar (I. 14), clarity (I. 18), and adaptation to the audience (III. 1). Alcuin recommends the use of common words for accuracy and figures for ornament (*Rhet.*, pp. 134–5), and Augustine lists "perspicuity, beauty of style, and persuasive power" as the three goals at which all discourse ought to aim (*Chris. Doc.*, IV. 26).

In discussing the first criterion, medieval and Renaissance theorists make much the same kind of remarks as the classical theorists did. They recommend study of grammar, reference to common usage, study of great speakers and writers, and practice in composition.

Classical theorists devoted most attention to the third criterion, propriety, discussing it in terms of appropriateness of symbolization to the audience, place, time, speaker, subject, and occasion. Medieval and Renaissance scholars consistently include propriety in their treatments of symbolization, although they tend to simply repeat classical statements with little elaboration. Alcuin, for instance, paraphrases Cicero by saying that the communicator

> should train himself to have above all an understanding of what befits himself and his subject, a sense of decorum in his choice of ideas and of words. He should not express himself in identical thoughts and phrases when he speaks to the different degrees of

fortune, rank, prestige, age; his style should not be insensitive to the adaptations suggested by the place and time of his speech, and by the audience he faces; in every part of his speech, as in every minute of life, he should let his sense of decorum be his guide (*Rhet.*, p. 137).

Likewise, John of Salisbury writes, "a good teacher dispenses his instruction in a way that is suited to the time and adapted to his students" (III. 1). Also, he says, communication is interactional:

It does not lie within the power of one person alone to bring to a successful conclusion, by himself, a joint enterprise, which requires the cooperation of another. One who is proceeding according to the art [of logic] is very often impeded by the slowness of his hearer, or the difficulty of the subject matter. . . . We should deal with a learned man in one way, but with an illiterate person in another. The former is convinced by syllogisms, whereas the latter's assent must be won by inductive reasoning (III. 10).

Augustine makes a similar remark, saying that there are some passages of scripture which are so complex that, however talented the preacher, they cannot be made clear to the multitude "and these should never be brought before the people at all" (IV. 9).

Bacon takes a somewhat broader and more theoretic view. Like John and Augustine, he says that the "bare facts" *ought* to be sufficient to lead people to "right" behavior. However, even the wisest and most learned are human, and human beings are not moved by reason alone. Inherent weaknesses, such as the tendency to be more affected by the present than the future, tend to get in the way of reasonable, logical choice-making. Thus, "it is eloquence that prevaileth" in everyday life (*Adv. Learn.*, II. xviii. 1).

Bacon treats symbolization under "tradition or delivery," the fourth intellectual art. Tradition, he says, concerns the transmission of knowledge. It consists of three parts: the organ (speech and writing), the method (of organizing), and illustration (eloquent expression). Illustration is "comprehended in that science which we call rhetoric, or art of eloquence; a science excellent, and excellently well-labored" (II. xviii. 1). Bacon cites Aristotle and Cicero as the "laborers" who have perfected this science. If there are any deficiencies in this art, he says, they are not in its classical roots, but in the work since then, the "collections, which may as handmaids attend the art" (II. xviii. 1).

Bacon's discussion of symbolication is highly Aristotelian. He attacks current conceptions for focusing on the use of symbols to arouse emotion and thus prevent rational decision-making. This fault is not inherent in the art itself, however, for "the duty and office of rhetoric is to apply reason to the imagination for the better moving of the will" (II. xviii. 2). That is, the function of symbols is to show "virtue . . . to the imagination in lively representation," to make the future consequences of current decisions present in the mind and thus to "second reason" (II. xviii. 2–4). Although reason should be the key factor in the transmission of knowledge, reason must be assisted by graphic immediacy in symbolization.

The Technical Approach   Aside from these rare and attenuated references, there are few theoretic treatments of the criteria of symbolization in medieval and Renaissance communication literature. Clarity is discussed in terms of the technicalities of grammar. Most treatments of propriety consist of listings of audience types and formulary examples. Allain de Lille, in *On the Preacher's Art*, lists nine special audiences, e. g., soldiers, lawyers, married persons, virgins, etc. In *Pastoral Care* (591), Gregory lists thirty-six pairs of characters based on habits, social position, sex, state of knowledge, etc., and provides a sample sermon to suit each pair.[34] We have seen that in the letter-writing manuals correspondents are encouraged to suit their wording, especially in the salutation, to the relationship between them and their reader, and sample letters are provided as formulas.

It is in the medieval and Renaissance approach to the second criterion, aesthetics, however, that we see the greatest divergence from classical concepts. The focus in classical treatments was on the function of figurative language. Aristotle, for instance, discusses metaphor in terms of its function in helping the receiver "feel" and "see" complex relationships among ideas. Language, he said, should be lively and graphic. Figurative expressions catch attention through their novelty and also express relationships between ideas that cannot be expressed succinctly in literal expressions.

Erasmus provides a somewhat similar explanation for the effect of copia: "Just as the eye is held more by a varying scene, in the same way the mind always eagerly examines whatever it sees as new" (*On Copia*, p. 16). Augustine, too, provides a classical, though Christianized, explanation of the function of figurative language. He points out that the scriptures are full of such language and are therefore often difficult to interpret. This, however, is no accident: "All this was divinely arranged for the purpose of subduing pride by toil and of preventing a feeling of satiety in the intellect which generally holds in small esteem what is discovered without difficulty" (*Chris. Doc.*, II. 6). Augustine expands on this notion with an analogy, explaining that literal passages "satisfy our hunger" while "the more obscure . . . stimulate our appetite" (II. 7). Thus, figurative language is a source of intellectual pleasure: "It is pleasanter in

---

[34] Murphy, *Rhetoric in the Middle Ages*, pp. 293–308.

some cases to have knowledge communicated through figures, and . . . what is attended with difficulty in the seeking gives greater pleasure in the finding" (II. 7).

Although these comments show some resemblance to classical theory, it is in their treatment of figurative language that we see one of the major differences between classical and medieval and Renaissance approaches to symbolization. We have seen that, at the end of the Renaissance, Francis Bacon thought of language as one of the fundamental obstacles to the development of scientific knowledge. His "idols of the market" are those "false notions" that spring from the abstract and arbitrary nature of words. Though Bacon's complaint springs from a concern for science, it is not without precedent. The semantic approach of the early medieval scholars sprang from their concern for the transmission of Christian ideology and their focus on scriptures as the ultimate source of truth. Given these concerns, scholars began to view language as an "obstacle" to understanding. John of Salisbury lists three sources of misunderstanding: schemes and tropes, sophisms, and failure to understand the motives of the speaker ("motives" grow out of the nature of the speaker and the listeners, the occasion, place, time, etc.). Furthermore, he says, "one must learn to discriminate between what is said literally, what is said figuratively, and what is said correctly [truthfully], if one is ever easily and accurately to comprehend what he reads" (I. 18).

Augustine devotes the first three books of On Christian Doctrine to these problems. He focuses on interpreting symbols, especially words, which are the most important class of conventional signs. Difficulties in interpreting written messages, he says, spring from two primary sources: unknown signs and ambiguous signs. When the reader encounters a word or phrase with which he is unfamiliar, Augustine advises using "old" information to interpret this "new" information. He offers three general strategies: (1) The reader should be familiar with the original languages of the scriptures, Greek and Hebrew, and with conventional usages in these languages. This general knowledge, then, can be used to compare different translations of the passage to arrive at understanding of the meaning. (2) The reader should interpret the surrounding words and phrases and then consult the context, "both what goes before and what comes after, to see which interpretation of the many that offer themselves, it pronounces for and allows to be dovetailed into itself" (III. 2). If neither of these strategies serves to reveal the meaning of the "unknown sign," Augustine advises the reader to memorize the word or phrase and look for it in other writings or, if the chance arises, ask a more learned person to explain its referent (II. 4).

Ambiguous signs present a slightly different problem. Signs are ambiguous if they allow for a diversity of interpretations (II. 12). The scriptures, he says, are full of such signs, and "hasty and careless readers are led astray by [these] many and manifold obscurities and ambiguities"

(II. 6). If careful reading does not solve the problem, the next step is to determine if the sign is being used literally, "to point out the objects they were designed to point out," or figuratively, "to signify something else" (II. 10). The word "ox," for instance, may be used to refer to a particular animal, or it may be used to signify the "ox-like" characteristics of a person or thing. First, the sign should be interpreted literally. This interpretation can then be tested for accuracy by its "harmony" with other passages in the context and with Christian doctrine. If the reader "takes up rashly a meaning which the author whom he is reading did not intend, he often falls in with other statements which he cannot harmonize with this meaning" (I. 37). Also, if the literal interpretation is inconsistent with Christian categorizations, if it "commands crime" and "forbids virtue," then it is inaccurate (III. 15–18).

If, by these tests, the passage cannot be interpreted literally, then it must be interpreted figuratively. The strategy Augustine recommends here again uses old information to interpret new. He recommends a broad general education, for figurative expressions are based on the nature of things—the habits and characteristics of natural phenomena and the received notions growing out of human intercourse, i. e., weights and measures, monetary systems, the organization of the arts and sciences, etc. (II. 25). He also urges study of the secular arts, especially grammar, which teaches the various kinds of figures. The Christian communicator, he explains, should learn to recognize the most common of these (he lists allegory, enigma, parable, metaphor, catechresis, irony, and antiphrasis) and should learn how to interpret them (III. 29). He also recommends dialectic. This art teaches the communicator to recognize valid and invalid reasoning (sophisms) and teaches the art of arriving at and/or testing conclusions. It is therefore "of the greatest assistance in the discovery of meaning" (II. 37).

Other writers, though they devote little space to methods of avoiding misunderstanding, follow Augustine in dividing language into literal (simple) and figurative (complex) terms. Most, however, spend little time on semantics, focusing instead on syntactics. Wilson, for instance, devotes three-fourths of his discussion of symbolization to various figures: tropes (such as transumption, circumlocution, etc.), schemes (sentence structures "contrary to the common manner of speaking"), and colors (rhetorical questions, similes, fables, allegories, etc.).

The definitions of figures, schemes, tropes, and colors, and the names and classifications of the forms, vary widely in medieval and Renaissance usage. Bede's treatment, however, is typical. He defines a scheme (which is a particular class of figures) as a shift in normal word order that is used to "clothe or adorn" discourse. Among his list of schemes, there are none that are familiar to the average twentieth-century reader, e. g., anaphora, epizeuxis, hirmos, etc. A trope differs from a scheme. It "is a figure in which a word, either from need or from purpose of embellishment, is shifted from its proper meaning to one similar but not proper to it." Among tropes he lists metaphor, synecdoche, metonymy, allegory, etc. (*Figures and Tropes*, p. 242). As we have seen, after giving his definitions, Bede proceeds to cite numerous examples of figures from "holy scripture."

This heavy focus on the nature and classification of figurative language is an important departure from classical pragmatism. It also highlights another important difference in the medieval and Renaissance conception of symbolization, the tendency to view symbolization not as a fundamental part of the communication process but as an afterthought, a sort of "frosting on the cake." Common definitions of symbolization reveal this shift. Alcuin defines it as "the adornment of speech" and explains the nature of figurative expressions:

> As clothing was first devised to protect him [mankind] from the cold, and in course of time became an ornament of his person and a symbol of his rank, so figurative language was first used to satisfy a need, and later was given new popularity by the pleasure it provided, and by the ornamental effect it produced (*Rhet.*, pp. 134–135).

Erasmus writes, "What clothing is to our body, diction [symbolization] is to the expression of our thoughts" (*De Copia*, p. 11). Given this analogy, he continues, "consequently, let this be the primary concern, that the clothes be not dirty, or ill fitting, or improperly arranged" (p. 18).

John of Salisbury defines symbolization as the province of rhetoric and calls it the art of "clothing with words" (*Met.*, IV. 3). Wilson calls symbolization "elocution" and characterizes it as the "most beautiful" part of rhetoric: "For whereas Invention helpeth to find matter, and Disposition serveth to place arguments: Elocution getteth words to set forth invention, and with such beauty commendeth the matter, that reason seemeth to be clad in Purple" (*Rhet.*, pp. 160–161). The art of elocution, he says, consists of "apt words and sentences together and beautifieth the tongue with great change of colors, and variety of figures" (p. 161).

Thus, in medieval and Renaissance approaches to human communication, words and thoughts came to be thought of as separate, sometimes conflicting, phenomena. Due to this separation, pragmatics began to take second place to semantics and syntactics. The classical concept of language as symbolic action was replaced with a concept of language as ornament. As we will see, this divorce between words and reality became a major topic of debate in the modern period.

Organization

Organization is that part of human communication concerned with order and relationships. In terms of the communication act, it is the adaptation of symbols to social contingencies. In classical theory, organization consisted of the final selection, ordering, and proportioning of concepts (see Fig. 2.7). This process depended upon *definition*, or analysis of the subject, *division*, or analysis of the subject in a specific context (under the general headings of deliberative, forensic, and epideictic situations), and *proportion*, or analysis of the sender/receiver relationship (again in terms of the genres of situations). There was also a well-established prescriptive system specifying four to six basic parts of a message with their concomitant contents.

Fig. 3.10   Organization in Medieval and Renaissance Theory

I. Functional—Ordering based on audience classification
    A. Learned audiences—Dialectic or syllogistic logic
    B. Popular audiences—Rhetoric (see Prescriptive)
II. Prescriptive—Ordering based on parts of an oration
    A. Rhetorics and letter-writing manuals (four to six classical parts: introduction, narration, division, proof, refutation, and conclusion)
    B. Preaching manuals (parts of an oration, topics of expansion, homily, four senses of interpretation)

The Functional Approach   For all practical purposes, the first of these approaches, the functional, disappears in medieval and Renaissance treatments of human communication (see Fig. 3.10). Definition and division were viewed as the province of logic (dialectic). For the most part, they were treated nonpragmatically, in terms of the technical analysis of syllogisms and the logical topics. Some scattered references are made to proportion in the context of appropriate wording of salutations and "decorum" in word choice and sentence construction. The central classification system, however, was based not upon the sender/receiver relationships within the three genres of situations, but upon the distinction between dialectic and rhetoric. Definition and division were viewed as the methods to be used in "disputation" among "the learned," when the goal was to arrive at truth or, later in the period, scientific knowledge. Thus, John of Salisbury reserves the use of syllogisms for sophisticated audiences (*Met.*, III. 10). Augustine recommends reserving complex, "syllogistic" definition and division for books and private conversations with those who "have the capacity of mind to understand it" (*Chris. Doc.*, IV. 9). Bacon distinguishes between two kinds of audiences, those who have special knowledge and those who do not. For the first sort, he recommends an organization which allows "examination," that is, one which presents knowledge "in the same method wherein it was invented." For the second kind of audience, he says it is necessary to present information in an order which is most easily understood and most likely to be believed. The first method is dialectical; it leads to further development and refinement of knowledge. The second is rhetorical; it leads only to persuasion (*Adv. Learn.*, II. xvii. 3).

The Prescriptive Approach   Not surprisingly, the primary focus in the medieval and Renaissance periods was on the prescriptive approach. Rhetorics and letter-writing and preaching manuals relied heavily on the traditional four- to six-part system of message organization.

Alciun defines organization as the second part of rhetoric and defines it as the arrangement, or distributing, of the subject matter (*Rhet.*, p. 71). He says there are six parts to any message. First, the introduction; it should make "the listener well-disposed, and attentive, and compliant" (p. 97). These purposes are achieved, as we have noted previously, through the use of the topics "for praise and blame of persons." The second part is the narration, which is "a story of events which have or could have taken place." The narration should be characterized by "brevity, clarity, probability" (p. 101). The third part is the division. Here the speaker gives a "rapid survey" of the remaining content of the message; he explains the central issue (the position or status) and the order and topics he will use to discuss it (p. 103). Fourth comes the proof. Proof is established through arguments (example, enthymeme, epichireme, and syllogism) drawn from logical and rhetorical topics having to do with persons—i. e., heredity, habits, fortunes, activities, etc.—or with events—i. e., in terms of motive, capability, opportunity, etc. (pp. 105–121). The fifth part is the refutation. Here the speader or writer responds to "the other side," refuting opposing arguments using the same topics and methods he used in the proof (pp. 121–125). Finally, the sixth part is the conclusion. The purposes here are to summarize, arouse indignation or antipathy toward opposing views, and arouse sympathy for the advocate and his position (pp. 125–129).

Alciun's discussion of organization demonstrates the continuance of the prescriptive, technical approach presented in such early Roman handbooks as the *Rhetorica ad Herrenium*. Thomas Wilson's presentation, though somewhat less technical and dry, follows essentially the same pattern. He also calls organization the second part of rhetoric. Having "invented," one's next step is to organize:

> But what availeth much treasure and apt matter, if man cannot apply it to his purpose. Therefore, in the second place is mentioned, the settling or ordering of things invented for the purpose,

called in Latin *Dispositio*, the which is nothing else but an apt bestowing, and orderly placing of things, declaring where every argument shall be set, and in what manner every reason shall be applied for confirmation of the purpose (*Rhetorique*, p. 6).

Wilson lists seven parts, adding the "proposition" between the narration and division. The proposition is the announcement of the issue, "a pithy sentence comprehending in small room, the sum of the whole matter" (p. 7). Alcuin had included this as a part of division. Like Alcuin, Wilson includes the logical and rhetorical topics in his discussion of the various parts. He also includes a rather detailed analysis of amplification, or "copia."

Preaching manuals, though they usually give little attention to organization *per se*, also used the prescriptive system. Alexander of Ashby, in *On the Mode of Preaching* (1200?), says, "The mode of preaching consists in the parts of a sermon, to wit: prologue, division, proof, and conclusion."[35] Alberic and John likewise list four parts for letters: exordium, narration, argument, and conclusion. The anonymous *Principles of Letter-Writing* (1135?) lists five parts: salutation, securing of good will, narration, petition, and conclusion.[36] As we have seen, the salutation was generally discussed in terms of the relative status of the correspondents and the other parts in terms of topics of expansion and figures of speech. Both preaching and letter writing manuals followed the example of the rhetorics in their definitions of these parts and in the recommendation of topics as sources or argument and both topics and figures as methods of amplification. The preaching manuals, of course, added Biblical citation to the arsenal, both as sources of proof and argument and as sources of amplification and ornament.

The recommendation of topics as sources of argument and as methods of expansion highlights the typical medieval and Renaissance tendency to confound various parts of the paradigm. Speaking of organization, Alcuin says, "Its rules may be found among the precepts of invention and style" (*Rhet.*, p. 71), and he presents his discussion of invention (conceptualization) in the context of topics relevant to each part of a message. Symbolization is often discussed in terms of the orderly progression of levels of style and of figures within each part of a message. Augustine, for instance, says that the introduction should usually be in the temperate style (*Chris. Doc.*, IV. 23). Preaching manuals recommended the conceptual topics as methods of expansion, and Erasmus treats them as methods of varying. Erasmus also treats classical organizational theory as a method of varying. He writes:

[35] Quoted in Murphy, *Rhetoric in the Middle Ages*, pp. 313.
[36] *Ibid.*, p. 205.

An oration may be enlarged by increasing the number of its parts. For as he who wishes to be most brief uses as few parts as possible, so he who desires to amplify will take care to add those legitimate parts prescribed by art. For although in general the purposes of an orator are three, to instruct, to please, and to persuade, anyone who likes brevity, content with one, will only instruct, which is done by narration and adducing proof; and he who likes copia will employ everything at once, and that in all parts of the speech, not only in the peroration or exordium. . . . he who aims at copia not only will use those six, *exordium, narration, division, proof, refutation, peroration,* but also as concerns the exordium, will develop its places rather fully at the beginning of the speech and then throughout the oration, wherever the subject permits, will intermingle certain small exordia, by which he may render his audience well disposed, attentive, and receptive, or dispel tedium, or soften beforehand something he is about to say (*On Copia,* pp. 97–98; emphases mine).

As we have seen, preaching manuals recommended certain conceptual methods, e. g., use of scriptural exegesis (homily) and analysis of the "four senses of interpretation," as organizational methods and justified them as aids to memory (categorization).

For the most part, medieval and Renaissance scholars' approaches to organization tend to be as technical, abstract, and nonpragmatic as their approaches to symbolization. The classical emphasis on organic organization based on careful conceptualization of the persons involved ("souls"), the subject, and the occasion virtually disappears from the literature. In large part, this may be accounted for by the extreme dichotomy between truth or reality (the province of dialectic) and probability or appearance (the province of rhetoric). Since both early Christians and later "scientists" were primarily concerned with "truth," their emphasis was on demonstration based on interpretation of scripture, on the one hand, and the rules of logical validity, on the other, rather than on the formation of probable opinion growing out of human intercourse and based on the premises of psychological inference. Thus, much of the content of classical organization theory was reduced to academic formulas having little reference to the process of communicative interaction.

Operationalization

Operationalization is the embodiment of a message in some physical form—a book, a speech, a letter, etc. In terms of human communication theory, it is the study of the use of media, the nature of information transmission, and the processes of symbolic interaction.

Classical theorists had little to say about operationalization. All granted the importance of appropriate control of media in communicating, but given that most communication was oral and face-to-face, there seemed to be little material for theorizing. Cicero pointed out that the voice and body naturally express emotions and asserted that these expressions are cross-cultural and can be understood even when the words of a message are foreign or unintelligible. The face and eyes, he claimed, are the most expressive features. In general, the classical theorists urged that the communicator be natural; either the absence or the exaggeration of gestures or voice inflections, they pointed out, could damage the speaker's ethos. For improvement of skill, they recommended study of music and theatre, private conversation, and physical exercise such as gymnastics. A few attempts were made to prescribe appropriate combinations of voice, gesture, and emotion, such as in the *Rhetorica ad Herenium*, but these were generally seen as futile, even by their authors.

The "Oral" Tradition   Though written communication was of extreme importance in the medieval and Reanissance periods and printing presses were fairly widespread by 1500, there is virtually no theorizing about writing as operationalization. Letter-writing manuals say little beyond urging personal handwriting and use of official seals. The oral tradition in operationalization remains primary throughout the period. Although scholars have, in general, even less to say about it than did the classical theorists, the essential features of the classical approach are summarized in the rhetorics and referred to in preaching manuals (see Fig. 3.11).

Fig. 3.11   Operationalization in Medieval and Renaissance Theory

I. Oral Delivery
   A. Graceful use of voice and body; avoidance of faults
   B. Source of pleasure or adornment
II. Nonverbal Communication
   A. Visual and aural symbols as extra meaningful
   B. Natural signs vs. arbitrary signs

Alcuin defines "delivery" as the fifth part of rhetoric, as "the regulating of the voice and body according to the dignity of thought and word" (*Rhet.*, p. 71). Wilson calls it "pronunciation" and says it is "apt ordering" of the voice, the face, and the entire body (*Rhetorique*, p. 218). Ramistic rhetorics defined operationalization as one of the two parts of the art (the other part was "style") and defined it as the expression of "the speech as conceived in the mind." In *Rhetorique Francoise* (1555),

Antoine Foclin says that the art of delivery requires that "one takes pain that the utterance may be such as the conception and thought of the mind have been."[37]

Alcuin points out that what is important about operationalization is that it be "fashioned to accord with the nature of the place where the speech is made, with the materials available to the speaker, with the persons concerned in the case, with the speaker's subject, and with the particular occasion" (p. 139). About how this accord is achieved he is silent. Foclin goes a bit further, explaining that "each thing that is said has some proper sound" and the speaker must learn these sounds (tones) and use his voice like a musician uses a lute.[38] Both Foclin and Wilson cite Demosthenes' habit of practicing his pronunciation against the roar of the surf and Cicero's characterization of gestures as the universal language of the body. Wilson and Alcuin recommend practice as the key to good delivery, together with exercise and study of music. Both also give some general hints about bad habits to be avoided, e. g., face the audience; do not look at the floor; be audible, but do not scream; do not bounce up and down on your feet. Alcuin's list of things to avoid is brief and rather dry. Wilson's, however, is a graphic and entertaining description of poor speakers he has observed. For instance, he writes, "Some sup their words up, as a poor man does his porridge. Some nod their heads at every sentence. Another winks with one eye and some with both" (p. 220). The descriptions continue for some three pages and constitute the major part of Wilson's treatment of operationalization.

Treatment of operationalization in the preaching manuals is even more brief than that in the rhetorics. Though Wilson reports that the clergy were the one group most seriously in need of improvement, the manuals tended to focus more on the what of sermonizing than on the how. Alexander of Ashby includes a brief comment on operationalization, saying that the delivery should be modest, humble, agreeable, and appropriate to the subject and to the organization of the sermon. Thomas Walsys, in On the Mode of Composing Sermons (1350), includes skillful operationalization as one of the twelve attributes of the preacher: "Let the preacher take care . . . to have a way of speaking that is intelligible and comprehensible, because the way of speaking itself will carry to the hearers no less than the thing said."[39] Another manual of about the same period, Robert of Basevorn's Form of Preaching, includes voice modulation and appropriate gesture as "extrinsic ornaments of form and execution."[40] Robert cites Augustine as his authority for this inclusion. Augustine does make a similar argument for skill in operationlization as an "ornament" and source of pleasure. He points out that even if the sub-

---

[37] Foclin, quoted in Howell, Logic and Rhetoric in England, p. 170.
[38] Ibid., p. 171.
[39] Quoted in Murphy, Rhetoric in the Middle Ages, p. 334.
[40] Ibid., p. 355.

jects to be discussed are well-known to the audience, they can be retold "for the sake of the pleasure they give, if the attention be directed not to the things themselves but to the way they are told." This is the same principle, he says, which accounts for the fact that some books are read and reread; people enjoy reading an old story if it is "gracefully written" (*Chris. Doc.*, IV. 10).

Nonverbal Communication In Augustine's brief explanation of the function of operationalization, we can see an early version of the idea that "the medium is the message." Similarly, in his explanation of the nature of signs, we can see an embryonic theory of nonverbal communication. As we have seen, Augustine divides signs into natural and conventional. Within conventional signs he includes not only words but nods, motions of the hands and limbs, pictures, statues, bodily dress, the sound of a bugle, flags, perfumes, etc., all of which he says are means "by which men communicate their thoughts to one another" (*Chris. Doc.*, II. 3–26). Thus, while traditional approaches limit operationalization primarily to the sounds of the voice and movements of the body in purposeful communication acts, Augustine includes a variety of nonverbal sounds, presentational symbols, and even scents. These, he says, have meaning and are constantly communicating with us.

Within purposive communication acts, Augustine notes similar phenomena. Although John of Salisbury, in 1159, wrote that "nods and signs" should not be classified as communicative (*Met.*, I. 18), Augustine clearly disagrees. For instance, he advises the preacher to take careful note of the nonverbal behavoir of his congregation. Since, he says, the audience cannot interru >t to ask questions in the middle of a sermon, the preacher must understa,d unspoken questions: "A crowd anxious for instruction shows by its movements if it understands what is said." The preacher should watch for such indications and continue explaining and elaborating a point until he sees by their "movement" that his congregation is satisfied (*Chris. Doc.*, IV. 10).

Bacon's analysis of operationalization, which he calls "tradition of delivery," is similar to Augustine's. He defines it as the fourth part of rational knowledge and explains that it has to do with "the expressing or transferring our knowledge to others" (*Adv. Learn.*, II. xvi. 1). The "organ" of operationalization, he says, "is either speech or writing: for Aristotle saith well, 'Words are the images of cogitations, and letters are the images of words.' But yet it is not of necessity that cogitations be expressed by the medium of words" (II. xvi. 2). He observes that people who do not share a common language and people who are deaf and dumb often communicate adequately by gestures. Furthermore, he notes that the Chinese use characters, which do not represent a word or a sound but stand for notions or series of words. Thus, he concludes, there are two kinds of "notes of cogitations," those that resemble the notation (such as gestures) and those that are agreed upon by social contract (such as words and ciphers).

Neither Bacon nor Augustine develop an elaborated theory of non-verbal communication. However, their extension of the notion of operationalization provides a precedent for the highly elaborated theory of "body talk" in the elocutionary movement of the modern period and may be seen as a precursor of the renewed interest in nonverbal behavior in the contemporary period.

Conclusion

Alexander Pope, in his *Essay on Criticism*, provides a succinct characterization of the fate of scholarship in the medieval and Renaissance periods.

Learning and Rome alike in empire grew;
And arts still follow'd where her eagles flew;
From the same foes, at last, both felt their doom.
And the same age saw Learning fall, and Rome.
With Tyranny then Superstition join'd,
As that the body, this enslaved the mind;
Much was believed, but little understood,
And to be dull was construed to be good;
A second deluge Learning thus o'er run,
And the Monks finish'd what the Goths begun.[41]

Though there was little advance, and much decline, in human communication theory during the medieval and Renaissance periods, there were a number of developments important to the continuation of the discipline. The inclusion of much of classical theory in theology assured the survival of many of the central tenets of human communication. The use of the paradigm in letter-writing and preaching manuals demonstrated its universality and adaptability. The rhetorics and comprehensive treatises reinforced the essential unity of the parts of the paradigm, counteracting to some extent the fragmenting tendencies of the seven liberal arts taxonomy and the specialized treatises focusing on isolated parts.

In terms of future developments, the disputes over overlapping among the arts of the trivium, and the occasional attempts to reintegrate the arts into a single discipline, demonstrated to modern theorists the essential unity of the paradigm and led to the revival of holistic theory. The focus on the topical system of conceptualization led to a system so complex and cumbersome that modern theorists rejected scholastic logic

[41] Alexander Pope, An *Essay on Criticism*, lines 684–693.

and began to reinvestigate the psychological bases of the process by which people come to know, believe, and act. The elaborate syntactic approaches to language led to a similar reaction—a return to broader, more theoretic and pragmatic conceptions of language as instrumental symbolic behavior.

The importance of writing and books in the medieval and Renaissance periods also led to new directions in modern theory. The oral tradition began to take a backseat to print. Fine literature (belles-lettres) began to be a central part of human communication theory. Theories of literary criticism, based on classical rhetorical theory, were developed. The precedent set by Augustine, in his lengthy analysis of "the mode of ascertaining the meaning" of written messages, finally bore fruit in the modern period in the emergence of receiver-oriented theories of human communication.

Although the medieval and Renaissance scholars, for the most part, preserved only the dry husks, these were the mulch for a revitalized theory in the following centuries.

Chapter 4

The Modern Period: An Overview

The modern period spanned approximately three centuries, from 1600 to 1900. It was a period of rapid growth and active theory building. In contrast to the medieval and Renaissance periods, human communication was a central concern of modern scholars. During this period a large body of theoretic and practical literature emerged. Because modern theory is so extensive, we will devote two chapters to it. The present chapter will examine the general content of the mainstream theoretic literature and note the modern conception of the nature and province of human communication. The major theorists covered are Fenelon, Lord Kames, George Campbell, Joseph Priestly, Hugh Blair, Richard Whately, Thomas De Quincey, and Herbert Spencer. The following chapter will examine in detail the modern treatment of the individual parts of the basic paradigm.

The central contrast between the medieval and Renaissance periods and the modern period is the contrast between chaos and order. In discussing the former periods, it was impossible to formulate any coherent or dominant theoretic picture. The treatment of the paradigm was scattered and inconsistent. Neither pragmatic nor theoretic principles dominated. If there was a focus, it was "scholastic." Classical precepts and concepts were preserved in a variety of forms and contexts—in theologies, rhetorics, logics, grammars, and manuals on letter writing and preaching. For the most part, however, this preservation was piecemeal. No one made any real attempt to gather these scattered parts into a coherent whole until the very end of the period. Bacon, as we have seen, began the process. His concern was to contribute to a general revival of secular knowledge. Though he did not conceive of his objective as the renovation of a particular discipline, his efforts were especially influential in the field of communication. Much of the theory of communication from the seventeenth through the nineteenth century can be viewed as the implementation of basic principles laid down by Bacon.

Extensive social changes in the modern world led to an approach to knowledge that differed sharply from medieval and early Renaissance approaches. The Church ceased to be a monolithic source of power; thus secular disciplines were allowed to resume a position comparable to that they held in the classical period. Though a number of the important modern theorists are clergymen, theology ceased to be *the* justification for studying human communication. Feudalism was replaced by nationalism and, especially in Great Britain, more democratic government opened renewed opportunities for public communication on significant social issues. Universities were firmly established as institutions for higher learning designed to prepare people for professions not only in the Church, but in law and government. Literacy became the norm rather than the exception. The growth of printing and the publishing of general interest books, periodicals, and newspapers proliferated with the spread of literacy. What has since become the most common criticism of mass communication, the "leveling" effects of popular media, made its first appearance in the literature.

In terms of this study, the most important change in the modern period was a renewed interest in the *discipline* of human communication. Modern theorists explicitly recognize that there was a coherent discipline in the classical period and that it was fragmented and dispersed in the medieval and Renaissance periods. They consciously set out to recover what was relevant from classical sources, to adapt it to the modern world, and to build upon it in terms of modern "advances" in knowledge. A number of twentieth century scholars have observed this phenomenon and provide detailed analyses of the process.[1]

Although close analysis of modern theorists reveals a variety of approaches and individual differences, the principal characteristic of the period was the homogeneity of thought. In reading the major theorists from Fenelon to Spencer (1679 to 1871), one is struck by the overwhelming consistency of topics and fundamental assumptions. One might liter-

[1] Wilbur Samuel Howell's *Eighteenth Century British Logic and Rhetoric* (Princeton: Princeton University Press, 1971) provides a detailed analysis of changes in the taxonomy of knowledge from 1700-1900. Howell especially emphasizes the development of empiricism and the experimental scientific method in terms of changes in human communication theory. He provides extensive background on the nature of communication theory throughout western Europe and in America. Hugh M. Davidson, *Audience, Words, and Art: Studies in Seventeenth Century French Rhetoric* (Columbus: Ohio State University Press, 1965) details the nature and extent of the French theorists' influence on modern theory, especially the influences of the "Port-Royal" revision of logic and rhetoric.

More general histories of thought include Ernst Cassirer, *Philosophy of the Enlightenment*, translated by Fritz C. A. Koelin and James P. Pettegrove (Boston: Beacon Press, 1951); F. Copelston, *A History of Philosophy* (New York: Doubleday, 1964); Carl L. Becker, *The Heavenly City of the Eighteenth-Century Philosophers* (New Haven: Yale University Press, 1966); and Sir Leslie Stephen, *History of English Thought in the Eighteenth Century* (New York: Harcourt, Brace & World, 1963).

ally imagine that the major writers composed while sitting in a large room looking over one another's shoulders. We will, of course, see differences and disagreements in terms of the specific treatments of the paradigm. These, however, can be best understood in the context of the similarities.

Approaches of the Major Communication Theorists

Ehninger's macroscopic view of modern communication theory provides a useful framework for an analysis of the major theorists and their approaches to the revitalization of the discipline. Ehninger identifies four "dominant trends" in modern theory.[2] *Classical* approaches focus on recovering the central tenets of Greek and Roman theory. *Psychological-Epistemological* approaches focus on reinterpretation of classical doctrine in terms of modern theories of human behavior. *Belletristic* approaches focus on developing universal standards of criticism for all the symbolic arts. *Elocutionist* approaches focus on the use of the voice and body in oral communication.

All of the major theorists were influenced by these trends. The first three are important in accounting for the content of mainstream theory. The fourth, elocution, is essentially an atheoretic movement representing a continuing tradition of specialization and prescriptivism. It is important to the history of human communication theory primarily in the sense that it emphasizes the fragmenting effect of approaches that concentrate on one part of the paradigm to the exclusion of others. Elocution is important to modern theory of operationalization primarily because the major theorists reacted so strongly against it.

Classical Approaches

Early in the modern period appeared a number of minor works usually referred to as "Ciceronian rhetorics." These are reminiscent of Alcuin's late medieval *Rhetoric*; that is, they are essentially summaries and restatements of classical doctrine. Examples of such works are Vossius' *Institutes of Oratory* (1622), Farnaby's *Index Rhetoricus* (1625), Lawson's *Lectures Concerning Oratory* (1752), and Ward's *A System of Oratory* (1759).

Fenelon   Among the major theoretic works of the period, Fenelon's *Dialogues on Eloquence* (1679)[3] is the most clearly classical. Unlike the minor theorists, however, Fenelon did not simply rehash classical theory; he selected central concepts and adapted them to the needs of the modern world.

---

[2] Douglas Ehninger, "Dominant Trends in English Rhetorical Thought, 1750–1800," *Southern Speech Journal* (September, 1952), pp. 3–11.
[3] *Dialogues* was composed in 1679 but first published (posthumously) in 1717.

Fenelon (1651–1715) is the first of the major modern theorists. His *Dialogues* is, in both structure and content, highly reminiscent of Plato's *Phaedrus*, a dialogue on "true," or "philosophic," rhetoric. Like *Phaedrus*, Fenelon's *Dialogues* involves a discussion of the "real" nature of human communication. A young man, called "B," comes to the philospher, called "A," who is Fenelon's spokesman (as Socrates was Plato's). "B" has just heard a "beautiful sermon." As he describes it, "A," with the assistance of the third character, "C," explains why the sermon could not have been "truly eloquent," though it may have been beautiful. The culmination of the dialogue among the characters is a sketch of the "ideal preacher."[4]

Fenelon's primary sources are three of the chief classical communication theorists, Plato, Cicero, and Augustine.[5] Unlike the later medieval and early Renaissance scholars, Fenelon focuses on the theoretic, communication-oriented works of these theorists. From their concepts he constructs a modern synthesis, the basic tenets of which are fundamental to later theorists of the period. Though Fenelon concentrates explicity on preaching, *Dialogues* is not an *artes praedicandi*. He applies his observations to both oral and written communication in general, and to "poetic" as well as "rhetorical" discourse. Though he was by profession a preacher, his interests, as revealed in the work, extend to all the fine arts, including music, painting, and architecture. He acknowledges the application of communication theory to the three classical genres, forensic, deliberative, and epideictic, though he does not deal with them explicitly.

Fenelon defines his subject as "eloquence," which, we soon discover, means "effective" communication. Eloquence, he affirms, "is nothing but the art of instructing and persuading men by moving them" (p. 125). These, of course, are the three classical "ends" of communication. Fenelon, however, gives them a modern twist. Instruction and persuasion are the ends; moving or pleasing or "delighting" is a means to that end. The implications of this view will become apparent in our subsequent discussion of the functions of communication.

Fenelon refers to the practitioner as an "orator." Like Plato, he says that an orator must first be "a philosopher, a man who knows how to establish the truth." In order to make an orator, he says, "we must add to the exactitude of his [the philosopher's] arguments the beauty and vehemence of a living discourse" (p. 89). Also like Plato and Augustine, he says that an orator must know his subject ("scripture and religion" for the preacher) and the "souls" of his auditors (p. 122). Like Cicero, he says

---

[4] Fenelon, *Dialogues on Eloquence*, trans. by Wilbur S. Howell (Princeton: Princeton University Press, 1951). All subsequent references within the text are to this translation.
[5] Fenelon also exhibits acquaintance with Aristotle, Quintilian, and "Longinus," though he relies on them less heavily.

that the orator must also have "order, a method of instructing, soundness of argument, movements of feeling, that is to say, things which strike and arouse the heart" (p. 126). The "true orator," he says, needs skill in dialectic, rhetoric, moral reasoning, history and poetics. He needs "the subtlety of dialecticians, the knowledge of the philosopher, something close to the diction of poets, the voice and gestures of the finest actors" (p. 84). Thus, Fenelon defines eloquence as the result of skill in four of the five classical cannons, conceptualization, symbolization, organization, and operationalization. Categorization he treats as Augustine did, in terms of the store of general and specific information prerequisite to effective interpretation and dissemination of "truth." Fenelon does not explicitly refer to the classical paradigm; however, his definitions of eloquence and oratory indicate that he takes his readers' knowledge of it for granted.

Fenelon's primary emphasis is on the central theoretic concepts within each of the parts of the paradigm. He rejects, primarily by omission, the prescriptive tenets of medieval and Renaissance treatment, e. g., the four to six part formula of organization, the four senses of interpretation, the doctrine of schemes and tropes, the dialectical and rhetorical "topics," etc. He makes his general rejection of most of the scholarship since Augustine explicit. His spokesman, "A," says that social conditions account for the poor communication practices of a number of Church scholars in the Middle Ages. Upon hearing this, "C" asks, "What? Is it true, as you would have it, that everything was decadent in respect to eloquence during the very centuries which were so favorable to religion?" (p. 147). "A" responds by explaining that he believes this to be true, and that the false theory of the age following Augustine is only now coming to an end: "And we are not yet rid of it. . . . The barbarians who overran the Roman Empire tended everywhere to show ignorance and poor taste. We are descended from them. And although literature may have begun to revive during the fifteenth century, its recovery has been slow" (p. 148). Fenelon's *Dialogues*, as it turns out, made a major contribution to this recovery. As Augustine's comparable work, *On Christian Doctrine*, begins the medieval period, the *Dialogues* begins the modern period. Both returned to Platonic and Ciceronian theory, interpreting it in terms of the needs of a new social order. Fortunately, unlike Augustine's ill-fated work, Fenelon's was not destined to be ignored. Rather it establishes a base for those who followed.

Fenelon stands out because he was one of the first to reverse the prescriptive, scholastic trends of the medieval and Renaissance periods and to renovate classical theory in terms of modern concerns. Classicism is fundamental to the renewal of theoretic development in the modern period. All of the major theorists, are, to some extent, classicists. Of medieval and Renaissance scholars, only Augustine and Bacon are viewed as heuristic. For the most part, modern theorists find it necessary to turn to classical sources for a theoretic foundation.

Psychological-Epistemological Approaches

Psychological-epistemological approaches focus on the mental processes underlying human communication. Hartley's associationism, Woeff's faculty psychology, and Reid's common sense philosophy have served as bases for modern communication theory that focuses on the effects of messages from the point of view of the receiver. Again, all of the major theorists were influenced by this trend. In fact, we can most accurately summarize modern human communication theory as classical doctrine, reinterpreted in accordance with dominant psychological-epistemological theory.

Faculty psychology provides the framework for modern definitions of the "ends" of communication. Associationism serves as a rationale for the effects of symbolic behavior. Common sense philosophy serves to account for the uniformity of these effects. These theories are fundamental to Kames' Elements of Criticism (1762), Campbell's Philosophy of Rhetoric (1776), Priestley's Lectures on Oratory and Criticism (1777), Blair's Lectures on Rhetoric and Belles Lettres (1783), Whately's Elements of Rhetoric (1828), De Quincey's essays on communication, Style, Rhetoric, Conversation, and Language (1823–1858), and Spencer's Philosophy of Style (1871).

Though all of these major theorists used current psychology and epistemology as support for their theoretic constructs, Campbell and Priestly are the two who used them most fully and consciously. Both viewed their central task as the construction of a theory of communication firmly rooted in principles of human nature. Though in some senses he is more of a classicist than either Campbell or Priestly, Whately also makes extensive use of modern psychology and epistemology. He viewed his task as the renovation of basic Aristotelian theory in terms of modern advances in knowledge.

Campbell   George Campbell (1719–1796) was a clergyman and theologian of the Church of Scotland. He also served as a teacher and principal at Marischal College in Aberdeen. In 1758 he helped found the Philosophical Society of Aberdeen, a society composed of leading thinkers who met regularly to discuss philosophical questions. David Hume was a primary influence on both the Society and on Campbell. Campbell is the author of a number of literary and theological works. His work on communication, Philosophy of Rhetoric (1776), is generally viewed as the outstanding theoretic treatise of the modern period. Though it was not an extremely popular textbook like Blair's and Whately's, it was used as a text in many colleges and went through forty-two reprintings in the eighteenth and nineteenth centuries.[6]

Campbell's chief sources in the *Philosophy of Rhetoric* include the major works of Aristotle, Cicero, and Quintilian side by side with those of John Locke, Thomas Reid, David Hartley, and David Hume (see Appendix for major works).

In order to understand Campbell's *Philosophy* we must have a general understanding of faculty and associational psychology, common sense philosophy, and modern empiricism. Faculty psychology is fundamental to Campbell's communication theory. It proposes that human behavior can be accounted for in terms of five "powers" of the mind: understanding (judgment), memory, imagination, passion, and will. These faculties are viewed as hierarchical in nature, the first four being subordinate and instrumental to the ultimate power, the will, or the power of action. Campbell ties the functions of communicative acts directly to the faculties. Communicating, he says, is an attempt "to enlighten the understanding, to please the imagination, to move the passions, or to influence the will" (p. 1).

Associational psychology serves an explanation for how the faculties work together. For instance, through association (categorizing of perceptions into classes on the basis of analogy and the principles of cause and effect, etc.) the imagination transforms perceptual data stored in the memory into general information, or conceptual understandings.[7] Common sense philosophy provides a rationale for association. The principles by which perceptions are associated and transformed into ideas are viewed as inherent in all human beings. Campbell takes the position that through these inherent abilities, e. g., the ability to perceive cause/effect relations, simple ideas are associated and become beliefs, opinions, attitudes, and ideologies.

Empiricism is fundamental to Campbell's philosophic approach to communication. In a brief history of the development of communication theory, he explains that his purpose is essentially "scientific" in the Newtonian sense. Working on the basis of past discoveries, his purpose is to contruct a scientific theory of human communication. He identifies four stages of development in the history of communication research. *First* came the observation of specific effects, or the discovery of the basic materials of the discipline. This grew out of "the consciousness a man has of what operates on his own mind, aided by the sympathetic feelings, and by that practical experience of mankind, which individuals, even in the rudest state of society, are capable of acquiring" (Preface, 1). In this stage, people discovered that certain symbolic behaviors seemed to lead

[6] Lloyd F. Bitzer, "Editor's Introduction" to George Campbell, *Philosophy of Rhetoric* (Carbondale: Southern Illinois University Press, 1963). All subsequent references to this work within the text are to this edition.
[7] This process is fully explained in the discussion of categorization below. Its similarity to John of Salisbury's twelfth century taxonomy of categorization is obvious. This taxonomy and Bacon's elaboration of it were discussed in Chap. 3.

to certain kinds of responses. The *second* stage was the classification of these materials, or the discovery of specific causes for the effects. Scientists began to distinguish and identify forms and modes that could be "employed for the purpose of explaining, convincing, pleasing, moving, and persuading." This, says Campbelll, was "the beginning of a critical science" (Preface, 1). The *third* stage was the discovery of more general causes, or of the rules for combining forms and modes in order to achieve specific purposes. Scientists compared the effects of various attempts to influence, taking into account all the circumstances that might be relevant to success or failure. They attempted to discover purposes and situations appropriate to each mode and form. This resulted in the "practical rhetoric" of the medieval and Renaissance period.

The *fourth* stage is where Campbell places himself and the other moderns. In this stage the scientist turns philosopher. He elaborates a theory. Taking the general causes previously formulated, he devises principles which, if they are true, will account for the effects observed, and he specifies all the consequences of his principles. Specifically, Campbell says, his approach will be to "canvass those principles in our nature to which the various attempts to influence others are adapted, and by which, in any instance, their success or want of success may be accounted for" (Preface, 1i). The result of this, he says, will be a *theory* of communication, or a "philosophical rhetoric." It will be grounded in, and tested through reference to, empirical observations.

Campbell recognizes the possible disadvantages of calling his subject "rhetoric." Clearly he is not dealing with the Ramistic "art of speaking well," nor with "mere bombast," nor with demogoguery. Rhetoric, he says, is the theory of "eloquence," meaning "effective" communication. "Eloquence," he says, can be defined as, "that art or talent by which the discourse is adapted to its end" (p. 1). He notes that he means to use the term eloquence in its "greatest latitude" as corresponding to the broad range of skills Cicero defined as characteristic of the orator. In other words, eloquence is the skillful *use* of the classical paradigm, the processes of classifying, conceiving, symbolizing, ordering, and transmitting information designed to accomplish specific purposes. Campbell uses the term "rhetoric" in his title, however, for his concern is not with skills, but with theory. As we have said, rhetoric, in its ancient sense, referred to the theory rather than to the practice of communication.[8] Campbell recognizes that some readers may mistake his subject, given the historical variations in the use of such key terms. He thus explains that his subject is "the grand art of communication,"[9] the theory of how people com-

[8] "Oratory" was the ancient equivalent of "eloquence," or the practice of communicating.

[9] Here Campbell uses "art" in the sense of "liberal arts"; that is, an art is an area of study or an academic discipline. Art, of course, carries the additional connotation of practice or operation. Campbell recognizes that communication is an "art" in both senses of the term.

municate their "ideas . . . sentiments, passions, dispositions, and purposes" (Preface, xlix). Communication, he points out, is an operational discipline. It is both a theoretic and a practical art. It is fundamental to any theory of how human beings come to know, believe, and act; no other area of study, he says, "hath so close a connection with all the faculties and powers of the mind" (Preface, xlix).[10] As a practical art, it can be viewed as both "fine" and "useful." It is a fine art, like poetry and music, because "it requires the aid of the imagination." It "not only pleases, but by pleasing demands attention, arouses passions, and often at last subdues the most stubborn resolution." It is a useful art, like architecture, because it teaches us to use symbols to achieve goals. It thus teaches the *use* of other arts, like logic, ethics, and grammar, and it is *the* vehicle of socialization. The "wisdom" of society is essentially impotent without communication. Campbell says that Solomon put it best when he said, "The wise in heart shall be called prudent, but the sweetness of the lips increaseth learning" (Preface, xlix).

Campbell notes that, traditionally, logic and grammar have also been classed as arts of discourse. Although these have important relationships with rhetoric, he explains that rhetoric is *the* theory of communication. Neither logic nor grammar deal with communication *per se*. Logic is a method of categorizing and conceptualizing subject matter: "The sole and ultimate end of logic is the eviction of truth"; logic "regards only the subject, which is examined solely for the sake of information" (p. 33). The "information" which results from logical analysis is useful to rhetoric, but communication is more than discovery of information; it is the human *use* of information in decision-making. Grammar likewise is relevant to rhetoric in a preliminary sort of way. Grammar, Campbell says, studies syntax, the rules of languages based on the "arbitrary conventions" of common usage. Grammar is concerned only with formal rules for combining words into sentences. Communication is concerned with "style," the *use* of words and sentences in constructing a social reality (p. 35). Logic, Campbell says, "forges the arms which eloquence teacheth us to wield" (p. 34). In terms of grammar, he says that its "highest aim" is "the lowest aim" of rhetoric; "where grammar ends, eloquence begins" (p. 35).

The *Philosophy of Rhetoric* is organized into three books. The first focuses on definitions of communication and basic principles of human behavior. Approximately half of the first book is devoted to the nature and process of message receiving. More than any previous theorist, Campbell makes the audience the center of human communication theory. He says that a human being "is much more an active than a

---

[10] Campbell's spelling, like that of his contemporaries, is inconsistent, but frequently departs from twentieth-century practices. Modern punctuation likewise deviates from contemporary practice. However, I assume, in both cases, that the reader will be able to interpret most of these differences more easily without the distractions caused by placing "sic" after each one.

contemplative being" and therefore behaves in terms of purpose. The professional communicator must take into account that he is dealing not with a passive but with an active auditor whose purposes may or may not coincide with his own. He must take into account the generic processes by which human beings sense and make sense of their "realities," as well as the specific habits, abilities, attitudes, etc., which distinguish individuals.

Book I comprises approximately half of the total pages of the *Philosophy*. Books II and III focus on "elocution," or symbolization, and comprise the second half.[11] Campbell explains this division when he says, "There are two things in every discourse which principally claim our attention, the sense and the expression; or in other words, the thought and the symbol by which it is communicated" (p. 32). Under "thought" Campbell discusses categorization and conceptualization. Under "expression" he discusses symbolization primarily, though he also deals with organization and operationalization. Book II is an analysis of symbols in terms of the principles of human nature outlined in Book I. Book III discusses the use of symbols in light of theoretic conclusions from the first two books.

Priestley   Joseph Priestley's *Lectures on Oratory and Criticism* (1777) is similar to Campbell's *Philosophy* in both structure and content. Priestley is known primarily as a scientist, as the discoverer of oxygen and soda water among other things. Like Campbell, however, he was also a theologian and an educator. He published more than twenty volumes of nonscientific writing.[12] His *Oratory and Criticism* is a collection of lectures first delivered in 1762 at Warrington Academy where he was an instructor of languages and belles-lettres. His purpose in publishing them, Priestley says, is to illustrate the application of "the doctrine of the association of ideas" to the study of communication. (Preface, i).

Priestley's view of communication is highly compatible with Campbell's though his terminology differs somewhat. He defines his subject as "oratory," which is "the natural faculty of speech [written or oral language] improved by art" (p. 1). The study of oratory, he says, has both aesthetic and instrumental value. Through the development of critical standards based on an understanding of human behavior we can improve our ability to both appreciate and use discourse (p. 1). Priestley says that the study of communication includes four specific areas: invention or recollection (conceptualization), style or expression (symbolization),

[11] Campbell prefers to use the classical terms "elocution" or "style" for symbolization in spite of the fact that the "elocutionists" had begun to use this as their term for "oral delivery."

[12] Vincent M. Bevilacque and Richard Murphy, "Editor's Introduction" to Joseph Priestley, *A Course of Lectures on Oratory and Criticism* (Carbondale: Southern Illinois University Press, 1965). All subsequent references to this work within the text are to this edition.

method or disposition (organization), and delivery (operationalization). Categorization is the fundamental aspect of communication. It is the theory of how judgment, memory, imagination, passion, and will work together through associational principles, or of how the faculties can be addressed to bring about certain kinds of effects in the human mind.

Priestley differs from Campbell, and from most of the other modern theorists, primarily in his inclusion of the rhetorical "topics" under conceptualization and in his rejection of common sense philosophy.[13] He resembles the more belletristic theorists in his special emphasis on criticism.

Whately   Richard Whately's *Elements of Rhetoric* (1828) has a number of resemblances to Fenelon's *Dialogues* as well as to Campbell's and Priestley's works. Whately (1787–1863) has some of the same purposes as Fenelon. He too was primarily a preacher and theologian. As Archbishop of Dublin, Whately seemed to view the primary function of communication as the means of propagating faith and of defending the inevitable and unquestionable truths of Christianity.[14]

His treatment and examples are, however, less archaic sounding than Fenelon's, and he includes more references to nonreligious communication. On the other hand, he tends to view communication less broadly than did Fenelon and other major modern theorists. Though he includes discussion of categorization, symbolization, and operationalization, he limits "rhetoric," *per se*, to conceptualization and organization: "The *finding* of suitable Arguments to prove a given point, and the skillful *arrangement* of them, may be considered as the immediate and proper province of Rhetoric, and of that alone" (p. 39). Knowledge, Whately says, comes from the subject matter; moving the passions belongs to both poetic and rhetoric; and "style" and "elocution," or delivery, belong to any kind of composition. Rhetoric has special claim only to instrumental composition, that is, any oral or written use of language to convince and persuade (p. 40).

Aside from his insistence on this narrower conception of communication, Whately's treatment of communication is very similar to Campbell's. Like Campbell, Whately views address to the faculties as the route to influence. Persuasion, he says, is the ultimate goal of communication and it depends upon "conviction of the understanding" and on "influencing of the will" through moving the passions (p. 175). He also says that logic and grammar are prior to rhetoric. However, he claims that logic is more important to rhetoric than Campbell implied, and that

[13] The implications of these differences are discussed in Chap. 5.
[14] Douglas Ehninger, "Introduction" to Richard Whately, *Elements of Rhetoric* (Carbondale: Southern Illinois University Press, 1963). All subsequent references to this work within the text are to this edition.

this is the only area in which Campbell's treatment is seriously insufficient (p. 9). Rhetoric, he says, depends upon "ascertainment of the truth," and this is the province of logic, or philosophy. Without logic, rhetoric, "the *establishment* of it [truth] to the *satisfaction of another*," would have no substance. (p. 5).

Again like Campbell, Whately notes in the Preface that he has chosen to call his subject "rhetoric," though he knows the term has some bad connotations, e. g., "bewildering the learned" or "deluding the multitude" (xxxiv). Also, he says, it has been used more narrowly than is proper, to refer to the study of figures of speech or to the art of public speaking. However, rhetoric is the ancient term for the broad study of the "art of composition" and it includes both the process of composing (sending) and the process of interpreting (receiving) written and oral communication (xxxiv). It includes all public discourse, including preaching, legal and political communication, and reporting in "the Medium of the Press" (Introduction, p. 2). Of all the modes of communication, it generally excludes only poetry and social conversation.

In reference to the history of communication research, Whately disagrees with Campbell's view of the systematic development of theory. He says that rhetoric "is not one of those branches of study in which we can trace with interest a progressive improvement from age to age" (p. 7). Among the more recent theorists, he says that Bacon is one of the "few moderns" to add anything to the study. Campbell is one of the others, for he is superior in both "depth of thought and ingenious original research" (pp. 8–9). Prior to the seventeenth century, however, the only really systematic thinker was Aristotle. Whately therefore seems to see his mission as the renovation of Aristotelian theory in the context of modern psychology and philosophy.

For many centuries, Whately says, rhetoric has been neglected because there was little scope for public communication. That, however, has changed. There is now great need for skilled communicators. Though Campbell makes many of the same points, Whately cites Aristotle as his authority for a number of observations which follow. For instance, he says that the advancement of knowledge depends upon communication. Knowledge which is not shared, he explains, might as well never have been discovered (p. 10). The use of rhetoric, he says, is to assist decision-making in contingent affairs (pp. 80–81). Also, "truth" naturally triumphs, but only if those who contend for it are as skilled as their adversaries (p. 12);[15] communication skill is a natural gift which can be improved through study (pp. 13–19); communication is clearly a science, for although nearly everyone can do it, some do it more effectively (p. 16). Finally, Whately reinforces the Platonic-Aristotelian (and very modern) emphasis on the role of the audience. He points out that "there

[15] This is also a major emphasis in Augustine's *On Christian Doctrine*.

can be no excellence of writing or speaking, in the abstract," for effectiveness depends upon "knowing for whom it is intended" (p. 204).

Thus, in Whately, we see that near the end of the modern period classical approaches and psychological-epistemological approaches are almost indistinguishably interwoven. The central tenets of classical theory presented in "pure" form by Fenelon have become the central tenets of modern theory.

Belletristic Approaches

The belletristic approach focuses on developing a general theory of criticism. The "arts"—poetry, rhetoric, fiction, drama, music, painting, gardening, architecture, etc.—are viewed as "branches" of the same "tree," and thus as susceptible to the same basic critical standards. Though Priestley (to some extent), De Quincey, and Spencer are essentially belletristic, Kames and Blair are the most typical representatives of this approach. They tend to see their principal object as the formulation of universal critical standards that will discriminate equally well whether applied to a country garden or to a parliamentary address. Though most major theorists do not see the presentational arts as central communication activities, they do include all discursive modes. Thus, terms like "eloquence," "oratory," "discourse," and "speech" are used generically to mean any message that is primarily verbal. Poetry and drama, for instance, are generally viewed as kinds of "oratory" rather than as separate genres. Likewise, to most major theorists, criticism is not a separate, but an inherent, part of theory construction. General principles, they agree, grow out of empirical observation of messages and their effects.

Kames   Henry Home, Lord Kames (1696–1782) was a noted lawyer and agriculturalist. His earliest works were collections and classifications of court decisions. Later in his life he developed an interest in scientific experiments in farming and published a book and several articles on the subject.He was also very interested in philosophy, religion, and education. In 1751 he published *Essays on the Principles of Morality and Natural Religion* in which he disagreed with a number of Locke's and Hume's fundamental positions. Others of his works in these areas include *Sketches of the History of Man* (1774) and *Loose Hints on Education* (1781). Kames was also known in his time as an amateur architect and planner of gardens. People traveled for miles to view his house and garden in New Street, the Canongate.[16]

Kames's *Elements of Criticism* (1762) is his contribution to communication theory. It is a one-thousand page treatise on "the fine arts." His purpose, he says, is "to exhibit their fundamental principles drawn

[16] Helen Whitcomb Randall, "The Critical Theory of Lord Kames" (*Smith College Studies of Modern Languages*, October 1940 to July 1941), pp. 1–22.

from human nature, the true source of criticism."[17] His plan is "to ascend gradually to principles, from facts and experiments. . . . to explain the nature of man, considered as a sensitive being capable of pleasure and pain" (I., p. 13). Structurally, *Elements* follows this basic plan. The first volume focuses on the fundamental principles of human nature (the faculties, association, and common sense) and the principles of the arts that grow out of them. The second volume focuses on rhetoric and poetics, especially emphasizing the analysis of specific examples of discourse that illustrate the principles identified in the first volume.

Although Kames includes a chapter on gardening and architecture, and uses them, as well as music and painting, to illustrate a number of his principles, his primary focus is on "language arts." These (poetry, oratory, drama, etc.) are, he says, the most important studies for they "unfold the human heart" (II., p. 19). Language, he says, makes society possible: "To connect individuals in the social state, no particular contributes more than language, by the power it possesses of an expeditious communication of thought, and a lively representation of transactions" (II., p. 357). Public use of language, he explains, tends to overcome the ill effects of class and status differences. This potential source of disunity "is in a good measure prevented by the access all ranks of people have to public spectacles. . . . Such meetings, where every one partakes of the same pleasures in common, are no slight support to the social affections" (II., p. 490). The language arts, he says, are what divert us from sorrow, allow us to share mirth, reveal secrets, give advice, and make compacts and agreements. Without them, the most important functions of human society would be impossible (II., p. 18). In his dedication to King George, Kames emphasizes that the fine arts are not merely diversionary:

> The fine arts have ever been encouraged by wise princes, not singly for private amusement, but for their beneficial influence in society. By uniting different ranks in the same elegant pleasures, they promote benevolence: by cherishing love of order, they enforce submission to government: and by inspiring delicacy of feeling, they make regular government a regular blessing (I., v).

Given that the arts are so central to society, and that criticism studies them, Kames asks, rhetorically, "what other science is more worthy of human beings?" (II., p. 19). The benefits of studying criticism as "a rational science," Kames says, are boundless. Scientific understanding of the nature of communication, he explains, improves the pleasure we receive from the arts. It strengthens the "reasoning faculties" through frequent exercise, for people enjoy reasoning about pleasant objects. It

---

[17] Henry Home, Lord Kames, *Elements of Criticism*, 3rd ed., two volumes (Edinburgh: A. Kincaid and J. Bell, 1765), I. p. 12. All subsequent references within the text are to this edition.

forms habits that are "sufficient to unravel all the intricacies of philosophy" (I., pp. 6–8). It improves our sociability, for it "furnishes elegant subjects for conversation, and prepares us finely for acting in the social state with dignity and propriety." It improves character because it tends "to moderate the selfish affections," and it is an antidote to such violent activities as hunting, drinking, and gambling and to such vices as ambition and avarice (I., pp. 8–10). Most important, it heightens sympathy and morality.[18] Sympathy, Kames says, "is the capital branch of every social passion. Sympathy in particular invites a communication of joys and sorrows, hopes and fears: such exercise, soothing and satisfactory in itself, is necessarily productive of mutual goodwill and affection" (I., p. 10). In terms of morality, critical study of communication creates "a conviction derived from experience, that disregard to justice or propriety never fails to be punished with shame and remorse" (I., pp. 10–11).

Kames' view of the importance of criticism is, of course, simply a slight twist on the traditional justifications for the study of rhetoric such as those we have observed in Isocrates, Cicero, Augustine, Alcuin, et al. Most modern theorists make similar observations about the value of the study of communication acts and of communication theory.

Blair   Hugh Blair (1718–1800) has little to add to Kames' discussion. Blair, like Fenelon, Campbell, and Priestley was an educator and preacher. He was minister of the High Church at St. Giles, the most prestigious pulpit in Scotland, and served for twenty-one years as Regius Professor of Rhetoric and Belles-Lettres at the University of Edinburgh. In addition to his major work, *Lectures on Rhetoric and Belles-Lettres* (1783), Blair published four volumes of sermons, a variety of moral and religious works, and a specialized treatise on communication, *Lectures on Pulpit Eloquence*. In spite of (or perhaps, because of) its derivative and ethnocentric character, *Rhetoric and Belles-Lettres* was one of the most popular textbooks of the period. It had twenty-six editions in Great Britain, thirty-seven in America, fifty-two abridged editions, and thirteen translations.[19]

Blair says that the purpose of his lectures is to initiate "Youth" into the study of fine literature and composition. His purpose is to help them develop "taste" in judging written and oral communication and "style" in writing and public speaking (Preface, iii–iv). In three volumes, nearly fifteen-hundred pages, Blair manages to include almost everything that has ever been said about communication. He includes the five-part paradigm in his discussion of the skills of the orator (II., p. 425), the three classical genres of communication, and the three classical "ends" of

---

[18] "Sympathy" is a key term in modern theory. Though its uses and meanings tend to become highly complex, essentially it means "empathy" of thought and feeling.

[19] Robert M. Schmitz, *Hugh Blair* (Morningside Heights, New York: King's Crown Press, 1948), pp. 1–5.

instructing, pleasing, and persuading (I., pp. 163–164). He explains that "the power of communicating their thoughts to one another" is what has allowed human beings to make important advancements in knowledge (I., pp. 1–2). As society becomes more complex, he says, the study of communication increases in importance: "Hence we find, that, in all the polished nations of Europe, this study has been treated as highly important, and has possessed a considerable place in every plan of liberal education" (I., pp. 2–3).

Blair explains that, in these lectures, he will draw on the ancient principles of rhetoric and the modern principles of human nature, substituting these for the "artificial and scholastic" principles of the medieval period. He proposes "to direct attention more towards substance than show, to recommend good sense as the foundation of all good composition, and simplicity as essential to all true ornament" (I., p. 3). He defines his general subject as "eloquence," which he says is "the art of placing truth in the most advantageous light for conviction and persuasion" (II., p. 281). He focuses on discourse, including both consummatory and instrumental modes under the general heading of "oratory."

De Quincey   Thomas De Quincey (1785–1859) is also generally classified as a belletristic theorist, though his approach differs in important ways from that of Kames and Blair. De Quincey did not write a full-length treatise on communication. Rather, he wrote a series of essays that appeared at varying intervals and that are often contradictory and inconsistent in terminology, if not in conception. His four most pertinent essays are *Rhetoric* (1828), *Style* (1841), *Conversation* (1847), and *Language* (1853). De Quincey also differs from other modern theorists in that he had no advanced degree or established profession. He was a "freelance" scholar, a drug addict, and a "hack" journalist.[20] He was also, as we will see, one of the most "contemporary" of modern thinkers and writers on communication.

De Quincey is belletristic in the sense that he includes a broad range of activities in his conception of communication. He is also, however, classical, relying upon Aristotle as one of his primary sources, and he is heavily influenced by faculty and associational psychology.

Although De Quincey never attempts to elaborate a single coherent theory of communication, analysis of his four essays on the subject reveals a fairly consistent view. He sees communication as primarily concerned with discourse. He seems to conceive of it in terms of what we might call a "universe of discourse" (see Fig. 4.1). Essentially, he proposes two genera: (1) objective, or scientific, discourse, and (2) subjective, or poetic, discourse. Scientific discourse is the "language of knowledge"; it is content-oriented, aims at conviction of the understanding,

[20] Frederick Burwick, "Introduction" to *Selected Essays on Rhetoric by Thomas De Quincey* (Carbondale: Southern Illinois University Press, 1967). All subsequent references to the essays within the text are to this edition.

Fig. 4.1   De Quincey's Universe of Discourse

I. Objective (Scientific) Discourse—The "language of knowledge"
   A. Content-oriented
   B. Conviction the goal—Addresses the understanding
   C. A useful art—Disseminates information
II. Subjective (Poetic) Discourse—The "language of power"
   A. Style-oriented
   B. Persuasion the goal—Addresses the passions
   C. An influential and fine art—Engages the will and gives intellectual pleasure
       1. Eloquence—Expression of spontaneous passion; its style appeals primarily to the passions, aims at emotional involvement, arouses strong feelings of preference by its manner rather than matter, works through imagery
       2. Rhetoric—Expression of rational decisions; its style appeals primarily to the understanding, aims at intellectual pleasure, rejuvenates old truths through new understanding, works through analogy
       3. Corinthian Rhetoric—Passionate expression of rational decisions; its style combines the attributes of eloquence and rhetoric

---

and is essentially a literature of statement, the use of which is dissemination of information. De Quincey has little to say about the language of knowledge. He finds it both uninteresting and of little use in a world where most of the things people discuss are contingent, and the primary function of communication is persuasion. Poetic discourse is the persuasive mode. It is the "language of power," and, being style-oriented, is essentially a literature of representation. Poetic discourse has three species. The first, eloquence, is spontaneous, passionate communication that achieves persuasion through the emotional involvement of the source and receiver (*Rhetoric*, p. 93). The second, rhetoric, is calmer, more "reasonable" communication that achieves persuasion through intellectual involvement (*Style*, p. 140). Eloquence works through imagery; rhetoric works through analogy. The third species, Corinthian Rhetoric, is the most powerful of all. It includes the attributes of both rhetoric and eloquence and thus achieves the strongest persuasion. It uses both analogy and imagery and appeals to both the understanding and the passions (*Rhetoric*, pp. 104–106).

De Quincey describes the rhetorical mode in Aristotelian terms. It depends primarily on "finding enthymemes," that is, "upon finding such arguments for any given thesis as, without positively proving or disproving it, should give it colourable support" (*Rhetoric*, p. 85). Rhetoric is planned discourse, carefully researched, organized, and rehearsed. Eloquence, on the other hand, is extemporaneous. It grows out of the sentiments of the moment and is ordered and expressed in accord with the natural demends of the emotions. Corinthian rhetoric is composed and delivered "eloquently" but planned and rehearsed "rhetorically." Forensic oratory is usually limited to rhetoric, whereas political oratory can often be eloquent (*Style*, p. 228). Either one, however, can become "Corinthian," given a suitable subject and occasion, e. g., a matter of life and death or war and peace. Pulpit oratory can always be Corinthian, for it is planned, yet it deals with great issues (*Rhetoric*, p. 110). For the most part, however, preachers must be content with rhetoric, for their tasks is the "rejuvenation" of old truths rather than the passionate eviction of "preference" (*Rhetoric*, p. 92). In short, De Quincey views poetic as the prototypical mode of communication (*Language*, p. 249). Rhetoric and eloquence are "toned down" poetry. Scientific discourse is neutral, non-poetic, and "useful" rather than "influential." "Style" is the central concern of communicating and the distinguishing characteristic of the genera and species.

Beyond his conceptualization of the universe of discourse, De Quincey's major contributions to modern theory are his insistence upon the organic nature of language and thought and upon the natural approach to operationalization. Also important is his broadening of the conception of criticism. He applies his critical standards to a range of public communication events, including not only "fine" literature but everyday journalism. Most important, he extends his criticism to private discourse and develops one of the first theories of informal social conversation.

De Quincey's observations on the impact of newspapers focus primarily on two "evil" influences of journalistic discourse. First, he says, they are corrupting the "national style." People are ceasing to speak naturally, even in informal conversation, preferring instead to use a stiff "bookish idiom," which they have learned from their morning paper and which they seem to think sounds sophisticated. Also, journalistic writing tends to favor exceptionally long and complex sentences, and these are beginning to appear everywhere in literature. The second evil grows out of the substance of newspapers. Rather than containing reasoned discourse on substantive matters, they tend to contain brief "jottings" that give the appearance of information but are in fact little more than hasty notes, or "pre-information." Thus, people believe that they are informed but are probably more ignorant of important issues than before they began to read. In short, a little pseudo-knowledge is a dangerous thing (*Style*, pp. 149–150).[21]

[21] These ideas are developed in an extensive passage. Since De Quincey's style is so much a part of his content, I have chosen to paraphrase these statements rather than try to select representative samples. However, because it may be interesting to some readers, I include most of the passage in the following quotation:

'One single number of a London morning paper—which in half a century has expanded from the size of a dinner napkin to that of a breakfast tablecloth, from that to a carpet, and will soon be forced by the expansions of public business into something resembling the mainsail of a frigate—is already equal in printed matter to a very large octavo volume. Every old woman in the nation now reads daily a vast miscellany in one volume royal octavo. The evil of this, as regards the quality of knowledge communicated, admits of no remedy. Public business, in its whole

De Quincey's "theory" of conversation is in reality more of a pre-theory. It consists of a number of critical observations and hints. However, it is certainly more fully developed than previous theories.[22] Conversation, De Quincey says, is like Corinthian rhetoric; it is both a fine and useful art and both pleases and influences. However, conversation has not been systematically studied (*Conversation*, p. 264). The importance of conversation cannot be overlooked, for it is "the great paramount purpose of social meetings" (p. 265). In structure, it is spontaneous and more related to "manners" than to intellect; that is, a theory of conversation would focus not on prescriptions, but proscriptions. Conversation is "a system of forebearances" (p. 266). In reference to other modes of communication, De Quincey says that conversation essentially functions to assist us in conceptualizing. He quotes Bacon's observation that "Reading maketh a full man; conference a ready man; and writing an exact man" (p. 268). Like Aristotle, he says that conversation is the best place to try out our ideas and to discover new ones. From "the electric kindling of life between two minds," we often discover ideas we would never have found through private study (p. 268).

> unwieldy compass, must always form the subject of these daily chronicles. Nor is there much room to expect any change in the style. The evil effect of this upon the style of the age may be reduced to two forms. Formerly the natural impulse of every man was spontaneously to use the language of life; the language of books was a secondary attainment, not made without effort. Now, on the contrary, the daily composers of newspapers have so long dealt in the professional idiom of books as to have brought it home to every reader in the nation who does not violently resist it by some domestic advantages. . . . The whole artificial dialect of books has come into play as the dialect of ordinary life. This is one form of the evil impressed upon our style by journalism: a dire monotony of bookish idiom has encrusted and stiffened all native freedom of expression, like some scaly leprosy or elephantiasis, barking and hide-binding the fine natural pulses of the elastic flesh. Another and almost a worse evil has established itself in the prevailing structure of sentences. Every man who has had any experience in writing knows how natural it is for hurry and fulness of matter to discharge itself by vast sentences, involving clause within clause *ad infinitum*; how difficult it is, and how much a work of art to break up this hugh fasciculus of cycle and epicycle into a graceful succession of sentences, long intermingled with short, each modifying the other, and arising musically by links of spontaneous connexion. Now, the plethoric form of period, this monster model of sentence, bloated with decomplex intercalations, and exactly repeating the form of syntax which distinguishes an act of Parliament, is the prevailing model in newspaper eloquence. Crude undigested masses of suggestion, furnishing rather raw materials for composition and jottings for the memory than any formal developments of the ideas, describe the quality of writing which must prevail in journalism . . . from the necessities of hurry and of instant compliance with an instant emergency, granting no possibility for revision or opening for amended thought, which are evils attached to the flying velocities of public business' (*Style*, pp. 149–150).

[22] Nearly every major classical theorist at least mentions "conversation." Augustine includes it in his discussion of "teaching." Bacon includes it with "negotiation" and "government" as one of the three most important communication activities (*Advancement of Learning*, XXIII).

In terms of the "rules" of conversation, De Quincey says that social communication may take the form of "colloquium," or "talking *with*" another, or of "alloquium," that is, "talking to" another (p. 281). The latter, he explains, is fatal to communication, for it is a "systematic trespass upon the conversational rights" of others and is a "violent interruption" of the "silent contract" of social intercourse. (pp. 281–282). Alloquium destroys empathy ("sympathy") between conversants and therefore makes sharing of ideas and sentiments impossible: "to be acted upon for ever, but never to react, is fatal to the very powers by which sympathy must grow, or by which intelligent admiration can be evoked" (p. 282).

De Quincey observes that there are a number of "diseases" that can destroy conversation. The central of these is failing to take turns, that is, proceeding by alloquium. Another is maintaining the floor for an inordinate amount of time. It is, he says, "an infringement of the general rights for any man to detain the conversation, or arrest its movements, for more than a short space of time" (p. 285). In *Style*, he points out that the English are especially inclined to usurp the floor. The French, he says, know that the right to speak is a "personal" one granted by the participants. In contrast:

> To an Englishman, the right of occupying the attention of the company seems to inhere in *things* rather than in persons; if the particular subject under discussion should happen to be a grave one, then, in right of *that*, and not by any right of his own, a speaker will seem to an Englishman invested with the privilege of drawing largely upon the attention of a company (pp. 156–157).

Two other "diseases" can interfere with informal social communication. One is a habit of interrupting. De Quincey says that "timing" our contributions so as not to cut short another's train of thought and expression is an important skill (p. 285). The other is "moving" the conversation. People who do not listen to the content of others' talk tend to "move" the topic, that is, to introduce what in more formal discourse would be called digressions. The inherent "excursiveness" of conversation makes it especially easy for people to voice their idiosyncratic associations, thus throwing the company off the more general topic. These incursions often lead to the dominance of "boring" personal indulgence (p. 287).

Somewhat seriously, De Quincey says that perhaps all conversations should be ruled over by a "symposiarch," whose role is to guard against these various diseases (p. 286). At least, he says, we need to pay more attention to developing a theory of social conversation. If we can develop "theories" of activities such as "spitting," and "soup-eating," and "betting," then we can surely devise a theory of this central human activity (p. 264).

Spencer   The central concern of the more belletristic theorists was with "style," both the aesthetics and the pragmatics of symbolization in terms of common psychological and epistemological theories. Kames, Blair, and De Quincey all devote considerable space to theories of language. The last major theorist of the period, Herbert Spencer, makes this approach the primary topic of his *Philosophy of Style* (1871). He says that previous treatments of rhetoric and composition have not done a good job of accounting for the nature of language in relationship to the nature of language users: "Standing as isolated dogmas—as empirical generalizations, they [precepts of style] are neither so clearly apprehended, nor so much respected, as they would be were they deduced from simple first principles."[23]

The "simple first principles" Spencer proposes grow out of modern psychology, especially associationism. Basically, he explains, the "meaning" of a message is created by the receiver. He or she must categorize and conceptualize the symbols presented and thus must use "mental energy." All precepts of symbolization, as well as a number of those of organization and operationalization, Spencer claims, can be accounted for in terms of the principle of conserving the "recipient's mental energy" (p. 2). Thus, he explains, nonverbal symbols, because they require less cognitive energy, communicate more quickly and forcibly (p. 2). Short words, because they are learned first and have more immediate associations, are more effective than long ones (p. 4). Figurative language, because it is naturally associated with strong feeling, arouses passion more quickly than literal language (p. 12).

A second, but related, principle, "economy of the mental sensibilities," accounts for such things as the proscription against using strong emotional appeal in the early portions of messages and the general superiority of climax order:

> It may be shown that alike in the reflective faculties, in the imagination, in the perceptions of the beautiful, the ludicrous, the sublime, in the sentiments, the instincts in all the mental powers, however we may classify them—action exhausts; and that in proportion as the action is violent, the subsequent prostration is great . . . Every perception received, and every conception realized, entailing some amount of waste . . . the resulting partial inability must affect the acts of perception and conception that immediately succeed (p. 17).

Thus, a variety of the precepts of symbolization and organization can be accounted for in terms of conserving the sensibilities of the receiver for the final, and most important, appeals.

Elocutionist Approaches

The fourth dominant trend in modern approaches to communication, elocution, seems to have had little influence on theory. The major theorists are adamant in their rejection of the "artificial" approach to operationalization developed by elocutionists.

A number of contemporary scholars have analyzed the nature, development, and rationale of the elocutionary movement.[24] As Fig. 4.2 reveals, the movement began in the early years of the modern period, reached a peak in the mid-eighteenth century, and began to slow in the mid-nineteenth century. Most scholars agree that elocutionary approaches grew out of two main areas of concern. First was a growing body of criticism expressing dismay at the poor delivery of contemporary speakers, especially preachers. Second was a new awareness of the inhibiting effects of regional dialects in terms of such professions as politics and acting.

Thomas Wilson was one of the earliest communication theorists to single preachers out as the "worst" public speakers. In his critique of sixteenth-century practice, he especially emphasized operational faults such as poor posture and poor articulation. Too many speakers, he says, are inclined to "weave" rather than stand comfortably, and to "bark" or "cackle" rather than talk naturally (*Arte of Rhetorique*, pp. 219–220). In the modern period, the delivery of preachers apparently did not improve. In his *Letter to a Young Clergyman*, Jonathan Swift critiques late seventeenth-century practices:

[23] Herbert Spencer, *The Philosophy of Style*, in *Humbolt Library of Popular Science Literature* (July, 1882), pp. 1–20.

[24] See, for instance, Frederick W. Haberman, "English Sources of American Elocution," *History of Speech Education in America*, ed. by Karl R. Wallace (New York, 1954), pp. 105–126; Wilbur S. Howell, "Sources of the Elocutionary Movement in England: 1700–1748," *Quarterly Journal of Speech* (February 1959), pp. 1–18; Wallace Bacon, "The Elocutionary Career of Thomas Sheridan," *Speech Monographs* (January 1963), pp. 1–53; and Warren Guthrie, "The Elocution Movement—England," in *The Province of Rhetoric*, ed. by Joseph Schwartz and John A. Rycenga (New York: Ronald Press, 1965), pp. 255–275.

Fig. 4.2   Elocution: A Chronology of Selected Authors and Works

Robert Robinson	*Art of Pronunciation*	1617
Louis de Cresolles	*Vacationes Automnales*	1620
Michel Le Faucheur	*Traitte de L'action de*	1657
	L'orateur	1657
John Bulwer	*Chirologia . . . Chironomia*	1644
Anonymous	*Some Rules for Speaking and Action*	1715
John Henley	*The Appeal of the Oratory to the First Ages of Christianity*	1727
John Mason	*An Essay on Elocution, or, Pronunciation*	1748

Fig. 4.2 Elocution (Cont'd)

Anonymous	An Essay on the Action Proper to the Pulpit	1753
Anonymous	Art of Speaking in Public	1755
Thomas Sheridan	British Education	1756
	Lessons in Elocution	1759
	Lectures on Elocution	1762
	Lectures on Reading	1775
	A Rhetorical Grammar of the English Language	
James Burgh	The Art of Speaking	1761
John Rice	An Introduction to the Art of Reading with Energy & Propriety	1765
Anselm Bayly	A Practical Treatise on Singing and Playing	1771
	The Alliance of Music, Poetry and Oratory	1789
John Harris	The Elements of Speech	1773
William Enfield	The Speaker	1774
Joshua Steele	Prosodia Rationalis	1775
William Cockin	The Art of Delivering Written Language	1775
William Scott	Lessons in Elocution	1779
John Walker	Exercises for Improvement in Elocution	1777
	Elements of Elocution	1781
	Rhetorical Grammar	1785
	The Melody of Speech	1787
	The Teacher's Assistant	1787
	The Academic Speaker	1801
Robert Dodsley	Precepts	1784
Richard Edgworth	Practical Elocution	1789
Gilbert Austin	Chironomia: or a Treatise on Rhetorical Delivery	1806
Johann J. Engel	Practical Illustrations of Rhetorical Gestures and Action Adapted to the English Drama	1807
Thomas Ewing	Principles of Elocution	1816
John H. Howlett	Instructions in Reading the Liturgy	1826
Henry Inness	The Rhetorical Class Book, or Principles and Practice of Elocution Defined and Illustrated	1834
Richard Cull	Garrick's Mode of Reading the Liturgy	1840
A.M. Hartley	The Academic Speaker: A System of Elocution Designed for Schools and Self-Instruction	1846

You will observe some clergymen with their heads held down from the beginning to the end within an inch of the cushion to read what is clearly legible; which, beside the untoward manner, hinders them from making the best advantage of their voice; others again have a trick of popping up and down every moment from their paper to the audience, like an idle school boy on repetition day.[25]

A number of similar observations appeared from time to time in popular periodicals like the *Tatler* and *Spectator*. Addison notes that preachers are not the only offenders against proper use of voice and body. He says, "Nothing could be more ridiculous than the gestures of most of our English Speakers." He notes that hands in pockets and hat-twisting are common faults (*Spectator*, No. 907).[26]

Thomas Sheridan, who is frequently viewed as the leader of the elocutionary movement in the eighteenth cenutry, viewed dialects and regional accents as a primary hindrance to political and social mobility and hence as an important justification for a focus on voice and pronunciation. His career on the English stage having been, he believed, impeded by his Irish accent, he had a personal stake in establishing standards.[27] Gilbert Austin, an early nineteenth-century elocutionist, cites the criticism of communication theorists, the popular press, and the need for standardization of dialect as the justification for his interest.[28]

Howell explains that a third possible explanation for the elocutionary movement may have been that operationalization was the only part of the classical paradigm that had never been "claimed" by another discipline. Thus, modern scholars may have seen it as the central aspect of communication and emphasis on it as the most fruitful focus for reconstruction of the field.[29] Sheridan says that his purpose is, in fact, "to revive the long lost art of oratory."[30] An earlier elocutionary author, John Bulwer, says that his *Chirologia . . . Chironomia* (1644) is inspired by a desire to make up for a deficiency in our knowledge of the use of gestures.[31] This deficiency, he explains, was first noted by Bacon in the *Advancement of Knolwedge*. Bulwer cites Bacon as having said that Aristotle "hath very ingeniously and diligently handled the features of the body

---

[25] Jonathan Swift. *Wo.ks*, ed. by Thomas Sheridan (London, 1803), VIII, p. 15.
[26] Quoted in Guthrie, "The Elocution Movement—England," p. 255.
[27] Howell, *Eighteenth Century British Logic and Rhetoric*, pp. 156–158.
[28] Gilbert Austin, *Chironomia; or a Treatise on Rhetorical Delivery* (London, 1806), pp. 6–11. Subsequent references within the text are to this edition.
[29] Howell, *Eighteenth Century British Logic and Rhetoric*, p. 152.
[30] Thomas Sheridan, *British Education* (London, 1756), p. vi (quoted in Howell, p. 222).
[31] John Bulwer, *Chirologia: or the Natural Language of the Hand, and Chironomia: or the Art of Manual Rhetoric*, ed. by James Cleary (Carbondale: Southern Illinois University Press, 1974). All subsequent references within the text are to this translation.

in Physiognomy, but not the gestures of the body, which are no less comprehensible by art, and of great use and advantage" (p. 5). Therefore, Bulwer says, his purpose is to discover and trace the theory of gesture through the classical authors and "to handle gesture, as the only speech and general language of human nature" (p. 6). Thus, in a certain sense, the elocutionists' purposes were similar to those of Fenelon and other major theorists, the reconstruction of the discipline on the basis of classical thought. Their narrow focus on one part of the paradigm, however, led them into prescription rather than theory.

Bulwer   A brief look as some of the typical works reveals the content and nature of elocutionary approaches. Bulwer's *Chirologia* is typical of the more mechanistic approaches favored by authors like Burgh and Walker. Bulwer focuses specifically on the use of the hands and fingers. The hand, he says, is the most effective way to "emphatically vent and communicate a thought"; it is "generally understood and known by all nations and is the only speech that is natural to man" (pp. 15–16). Gesture is not only more effective and prior to speech, but it often obviates any need for speech: "Although speech and gesture are conceived together in the mind, yet the hand first appearing in the delivery, anticipates the tongue, insomuch as many times the tongue perceiving herself forestalled, spares itself a labor to prevent needless tautology" (p. 17). Gestures, he continues, are natural signs: "TO HOLD UP THE HAND is a natural token of *approbation, consent, election,* and of giving *suffrage*" (p. 49).

Although Bulwer claims simply to be describing the natural communicative use of hands and fingers, his detailed descriptions of movements in relation to their "meanings" rapidly take on the tone of prescriptions. Thus, he says, "both the turned out palms bent to the left side is a more passionate form of detestation, as being a redoubled action" (p. 187). The numerous charts and figures add to the mechanistic and prescriptive tone by showing the reader exactly how to position and move in order to accomplish specific purposes (see Fig. 4.3).

Austin   Gilbert Austin's *Chironomia; or A Treatise on Rhetorical Delivery* (1806) is somewhat less mechanistic and more broadly conceived than Bulwer's work. Austin includes use of voice and of the entire body in "chironomia." Thus he is also in the more "natural" tradition of Sheridan and Mason. Moreover, he connects himself to some extent with the mainstream communication theorists when he defines his subject as only one part of the larger discipline of communication. The first four parts, "invention, disposition, elocution (that is, choice of language),[32] and memory," he says, have been dealt with systematically and fully by both ancient and modern theorists. Neither group, however, has formulated "any sufficiently detailed and precise precepts for the fifth division . . . namely, *rhetorical delivery*, called by the ancients *actio and pronunciatio*" (p. ix). Austin describes his purpose as the development of a system of notation "to record and to communicate in writing" the variations in voice and gesture appropriate to particular occasions, and the "improvement and perfecting of public speaking in general" (pp. iv-v).

An Index of reference to the following Table, or Alphabet of naturall expreffions.

Which Geftures, befides their typicall figni-fications, are fo ordered to ferve for privy cyphers for any fecret intimation.

A   B   C   D
Figures out the I *Gefture.*II *Geft.*III *Geft.*IV *Geft.*

E   F   G   H
V *Geft.*   VI *Geft.*   VII *Geft.*   VIII *Geff.*

I   K   L   M
IX *Geft.*   X *Geft.*   XI *Geft.*   XII *Geff.*

N   O   P   Q
XIII *Geft.*   XIV *Geft.*   XV *Geft.*   XVI *Geft.*

R   S   T   V
XVII *Geft.*   XVIII *Geft.*   XIX *Geft.*   XX *Geft.*

W   X   Y   Z
XXI *Geft.*   XXII *Geft.*   XXIII *Geft.*   XXIV *Geft.*

The neceffary defeft of thefe Chirograms in point of motion and percuffion, which Art cannot expreffe, muft be fupplied with imagi-nation, and a topicall reference to the order and number of their Geftures.

Fig. 4.3   *A Chart of Sample Hand Movements from John Bulwer's Chirologia . . . Chironomia*

"Elocution" is, of course, the traditional term for "symbolization," and Austin uses it in that sense. Other "elocutionists" preferred to use it to mean operationalization because, apparently, they wanted to use a classical term but found "pronunciation" and "action," the traditional classical terms, too confusing for modern readers. Also, "elocution" had the advantage of implying "expression" of sense. It is unclear why only a few, like Austin, chose to use the English word "delivery."

As *Chironomia* proceeds, it soon becomes clear that Austin regards operationalization as more than "one-fifth" of communication. In the introductory pages he seems to say that it more like one-half. The first four parts, he says, have to do with the "internal" aspects of communication, while "the management of the voice, the expression of the countenance, and the gesture of the head, the body, and the limbs, constitute the external part of oratory" (p. 1). In fact, he says, without operationalization, the other four parts are nearly useless. A communicator who neglects "correct delivery . . . deprives his composition of its just effect" (p. 5). In discussing appropriateness of operationalization, Austin goes still further, making "delivery" the prior consideration to content: "The delivery and the composition mutually act upon and affect each other; where the delivery is to be cold, the composition must be dry and formal. Where it is to be animated . . . the very language glows and burns as it is formed under the pen" (pp. 18–19). Finally, he says, "on public occasions, men can be influenced only by what they hear." It is not *what* is said, he seems to claim, so much as *how*: "The sound of the human voice is imperious and awful; and we find it often used to terrify, as well as to convince" (p. 31).

Having placed his subject in its context and made it the pragmatic whole of communication, Austin proceeds to discuss the various rules for pronunciation, posture, facial expression, gesture, etc., which comprise the major bulk of the work. He develops a system of notation for marking messages to show proper delivery in each of these particulars. He includes a number of figures and sample compositions marked and cross-referenced to the figures. In a sense, *Chironomia* may be described as one of the first "self-instruction manuals." By the time he or she finishes reading the book, a careful student should have become an expert—at least on the notation system and the poses shown in the appendix.

In terms of its basic conceptions and assumptions, Austin's *Chironomia* is not sharply inconsistent with the operationalization theory of the major theorists. His focus on the "natural" meaning of nonverbal behavior is, in fact, extremely consistent. However, when he ceases describing what *does* happen, and begins prescribing what *should* happen, he tends to become as mechanistic and artificial as the other elocutionists. The minute distinctions between gestures for noting, pushing, beckoning, repressing, collecting, etc. (pp. 342–349), quickly become tiresome and unrealistic. Figures 4.4–4.9 indicate the nature of Austin's symbol system for noting variations in voice and body. They also show how the system can be used on a sample message and give an idea of the variety of postures and gestures he identifies. As Austin would say, these figures are much more eloquent indications of the nature of his work than any words could be.

As indicated earlier, the existence of these four dominent trends (classical, psychological-epistemological, belletristic, and elocutionist) and our classification of the major theorists in terms of them, should not be taken as an indication of serious divisions or disagreements. A relatively brief review of the general conception of the nature and province of modern communication theory, in fact, reveals the reverse, that is, extensive areas of consistency and general agreement.

Nature and Province of
Modern Human Communication Theory

Modern communication theorists take a fundamentally classical view of the nature and province of human communication theory. They agree that human communication is concerned primarily with contingent matters, that its ultimate end is persuasion, and that all communication acts are instrumental.

Contingent Subject Matter

In modern theory, communication is generally viewed as being primarily concerned with the process of decision-making in the realm of "contingent" affairs. Through communication, Blair says, people arrive at agreements concerning what is "true," what is morally right or a matter of duty, and what is profitable and good or in their own interest (II., p. 375). Campbell says that the study of the "philosophy of rhetoric" is worthwhile and useful because it concerns the use of symbolic means for the achievement of personal decision-making and also for "the conviction and persuasion of others" (p. xlix).

Campbell emphasizes that the "proper province" of communication is "moral reasoning" in contingent matters. Abstract or scientific "truth," he says, is seldom a subject for discussion. What we all agree upon needs merely to be "pointed to" in order to be accepted (p. 43). However, there are very few areas of human life where "truth" is either known or accepted. Nearly everything that affects human conduct, "the real but often changeable and contingent connexions that subsist among things," is subject to moral reasoning (p. 44). Moral reasoning "admits degrees" and is always inconclusive for "there is always real, not apparent, evidence on both sides. There are contrary experiences, contrary presumptions, contrary testimonies, to balance against one another" (p. 45). Because human communication theory is the study of moral reasoning in contingent affairs, Campbell says, it is essential to social organization. It includes study of the "laws and works of nature," the "arts and institutions of men," and all things in "the cognizance of the human mind with all their modification, operations, and effects." Without moral reasoning, "society must not only suffer but perish" (p. 46). Thus, in modern theory, human communication is not, as the medieval and Renaissance scholars viewed it, the simple presentation of known truth; it is the primary vehicle for the social construction of reality.

Alphabetical Arrangement of Symbolic Letters.

	Above the Line. Hands, Arms, Body and Head.				Capital B and double small Letters. Both Arms and both Hands.	Capitals for particular Parts.	Capitals for Head and Eyes.	Below the Line. Feet.		Capitals and small; significant Gestures.
	Small Letters relating to the Hand and Arm.							Small Letters. Steps.	Capitals. Positions.	
	1. Hand.	2. Elevation of the Arm.	3. Transverse Position of the Arm.	4 and 5. Motion and Force.						
A	-	-	-	ascending alternate	applied	-	assenting averted	advance	-	appealing attention admiration aversion
B	backwards	-	backwards	backwards beckoning	both	breast	-	-	both	-
C	clinched	-	across	collecting contracted clinching	crossed clasped	Chin	-	cross	-	commanding
D	-	downwards	-	descending	-	-	downwards denying	-	-	deprecation declaration
E	-	elevated	-	-	encumbered	Eyes	erect	-	-	encouragement.
F	forwards	-	forwards	forwards flourish	folded	Forehead	Forward	-	front	fear
G	grasping	-	-	grasping	-	-	-	-	-	Grief

H holding	horizontal						Horror
I index		inwards	inclosed	inclined		kneeling	⎰ Lamenta- tion
K collected			a kimbo				⎱ Listenng
L collected		left				left	
M thumb		moderate	Lips				
N natural inwards		noting	enumerating / Nose				
O outwards		outwards					
P prone	oblique	⎰ pushing ⎱ pressing					Pride
Q			reposed	rcund	retire	oblique / right	
R Rest		⎰ right re- coiling re- ⎱ pressing rejecting					
S supine		⎰ swecp springing, ⎱ striking shaking		⎰ shaking ⎱ aside	⎰ start stamp ⎱ shock	side	shame
T		⎰ touching ⎱ throwing		Tossing	traverse		threatning
U				Uwpards			
V Vertical		revolving		Vacancy			Veneration
W hollow		waving	wringing				side
X extended	extended	extreme					
Z	Zenith						

Fig. 4.4 Austin's System for Marking Body Movement

Although neither Campbell nor the other modern theorists go so far as to claim that "truth" and "reality" do not exist, they do agree that these are often difficult, and in many cases impossible, to discover or establish. As De Quincey puts it:

> Whatsoever is certain, or matter of fixed science, can be no subject for the rhetorician. . . . Absolute certainty and fixed science trans-

---

Symbols for Noting the Force and Rapidity or Interruption of the Voice in Delivery.

The symbols are to be marked in the margin near the commencement of the passage which they are to influence.

Symbols.

Piano	═══
Uniform loudness, or forte	∧∧∧
Crescendo (as in music)	◁
Diminuendo (as in music)	▷
Rapid	◡ ◡ ◡
Slow	▬▬▬
Suspension of the voice, the break or dash after a word }	▬ ▬
Long pause, or new paragraph	‖
Whisper or monotone	▬▬

Compound Symbols.

Piano and slow	≡≡≡
Piano and quick	◡ ◡ ◡ ═
Loud and slow	∧̿∧̿∧̿
Loud and quick	◡ ◡ ◡ ∧∧∧
Monotonous or whisper slow	≡≡≡
Monotone or whisper quick	◡ ◡ ◡

Fig. 4.5   Austin's System for Marking Voice Inflection

THE MISER AND PLUTUS.

GAY.

R Bvhf r——— q. peq n—pdq
1. 2. THE wind was high, the window shakes;
a.R.2.

veq c—vhx c
3. With sudden start the miser wakes!
sR1x

F pdb ad ————phq—
4. Along the silent room he stalks;
aR2

B vhx—vhq c Bvhf tr
5. 6. Looks back, and trembles as he walks!
sR1x

vhq— . . . . : . . —vhx c
7. Each lock and ev'ry bolt he tries,
aL2

shq o— . . . —shc i
8. In ev'ry creek and corner pries;
aR2

Bpdq ————n
9. Then opes his chest with treasure stor'd,

D Bseq
10. And stands in rapture o'er his hoard:
R2

Bvhf c
11. But now with sudden qualms possest,
rR1

Bfl. hf ————2 ———— ————Bfl.br.
12. He wrings his hands, he beats his breast.

g.br — . . . . — veq
13. By conscience stung he wildly stares;

Bshf sh.
14. And thus his guilty soul declares.

Bsdf d ——————————n
15. Had the deep earth her stores confin'd,
aR2

br—R
16. This heart had known sweet peace of mind,
R1

Fig. 4.6 A Sample Composition Marked with Austin's System

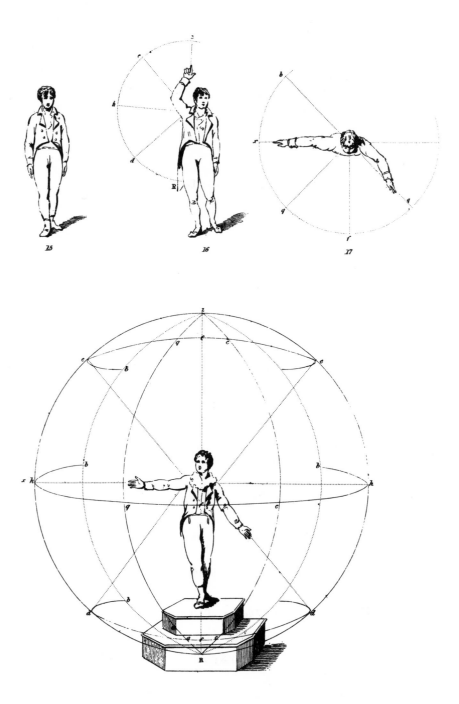

Fig. 4.7   Austin's Basic Body Positions

Fig. 4.8 Austin's Positions of the Feet

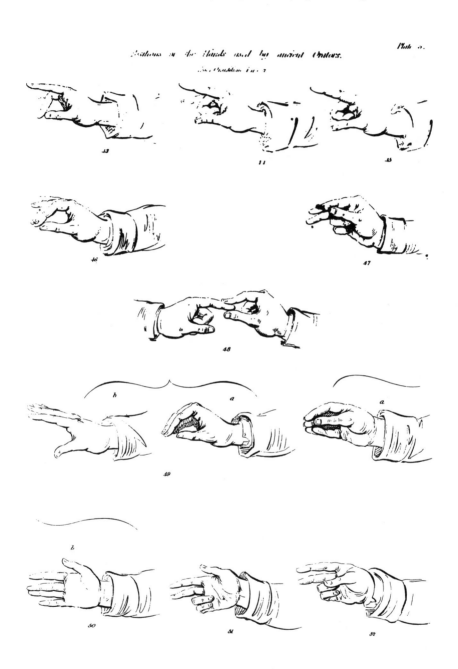

Fig. 4.9   Austin's Positions of the Hands and Fingers

cend opinion and exclude the probable. The province of Rhetoric, whether meant for an influence upon the actions, or simply upon the belief, lies among that vast field of cases where there is a *pro* and a *con*, with the chance of right and wrong, true and false, distributed in varying proportions between them (*Rhetoric*, p. 90).

De Quincey goes on to say that there are some cases where "the affirmative and negative are both true" and that these also come within the province of "rhetoric."

Similarly, Whately points out that though it would be preferable to have assurance that all our decisions are based on incontrovertible evidence, in practice we more often make decisions in spite of the fact that we are not "fully convinced" (pp. 80–81). Furthermore, even when we have made up our own minds, we constantly must deal with others who have no opinion on an "important" matter, who have contrary opinions, or who are in doubt about what to believe. For these reasons, rhetoric, which he defines as the study of "argument," or the means of establishing a belief "to the *satisfaction* of *another*," is essential to social organization (p. 5). Though most of the moderns conceived of communication theory more broadly than Whately, all agree that the ultimate function of communication, and therefore the justification for theory, is the study of how people influence each other.

The "Ends" of Communication   That influence is the ultimate function of human communication becomes clear when we examine the modern theory of the "ends" or outcomes of communicative acts. At first glance, it seems that modern theorists are simply continuing the classical tradition as maintained throughout the medieval and Renaissance periods. Blair, for instance, says that there are three ends toward which a communicator might aim: (1) informing, instructing, or convincing, (2) pleasing or entertaining, and (3) interesting, agitating, or persuading (I., p. 163). Fenelon says all communicative acts "can be reduced to proving, to portraying, and to striking" (p. 92).

Modern theorists, however, are not content to simply restate the three classical ends of instructing, pleasing, and persuading. Rather, upon this foundation they build a unique theory that contains most of the ancient precepts but which is elaborated in the context of faculty and associational psychology.

In general, modern theorists agree, there are four generic functions of communication—conviction, pleasure, passion, and persuasion. Campbell says that a communicative act may work "to enlighten the understanding, to please the imagination, to move the passions, or to influence the will" (p. 1). Though we might conceive of these outcomes or ends as separate "species," he says, in actual operation they are multi-plicative:

> In general it may be asserted, that each preceding species, in the order above exhibited, is preparatory to the subsequent; that each subsequent species is founded upon the preceding; and thus they ascend in a regular progression. Knowledge, the object of the intellect, furnisheth materials for the fancy; the fancy culls, compounds, and, by her mimic art, disposes these materials so as to affect the passions; the passions are the natural spurs to volition or action, and so need only to be right directed (p. 2).

This "progressive" approach to function grows out of the hierarchial nature of the faculties of the mind. As Campbell explains, the faculties of understanding, imagination, memory, and passion are "mutually subservient" to the will, the ultimate faculty. Thus, in order to influence a person to act, or in order to engage the will, all four faculties must be activated:

> It is not therefore the understanding alone that is here concerned. If the orator would prove successful, it is necessary that he engage in his service all these different powers of the mind, the imagination, the memory, and the passions. These are not the supplantors of reason, or even rivals in her sway; they are her handmaids, by whose ministry she is enabled to usher truth into the heart, and procure it there a favourable reception (p. 72).

As Campbell's description of the operations of the faculties implies, modern theorists tended to view pleasure and passion not as ends, in the classical sense, but as necessary outcomes of "effective" communication and as means to the ultimate end of persuading. Conviction, or informing the understanding, is generally viewed as a necessary adjunct of persuasion, but seldom as an end in itself. Even in instruction the purpose is "persuasive," to influence belief. In short, we might say that modern theorists take the position that "communication cannot *not* influence."

In his discussion of the nature of communication, Priestley blends conviction and persuasion into one goal. He says, "the *informing of the judgment,* and influencing the practice . . . is the only direct and proper, at least ultimate end" (p. 68). Pleasing the imagination and moving the passions, he says, are means to influencing judgments and resolution and "thereby to *direct the practice*" (p. 69). As we have seen, Fenelon emphasizes the interdependence of understanding, passion, and influence when he says that "eloquence is nothing but the art of instructing and persuading men by moving them" (p. 125). He bases his definition on the "ancient theorists' conception" of the nature of communication theory and says it is still the best one: "According to them," he says, it is the study of how discourse works "to establish truth and to arouse a love for it in the hearts of men" (p. 126). Thus, an effective communicator is "a man who knows how to establish truth" and also a person whose skill consists in adding "everything capable of arousing your sentiments, of making you love demonstrated truth" (p. 89). Blair adds that the communicator must engage not only the understanding and the passions, but also the imagination and memory. This art, he says, is complex:

> It is the art not of pleasing the fancy merely; but of speaking both to the understanding and to the heart; of interesting the hearers in such a degree, as to seize and carry them along with us; and to leave them with a deep and strong impression of what they have heard (II., pp. 424–425).

Modern theorists agree that conviction is the necessary adjunct of persuasion. Fenelon says that it is the basic requirement: "In eloquence, everything consists in adding to solid proof the means of interesting the listener" (p. 90). Blair says, "No persuasion is stable, which is not founded on conviction" (I., p. 162). In fact, he says, we must not only establish conviction in order to persuade, but we must maintain it: "The hearers must be convinced that there are good and sufficient grounds for their entering with warmth into the cause; and remain satisfied that they are not carried away by mere delusion" (II., p. 383).

The conviction-persuasion process is somewhat more complex than Blair's statement may imply. As a number of theorists point out, conviction enters in at a variety of points. For instance, Whately points out that conviction includes instruction. Often we must "convince" people that there is a problem, that they need to act on or form an opinion about some matter, that they need to resolve a doubt, or that they need to change an opinion or behavior (p. 36). In any of these cases, the first requirement is to establish the "fact." The next step is to elicit a willingness to deal with it. Here, of course, memory, imagination, and passion come into play. Once the problem is established and the desire aroused, however, the auditor must be instructed as to the choices available to him and convinced that the decision he is being asked to make will "solve" the problem. Hence, Whately points out, "the conviction of the understanding . . . is an essential *part* of persuasion," for in order to influence opinions or behavior it is necessary "1. that the proposed *Object* should appear desirable; and 2. that the *Means* suggested should be proved to be conducive to the attainment of that object" (p. 175).

This view of conviction-persuasion has been called the "wish-fulfillment" theory. In more contemporary terms, however, we might call it a probability-utility approach. When confronted with a decision, an individual must assign values to the outcomes and weigh the probabilities of success in terms of the effort, costs, and potential rewards. Campbell reminds us that since there are a number of such factors which influence our decisions in contingent matters, the communicator must take into account the interaction of "rational" and "emotional" factors:

> [T]he principal scope for employing persuasion is, when the mind balances, or may be supposed to balance, in determining what choice to make in respect to conduct, whether to do this or to do that, or at least whether to do or to forbear. And it is equally evident that the mind would never balance a moment in choosing, unless there were motives to influence it on each of the opposite sides. . . . Now, whichever side the orator espouses, there are two things that must carefully be studied by him; . . . The first is to excite in his hearers that desire or passion which favours his design; the second is, to satisfy their judgments that there is a connexion between the conduct to which he would persuade them, and the gratification of the desire or passion which he excites (p. 274).

Thus, says Campbell, persuasion "is in reality an artful mixture of that which proposes to convince the judgment, and that which interests the passions" (p. 4). Whately says that persuasion "depends on, first *Argument*, (to prove the expediency of the Means proposed,) and secondly, what is usually called *Exhortation*, i. e., the excitement of men to adopt those Means, by representing the end as sufficiently desirable" (p. 176).

This emphasis on persuasion as the ultimate end of communication and central concern of theory may seem restrictive to the contemporary reader. Most modern theorists do not deny that a particular communicative act may be undertaken primarily to inform or to entertain. However, they are operating on an assumption about the nature of "good," or "effective," communication, which essentially rules out the purely informative or entertaining. Communication ("eloquence," or "oratory," or symbolic "art"), they argue, is essentially instrumental. It takes place in social interaction and deals almost exclusively with "moral" questions, which are infinitely inconclusive: Our opinions, behavior, and values are originally formed through social intercourse and are thus continually subject to change through the same process.

Even "simple information" influences our preferences and thus leads to change. Kames gives as an instance of the process the mutation of affection between lovers who live together. Over time, as they become more well-known and predictable to each other, passionate love weakens into affection and eventually is replaced by habit. If the individuals cease to change, even habitual affection can die. Kames says all preferences feed on change and growth; if they become "stationary," they "must begin to decay" (II., p 115). Thus, human beings are constantly processing and using information and constantly undergoing change. Any "message" that impinges upon our consciousness "affects" us. A message that does not affect us simply has not been "received." The modern identification of communication with persuasion is not a simplistic reduction; rather, it is an elegant representation of a complex conception.

The Social Instrumental Function of Communication The "social instrumental" concept of communication accounts for Campbell's virtual exclusion of "purely" informative messages from the province of human communication theory. Campbell says that mathematical demonstration is the only genre of discourse that does not require appeal to the imagination, passions, or will. "Pure" conviction is the province of abstract logic. Logic, he says, "regards only the subject, which is examined solely for the sake of information"; however, such examination is socially impotent without persuasion. As he explains: "By the former [logic] a man's own conduct may be well-regulated, but the latter [persuasion] is absolutely necessary for diffusing valuable knowledge, and enforcing right rules of action upon others" (p. xlix). Whately points out that logic ascertains or judges truth; rhetoric communicates or establishes it. Each requires the other. When the philosopher expresses himself, he becomes a rhetorician (p. 5).

If a focus on pure information is socially impotent, a focus on pure entertainment is socially dysfunctional. Fenelon says that a "good" person seeks to please "only that he may urge justice and the other virtues by making them attractive" (p. 62). He takes the Platonic position that pleasure is not only a trivial, but a morally reprehensible, end. He says that some people use the example of the ancients to argue that many symbolic arts exist only to entertain. This, he says, is not true. Music, dancing, eloquence, and poetry "appeared to be for pleasure, but were in reality among the ancients a part of their deepest striving for morality and religion" (p. 68). Even eulogies, he continues, which classical theorists viewed as a species of epideictic, or ceremonial, address designed to elicit pleasure, should be thought of as opportunities for moral persuasion:

> A man must speak only to instruct. He must praise the great only in order that he may teach their virtues to the people, in order that he may induce the people to imitate them, in order that he may show glory and virtue to be inseparable (p. 73).

Implicit in Fenelon's precepts is the proposition that all communication influences. If a good person may use pleasure to teach virtue, an "evil person may use pleasure to teach vice." Or, more likely, a careless person may miscommunicate, that is, fail to take advantage of the opportunity to reinforce moral values and as a result reinforce social irresponsibility.

For the most part, later theorists of the modern period take for granted that commending truth is the function of pleasure. They generally reject the possibility of purely consummatory communication. They tend to ignore the possibility that pleasure may be used to commend "vice," for evil cannot be pleasurable.

Kames exemplifies the modern position that even those communication events that we might regard as recreational, if they make sense and produce pleasure, necessarily influence us. He points out that the fine arts, poetry, fiction, painting, etc., produce conviction and persuasion. For instance, the pleasure we obtain from literature grows out of sympathy. As we feel with the hero against the villain, we "exercise" our emotions. Over time this exercise results in a habitual response that can be activated whenever it is appropriate. Thus literary works—novels, poetry, and drama, especially—"teach" us to love virtue and hate vice. They build "propensities," the bases of emotions. Indirectly, then, literary works influence actions, because emotions are the bases of behavior (II., pp. 56–77).

Even informal communication, modern theorists point out, has impact above and beyond simple pleasure. Whately cautions us about the dangers of talking informally with those whose intellectual abilities are inferior to ours, for our own judgment will tend to atrophy as a result. Furthermore, discussion with friends who generally agree with our opinions is a form of influence—self-persuasion. A person in such a situation, he says, is "disposed to overrate [his friends'] judgment when it coincides with his own; and thence to find himself confirmed in what he thinks and feels, by listening to what is, in fact, the echo of his own voice" (p. 375).

De Quincey, as we have seen, emphasizes the influence of "good" conversation upon our conceptual abilities: From the exchange of ideas, "through sympathy . . . there sometimes arise glimpses and shy revelations of affinity, suggestion, relation, analogy, that could not have been approached through any avenues of mechanical study" (*Conversation*, p. 268). De Quincey points out that some conversants may aim simply at ornamental discourse. However, when this occurs, it tends to produce the opposite of pleasure. First, people may physically withdraw from the interaction, for "the elastic spring of conversation is gone if the talker is a mere showy man of talent" (p. 273). Second, people may withdraw psychologically: "If the great talker attempts the plan of showing off by firing cannonshot when everybody else is content with musketry, then undoubtedly he produces an impression, but at the expense of insulating himself from the sympathies of the company" (p. 280). Hence, as most modern theorists would agree, the "impact" of an address aimed solely to the imagination can, at most, be social rejection and is thus dysfunctional even in the limited sense in which it can exist.

Modern theorists' view of the nature of emotion prevents them from even considering the possibility of communication for the sole purpose of arousing the passions. As it is impossible to influence or persuade without awakening passions, so it is impossible to awaken passions without influencing or persuading. "Feelings" can and do exist independently of, and prior to, a particular communication act, but whenever people interact, certain feelings are necessarily made salient and become desires and motives. These awakened feelings must be resolved by action, which may be either mental or physical.

Kames explains the centrality of passion to human communication. Feelings, he says, grow out of perception. Those feelings which "arise from seeing and hearing are honoured with the name of *passion* or *emotion*" (II., p. 31). He distinguishes between passion and emotions. Emotions are simply notices of pleasure and pain. They do not necessarily lead to any additional action. Passion, however, is activated emotion; it leads to desire (II., p. 39). Furthermore, "the same mental act, that is termed a *desire* with respect to an end in view, is termed a *motive* with respect to its power of determining the will" (II., p. 44). Thus, emotion activated becomes passion, which creates desires for outcomes or motivation to act. This is the basic principle governing human behavior, for "no man ever proceeds to action but through some antecedent desire or impulse" (II., p. 41). The principle is in turn based on human nature: "Man is framed to be governed by reason: he generally acts with deliberation, and in order to bring about some desirable end . . ." (II., p. 43). Whether that end is "rational," or the behavior is consonant with it, may be questionable, but that activity is purposeful and is stimulated by passionate motivation is a "given" that the "successful" communicator necessarily takes into account.

Blair claims that "all high eloquence flows from passion" (I., p. 166). De Quincey says that sentiment is inherent in human communication; to express a thought is to express a feeling (*Rhetoric*, p. 119). Furthermore, he points out that discourse that does not engage the feelings has no possibility of lasting effect: "From the heart, from an interest of love or hatred, of hope or care, springs all permanent eloquence" (*Conversation*, p. 273). Likewise, Fenelon says: "Any speech which leaves you cold, which only acts to amuse you, and which does not affect your feelings, your heart, is not eloquent" (p. 87). Whately says that emotion is a constant factor in human nature and cannot be ignored: "Wherever there are men, learned or ignorant, civilized or barbarous, there are passions" (p. 206). He attacks those who claim that passions interfere with reason. They act, he says, "as if Reason alone could influence the Will which it no more can, than the eyes, which show a man his road, can enable him to move from place to place ' (p. 180). The only legitimate complaint one may make about emotional appeal, he says, is when one arouses passions that are inappropriate to the action urged. For instance, anger and pity should not be brought into play when the "expediency" of procedures is the question being considered (p. 177). Campbell, however, points out that such practices are likely to have at best temporary effects. If no convincing connection has been made between the motive and the objective, people are unlikely to take the action advocated. As he says, "If you would be ascertained of the truth of this, allow the assembly to disperse immediately after hearing you; give them time to cool, and then collect their votes, and it is a thousand to one you shall find that the charm is dissolved" (p. 108).

Conclusion

The full extent of the modern theorists' rational/emotional view of human nature, and the communication strategies they conceive to suit that nature, will become apparent in the following chapter, in which we shall investigate the modern treatment of the paradigm. For now, it is sufficient to note the modern insistence that all "effective" communication must make sense and must awaken feelings. Treatment of each of the parts of the paradigm reveals the pervasiveness of this view. Categorization is discussed in terms of the association of ideas and the association of passions. Conceptualization is discussed in terms of evidence (hard data) and argument (passionate proof). Symbolism is discussed in terms of literal clarity (factual language) and figurative force (vivid portraiture). Organization is discussed in terms of logical method (analysis and synthesis) and organic division (adjustment to "pathetic" perception). Finally, operationalization is discussed in terms of logical unities (of form and content) and spontaneous unities (interaction of ethos, pathos, and logos).

Chapter 5

The Modern Period: Treatment of the Paradigm

With the overview of the modern period in mind, we can now turn to a detailed analysis of the individual parts of the paradigm. Within each part we will note similarities and differences between modern and classical approaches and between modern and medieval and Renaissance approaches.

Categorization

Categorization has been defined as the perception, storage, and recall of data, or as the process by which data is transformed into information. Classical theorists tended to focus almost exclusively on the nature of recall, especially in terms of oral and unmediated public address. Though medieval and Renaissance scholars preserved the artificial memory systems that grew out of this tradition, they tended to focus on "right learning" and classification systems for storing information. In the later centuries of that period, the revival of secular education and spread of literacy led to a stirring of interest in the nature of perception. Especially in the writings of Francis Bacon we saw the beginning of what was to become the central focus in modern categorization theory: the study of how human beings sense and make sense of their world.

In the classical taxonomy of categorization, "natural memory" was conceived as an inherent ability of the human being to perceive, classify, store, and access experience and ideas. "Artificial memory" was conceived as a system for assisting natural memory by mentally visualizing symbolic, nonverbal images that would stimulate verbal recall. The main components of the system were analogy (visualizing an object or series of actions symbolic of the concept you want to express), vivid representation (selecting image objects or series of actions that are novel or dramatic), and order (mentally placing the images in coherent backgrounds, e.g., in the rooms of a house you know well).

181

As we have said, medieval scholars maintained this taxonomy, elaborating on it primarily by including the classical topics of conceptualization and adding the precepts of scriptual exegisis to classical methods of "artificial memory." These were treated as methods of storing information for later recall rather than as aids to extemporaneous communication. In the Renaissance, the emphasis on artificial methods of categorization began to give way to a focus on the natural processes of perception. John of Salisbury (1159) defined "natural" categorization as the "power" by which human beings sense, remember, imaginatively order and discriminate (classify), and comprehend reality (*Metalogicon*, IV. 9). Several centuries later, Francis Bacon (1620) presented a similar analysis. Human beings, he said, sense or perceive, form a prenotion (store sense perceptions in categories), develop emblems (ideas), and form hypotheses (imaginatively order ideas). These tentative beliefs can then be tested to discover their "fit" with reality (*Novum Organum*, I. 38-50).

Modern categorization theory is an elaboration of basic notions developed in the preceding periods. The emphasis in modern theory is upon "natural memory," which is treated in terms of concepts central to artificial classical systems, especially the processes of analogy and ordering, and in terms of the perceptual process outlined in the early Renaissance. Modern theories of what we might call "artificial" categorization, that is, of mediated or indirect stimulation of perception, focus on the classical notions of vivid representation and natural order as aids to imaginative recall. In modern taxonomy, "natural memory" is conceived of as the basic process by which human beings sense and make sense of reality. It is thus fundamental to human communication, the sharing, and mutual shaping, of perceptions of reality. "Artificial memory" is conceived as the conscious use of natural processes in communicating to and in being communicated with (see Fig. 5.1). Memorizing, which was of major importance in the predominantly oral culture of the classical and medieval periods, had ceased to be relevant to the print culture of the late Renaissance. By the beginning of the modern period, as we shall see in the discussion of operationalization, memorizing a formal public address had come to be considered a detriment to "natural" oral communication. Memorizing was, of course, irrelevant to written communication, which was the predominant mode.

Natural Memory

Experience is the key term in modern categorization theory, for experience is viewed as the fundamental source of knowledge, beliefs, and, ultimately, of action. Campbell's discussion of experience serves as a coherent outline of the basic tenets of modern theory. The process, as he outlines it, begins when an individual senses or perceives an object or event. This perception is then stored in the memory and associated with

---

Fig. 5.1   Modern Taxonomy of Categorization

I. "Natural Memory"—Perception as the basis of conception; the transformation of data into knowledge
    A. Sensing or perceiving objects and events
    B. Storing or retaining impressions in memory
    C. Association or classification of like impressions in terms of natural principles
    D. Generalizations or habitual associations
II. "Artificial Memory"—Mediated or indirect experience created through communication.
    A. Ideal presence—Selection and use of vivid images arranged in accordance with natural order and principles of association
    B. Taste—Natural reaction to symbolic products, formed by experience, based on perception and association

---

similar perceptions. These groupings of associations serve as the data for conceptions or generalizations. In other words, experience is the end result of the process of categorization.

Campbell explains that there are two initial sources of experiential knowledge, sense and memory. The senses "are the original inlets of perceptions." As soon as an individual perceives "any particular instance," then "the articles of information exhibited by them are developed on the memory. Remembrance instantly succeeds sensation, insomuch that the memory becomes the sole repository of the knowledge received from sense." The memory of the sense perception is a "voucher extant of past realities" or "prints that have been left by sensible impressions." These prints or vouchers, however, give us "knowledge only of individual facts"; a further operation is necessary before they are of practical use (*Phil. of Rhet.* p. 47).

Campbell explains: "Now, in order to render this knowledge useful to us, in discovering the nature of things and in regulating our conduct, we must associate the individual facts into classes about which we can make generalizations. Taking a number of like ideas (such as apples falling from trees, rocks falling from mountainsides, etc.) we tend to "forget" the specific instances and "remember" only the general idea (in this case, the law of gravity). The conclusion we draw is a belief based on experience or "habitual association" and is fundamental to all future learning. Campbell concludes his summary of the process of natural categorization by saying that this "classing and . . . generalizing" ability is what distinguishes human beings from other animals, allows the development and use of language, and makes one person intellectually superior to another (pp. 47–48).

This basic approach is fundamental to understanding modern communication theory. Every major theorist devotes at least some attention to these ideas and uses them as support for various precepts concerning symbolization, conceptualization, organization, and operationalization. In this section, we will summarize some of the central points; the application will be spelled out more fully in the discussion of each of the other parts of the paradigm.

In his discussion of categorization, Kames distinguishes between perception and sensing:

> *Perceiving* is a general term for hearing, seeing, tasting, touching, smelling, and therefore *perception* signifies every act by which we are made acquainted with external objects. . . . *Sensation* properly signifies that internal act by which we are made conscious of pleasure or pain felt at the organ of sense (II., p. 501).

Thus sensing is an internal response that may be activated by a wide variety of kinds of objects; perceiving is a physical activity. The primary importance of this distinction is that we do not sense everything we perceive. We select certain things to attend to. Those that we attend to we store in the memory and, as Kames says, "This indistinct secondary perception of an object is termed *an idea*" (II., p. 505).

Ideas are important, for they are the fundamental units of thought, "the chief materials employ'd in reasoning and reflecting" (II., p. 501), and thought is the process by which data is transformed into knowledge. Thought, says Kames, is the association of ideas "in a train" by natural principles: "We find by experience that ideas are connected in the mind precisely as their objects are externally," by cause and effect, contiguity in space and time, resemblance, contrast, antecedent and consequent; through these connectives, one idea can "suggest" another (I., p. 17). Campbell says that thought results from the natural "tendency of the mind to associate ideas under the notions of causes, effects, or adjuncts" (p. 50). The "naturalness," or inevitability, of this process is attested to by Kames:

> "A man while awake is sensible of a continued train of perceptions and ideas passing in his mind. It requires no activity on his part to carry on the train: nor can he at will add to the train any idea which has no connection with it" (I., p. 15).

This notion of a "train" of ideas and perceptions—what the other major theorists call "association"—is fundamental to modern categorization theory.

Priestley says that "The principle of association is predominant in every thing relating to our intellectual faculties" (p. 129), and the general principles by which we associate ideas are the product "of the analogy or uniformity of things" (p. 165). Thus, all pleasurable objects are alike in their basic properties: "*uniformity, variety, proportion,* or *a fitness to some useful end"* (p. 132). These complex ideas grow out of initial, discrete sense perceptions: "All our intellectual pleasures and pains consist of nothing but the simple pleasures and pains of sense, commixed and combined together in infinitely-various degrees and proportions, so as to be separately indistinguishable" (p. 137).

De Quincey likewise describes the generalizing faculty as the product of association of like ideas to derive new and more complex ideas: "All reasoning is carried on discursively; that is . . . by running about to the right and to the left, laying the separate notices together, and thence mediately deriving some third apprehension" (*Rhetoric*, p. 103). Furthermore, he too says that this process depends upon analogy:

> Now, to apprehend and detect more relations, or to pursue them steadily, is a process absolutely impossible without the intervention of physical analogies. To say, therefore, that a man is a great thinker, or a fine thinker, is but another expression for saying that he has a *schematizing* (or to use a plainer but less accurate expression, a figurative) understanding (*Rhetoric*, p. 103).

Edmund Burke, says De Quincey, is one of these great thinkers, for he argues in analogies, his figures "incarnate" rather than "dress" his thoughts.[1]

"Artificial Memory"

The experiential basis of human categorization, modern theorists explain, has important implications for communicating to others. Kames writes that "Our first perceptions are of external objects, and our first attachments are to them"; thus all other sensations (internal responses) are more or less weak in comparison (I., p. 4). Blair explains that our internal responses are "most strongly excited by sensation. . . . Next to the influence of sense, is that of memory; and next to memory, is the influence of the imagination" (II., p. 385). Likewise, Campbell says that our strongest excitement comes from the senses first, the memory second, and the imagination third (p. 81). Unfortunately, in communicating with others, it is the weakest of these, the imagination, which is addressed. Language, Kames says, is the means by which an individual attempts to "communicate his perceptions" to others (II., p. 510); however, language results not in immediate sense perception but in "conception." Kames explains, "Conception is different from perception. The latter includes a conviction of the reality of its object; the former does

---

[1] De Quincey's assertion that Burke argues in analogies has since been tested and supported. See Nancy L. Harper, "The Role of Imagery in Edmund Burke's *Reflections on the Revolution in France (A Computer Assisted Analysis)."* (Unpublished Ph.D. Dissertation, University of Iowa, 1973).

not. . . . When I describe a picture [idea or notion] to another, the idea he forms of it is termed a conception" (II., p. 502). Thus the central problem for the communicator is, as Campbell explains, to "make the ideas he summons up in the imaginations of his hearers, resemble, in lustre and steadiness, those of sensation and remembrance" (p. 81). Blair, though he does not cite Campbell, makes a similar statement. The communicator, he says, must "strike the imagination of the hearers with circumstances, which, in lustre and steadiness, resemble those of sensation and remembrance" (II., p. 384).

Ideal Presence   The manner in which ideas of imagination may be made to resemble those of sense and memory is most succinctly explained by Kames. First, he says, it is important to note that "By the power of memory a thing formerly seen may be recalled to the mind with different degrees of accuracy" (I. p. 80). Now, he says, "In a complete idea of memory there is no past or future: a thing recalled to the mind . . . is perceived as in our view, and consequently as existing at present" (I., p. 81). This "complete idea" he calls "ideal presence." As he explains, "In contradistinction to real presence, ideal presence may be properly termed *a waking dream*; because, like a dream, it vanisheth the moment we reflect on our present situation . . ." (I., p. 82). Ideal presence is distinguished from "reflective remembrance," which is recalling *that* you experienced something as opposed to re-experiencing it. Reflective remembrance, says Kames, makes little impression for it "cannot warm us into any emotion," while ideal presence brings with it all the sensations which would attend a real event (I., pp. 83–85). Because, as Kames has explained, sensation is an internal act, we do not necessarily need to perceive a physical object in order to react "as if" it were present. In fact, he says, "Every thing one is conscious of, whether external or internal, passions, emotions, thinking, resolving, willing, heat, cold, etc. as well as external objects, may be recalled . . . by the power of memory" (II., p. 508).

In terms of the application of the notion of ideal presence, Kames explains that the senses of sight and hearing are the highest senses. Because visual and aural sensations enter the mind without any conscious organic impression, they combine the attributes of both organic and intellectual pleasures. Priestley, citing Kames, makes similar observations. Of the "pleasures of the imagination," he says, those arising from the eye and the ear are the strongest for they are least inhibited by the awareness of physical sensation. Thus, in the presence of visual and aural stimuli, "a person, for the time, enters into, adopts, and is activated by, the sentiments that are presented to his mind" (pp. 125–126).

Although, in theory, sight and hearing seem to be treated as equally strong, it is sight that emerges as the primary topic of concern. (Given that this is the age of print, such an occurence should not be surprising.)

Kames provides the rationale: "The original perception of an object of sight is more complete, lively, and distinct than that of any other object" (II., p. 509). Thus, the secondary perception of visuals, through eliciting "pictures" in the mind, is likely to have the most affect on a receiver of messages. It is axiomatic with the modern theorists that "to see is to feel and to feel is to believe."

We can summarize the importance of modern categorization theory in terms of communicating with others as follows: Sight is the source of our strongest sense preceptions. In communicating, our goal is to approximate as closely as possible the sensation of direct experience, because experience creates the strongest beliefs. Therefore we should "paint" pictures in words that will create ideal presence. Also, since memory is second only to experience in strength of impression, we should endeavor to make our messages memorable—again, through vivid pictures. But since belief is as important as impression and memory, we should always attend to "natural order" in our paintings, for people will not believe a portrait that does not seem plausible. Finally, passion is the source of all human behavior, and the strongest emotional response is to experience; therefore we should make use of the natural associational principles of proximity, interest, etc., in order to involve our audience experientially. Obviously, this approach to categorization has important implications in terms of designing and responding to messages.

Blair says that the secret of successful communication is "to paint the object of that passion which we wish to raise, in the most natural and striking manner; to describe it with such circumstances as are likely to awaken it in the minds of others" (II., p. 385). Fenelon personifies persuasion saying that "not only does she reveal the truth, but she also paints it as pleasant" (p. 90). Campbell emphasizes the importance of "vivid" images because "nothing can operate on the mind which is not present to it" (p. 75). Furthermore, he says, it is a basic principle that

> passion to an absent object may be excited by eloquence, which, by enlivening and invigorating the ideas of the imagination, makes them resemble the impressions of sense and the traces of memory; and in this respect hath an effect on the mind similar to that produced by the telescope on the sight; things remote are brought near, things obscure rendered conspicuous (p. 94).

Modern theorists also agree that in order to make an impression, a communicator must, as Campbell puts it, "engage the help of memory" (p. 75). He explains that memory is a "means to some further end; and as such is more or less necessary on every occasion" (p. 76). One of the major criticisms one can make of a speaker, Fenelon says, is that "almost nothing of all that he has said remains in the heads of those who have listened to him" (p. 103).

The memory can be engaged and assist the workings of the imagination in two ways. First, as Campbell explains, "the credibility of the fact is the sum of the evidence of all the arguments, often independent of one another, brought to support it." Thus, in order for the receiver to make sense of the evidence, it must be presented in terms of "natural connexions," or the habitual associational patterns that the receivers have learned from experience, i.e., cause, effect, adjuncts, (p. 75). Natural order thus contributes to ideal presence by approximating actual perception. It also, as Whately puts it, awakens a "multitude of associations" and thus "serves as a help to the [long-term] memory" (p. 93). Finally, natural order contributes to belief and accounts for the working of loops in messages. If the chain of ideas seems plausible, has internal consistency, and does not thwart the hearers' habitual "conclusions and anticipations," then they are more likely to make the initial commitment to believe that it "could be" true (Campbell, p. 82). Kames adds the further justification that natural order is pleasurable: "Every work of art that is conformable to the natural course of our ideas, is so far agreeable; and every work of art that reverses that course, is so far disagreeable" (I., p. 25).

The second way that memory is involved in making an impression on a receiver is through the emotions. As Fenelon explains, "In order to make a durable impression, one must help the mind by touching the passions" (pp. 103–104). Kames says, "It is by means of ideal presence that our passions are excited; and till words produce that charm, they avail nothing; even real events entitled to our belief, must be conceived as present and passing in our sight, before they can move us" (II., p. 89). Furthermore, he says, "Emotions and passions are connected with perceptions and ideas so intimately as not to have any independent existence" (II., p. 107). Priestley explains that certain subjects have more associations that, by exciting the passions, stimulate memory and hence approximate experience:

> As the sentiments and actions of our fellow-creatures are more interesting to us than anything belonging to inanimate nature, or the actions of brute animals, a much greater variety of sensations and ideas must have been excited by them, and consequently adhere to them by the principles of association (p. 247).

Thus association of ideas accounts for the impact of figures of speech such as personification. Thus also it accounts for what Campbell calls the "sources of argument" affecting the passions. We will deal with these in more detail in discussing conceptualization; however, for example, proximity of time and place tend to excite more associations and stronger emotions. The general subject of murder is not likely to be as involving as is an account of murder which occurred last night in "our own neighborhood," or to someone we at least knew by sight (pp. 87–88).

From observations such as these, modern theorists are led to conclude that not only is there natural association among ideas, but that
emotions also associate. Priestley says, "All passions are communicative,
and are universally propagated by the genuine expressions of them" (p.
110). This principle is basic to the functions of sympathy, ethos, and
logos discussed under conceptualization as well as to the advocacy of the
"natural manner" of operationalization. What is important here, however, is the affect of the "communication of passions" on perception.[2]

Kames gives what is probably the most elaborate and detailed account of the nature of this effect. He writes:

> That our actions are too much influenced by passion is a known
> truth; but it is not less certain, though not so commonly observed,
> that passion hath also an influence upon our perceptions, opinions,
> and beliefs. For example, the opinions we form of men and things,
> are generally directed by affection: an advice given by a man of
> figure hath greater weight; the same advice from one in a low
> condition is utterly neglected . . . (p. 142).

Kames continues with a number of other examples of the influence of
passion on categorization. For instance, he says that the communication
of passions accounts for selective retention; that prejudice or "tone of
mind" affects our memory is obvious because "the arguments of a favorite
opinion are always at hand, while we often search in vain for those that
cross our inclination" (II., p. 144).

Along the same lines, gratitude tends to magnify good qualities
while envy magnifies bad (II., pp. 145–146). Anger can lead us to
"believe" that an accident was purposeful as when we personify "a rock or
stone when it occasions bodily pain" in order to justify our feeling of
"resentment" and desire for revenge (II., p. 148). Justification leads to a
number of kinds of distortion. For instance, good news is accepted "upon
very slender evidence" and "if a future event be either much wished or
dreaded, the mind never fails to augment the probability beyond truth"
(II., pp. 151–153). Our measurement of time and conception of space
can likewise be distorted by passions. Busyness makes the time seem
shorter and a cluttered room seems smaller (II., pp. 155–157). Not only
the number, but the kind, of perceptions impinging upon us affects our
judgments. Thus, time spent perceiving a number of real objects seems
longer than the same time spent with a number of ideas, because the real
objects are easier to remember as separate instances (II., p. 160).

Finally, Kames says, emotions resemble their causes: "Sluggish motion, for example, causeth a languid, unpleasant feeling. . . . A sound in
a high key, cheers the mind by raising it. . . . A constrained posture,

---

[2] In contemporary terminology, we usually refer to this phenomenon as "selectivity" and
speak of selective perception, selective retention, and selective attention.

uneasy to the man himself, is disagreeable to the spectator. . . . A part-
ing scene between lovers or friends produceth in the spectator a sort of
pity . . . (II., pp. 167–170). This principle accounts for the salutory
effects of good literature. Virtuous scenes "warm the mind" and enliven
"the propensity we have to such action" to the extent that we actually
feel the emotion being portrayed (II., p. 56). Kames concludes that the
strongest emotion is self-love (II., p. 63) and that this accounts for "a
strong tendency in our nature to justify our passions as well as our actions, not to others only, but even to ourselves" (II., p. 143). Thus,
when we feel desire we seek to gratify it. In either case, rationality often
takes a backseat to emotion: "Reason may proclaim our duty, but the
Will, influenced by passion, makes gratification always welcome. . . .
and where proper objects are wanting, it clings to any object at hand
without distinction" (II., p. 182).

To modern theorists, categorization is thus extremely important in
terms of communicating to others. When communication is viewed as
mediated, or indirectly experienced, the concepts which cluster around
"ideal presence" (vivid, natural expression; the association of ideas and
of emotions) become truly fundamental to all the communicator's
message-related decisions. As we have indicated, this unique emphasis
on categorization significantly affects modern treatment of the basic
paradigm. It also serves as the basis of the pervasive concern of modern
theorists with "taste."

Taste   If ideal presence can be viewed as a theory of categorization in terms of message sending, then taste can be viewed as a theory of
categorization in terms of message receiving. Essentially, "taste" is conceived of as the faculty or power that allows individuals to judge the
artistic merits of human products. Kames, for instance, defines the objects of taste as "painting, sculpture, music, gardening, and architecture"
as well as "eloquence" (I., p. 5). In other words, any human creation
that appeals primarily to the "higher senses" of sight and hearing is a
"fine art" and thus appeals to the "taste" (I., pp. 2–4). For the most part,
however, taste is discussed in terms of discourse, being the central concept in modern rhetorical and literary criticism.[3] Though nearly every

[3] Modern theorists tend not to view rhetorical discourse (oratory, essays, or instrumental
symbolic behavior) and literary discourse (poetry, fiction, or consummatory symbolic
behavior) as distinct in any important way. Both kinds of discourse, they argue, work for
the three ends of informing, pleasing, and persuading, and both achieve these ends
through vivid portraiture. Blair says that there is no need to be "precise about the
boundaries" (III., pp. 80–81). Fenelon says that the only difference is the higher degree
of "ecstasy" in the poet's language (p. 93). Thus the standards of taste are the same for
critiquing a newspaper editorial and a novel. In fact, say critics like Priestley and Kames,
the principles of harmony, uniformity, etc., apply to architecture, gardening, interior
decorating, etc., as well as to verbal messages. A poorly organized essay offends the same
sensibilities, and in the same manner, as does an unweeded flower plot!

modern literary figure, communication theorist, and philosopher has written an essay on taste, and although there have been a number of controversies surrounding the concept, here we will review not the history of "taste," but the communicative principles most theroists seem to agree are subsumed under that concept.

Blair defines taste as "the power of receiving pleasures from the beauties of nature and of art" and as "a faculty common to all men" (I., pp. 18–19). This power or faculty, he says, is an innate ability, like our ability to perceive colors, shapes, etc.: "The faculty by which we relish [artistic] beauties seems more allied to a feeling of sense, than to a process of the understanding" (I. 18). Thus the peasant and the philosopher, the boy and the man, are alike in their inherent ability to perceive and respond to beauty and ugliness.

Priestley explains that this inherent ability is the product of the association of ideas. He says that the experience we have of a pleasurable place or event has "connected with it a variety of distinct pleasures," which become "separately indistinguishable" (p. 129). Thus, when taking a walk in the country, we may experience the pleasant smell of grass, the songs of birds, etc., and these sensations form a complex emotion that is awakened when we are reminded of it in reading a book or viewing a landscape painting. In other words, through the communication of passions, complex associations "transfer" to other, similar objects (pp. 130–132).

Kames likewise views the ability to respond to the beauties of art as inherent and analogous to experiential knowledge, especially to moral knowledge:

> [A] taste in the fine arts goes hand in hand with the moral sense, to which indeed it is nearly allied: both of them discover what is right and what is wrong: fashion, temper, and education, have an influence upon both to vitiate them, or to preserve them pure and untainted: neither of them are arbitrary and local; being rooted in human nature, and governed by principles common to all men (I., p. 5).

Thus, says Kames, that "there is no disputing about taste" is true only with respect to trivialities, not with respect to morals or fine arts. This, he says, is founded in nature: "There appears a remarkable uniformity among creatures of the same kind. . . . This common nature is conceived to be a model or standard for each individual that belongs to the kind" (II., p. 484). Furthermore, "We are so constituted as to conceive that this common nature, is not only invariable, but also *perfect* or *right*; and consequently that individuals *ought* to be made conformable to it" (II., p. 485). This accounts for standards of taste in morals and arts: What conforms is good, what strays is bad. We can readily see the truth of this observation, Kames says, if we consider our own daily interactions: "The uneasiness a man feels when in matters of importance his opinions are rejected by others" and "the pleasure we take in those who espouse the same principles and opinions as ourselves, as well as the aversion we have at those who differ from us" can be accounted for only in terms of a basic belief in a common standard (II., pp. 486–487).

In other words, in the modern framework of message perception, human beings react to "art" as they do to all other external data. The ability to perceive harmony, discord, uniformity, variety, etc., is inherent. The associational patterns by which these perceptions are ordered are more or less normative. It is the "more or less," however, which accounts for differences in the way individuals react to symbolic data. Blair says that some people may be more sensitive to artistic excellence because they have "nicer organs and finer internal powers" (II., p. 21). Whately, like Kames, distinguishes between sensing and perceiving. He explains that people can "see" the same thing differently: "The object that strikes the eye is to all of these persons the same; the difference of the impressions produced on the minds of each is referable to the differences in their minds" (p. 89). Priestley explains that some individuals may be more capable of responding to ideal presence: "The more vivid are a man's ideas, and the greater is his general sensibility, the more entirely, and with the greater facility, doth he adapt himself to the situations he is viewing" (p. 127). For the most part, however, most modern communication theorists agree with Blair that differences in taste are more attributable to difference in "education and culture" than to differences in perceptual ability (I. 21).

As we have seen, modern categorization theory posits that responses to literary and visual arts are not exactly analogous to sensual perceptions of "real" objects and events. The sensual response is mediated by memory and imagination. Thus, as Edmund Burke points out, taste is not a simple faculty; it is "partly made up of a perception of the primary pleasures of the sense, of the secondary pleasures of the imagination, and of the conclusions of the reasoning faculty, concerning the various relations of these, and concerning the human passions, manners and actions."[4]

Priestley explains that because people have different primary experiences, they develop different associations. For instance, a person who was forced to study Shakespeare in a cruel and harsh environment may never be able to appreciate Hamlet. Contact with this object, rather than raising pleasurable associations in the imagination, may provoke painful images in the memory. This accounts for diversity of taste. On the other hand, says Priestley, there is great similarity of taste throughout the civilized world. The relatively recent advancements in printing and

---

[4] Edmund Burke, "A Philosophical Inquiry into the Origins of Our Ideas of the Sublime and Beautiful; with an Introductory Essay on Taste," Works of the Right Honorable Edmund Burke (London, 1826), pp. 99–100.

the increasing literacy due to common education seems to be leading to what we might call a "mass society" and therefore to a universal standard of taste.

Unfortunately, most modern theorists are both vague and ethnocentric about this "universal standard."[5] Reduced to its basics, good taste turns out to be "what I and people like me agree upon." Blair says that for the standard we should look to civilized, enlightened, and unperverted cultures. Kames adds that, within such cultures, we should look to the "general opinion and general practice" of the most advantaged and educated. Savages, laborers, and the voluptuously wealthy must be excluded. Only those with "good" education, much experience, natural delicacy, and habits of reflection and moderation can provide the standard (II., pp. 489–496).[6]

Although the concept of taste seems to degenerate into elitist generalities, the widespread attention it began to receive contributed to the new focus on message-receiving as an active and vital communication activity. Thus embryonic trends noted in medieval and Renaissance theory—Augustine's treatment of "interpretation" in Christian writing and John of Salisbury's and Francis Bacon's perception-based approach to categorization—are brought to fruition in the modern period. As we have seen, more philosophic and theoretic scholars, such as Campbell, paid little attention to the controversy over taste; rather they concentrated on building a theory of differential response grounded in principles of experiential learning.

Conceptualization

We have defined conceptualization as the process by which an individual assigns meaning to data in light of some present concern. More generally, it is that branch of human communication theory concerned with the nature of knowledge and the processes of information acquisition and interpretation. Classical theorists viewed conceptualization ("invention") as a creative process and as the focal point of communication theory. The complex theoretic taxonomy they developed was based on a thorough analysis of the subject, the occasion, and the basic principles of human nature buttressed by an extensive liberal education.

As we have seen, in the medieval and Renaissance periods, "invention became revelation." Authorized Christian doctrine dictated "truth." The analytic topics of classical theory were reduced to a system for storing commonplaces, prepackaged materials for copia and adornment. Communication ceased to be thought of as essentially creative and

[5] For a more detailed discussion of the various approaches of modern theorists and philosophers, see John Waite Bowers, "A Comparative Analysis of Hugh Blair's Essay on Taste," *Quarterly Journal of Speech*, 47 (1961), pp. 384–389.
[6] In other words, the arbiters of taste are "recognized authorities" like Blair and Kames!

began to be viewed as essentially presentational. "What to say" was given by the absolute authority of the Church and the mechanical authority of the topics. About the only choices left to a communicator were in terms of "how to say it."

In spirit, modern theorists are much closer to Aristotle and Cicero than to Cassiodorus and Erasmus. In reference to medieval and Renaissance scholars, we have said that they preserved the form but discarded the substance of classical conceptualization theory. In the modern period, the reverse is true. Modern theorists resurrect the substance but, for the most part, discard the form (see Fig. 5.2). For example, most reject the topical system of analysis, replacing it with a system based on the nature of evidence and the functioning of the intellectual faculties. The modes of proof are treated neither as methods for analyzing subjects and situations nor as "appeals" to be superadded to messages. Instead, they are used as general principles to account for the effects of evidence

---

Fig. 5.2   Modern Taxonomy of Conceptualization

I. Inartistic—Evidence; research; information acquisition
   A. General—Broad liberal education; culturally defined knowledge
   B. Specific—Investigation of the subject matter; expert knowledge
   C. Intuitive—Knowledge based on intellection, consciousness, and common sense
II. Artistic—Interpretation and use; information management
   A. Deductive reasoning
      1. Demonstrative—"Scientific" reasoning based on intellection; revelation of truth through "necessary" relationship of ideas; "pure" logos
      2. Moral—Probable reasoning leading to opinions, beliefs, and attitudes on contingent matters
         a. Experience—Appeal to natural principles
         b. Analogy—Appeal to resemblances
         c. Testimony—Appeal to the experience of another; dependence on ethos
         d. Calculation of chances—Statistical probability
   B. Argumentative reasoning—Address to the faculties in order to convince and persuade
      1. Understanding—Establishment of ethos and logos through reference to familiar ideas, habitual thought patterns, and appropriate level of abstraction
      2. Memory—Establishment of logos and pathos through visualization of ideas in natural relationships
      3. Imagination—Creation of sympathy through introduction of vivid, sublime, novel ideas; creation of ideal presence
      4. Passion—Creation of pathos; evocation and fulfillment of desire
         a. Circumstances affecting pathos—Probability, plausibility, importance, proximity of time, connection of place, relation to persons involved, interest in consequences, auxiliaries
         b. Circumstances calming passions—Wit and ridicule, excitation of contrary motives and passions, opposites of affecting circumstances (i.e., improbability, etc.)

and argumentation. A "new" mode of proof, sympathy, becomes a central explanatory concept that works through combining ethos and pathos or, sometimes, logos and pathos. The three basic genres of communication situations (deliberative, forensic, and epideictic) are retained, though the epideictic genre is expanded to include preaching, on the one hand, and "fine" literature, on the other.[7] Finally, audience analysis becomes a much more central concern than it had been in either the classical or the medieval and Renaissance periods. The uniquely modern emphasis on categorization provides a new and firmer foundation for analysis of the interaction of the basic variables of subject, source, situation, and receiver. In other words, conceptualization theory is developed in the context of the central question of the period: "How do human beings come to know, to believe, and to act?"

Like classical theorists, modern theorists discuss conceptualization in terms of two basic classifications. The first, *inartistic conceptualization*, posits that certain kinds of information exist prior to, and independent of, a particular communication situation. Some of this information "belongs" to particular subject matters and can be acquired through research and education. Other inartistic information may be referred to as that to which everyone has access because of inherent characteristics of human nature. Both classical and modern theorists view inartistic conceptualization as essentially "pre-rhetorical," or outside the domain of communication theory *per se*.

The second classification, *artistic conceptualization*, is the management of information. It requires judgment and creative decision-making and is therefore the more proper and central object of communication theory. The basic principle here is that the outcome of any particular communicative interaction is dependent upon a complex of decisions taking into account relationships between information and people. As Campbell puts it:

> Eloquence [the art of effective communication] not only considers the subject, but also the speaker and the hearers, and both the subject and the speaker for the sake of the hearers, or rather for the sake of the effect intended to be produced in them (p. 33).

The balance between inartistic and artistic considerations implied in this statement is essentially classical. The central focus in both ancient and modern theory is on artistic conceptualization.[8] Modern theorists,

---

[7] Before the modern period, preaching, literature, and other forms of discourse (e.g., letters and essays) had been treated as having a "rhetoric" of their own, parallel to, but separate from, instrumental oral communication.

[8] A number of contemporary scholars argue that modern theorists reverse the classical balance between inartistic and artistic, focusing on "research" and slighting "invention." For examples of this position, see Douglas Ehninger, "Introduction," in Richard Whate-

however, tend to redress the extreme imbalance that existed in the classical approach. Given that this period is an age of science and psychology, it is not surprising that modern theorists place more emphasis on research and intuitive knowledge than did classical theorists.

Inartistic Conceptualization

General Knowledge   Harking back to the example of Aristotle and the precepts of theorists like Cicero and Quintilian, most modern theorists assert the need for a broad general education. Blair writes, "The study of Rhetoric and Belles Lettres supposes and requires a proper acquaintance with the rest of the liberal arts. It embraces them all within its circle . . ." (I., p. 4). In other words, he explains, the best communicators are also scholars; they have a ready store of knowledge from literature, history, biography, science, etc. This knowledge beautifies and commends their discourse, but, more important, it serves as a basis for arguments, proofs, and illustrations. For example, predictions about future events can be supported through reference to trends in history (pp. 443–435). Along these same lines, Priestley recommends general knowledge of grammar, logical reasoning, and human nature, especially the "passions, prejudices, interest, and views" of identifiable social and cultural groups (p. 3).

Echoing a number of previous writers on communication (e.g., Plato, Aristotle, John of Salisbury, Bacon, etc.), De Quincey reminds us that formal education and academic research may be one way of acquiring ideas, but people are also good sources: "Social discussion supplies the natural integration for the deficiencies of private and sequestered study" (*Conversation*, p. 270). He even goes so far as to claim that of all the means for clearing up "intellectual perplexities," arriving at "sudden revelation," and seeing a complex question "under some difference of angle," the "chief by right and potentiality is CONVERSATION" (*Conversation*, pp. 270–279).

ly, *Elements of Rhetoric* (Carbondale: Southern Illinois University Press, 1963); Lloyd F. Bitzer, "Introduction," in George Campbell, *The Philosphy of Rhetoric* (Carbondale: Southern Illinois University Press, 1963); Wilbur Samuel Howell, *Eighteenth-Century British Logic and Rhetoric* (Princeton: Princeton University Press, 1971), pp. 442–443. The observation of these scholars is certainly true in the sense that modern theorists reject the "artificial" topical system and the primacy of the syllogism. They also give somewhat more space to inartistic information acquisition than did classical theorists, and they verbally emphasize its importance. On the other hand, as a glance at the taxonomy reveals, (Fig. 5.2) the modern theorists find little scope in theorizing about "research"; they focus on the creative interpretation and use of such information. Spatially, modern treatises seldom devote more than a few, usually introductory, pages to inartistic conceptualization. The bulk of most modern treatments of conceptualization is devoted to the process of reasoning, the nature of argument and use of evidence, and the analysis of form, of situational constraints, and of source and receiver characteristics—in other words, to the "artistic" management of information.

Fenelon sums up the issue of general study in preparation for specific analysis of a subject, saying that though it takes "many years" to develop the necessary resources, it is nevertheless essential to spend this time.

[I]f you have only applied yourself to the preparation of particular subjects, you are reduced to paying off in the currency of aphorisms and antithesis; you treat only the commonplaces; you utter nothing but incoherencies; you sew up rags not made for each other; you do not show the real principles of things; you are restricted to superficial and often false arguments; you are incapable of showing the full extent of truth, because all general truths have necessary interconnections, and it is obligatory to know almost all of them in order to handle adequately a particular one (p. 85).

In addition to providing a rationale for broad learning, Fenelon's statement has other important implications. First, it continues the long tradition (from Plato to the present) of insisting that the "orator" be a "philosopher" first, or, as the medieval and Renaissance scholars would say, that since every particular question is a species of a more general one, "dialectic" precedes "rhetoric." Second, and more important, it exemplifies the almost universal modern rejection of the topical system of analysis as developed by medieval and Renaissance scholars.

Investigation of the Subject   Modern theorists are united in their agreement that the first requirement for a communicator is that he know what he is talking about. Furthermore, they agree that this "expert knowledge" grows out of research into the subject matter. Speaking of the Christian preacher, Fenelon says, "The most essential trait of a preacher is to be instructive. But he must be well-instructed in order to instruct others . . ." (p. 121). On the authority of Bacon,[9] Priestley calls conceptualization "recollection" and explains its fundamental principle: "In order to speak, or write, well upon any subject, it is necessary that that subject be thoroughly understood, that every argument which is to be used be previously collected, and the value of it ascertained" (p. 3). In other words, "recollection" requires thorough research and analysis in order to discover what *can* be said and to select "what is proper" to be said given a particular purpose.

Whately explains that "*conveying truth*," which is the "*Rhetorical Process*," requires first "*Investigation*," then "*Proofs*." The first step for the communicator "is to lay down distinctly in his own mind the proposition or propositions to be proved" (p. 35). Limited propositions are necessary,

---

[9] See the discussion of Bacon's critique of medieval "inventional" theory in Chap. 3. In the *Advancement of Learning,* Bacon explains that the topical system is a method for recovering or recollecting knowledge, not a method of discovering new knowledge (II.xiii.6).

he explains, because they narrow the field of inquiry, thus preventing the kind of "vague and trite" remarks prompted by general and extensive subjects like "love" or "friendship" (pp. 36–38). In order to arrive at such propositions, Whately recommends a modified version of the Roman "status" system for analysis of legal questions.[10] He advises the communicator to ask, "What is the fact? secondly, Why (i.e., from what Cause) is it? or, in other words, how is it to be accounted for? and thirdly, What Consequence results from it?" Though this method was originally a part of the artistic system of topics, Whately, like most modern theorists, views it as a general method for researching any subject. The "knowledge" which results from it is not "rhetorical"; it is "borrowed" from the subject matter, that is, from politics, law, ethics, etc. (p. 40).

Fenelon was one of the earliest (1679) and most adamant opponents of the medieval "commonplace" approach to conceptualization. He says that research, knowing the subject, will yield sufficient and relevant material as well as substantive arguments and convincing proof. In terms of conceptualizing sermons, he says, "A preacher who knows that book [the Bible] well" will not need artificial stimuli, for "one speaks easily of things when he fully knows and loves them" (p. 135). Furthermore, he says, "The real way to prove the truth of religion is to explain it well. It proves itself when you give the true idea of it" (p. 141). Going beyond the special situation of the preacher, he criticizes the topics for epideictic discourse "in praise of a person." He says, "The real way to make a portrait that will be a genuine likeness is to paint the whole man. He must be put before the eyes of the listeners precisely as he speaks and acts" (p. 152). Such a portrait might include many of the classical topics (events, deeds, life phases, etc.), but these will emerge from the consideration of the particular individual who is the subject rather than being imposed, whether or not appropriate, by a prior formula.

A few of the modern theorists do attempt to defend the worth of the topical system. Priestley explains that the topics are not really useful for "inventing" knowledge but can sometimes aid in analyzing and researching a subject, that is, "recollection" or the "recovery" of knowledge. Defining topical conceptualization as "artificial recollection," he says that it is a method of summoning to mind information the communicator knows but might not remember in relation to a particular need. It is also useful because it insures thorough research.

Priestley devotes about ten pages (pp. 10–20) to listing and defining the two classes of topics: (1) commonplaces or general topics— definition, adjuncts, antecedents, consequents, means, analogy, contrariety, example, authority, and (2) particular topics—facts (the time,

---

[10] The status system was the basis of forensic argument. It consisted of three topics: *an sit* (what happened), *quid sit* (what the result was), and *qual sit* (why it happened).

place, motive, manner, instrument, etc.), persons (the sex, age, qualifications, education, profession, etc.), and laws (their ambiguity, intention, form, etc.). These topics, he says, work through the laws of association. They can help the communicator decide how to handle his subject, for recollection is "the introduction of one idea into the mind by means of another with which it was previously associated" (p. 22). He does not claim that everyone must know this artificial system, but he insists that all use it, whether or not they know the names of the ideas. Furthermore, he says it can be useful to know the system consciously, for "is it not better to sit down to composition provided with a tolerably complete list of these topics digested with care and precision" than to find materials haphazardly? (p. 23). Other advantages are that a list of topics can assist in judging the works of others, in determining whether they have covered the subject thoroughly and selected the best arguments. A list is also useful to "young persons" who have little experience in formal communication and to preachers and moral essayists whose material is not original and who therefore need to find new ways to say old things.

In concluding his discussion, however, Priestley seems to admit that learning the topical system is probably unimportant in the long run. Through experience we all use them anyway, in a "secondarily automatic manner" that requires no conscious attention to a list. Thus, in spite of what seems a reasonable and sound defense of the classical (as opposed to medieval) topical system, Priestley seems to arrive at a position similar to that of his contemporaries. Blair summarizes this position when he says that the topics yield copious but often trivial declamation: "What is truly solid and persuasive must be drawn . . . from a thorough knowledge of the subject, and profound meditation on it" in the context of a broad liberal education (II., pp. 370–372).

Intuitive Knowledge   In addition to education and research, modern theorists posit a third kind of inartistic conceptualization. This source, generally referred to as "intuitive," grows out of modern categorization theory. Campbell calls conceptualization "the art of thinking" and claims that it is as essential to communication as is "the art of speaking" (p. 139). Drawing on associational psychology, faculty psychology, common sense philosophy, and classical rhetorical theory, he identifies two basic kinds of information. The first comes from intuitive sources. It is inartistic, for intuition is an inherent power of the human mind. The second, deductive, is artistic, for it grows out of conscious manipulation of data that is apprehended intuitively.

Intuitive knowledge, Campbell explains, is the most basic or central, for it has to do with our innate belief in "objective" physical realities. He identifies three "sources of evidence" that make up intuitive knowledge. The first, *intellection*, is the source of our beliefs in such things as mathematical operation, e.g., three plus two equals five. The second, *consciousness*, is our awareness of the existence of self and others, colors, shapes, etc. As Campbell says of it, "Hence every man derives the perfect assurance that he hath of his own existence" (p. 37). *Common sense*, the third kind of intuitive knowledge, is "an original source of knowledge common to all mankind" that allows us to observe such patterns as "whatever has a beginning has a cause. . . . the future will resemble the past," etc. Campbell explains that "without a full conviction" of the efficacy of intuitive beliefs it would be impossible "to advance a single step in the acquisition of knowledge, especially in all that regards mankind, life, and conduct." In other words, intuitive beliefs are to deductive beliefs as axioms are to math (pp. 38–42). In twentieth-century terminology, we might say that intuitive beliefs are formed by our early acceptance of objectified reality. We are born into and socialized by a "world view" that has been created by our parents and their parents and is therefore "given." Though we may question deductions growing out of these intuitive beliefs, to doubt the existence of the basic "realities" is to be "insane."

Most modern theorists seem to take it for granted that intuitive beliefs grow out of sense perception and are the basis of artistic conceptualization. Whately says that habitual associations of sense perceptions lead to experiential knowledge and that "experience, in its original and proper sense, is applicable to the *premises* from which we argue, not to the inferences we draw" (p. 88). Kames writes, "That the objects of our external senses really exist in the way and manner we perceive them, is a branch of intuitive knowledge . . ." (I., p. 80). Furthermore, he says, people "naturally" evaluate external objects in terms of such universal principles as regularity, propriety, and purpose, and that the judgments which result are generally viewed as unquestionable (ii., p. 34). De Quincey sums up the nature of, and difference between, intuitive and deductive beliefs: "An *intuition* is any knowledge, whatsoever, sensuous or intellectual, which is apprehended immediately: a notion, on the other hand, or product of the discursive faculty, is any knowledge whatsoever which is apprehended *mediately*" (p. 103). Thus, simple inartistic conceptualization is the basis of all complex ideas or artistic conceptualizations. If we understand how people "naturally" learn, then, by following this pattern, we can design messages that will also "naturally" engage the understanding, memory, imagination, passions, and will.

Artistic Conceptualization

Deductive Reasoning   Intuitive learning is the basis of deductive reasoning, and Campbell's discussion of "deductive sources of evidence" provides a coherent framework for modern artistic conceptualization theory. He identifies two kinds of deductive evidence, *demonstrative* and *moral*. As we have seen, Campbell's discussion of demonstration is very traditional. Like Aristotle, he defines it as the province of logic, as a method of conceiving abstract "scientific" truth in terms of necessary and unchangeable relationships. Thus, he says, it is based on "pure intellection, and consisteth in an uninterrupted series of axioms" leading to conclusions that we intuitively recognize and accept when they are pointed out to us (p. 43). Thus, beliefs that grow out of demonstration are of very little interest to communication theory, for people spend little time discussing things everyone accepts as indisputable. Furthermore, there are very few beliefs that are demonstrable. Most, in fact nearly all, beliefs that affect human conduct grow out of "moral reasoning," the second classification of deductive sources.

As we have seen, Campbell describes moral beliefs as "changeable and contingent" (p. 44). Any conclusion of moral reasoning, he says, "admits degrees" and is disputable, for "there is always real, not apparent, evidence on both sides" (p. 45). Thus, in contrast to demonstration, which consists of a coherent series or string of proofs leading irrevocably to a necessary conclusion, moral reasoning consists of bundles of "independent proofs" supporting probabilities that must be compared and weighed (p. 45). Campbell concludes that in spite of this openendedness, in spite of the fact that demonstration is "superior in point of authority," moral reasoning "excels in point of importance." It has a "wider empire," for "the whole world is comprised in her dominions" (p. 46). Most modern theorists agree with Campbell that the nature, formation, and function of beliefs based on moral reasoning should be the central focus of conceptualization theory, for human communication is essentially the process of discovering and establishing agreement on contingent matters.

Campbell identifies four basic sources of contingent beliefs. These are arranged in order of their strength of influence or their centrality in affecting belief (see Fig. 5.2). The first, of course, is *experience*, the sum of our intuitive beliefs about relationships such as cause and effect, whole and parts, etc. As we have seen, experience is the result of categorization. Experiential conclusions may be "morally certain" if they are never known to have exceptions, e.g., the conclusion that iron sinks in water. The degree of probability depends upon the proportion of occurrence to nonoccurrence. Thus, the truth of the assertion "It will snow this winter" is not certain but more probable than that of "It will snow this December." This kind of moral reasoning, Campbell says, is the "criterion and the principle organ" of truth in natural history, medicine, astronomy, psychology, etc. (pp. 50–52). As we will see in more detail later, the efficacy of experiential deductions depends upon both probability and plausibility.

The second source of moral reasoning is *analogy*, "a more indirect experience based on some remote similitude," e.g., the assertion that sap functions in plants like blood functions in humans. Analogical evidence is more or less strong in relation to the strength of the resemblance.

Campbell says that it is seldom regarded as proof and is "at best but feeble support." However, analogy can lead to creative hypotheses. It is the basis of the intellectual pleasure we receive from the figures of speech that work through comparison, and it is often effective in combatting refutation (pp. 53–54).

The nature and appeal of analogy has been explained in our discussion of categorization. It is the principle by which we perceive likenesses between apparently unrelated things and develop associational complexes. As De Quincey puts it, analogy is what allows us to discover "new" ideas: By putting "separate notices," or perceptions, together, we are often able to "mediately" derive new "apprehensions" (Rhetoric, p. 103).[11] Thus analogy has a strong "natural" appeal. Because analogy does have strong effects on conception and because it should not be considered "proof," Whately cautions the communicator to use it carefully. Analogy, he says, is based on "a resemblance of ratios" between otherwise unrelated objects or phenomena. Thus, we should strive to select analogies as remote as possible except in the one particular resemblance we wish to highlight in order to prevent the gross errors that can result from overextension of resemblances (pp. 90–93).

Testimony, that statement of an individual about what he remembers seeing, hearing, or observing, is the third source of moral reasoning. Testimony, Campbell says, "hath a natural influence on belief," for it "resembles memory." It is a kind of indirect experience and is the source of our concurrence about history, religion, language, etc. (pp. 54–55). As Kames points out, an individual cannot directly experience everything that may be important to him; hence, we all must rely on the experience of others to some extent (II., p. 510). In an important sense, all human communication is a form of testimony. Most of us believe that the earth is round because credible sources have said it is. Our belief in others' internal experiences (love, fear, pain, hunger, etc.) is based primarily on their reports.

Given the pervasiveness, the potential impact, and the necessity of relying on testimony in forming our beliefs, it is not surprising that modern theorists are united in their emphasis on the importance of ethos. Campbell says that the "moral truth" of testimony depends primarily on "the degree of credibility" of the source or sources. The concurrence of a number of witnesses increases the presumption of truth. In general, however, the degree of truth depends upon an interaction of senders and receivers: the "disposition of the hearers" in relation to the

---

[11] "An excellent example of this process is a conversation the author overheard recently: Graduate Student to Donovan Ochs: "You heard that Charlie is going to be gone next year?" Ochs: "Oh yeah?" Student: "Yeah. I guess we'll have to postpone that project he and I were going to do." Ochs: "Um, hum. Well—I guess you'll just have to put it in the foetus file."

source's "reputation . . . manner of address, the nature of the fact attested, the possible or probable design in giving it" (pp. 54–56).

Whately says that in reference to matters of fact (statements about things observable to the senses), ethos depends upon the "honesty of a witness, his accuracy, and his means of gaining information." In matters of opinion, we look to the witness's "ability to form a judgment"—his character and prejudices—and also to the numbers and kinds of persons who agree with him. Furthermore, he says, we are more likely to believe a person who has nothing to gain, and we are most likely to believe an "unwilling" witness or one who has something to lose as a result of his statement (pp. 60–64). Even if all these conditions are met, however, Whately says that there must still be some doubt. We should seek out as much "hard evidence" as possible by examining the correspondence between whatever physical evidence exists and the verbal statements, by examining the circumstances under which the statement was made (under duress, under oath, etc.), and by investigating the possibility of a conspiracy among witnesses (pp. 69–76).[12] In short, he says, "the generality of men are too much disposed to consider more, *who* proposes a measure, than *what* it is that is proposed." However, since everyone cannot have all relevant information on everything, we must still "take into consideration the characters of those who propose, support or disuade any measure . . ." (p. 219).

Most modern theorists agree with this statement. In contingent matters, there is often not sufficient inartistic evidence, and ethos becomes the deciding factor. In such cases, Campbell says, the source's "self" becomes the major consideration: "not that estimate of himself which is derived directly from consciousness or self-acquaintance, but that which is obtained reflexively from the opinion entertained of him by the hearers, or the character which he bears with them" (p. 96).

A number of modern theorists discuss the issue of whether a source must be, in Quintilian's terms, "a good man" in order to be credible. The general conclusion seems to be that "real" goodness is important because it is easier to "appear" to be what you really are. On the other hand, goodness is relative; ethos is always granted by the auditors.

Given the nature of ethos, Whately concludes, in agreement with Campbell and others, that though it is often all we have to go on, testimony is not the best evidence, and beliefs based on it are often readily susceptible to revision. Even the "authority of experience," Whately says, can often mislead us. Time spent at a job or in study does not always indicate competence. Experience in one context is often not

---

[12] Whately gives a number of examples of how testimony may be confirmed or refuted by physical evidence. For the contemporary reader, one of the best accounts of this process can be found in the description of the investigation of "the Manson murders" in Vincent Bugliosi (with Curt Gentry), *Helter Skelter* (New York: Bantam Books 1974).

readily transferable to another. The theoretic conclusions of an "amateur," when based on a "wide induction of facts," may often be superior to the practical conclusions of an expert whose experience may be with isolated details (pp. 221–222).

Campbell says that the fourth source of evidence for moral reasoning, *calculation of chances*, is even weaker than testimony. When all else fails, when the "cause of a thing is impossible to determine, we resort to statistical probability. As in tossing dice, we weigh the odds and take our chances (p. 56). Whately says that the criterion for judging conclusions based on chance is their relative probability: "The multitude of the chances . . . against any series of events, does not constitute it improbable; since the like happens to everyone everyday." The improbability of our seeing the same particular people, in the same particular order, on today's walk as on yesterday's comes "not from the number of chances against it, considered *independently*, but from the number of chances against it compared with those which lie against some *other* supposition" (pp. 77–78).

In contemporary scholarship, of course, statistical probability has come to be viewed as a superior form of moral reasoning. It is generally viewed as much more conclusive in contingent matters than experience, testimony, or analogy. For the most part, however, modern theorists seem to have had almost absolute faith in their power to observe reality, draw inferences, and judge the probability of their conclusions without the "intervention" of quantification. In the early seventeenth century, Bacon had pointed out the dangers of relying on our physical senses for evidence as to the operations of nature. Two and one-half centuries later, De Quincey points out that there is bias in the inferences we draw from sense perception, but that this is inherent and unavoidable: "The eye cannot see itself; we cannot project from ourselves, and contemplate as an object, our own contemplating faculty, or appreciate our own appreciating power" (*Style*, p. 153).

Whately likewise says that deductions from experience can be very misleading. For instance, he points out that sighted people tend to think that being blind is like closing their eyes. They assume that if a blind person's sight were restored, he would immediately recognize objects he had formerly known only by touch and that he would see colors though he had before known only texture. Visual literacy, however, is learned. Even sighted people do not all "see" the same world (p. 49). However, Whately does not conclude from this example that more "objective" means, such as statistics, would improve our ability to know reality. Instead, he urges more attention to rational analysis of observational data: "I believe it to be a prevailing fault of the present day not indeed to seek too much for knowledge, but to trust to accumulation of facts as a *substitute* for accuracy in the logical processes" (p. 15). He cites Bacon's "revolution" of logic as an instance of how improvement in reasoning expands knowledge. Those who followed Bacon, he says, increased their knowledge of physical facts; "they discovered new phenomena in consequence of a new system of philosophyzing" (p. 15). Though Whately admits that the scholastic logic of medieval scholarship, "the dark periods when the intellectual powers of mankind seemed nearly paralysed," served primarily to prevent the advancement of knowledge, he argues that the haphazard collection of facts can be just as dangerous (p. 125).

Whately's criticism of "natural logic" (the process of observation and generalization, which was previously discussed under categorization) is not without foundation. As Priestley points out in his defense of the topics, the strength of classical logic lay in the testing of conceptualization. The natural method preferred by Campbell and others seems to have no method of validation beyond the level of social concurrence—if we all agree, it must be true. Bacon, of course, had recommended experimental testing, and to some extent Campbell, Kames, Blair, et al., believed their careful observation of nature to be a form of experimentation. It was not until the twentieth century, when statistics came to be accepted as "objective" evidence, that naturally derived generalizations began to be tested under controlled conditions. Thus, Whately identified a problem that future generations were to view as central, but his solution was, for the most part, rejected not only by his contemporaries, but by his successors.

Argumentative Reasoning   The modern rejection of classical logic as the basic process of conceptualization led to the concurrent rejection of "syllogistic" argumentation.[13] To the classical theorists the discovery of examples and enthymemes was the focus of artistic conceptualization. Examples, of course, served as inductive proof and enthymemes as deductive proof. In the centuries between Aristotle and Campbell, however, the original notion of "rhetorical proof" or argumentation was thoroughly subjugated to scholastic or syllogistic logic. De Quincey

---

[13] After concluding his analysis of the deductive and moral "sources of evidence," Campbell devotes a brief chapter to refutation of the "scholastic art of syllogizing" (pp. 61–70). His critique is an eloquent summary of the position of major modern philosophers like Bacon, Descartes, and Locke. He cites Locke specifically when he says, "The syllogistic art, with its figures and moods, serves more to display the ingenuity of the inventor, and to exercise the address and fluency of the learner, than to assist the diligent inquirer in his researches after truth" (p. 62). In short, he says, syllogisms are tautological; because they work from the less well-known to the more well-known, they cannot serve to tell us anything new. For example, the syllogism "All animals feel; all horses are animals; therefore all horses feel" is meaningful only if we know what horses, animals, and feelings are, and if we understand the concept of genus and species. Of course, if we know all that, then the syllogism is unnecessary since it tells us nothing new. If fact, he says, a syllogism is simply a method of begging the question, or "proving a thing by itself," through the use of different words that mean the same thing or through assuming as part of the proof the principle that is to be proved.

points out that Aristotle had defined "the office of rhetoric" as the discovery of enthymemes and had defined an enthymeme as syllogistic only in appearance, not in substance. Substantively, De Quincey says, an enthymeme is simply a statement of probability based on common beliefs. This fact, he says, has been strangely overlooked as people have insisted on thinking of an enthymeme as a syllogism in which one or both of the premises is left unstated. He points out that it is ridiculous to believe that a "brilliant" theorist like Aristotle would base a whole science on the practice of omitting premises (pp. 86–87).

His description of the "real" difference is parallel to Campbell's distinction between demonstrative and moral reasoning:

> An enthymeme differs from a syllogism, not in the accident of suppressing one of its propositions; either may do this, or neither; the difference is essential, and in the nature of the *matter*: that of the syllogism proper being certain and apodictic: that of the enthymeme simply probable, and drawn from the province of opinion (p. 90).

Though De Quincey's analysis seems essentially correct, the weight of tradition was against him. Even into the mid-twentieth century, scholars continued to view the enthymeme as an "incomplete syllogism."[14] In the modern period, only one other theorist makes any attempt to revive the classical approach to argumentative conceptualization.

Whately says that his theory of rhetoric is an elaboration of Aristotle's. He defines rhetoric as dealing with " 'Argumentative Composition,' *generally* and *exclusively*" (p. 4). It is, he says, "an offshoot of logic," and it deals with all forms of instrumental communication, including "the medium of the Press," but not poetry and fiction (pp. 2–4).

Whately identifies two classes of argument based on the relationship between premises and conclusions. The first, *a priori*, is an argument from cause to effect. It is used "to *account for*" a fact or principle whose truth is granted. For instance, we all agree that X committed a murder; the only question is why. Was it jealousy? or anger? or greed? (pp. 43–46). The second class includes all other kinds of questions. It is "argument from an *Effect* to a *Condition*," or *a posteriori*. For instance, we see that a killing has occurred and that X has blood on his clothes; thus, we conclude that he might have committed murder (p. 53). The first class of arguments is essentially syllogistic. The second class, which works from signs and examples, is essentially enthymematic. It includes experience, analogy, and testimony (a kind of "sign" that a thing has occurred) and is based on the premise that what is true of an individual member is true of the class. Induction is the process of using such arguments in a series, of inferring

[14] See the discussion of enthymemes in Chap. 2.

from "a known Effect a certain Cause, and again, from that Cause, another unknown Effect" etc. (pp. 86–87).

In its substance, Whately's theory of argumentative reasoning is not inconsistent with the more dominant approach exemplified by Campbell. In form, however, it seems anachronistic in the modern context of faculty and associational psychology.[15] Also, though Whately's approach had extensive influence on theories of legal communication and formal debate, both in his own time and well into the twentieth century, the empirical-psychological approach has had a longer lived and more pervasive impact on general theories of communication.

Campbell is the best representative of this approach. He identifies four sources or arguments based on the "ends" of communication and the faculties of the mind. The basic premise is that in conceptualizing a message, the communicator who wants to convince and persuade must take into account fundamental principles of human nature. As Campbell says:

> In order to evince the truth considered by itself, conclusive arguments alone are requisite; but in order to convince me by these arguments, it is moreover requisite that they be understood, that they be attended to, that they be remembered by me; and in order to persuade me by them to any particular action or conduct, it is further requisite, that by interesting me in the subject, they may, as it were, be felt (pp. 71–72).

Thus, he explains, we must take into account people "in general" and people "in particular."

Address to the Understanding   Human beings, Campbell points out, have understanding in different degrees. Also, they have different abilities to imagine and remember and are activated by different passions. But the initial prerequisite is to adjust the message to the level of understanding:

> The first thing to be studied by the speaker is, that his arguments may be understood. If they be unintelligible, the cause must be either in the sense or in the expression. It lies in the sense if the mediums of proof be such as the hearers are unacquainted with

[15] For a thorough analysis of Whately's divergence from his contemporaries in regard to argument and the nature of knowledge, see Dale Leathers: "Whately's Logically Derived Rhetoric: A Stranger in Its Times," *Western Speech* (Winter, 1969), pp. 48–58. In partial defense of Whately, however, it might be fair to note here that he may have been a "stranger," but he was not the "lone stranger." Priestley, De Quincey, Ward, and Lawson, to name a few, also accepted and defended one or more of the tenets of classical logic, which we often tend to think were "universally rejected" by the modern theorists.

[they are totally new or too abstract or]. . . . if the train of reasoning (though no unusual ideas be introduced) be longer or more
complex, or more intricate, than they are accustomed to (p. 73).

Judgment of whether proof is too abstract or too complex depends
upon the particulars of the auditors. People differ in intellectual and
moral abilities. Their "cultivation of the understanding" through education, along with their "manner of life," their habits and occupations,
leads to different propensities. These also, then, influence their imagination and memory and incline them toward certain passions more than
others. For instance, Campbell says, we might say that Republicans are
inclined toward "the pomp and splendour of monarchy," merchants toward "interest," soldiers toward "glory," genius toward "fame," industrial
magnates toward "riches," and the very rich toward gratification of "pleasures" (p. 95).

Fenelon says Plato was the first to point out that a communicator
must know human nature: "He would have the speaker commence with
the study of men in general; and afterwards apply himself to knowing the
particular men to whom he will have to speak" (p. 82). People in general, Fenelon says, have a sense of destiny, interests, desire for happiness,
and passions. These are modified and regulated by the laws and customs
under which they live, the temperament and manners of their culture,
their education, and their particular prejudices and interests (p. 82).

In order to convince the understanding, the communicator must use
reasoning that, as Blair says, "attempts to satisfy another of what is true
or right, or just" (II., p. 381). To do so requires arguments drawn from
experience, analogy, testimony, and chance. These arguments must be
arranged and connected, Whately says, in order to show "on which side
the evidence proponderates" (p. 156). He points out that the fundamental idea is to raise a "presumption" in favor of the objective. A presumption is "a pre-occupation of the ground, as implies that it must stand good
ti.l some sufficient reason is adduced against it" (p. 112). In addition to
the artificial presumption raised by skillful address to the understanding,
Whately points out there is a natural presumption in favor of, for instance, existing institutions, recognized authorities, close associates,
loved persons, well-known phenomena, the decisions of an official coun-
cil or assembly, etc. These can be used to reinforce the source's position.
In fact, he says, a natural presumption is one of the "strongest arguments" (pp. 113–123).

Ethos, as we have seen, is also necessary for convincing the understanding, and ethos, Whately says, is a kind of presumption in favor of
the judgment of the source. The "deference" we have for communicators and those they cite and associate themselves with greatly affects our
willingness to attend to them and to believe them (p. 122). He goes on

to say that good principle and good will depend on "reference to the opinions and habits of the audience"; in proportion as the sources' opinions deviate from the auditors', their task becomes more difficult (p. 207). Campbell also says that the sources' perceived intellectual ability and moral qualities are relative to the receivers'. All individuals have prejudices based on such circumstances as party membership, national origin, religious affiliation, etc. The level of education of an audience determines the general importance of ethos. Ethos is important to the learned, he says, but it is everything to the uneducated, for they tend to forget the substance in favor of the source. In general, positive ethos adds to the other arguments as a kind of testimony (p. 97). When one's ethos is negative, however, it may be necessary to "build" ethos by shifting attention away from the sources' profession, which can detract from their ethos. The preacher has a special problem in that he must be a role model; he cannot have "minor failings." The lawyer is always somewhat suspect because everyone knows that he may argue either side of a case for money. Unfortunately, says Campbell, he cannot give many rules for handling these problems; the circumstances that must be taken into account are too many and too varied. The main thing, however, is to understand "those principles of the mind on which the rules are founded" and apply them to the particulars of the case (pp. 98–101).

Address to the Memory and Imagination   The importance and function of address to the memory and imagination has previously been discussed under categorization. Basically, modern theorists point out, the communicator must take into account that vivid ideas arranged in natural order are more likely to be remembered and thus more likely to have long term effects on the receiver. The creation of ideal presence also assists memory and, through the power of the imagination, arouses sympathy and passion. It is necessary to engage both on all occasions, Campbell says, but memory is the most important for convincing and imagination the most important for persuading (pp. 75–76).

Address to the Passions   It is in their discussion of the fourth faculty, passion, that the full scope of modern theory of argumentation is revealed. As we have seen, modern theorists are adamant about the importance of passion in affecting both belief and action. Medieval and Renaissance scholars viewed emotion as an obstruction to reason and regarded pathos, "appeal to emotion," as more or less unethical. The classical theorists, on the other hand, defined pathos as a mode of proof and generally agreed that since people inevitably respond emotionally, the communicator's task was to direct these responses toward empathy rather than antipathy. The modern theorists revive this classical view and elevate pathos to *the* central position in argumentative reasoning.

Modern theorists characterize emotion not as an obstruction but as an aid, or "handmaid," to reason. They also view it as inevitable. De Quincey says that we might think modern audiences are unemotional and prefer address that concentrates on "the facts." For instance, he says, in Parliament it seems that most of the discourse revolves around "business" affairs and dull calculations about topics such as road construction. The courts often seem to deal only with "dry technicalities" of contacts and precedents. "Peace and war, vengeance for public wrongs . . . justice, large and diffusive," the topics we might think would arouse strong emotional responses, are seldom discussed. However, he says, passionate persuasion still occurs; it is "immortal, and will never perish so long as there are human hearts moving under the agitation of hope and fear, love and passionate hatred" (pp. 97–100). Blair writes that in terms of "practice," no one influences another "but addresses himself to passions more or less" for "passions are the great springs of human action" (II., p. 381). Campbell explains that there is no activity without passion, saying, "Passion is the mover to action, reason is the guide" (p. 78). Thus, as long as there is *human* communication, and as long as people seek to influence each other's behavior, there will be *passionate* communication.

A number of theorists point out that since emotions are inherent in human interaction, the problem for a communicator is to determine how to stimulate those which are appropriate and to allay others. Whately explains that both processes are important (p. 185). He says that most people are overly concerned about allaying emotion. We are all fearful of being misled by our passions. However, he points out, being misled by the understanding is more likely and more dangerous. Sophistry is difficult to see, and conviction based on it is more long lasting. The passions cool quickly, and we easily change "wrong" opinions based on inappropriate emotional responses. An "ingenious reasoner," he says, can be infinitely more dangerous in the long run (pp. 184–187). Also, he points out, people are probably more often misled from a "defect of passion" than from an excess. Too often we are cold when we should be warm. An obvious example is in religion, where "familiarity" breeds boredom (p. 180).

In terms of raising passion, Whately explains that it is involuntary: "One may, by a deliberate act of the Will, set himself to calculate . . . on the other hand, a Volition to hope or fear, to love or hate . . . is as ineffectual as to will that the pulsation of the heart . . . should be altered" (p. 181). Thus a communicator cannot "argue" people into feeling, nor, by extension, into acting. The only way to arouse a passion is "By calling on the Imagination to present a vivid picture of all that is related and referred to" and leading the auditor into "thinking about, and attending to, such objects as are calculated to awaken it" (pp. 183–184). This process is, and must be, indirect. People tend to resent "the idea that they need to have motives urged upon them," for we all like to believe that we do "good" through our own will. Thus the communicator should address the reason first, prove that his objective is worthwhile, then present details and fix the attention so that emotions "spontaneously arise," in a sense, "out of that conviction" (pp. 189–201). This process is essential, he says, even in factual discourse such as history. For "unless we have before the mind a lively idea of the scenes in which the events took place, the habits of thought and feeling of the actors . . . [and can] transport ourselves out of our own age, and country, and persons" we cannot develop an accurate understanding of other times and places (p. 194).

Circumstances Affecting and Calming Passions   Given the principles of human nature, Campbell says that there are seven basic "circumstances" that serve to build pathos (see Fig. 5.2). In order for an individual to become caught up in a message, it must be perceived as both *probable* and *plausible*. An argument or depiction of reality seems probable if it has external validity. Given what we know from our own experience, it makes sense, seems likely. Probability grows out of presentation of facts and evidence and is based on reason (p. 82). Whately says that the strongest probability comes from *a priori* arguments where the cause seems to be fully sufficient, given no intervening obstacles, to the effect claimed (p. 48). Kames likewise says that the strongest sense of probability grows out of cause/effect reasoning (II., p. 398).

Plausibility is a somewhat weaker circumstance. It is the internal validity of the message. If the message seems plausible, the receiver accepts that the events "could happen." Campbell says that plausibility grows out of coherence within a chain of reasoning and depends upon presentation of events and relationships that do not thwart the auditors' habitual "conclusions and anticipations." In fiction, plausibility is usually called "verisimilitude"; it is necessary even if the narrative concerns the activities of improbable beings like dragons and demons (p. 82).

Modern theorists agree that both probability and plausibility are necessary on all occasions. Doubt that a thing would or could happen creates an obstacle to empathy and thus to the development of feelings appropriate to the object. As Kames says, "Any circumstance that obstructs the mind in passing and repassing between its objects, occasions a like obstruction in the communication [association] of passion" (II., p. 70).

The perceived *importance of the subject* is also a circumstance that affects pathos. Campbell says: "An action may derive its importance from its own nature, from those concerned in it as acting or suffering, or from its consequences" (p. 86). The central connection here, of course, is self. Because of the principle of the association of passions, the more a thing affects "me," the more important it is. The idea is, Whately explains, that "the flame spreads." If we want auditors to feel pity for another's misfortune, we might want to lead them "to consider how they would feel were such and such an injury done to themselves" (p. 198).

The next four circumstances that affect pathos grow out of this notion that what is "closer" to us is more likely to involve us. *Proximity in time*, for instance, increases our emotional response. Campbell says that future events are more relevant to us than past, for the past is over but the future is "approaching" and can therefore make a difference to our lives. Of course, the immediate past is more relevant than the remote future. Also, it is generally easier to "prove" past facts than future ones. Thus forensic discourse has a natural advantage (in terms of probability and plausibility) over deliberative discourse. We are somewhat inclined to view the lawyer's subjects as more "real" than those of the politician (p. 87). Whately points out that in discussing the past we can cite current "real signs" to establish past occurrences. In discussing the future, we are limited to using the examples of the past and these have only hypothetical relevance to the future (p. 132).

Campbell points out that *proximity in terms of place* also affects us emotionally. A thing that occurs in our own neighborhood is likely to involve us more than a thing that occurs in another country (p. 88). A number of theorists explain that this is, again, the result of a natural associational process. Love of self, Kames says, extends to love of one's possessions, relatives, nation, etc. (II., p. 60). This same principle accounts for Campbell's next circumstance, *relation to the persons involved*. The more closely we identify with the actor or victim, the more emotionally involved we become. Campbell says that a feeling of relationship may grow out of friendship, acquaintance, or similarity in national origin, language, religion, occupation, etc. (p. 89). Kames says that our natural sense of order determines the relative strength of such identification. Thus, he says, a man identifies more strongly with a son than with a daughter. Also, the nature of parental love dictates that a parent is likely to be more affected by fear for his children than by fear for himself (II., p. 68).

This identification leads to the last circumstance, *personal interest in the consequences*, which Campbell says is the most powerful of all. Through sympathy and the association of passions, self-love becomes an overwhelming motive. Campbell explains: "Sympathy is but a reflected feeling, and therefore, in ordinary cases, must be weaker than the original" (p. 89). To see an injustice is to be indignant and feel resentment, but to experience it is to seek revenge. Thus, when the consequences of an event can be made personal to the auditors, the passions elicited are likely to be much stronger: "The speaker, from engaging *pity* in his favour, can proceed to operate on a more powerful principle, *self-preservation*. The benevolence of his hearers he can work up into *gratitude*, their *indignation* into revenge" (pp. 89–90).

It is important to note here that pathos is not, in modern theory, simply a matter of eliciting emotions. The central idea is that from relatively simple emotional responses one builds complex passions that become motives for action. This process works through association. The first principle in this progressive approach, as a number of theorists point out, is that only "like" emotions associate. Priestley cites Hume as saying:

All resembling impressions are connected together; and not sooner one arises, than the rest naturally follow. Grief and disappointment give rise to anger, anger to envy, envy to malice, and malice to grief again. In like manner our temper, when elevated by joy, naturally throws itself into love, generosity, courage, pride, and other resembling affections (p. 98).

The association of like emotions should not, however, be interpreted to mean that an individual cannot feel conflicting emotions. If fact, Campbell says, a mixture of pleasurable and painful emotions associated with the same objects yields "a greater and more durable" impression (pp. 130–131). Kames says that a mixture of similar emotions gives "the pleasure of concord or harmony" (II., p. 119), but that a mixture of opposites is the basis of great drama (II., p. 138). Opposite emotions, he explains, can exist only in succession. For instance, we may feel both love and jealousy (hatred) for the same object. These passions "prevail alternately," and one of them eventually predominates. In responding to a message, this tension and its eventual resolution are primary sources of intellectual pleasure (II., p. 124). Priestley reinforces this observation when he says that both the body and the mind resist inactivity: "One property essential to everything that gives pleasure is, that it occasions a moderate exercise of our faculties" (p. 136). Also, Campbell points out, uneasiness such as that caused by attraction/avoidance may be temporarily unpleasant, but such conflicts "are the principle spurs to action" (p. 129).

Finally, in terms of the motive power of passions, it is important for the communicator to remember that emotions are not equal in their effects. Some are "inert" whereas others stimulate. Campbell says that sorrow, fear, shame, and humility depress, whereas hope, patriotism, ambition, emulation, and anger stimulate (p. 5). Also, he points out, some emotions are less associative than others. Joy, for instance, does not associate well with other emotions. This characteristic explains why, in novels and plays, authors tend to make joy the object of the briefest, and the last, scene (p. 131). Along these same lines, a painful emotion makes a "deeper impression on the imagination than pleasure does, and is longer retained by the memory" (p. 130). Also, it is easier to empathize with pain than with pleasure. Miserable people need sympathy; happy people are more likely to arouse envy (p. 131). This accounts, in part, for the popularity of dramatic tragedy (p. 135).

In concluding his discussion of the passions as argument, Campbell reminds us that raising emotion is not the sole concern. First, once aroused, passion must be maintained. Under the heading of "auxiliary circumstances," he says that we can keep passion alive and augment it by, for instance, quoting respected authorities and giving examples of popular heroes. These act as "a sort of reasoning." The motives evoked by them tend to serve as the major premises of enthymemes, premises which need not be stated, proved, or argued for because they draw on common beliefs (p. 92).

Second, Campbell says, we need to be concerned not only about raising appropriate passions, but also about calming inappropriate or unfavorable ones. This end can be accomplished by use of the "auxiliary circumstances" in refutation, by use of the opposites of the "affecting circumstances" (i.e., by showing that a thing is improbable, that it is really very distant in terms of time, place, or interest, etc.), by the use of humor (wit or ridicule), or by exciting another passion or disposition that will overrule the unfavorable one. For instance, we might show that an action that promotes immediate interest simultaneously destroys future interest through damaging reputation (p. 93). Whately says that prejudice is a particular problem and can often be overcome by exciting a contrary emotion or by giving a new direction to the emotion, that is, by changing the object of the perception rather than the perception of the object (pp. 227–230).

The modern theorists agree that the principles of conceptualization discussed above are not to be regarded as "rules." Their emphasis is upon pointing out why certain observed practices seem to work. The principles they infer are viewed as universal, but not as equally applicable to all communication situations. Campbell points out that their use depends upon careful analysis of five particulars: "the *speaker*, the *hearers* or persons addressed, the *subject*, the *occasion*, and the *end* in view or the effect intended to produced by the discourse" (p. 99; emphases mine). As we have seen, the analysis of each of these variables is complex and defies simplistic reduction or prescription. Determining what to say requires broad general knowledge, expert acquaintance with the subject, and creative management of information in light of a thorough understanding of how people come to know, believe, and act. Given that symbolization, organization, and operationalization depend directly upon decisions made in the conceptualization process, it is not difficult to "sympathize" with the modern theorists' claim that true "eloquence" grows out of a lifetime of preparation.

Symbolization

Symbolization is that part of human communication theory concerned with the nature of symbols. In terms of the communication act, it is the selection of symbols to represent meanings and the inferring of meanings from symbolic objects, events, and behaviors. In their discussion of symbolization, the classical theorists focused on the pragmatics of symbol use. They posited three levels of style—plain, middle, and vigorous—which were discussed in terms of their function in instructing, pleasing, and persuading. The plain style was viewed primarily in terms of its facility in creating ethos and leading to understanding. The primary criterion for the plain style was accuracy. The middle style was viewed as a primary means for the creation of conviction or logos. The middle style was defined as philosophical, highly metaphorical, and aesthetically pleasing. The vigorous style was the vehicle for pathos, or the creation of empathy and thus persuasion. The vigorous style was variously characterized as sublime, ornate, and copious. The overriding criterion for the use of style was propriety, appropriateness to purpose, source, receiver, place, time, and subject.

As we have seen, in the medieval and Renaissance periods, this pragmatic approach to symbolization was replaced by approaches that tended to focus on syntactics and semantics. Theorists of this period tended to view language as a technical study and thus devoted much time and effort to analysis of the linguistic structure, especially figures of speech. They also viewed language as "dressing" or "ornament" that was superadded to thought and that therefore tended to act as an obstacle to communication, as a primary source of misunderstanding. The levels of style and the classical criteria were viewed less in terms of function and more in terms of formulaic standards.

Modern theorists, for the most part, rebelled against the dry, sterile tradition of the medieval and Renaissance periods. They returned to the more pragmatic emphasis of the classical period. They tend, however, to focus not on the levels of style, but on the nature and function of language across situational contexts. Language is viewed as organic with thought, and symbolization in general is viewed as a form of human action. Style is discussed in terms of its effects on the faculties of the mind and in terms of the ultimate ends of conviction and persuasion (see Fig. 5.3).

Organic Nature of Language

Modern theorists agree that although in one sense language is an external representation of internal processes, and thus a "dressing" of thought, the relationship of language to thought is organic. Campbell explains, as do a number of other theorists, that language is an arbitrary invention of human beings. Although, as many speculate, it may have originated through some "natural" correspondence between sounds and objects, events, or processes (see Blair, I., p. 117), that natural connection is no longer obvious. In fact, Campbell says, signs (conventional symbols like words) "have no natural connexion with the things whereof

---

Fig. 5.3   Modern Taxonomy of Symbolization

I. Nature and Function of Language
   A. Organic—Language incarnates thought
   B. Instrumental—Language is a means of acting
   C. Pragmatic—Principles of language use depend on function
II. Criteria of Symbolization
   A. Perspicuity—Clarity; address to the understanding
   B. Vivacity—Liveliness, vividness, animation; address to the imagination, memory, and passions
   C. Conciseness—Brevity; stimulation of the imagination
   D. Propriety—Elegance; appropriateness to source, receiver, occasion, subject, purpose

---

they are signs"; rather signs are representations of generalized abstractions (p. 257). The fundamental process, he says, is that through frequent use we learn to associate certain signs with other signs. Eventually we "forget" the particulars of these associations and "we really think in signs as well as speak by them" (pp. 259–260). Thus, although "the perceptions of the senses" and "the conceptions of the intellect" are different in fact, language obscures that difference to the point where in practice they become indistinguishable (p. 261).

Priestley, operating on this same basic principle, draws an analogy between language and thought in terms of the human body. He explains that conceptualization is the "bones, muscles, and nerves of a composition," whereas language is "the external lineaments, the colour, the complexion, and graceful attitude of it" (p. 72). At one point, Campbell compares the relationship between thought and language to that between "body and soul" (p. 215); at another, he emphasizes the container/contained relationship, calling language the "vehicle" of sentiments (p. 139). De Quincey points out that the theoretical separableness of the "container" and that which it "contains" should not mislead us into thinking that we can be affected by one and not by the other. He says that the importance of style, the use of language in human communication, is often overlooked because of a common tendency to see subject and style "as in a separate relation" (*Style*, p. 138). However, he claims, "the intertexture of style and matter" is such that it is impossible that anyone could be affected by one "*otherwise than in connexion with the other*" (*Style*, p. 141). In attempting to account for the effects of messages, he says, "the interpenetration of the style and the matter" is so thorough that it is virtually impossible "to distribute the true proportions of their joint action" (*Style*, p. 139).

Whately points out that often what we call "failures" in style are really failures in conceptualization or they are instances of the operation of hidden purposes. For instance, a communicator whose message is so abstract and general that it makes no sense may be trying to seem "refined" or give the impression that he is covering the subject comprehensively. Of such abstract messages, Whately says, though "they *include* much, they *impress* little or nothing" (p. 278). Also, he points out, people often talk not for the purpose of communicating ideas, but to "veil sophistry," or "to appear to say something . . . so as to at least avoid the ignominy of being silenced" or to give the appearance of an excuse for an action; talking may also serve "to occupy time," as in delaying a decision or because custom requires that, for instance, a sermon last at least one hour (pp. 265–272). In such cases, of course, language is organic not with the apparent, but with the real, purposes of the communicator.

De Quincey claims that language which serves to advance a hidden purpose always seems artificial. For instance, a person who is trying to impress adds his imagery "afterwards, as so much embroidery or fringe" (*Rhetoric*, p. 110). Modern theorists tend to agree that the best standard for determining the "truth" of a communicator's style in regard to his purposes is everyday conversation. Whately makes this point when he says, "in conversation, a man naturally tries first one, then another mode of conveying his thoughts, and stops as soon as he perceives that his companion fully comprehends his sentiments, and is sufficiently impressed by them" (p. 310). Campbell says that the natural style of expression of reputable and educated people is the best standard for both speaking and writing (p. 141). De Quincey points out that "real situations are always pledges of real natural language" (*Style*, p. 145). Of the great communicators of the past, he says, "Men wrote eloquently because they wrote feelingly; they wrote idiomatically because they wrote naturally and without affectation" (*Rhetoric*, p. 126).

Instrumental Nature of Language

The fact that language and thought are organic does not mean that the communicator has no choices to make in symbolizing his message. A communicator who is aware of the instrumental nature of language, who understands, as Spencer puts it, that our responses to messages are "partially aroused by the forms" (p. 15), focuses his attention on the relationship between form and function.

That the modern theorists view instrumentality as an ultimate principle in symbolization is demonstrated in their approach to figurative language. Although they agree with medieval and Renaissance theorists that figures may be viewed as "ornaments," or sources of aesthetic and intellectual pleasure, their concept of language leads to a focus on the function of imagery in bringing about conviction and persuasion. Imagery, or figurative expression, they claim, serves to help create ideal presence, stimulate the imagination, and engage the passions. Because figures work through analogy, they also serve the general function of argumentation, or address to the understanding.

De Quincey points out that imagery serves not as "the mere alien apparelling of a thought . . . but is the coefficient that . . . absolutely *makes* the thought as a *third* and separate existence" (*Language*, p. 262). Imagery, he says, tends to "extend and amplify the thought, or to fortify it by some indirect argument of its truth" (*Rhetoric*, p. 125). As an example, he cites the excellence of Edmund Burke, who "grows a thought" rather than "dresses" it, who thinks "in and by his figures," incarnating "his thoughts in imagery" (*Rhetoric*, p. 115).

Campbell likewise points out that figures or tropes may be used to illustrate a point or to make it clearer. However, because figures "imply a likeness in the *things*, and not just in the *symbols*," they often function as "arguments from analogy." For instance, he says of metaphor: "Without anything like an explicit comparison, and commonly without any warning or apology, the name of one thing is obtruded upon us, for the name of another quite different, though resembling in some quality" (pp. 293–294).

Blair defines figurative language as "some departure from simplicity of expression which is designed to render the impression more strong and vivid" (I., p. 317). But, he says, this does not mean that figures are special forms used only on certain occasions. Metaphor, simile, personification, etc., are inherent in language and appear constantly in everyday conversation. In general, anytime discourse "is prompted either by the imagination or by the passions," we find abundance of figurative expression (I., p. 318–319). The conscious use of such expressions, of course, can add both depth and beauty to messages. Figures, he says, reveal subleties of thought, give us intellectual pleasure (because they are all founded on analogy, they allow us to "see one thing in another," to experience unexpected resemblances), make the abstract concrete, thus giving us clearer ideas, and highlight central aspects of a subject or event. They add to proof and arguments as confirmation and serve as motives to actions (I., pp. 331–420).

Kames makes much the same set of observations on the nature and use of imagery (see his summary, I, p. 182). Like Blair, he devotes several hundred pages to examples of effective and ineffective uses of language (especially of figurative language). His examples are drawn from great literature of the past as well as from current fiction, poetry, and journalism. Important principles concerning the nature and function of language are thus drawn empirically from observed instances and comparatively evaluated. The standards for this critical evaluation are those explained under categorization, especially ideal presence and taste, as well as those discussed under moral reasoning and argument in conceptualization.

For example, Kames writes that a good description is "lively and accurate"; it should elicit in the auditor a feeling of having been an "eye-witness" (II., p. 84). The necessity of creating ideal presence, he says, holds true "whether the subject be a fable or reality," for once it is established, the auditor has no time for the kind of reflection that tends to destroy sympathetic participation (II., p. 86). Ideal presence created by imaginative language not only affects sympathy, it affects "the understanding and contributes to belief. For when events are related in a lively manner, and every circumstance appears as passing before us, we suffer not patiently the truth of the facts to be questioned" (II., p. 92–93). Such descriptions, he continues, must be both probable and plausible through their accordance with our experiential knowledge of natural order: "A chain of imagined incidents linked together according to nature, finds easy admittance into the mind; and a lively narrative of such incidents, occasions complete images, including ideal presence" (II., p. 94).

Pragmatic Function of Language

Other modern theorists, though they devote less space to actual criticism, likewise base their analyses of symbolization on the instrumentality of language. Campbell says that *the* communicative standard for the use of language is not "grammatical," but "rhetorical." Grammar, he says, is concerned with collecting and methodizing rules for joining words together (p. 140). Grammar bears the same relation to rhetoric as "the art of the mason bears to that of the architect" (pp. 169–170). The architect uses the principles of masonry, but his major concern is to design and execute in terms of function. Likewise, the communicator is primarily concerned with function: "It is not ultimately the justness either of the thoughts or of the expression, which is the aim of the orator; but it is a certain effect to be produced in the hearers" (p. 215). De Quincey makes a similar distinction between approaches to language. The "mechanic" approach studies syntax, the "combination of words into sentences;" the "organic" approach, which is the one of interest to communication, *per se*, studies pragmatics: "all possible relations that can arise between thought and words—the total effect of a writer as derived from manner" (*Style*, p. 163). Whately says that in the purposive use of language, the central question is "not whether this or that is a *striking expression*, but whether it makes the *meaning* more striking" (p. 287).

Criteria of Symbolization

Modern theorists tend to agree that the criteria for the use and evaluation of symbolization must be based on the the principles of categorization and conceptualization. The criteria that emerge tend to fall into four basic categories: perspecuity (clarity), vivacity (liveliness, vividness, animation), conciseness (brevity), and propriety (elegance, appropriateness). The value of these qualities is justified in terms of the use of language in addressing the faculties of the mind.

Perspicuity   What we know of human nature, Campbell says, tells us that the first criterion for the use of language is that it engage the understanding. Thus, he says, of the qualities of style, "the first and most essential is *perspicuity* . . . whatever the ultimate intention of the orator, to inform, to convince, to please, to move, or to persuade, still he must speak so as to be understood, or he speaks to no purpose" (p. 216). Campbell points out that perspicuity "originally and properly implies *transparency*." The operational definition of a perspicuous message is "when the subject engrosses the attention of the hearer, and the diction is so little minded by him that he can scarcely be said to be conscious that it is through this medium he sees into the speaker's thought" (p. 221). "Purity" of grammar and syntax are a part of perspicuity only in the sense that violations of the rules will distract the auditor into trying mentally to "correct the imperfection of the speaker's language" (p. 221). Priestley makes a similar point, saying that semantic ambiguity and syntactic errors interfere with the receiver's associational processes (p. 281).

Kames says that perspicuity is one of the "beauties of language and that "communication of thought being the principal end of language, it is a rule, that perspicuity ought not to be sacrificed to any other beauty whatever" (I. p. 20). For the benefit of students, Kames, like Blair, offers detailed examples and analyses of violations of perspicuity. Campbell presents a brief summary of these. For instance, he says obscurity may result from omitting the antecedent for a pronoun or from using the same word in different senses. It may also result from equivocation or affectation (using remote analogies or farfetched metaphors) or from piling up too many synonyms (pp. 217–255).

These kinds of syntatic and semantic faults, the modern theorists agree, can be avoided by practice and study of the style of effective communicators. They are basically mechanical. The more difficult thing is to adjust the level of the language to the understanding of the audience—to take into account the members as people "in general" and "in particular." For instance, Whately points out that perspicuity is "a *relative* quality." Whether a message will be understood and attended to depends on "reference to the class of readers or hearers for whom it is designed." Some auditors are "slow" and need copious and gradual explanation. Others are "quick" and will not attend to long, detailed exposition. Also, auditors tend to have different degrees of prior exposure, they have formed different habits of "audiencing," and they have different expectations of the situation (p. 258). Whately also reminds us that some audiences are more mixed than others. Preachers especially have this problem. For increasing perspicuity in relation to a very diverse audience, he recommends repetition and the use of many brief expressions, recapitulation of the main point in a varied order, and synonyms and vivid metaphors. Variety will maintain the attention of the more intellectual and less patient, whereas repetition will impress ideas on the less intellectual (pp. 259–261).

Although being understood is the basic objective of communicating, it is usually not the ultimate objective. Campbell says that if the communicator wants to achieve conviction and persuasion, perspicuity alone is insufficient: "If he would not only inform the understanding, but please the imagination, he must add the charms of vivacity and elegance. . . . By vivacity, resemblance [of thoughts] is attained; by elegance, dignity of manner. . . . If he proposes to work upon the passions, his very diction, as well as his sentiments, must be animated" (p. 215).

Vivacity   Modern theorists agree that to engage the imagination and the passions, vivacity (or liveliness or vividness) is essential. Fenelon says that in order for a message to avoid being "dry, flat, and boring," in order to "impress things upon the soul of the listener," it is necessary to "paint" the facts (p. 94). The only way to "heat the imagination of a listener or arouse his passions" is, by "the power of imitation and of portraiture," to create a picture for the mind: "A simple story cannot move. It is necessary not only to acquaint the listeners with the facts, but to make the facts visible to them, and to strike their consciousness by means of a perfect representation of the arresting manner in which the facts have come to pass" (pp. 93–94).

Priestley says that the creation of mental images arouses passions because of the association of ideas. Because emotions are complex associations of feelings with sense perceptions, our affections are engaged and "we feel ourselves interested, in proportion to the *vividness of our ideas* of those objects and circumstances which contribute to excite them" (p. 79). Because in nature "we see nothing but particulars," he says that it is necessary "to be very *circumstantial,* and to introduce as many *sensible* images as possible." In so doing, we make our messages "resemble real and active life," and our listeners find themselves "strongly inclined to believe the scene to be real" (pp. 84–89). Thus, style of expression can be used to involve the auditor in an "imaginative reality," and he is more likely to believe and to act. Whately likewise points out that "copiousness of detail" and dwelling on the circumstances of an event are the most likely ways to engage the imagination and passions (p. 192). He also emphasizes the impact of vivid style in contributing to belief. Detailed description, he says, serves "to impress strongly on the mind the arguments adduced" (p. 275).

De Quincey explains that vivacity is necessary not only in engaging passions and imagination, but in impressing the memory. Also, he says, not only the content has these effects, but the symbolic strategies:

> [O]ften enough two orators have relied upon the same identical matter—the facts, for instance, of the slavetrade—and one has turned this to such good account by his arrangements, by his modes of vivifying dry statements, by his arts of illustration, by his science

of connecting things with human feeling, that he has left his hearers in convulsions of passion; whilst the other shall have used every tittle of the same matter without eliciting one scintillation of sympathy, without leaving behind one distinct impression on the memory or planting one murmur in the heart (pp. 138–139).

Spencer points out that the superiority of detail, images based on sense perceptions, particulars over generalities, and concrete terms over abstract can all be justified in terms of "economy of the recipient's mental energy" (p. 4). These qualities of style naturally have the most immediate and strong associations, and if we think of language as the "vehicle of thought," he explains then "there seems reason to think that in all cases the friction and inertia of the vehicle deduct from its efficiency" (p. 3). Thus, he says, what is grasped most quickly, without excessive intellection, is potentially more effective.

Campbell likewise says that "the imagination is more strongly affected by what is perceived by the senses, than by what is conceived by the understanding" (p. 304). For this reason, he says, the first step in persuasion, exciting a desire, depends on style; it is "affected by communicating natural and lively ideas of the object." The second step, making a connection between the conduct urged and the gratification of the desire excited, is slower and depends upon "arguments from experience, analogy, testimony, or the plurality of chances" (p. 275).

Figurative language is a special, and essential, aspect of vivacity. Blair says that it "always imports some colouring of the imagination, or some emotion of passion" (I., p. 320). It is wrong, he says, to think that figures are merely ornaments: "It is a very erroneous idea . . . as if they were things detached from the subject, and that could be stuck to it like lace upon a coat" (II., p. 3). For instance, Kames gives an example of the interdependence of figures and conceptualization when he explains that it is almost impossible to imagine abstract notions like numbers. Thus, it is more effective to "add" to "their army was 10,000 strong" the phrase, "they resembled a swarm of bees" (I., p. 194).

Campbell explains the function of various symbolic strategies that have sometimes been thought of as ornaments. For instance, he says, "correction, climax, and vision tend greatly to enliven the ideas, by the implicit but animated comparisons and opposition conveyed in them" (p. 94). Others, like exclamation and apostrophe, he explains, "operate chiefly by sympathy, as they are the most ardent expressions of perturbation in the speaker" (p. 94). Rhetorical questions, "interrogation," also work through sympathy:

[A rhetorical question] implies in the orator the strongest confidence in the rectitude of his sentiments, and in the concurrence of every reasonable being. The auditors, by sympathizing with this frame of spirit, find it impracticable to withhold an assent which is so confidently depended upon (p. 94).

Aside from their specific functions, figures of speech and other lively expressions, Campbell says, generally appeal to the human need for variety. A mixture of stylistic devices is the key, for "everything in nature is heightened and set off by its contrary, which by giving scope for comparison, enhances every excellence. The colours of a painting acquire a double lustre from the shades; the harmony in music is greatly improved by a judicious mix of discords" (p. 131).

Conciseness   The value of conciseness or brevity grows out of many of the same principles underlying vivacity. The basic principle is that "fewer words equals less friction." Kames explains that "to make a sudden and strong impression, some single circumstance happily selected, has more power than the most laboured description (I., p. 331). Priestley says: "In order to raise a very lively and tender sentiment, it is of advantage to describe the circumstances which raise it, in as *few words* as possible" (p. 101). A briefly expressed idea, he says, requires less transition time; it more closely resembles sensation. Also, since the writer or speaker tends to "disappear," the experience is less mediated. Brief expressions allow the reader or hearer to fill in the details in his own imagination, and he thus "sees" a complex whole which is consistent with his personal experience (p. 101). As Kames puts it, "when we are given the stimulus and the opportunity to use our imagination, we are pleased with the discovery [idea or conclusion] because it is our own work" (I., p. 276).

Campbell says that conciseness comes primarily from figures, for they tend to express complex relationships in compressed form (p. 337). Also, he says, brevity does not necessarily imply that a short message is better than a long one. Lack of conciseness is taking more time to express a thought than is required. Consequently, tautologies (for example, describing a fact as "plain and evident") are offenses against brevity (p. 338). Furthermore, conciseness is not a virtue on every occasion and with every audience. In oral situations, for instance, repetition is often necessary. Whately makes the same point. He suggests, however, that sometimes adding a pithy statement at the end of a long explanation will give a sense of brevity; the audience will *"understand* the longer, and *remember* the shorter" (p. 304).

Propriety   Modern theorists agree that one of the principal natural beauties is the fitness of means to ends, or propriety. It is also the ultimate criterion for symbolization. Priestley says that in judging any sort of composition we must fully understand the subject, identify the design, and evaluate the execution in terms of the purpose (p. 73). Campbell says that "perfection" in language is in proportion to its "fitness for serving the purposes" of the thought or sentiment to be communicated (p. 32). All of the decisions a communicator must make, all of the principles that must be taken into account in affecting the understanding, memory, imagination, and passions, must ultimately be based on propriety.

De Quincey expands on the importance of occasion and mode in making decisions with regard to degree of conciseness, level of abstraction, etc:

> That is good rhetoric for the hustings which is bad for a book. Even for the highest forms of popular eloquence the laws of style vary much from the general standard. In the senate, and for the same reason in a newspaper, it is a virtue to reiterate your meaning: tautology becomes a merit: variation of the words, with substantial identity of the sense and dilution of the truth, is oftentimes a necessity. A man who should content himself with a single condensed enunciation of a perplexed doctrine would be a madman. . . . you must shift your lights and vibrate your reflections at every possible angle, if you would agitate the popular mind extensively (*Style*, p. 139).

Following his own precepts, making his form fit his content and purpose, De Quincey continues:

> Every mode of intellectual communication has its separate strength and separate weaknesses,—its peculiar embarrassments, compensated by peculiar resources. It is the advantage of a book that you can return to the past page if anything in the present depends on it. But return being impossible in the case of a spoken harangue, where each sentence perishes as it is born, both the speaker and the hearer become aware of a mutual interest in a much looser style, and a perpetual dispensation from the severities of abstract discussion. It is for the benefit of both that the weightier propositions should be detained before the eye. . . . Time must be given for the intellect to eddy about a truth. . . . And this is obtained for the intellect by varying the modes of presenting it,—now putting it directly before the eye, now obliquely, now in an abstract shape, now in the concrete . . . (*Style*, pp. 139–140).

Blair is somewhat less eloquent in his discussion of propriety. He says simply that it is necessary "with respect to style, that we always study to adapt it to the subject, and also to the capacity of our hearers." In addition, he says, "Nothing merits the name of eloquent or beautiful which is not suited to the occasion" (II., p. 51). For example, in public deliberation, the speaker "must never kindle too soon; he must begin with moderation; and study to carry his hearers along with him, as he warms in the progress of his discourse" (II., p. 223). Also, he warns that though a diffuse style is generally better for public oral discourse, "every audience is very ready to be tired"; thus it is better to err through brevity than through length (II., p. 223).

Kames points out that the nature of the feelings to be expressed should affect our choice of language: "Elevated sentiments required elevated language; tender sentiments ought to be clothed in words that are soft and flowing. . . . Words are intimately connected with the ideas they represent: and if the former correspond not precisely to the latter our taste is not gratified" (II., p. 479). Campbell explains that lack of propriety can completely alienate our auditors. For instance, "against murder, cruelty, parricide, ingratitude, perfidy, to attempt to raise a laugh, would show such an unnatural insensibility in the speaker as would be excessively disgustful to any audience" (p. 21). Fenelon makes a similar point in explaining that "pleasure cannot be a part of every kind of message: Why seek the pleasant in a subject so terrifying? And why amuse the listener by a secular story of the grief of Artemisia, when one ought to thunder and present only the terrible images of death?" (p. 60).

Modern theorists leave no doubt that they consider symbolization, the styling of messages, as one of the most important processes in human communication. Language is, they agree, *the* means by which we express our feelings, intentions, desires, and thoughts (Campbell, p. 139). As we will see, they do not reject nonverbal communication, but verbal language is viewed as the primary organ of complex social organization. Whately points out that it is not language, *per se*, which distinguishes human beings from other animals. What is unique to humans, he says, is "the distinct use of language . . . as an *instrument of thought*,—a system of General Signs, without which the reasoning process could not be conducted" (p. 20).

The importance of the use of language in communicating our "reasoning" is heightened by the contingency of social reality. As Campbell has pointed out, in contingent questions there are always passions and arguments on both sides (p. 277). De Quincey explains that when we have "absolute facts to communicate from some [external] branch of study," we can be "careless of style." In such cases "the matter transcends and oppresses the manner" in a very high degree. On the other hand, in most cases we have no determinate *data*, what we say grows out of our internal sense, our "peculiar feelings" and our personal "way of viewing things." In these contingent areas, "the manner . . . *is* the matter" (*Style*, p. 226). As he explains:

> Ponderable facts and external realities are intelligible in almost any language; they are self-explained and self-sustained. But, the more

closely any exercise of mind is connected with what is internal and individual in the sensibilities . . . precisely in that degree, and the more subtly, does the style or the embodying of the thoughts cease to be a mere separable ornament (*Style*, p. 229).

Style, De Quincey says, has two basic functions: "first, to brighten the *intelligibility* of a subject which is obscure to the understanding; secondly, to regenerate the normal *power* and impressiveness of a subject which has become dormant to the sensibilities" (*Language*, p. 260). The latter function is the more important and pervasive. The former gives us knowledge, "*light* to see the road," but the latter gives us influence, "power to *advance along* it" (*Language*, p. 261). People who identify and popularize "truth" develop and maintain culture. Whately observes that identifying or knowing truth and making it intelligible and desireable do not always go hand in hand. Clarity of conception, he says, does not necessarily increase the likelihood of clarity in expression; "Universally, indeed, an unpracticed writer is liable to be misled by his own knowledge of his own meaning" (p. 264). This fact has led to an increased reliance on professionals who report the knowledge of experts. In the modern world, De Quincey explains, with the ever-increasing proliferation of professional communicators and or printed materials, it is style that more and more determines what will be read and who will be heard:

[I must insist] on the growing necessity of style as a practical interest in daily life. Upon subjects of public concern, and in proportion to that concern, there will always be a suitable (and as letters extend a growing) competition. Other things being equal, or appearing to be equal, the determining principle for the public choice will lie in the style (*Style*, p. 167).[16]

Organization

Organization is the process by which a communicator adapts symbols to social contingencies. It is that part of human communication theory which studies the nature of ordering and the process of relationship.

The traditional approach to organization in both the classical and the medieval and Renaissance periods was to consider a message as composed of from four to six parts, each of which had identifiable content and specific functions. This approach tended to be prescriptive and, especially in the Middle Ages, formulaic.

A second approach, which essentially disappeared at the end of the

---

[16] In this essay, De Quincey includes the attack on the deleterious effects of newspaper style cited in Chap. 4.

classical period, was more function-oriented and generic. This approach posited three basic processes in organizing information: definition, division, and proportion. Definition was viewed as the process of bringing scattered particulars together into a whole, as an analogic process dependent upon the ability to see "resemblances" or similarities. Division was the process of seeing differences, of distinguishing the parts of a whole in terms of natural or organic structure. Proportioning was the pragmatic focal point. It was the process of adapting the materials to the occasion. The emphasis was on the relationship between the source and receiver in a communication situation. Three classes of relationship were identified: (1) the teacher/student relationship, in which the purpose is instruction and the situation philosophical or epideictic, (2) the performer/judge relationship, in which the purpose is persuasion and the situation forensic, and (3) the leader/follower relationship, in which the purpose is advising and the situation deliberative. These relationships and situations, of course, overlap, and definition, division, and proportion were viewed as processes common to all communicative acts.

Modern theorists focus almost exclusively on this more generic functional approach to organization (see Fig. 5.4). Their primary concern is with the principles of ordering and the applications of these principles to conviction and persuasion. The traditional prescriptive approach is generally abandoned. In terms of a general scheme for organizing messages, the trend is to return to the Aristotelian position that a message must

---

Fig. 5.4   Modern Taxonomy of Organization

I. Definition—Initial ordering of information; limiting in light of subject, audience, and purpose
    A. Analysis—Ordering from general to particular, for learned audiences and more demonstrable subjects; investigation of truth
    B. Synthesis—Ordering from particular to general, for popular audiences and more contingent subjects; presentation of known truths
II. Division—Disposing arguments, facts, and functions throughout the message
    A. Prescriptive—Traditional four to six parts (see Blair's taxonomy, Fig. 5.5)
    B. Organic
        1. Natural—From experience and the laws of association
        2. "Artificial"—Adjustment to situational constraints
        3. Parts—Introductions and conclusions
        4. Word order
    C. Proportion—Influence of social contingencies, special contraints of the particular subject, the referent (things or persons) of the subject, the occasion (novel or routine), and the effect desired
        1. Forensic situations(lawyers)
        2. Deliberative situations(senators)
        3. Epideictic situations (preachers)

have at least two parts, statement and proof. At most, it might have an introduction, body (statement and proof), and a conclusion. Blair is one of the few who preserves the traditional six-part theory of organization. His presentation of it, however, is justified primarily as a guide to beginning students. His discussion emphasizes that not all six parts are always needed but that knowledge of the system may be an aid to creative ordering. Also, the six-part taxonomy provides him with a useful framework for synthesizing much of classical theory in the context of modern psychology (see Fig. 5.5 for an outline of Blair's synthesis).

Fig. 5.5   Blair's Prescriptive Taxonomy of Organization*

I. Introduction (Exordium)—Inducing the receiver to be benevolent, attentive, and receptive; may be explanatory or historical
    A. Should be natural and easy, grammatically correct, and in plain style
    B. Should be modest to establish ethos and subtle in tone rather than vehement
    C. Should be proportionate in length to the rest of the message
    D. Should not anticipate the substantive arguments (for that destroys novelty)
II. Proposition (announcement of the subject) and Division (optional announcement of the order to be followed)
    A. The proposition should be clear and distinct and expressed in few words
    B. The division should exhaust the subject, be natural, based on concise definition of terms, and divided into the fewest heads possible (e.g., five to six at most).
III. Narration—Explication of the facts without artifice
    A. Should be clear, for the understanding
    B. Should be probable, for belief (should reveal character and motives of the referents
    C. Should be concise, for memory and attention
IV. Argument
    A. Invention from study of the subject; best selection made by putting oneself in the receiver's position
    B. Disposition and arrangement, analytic, synthetic, or natural (by genre, by associational principles, by primacy or recency)
    C. Expression in style and manner (ideal presence, natural delivery)
V. Pathetic—Appeal to the emotions
    A. Follows understanding and conviction
    B. Must be introduced indirectly
    C. Uses methods resembling sensation and memory
    D. Requires real feeling from the communicator
    E. Uses natural language, avoids digressions, and is brief (warm feelings cool quickly)
VI. Conclusion (Peroration)—Whatever the cause rests on
    A. May be pathetic
    B. May be a summing up of arguments
    C. May be inferences from the body

* Deliberative situations serve as Blair's reference point in discussing each of the parts. In order to emphasize the fundamental flexibility of the taxonomy, however, he inserts a number of discussions of the special nature of each part in forensic and epideictic (religious) communication.

Rejection of Prescriptivism

Most modern theorists refer to the traditional prescriptive approach primarily in order to attack it. The classical lore of introductions and conclusions alone is exempt from attack. Fenelon says, for instance, that the "partition" or "division" prescribed by the medieval "scholastics" is unnatural, nonpragmatic, and more of a hindrance than an aid to either the receiver or the source. The partition usually came immediately after the introduction and consisted of a preview of the parts that would follow. Fenelon says that the partition was usually justified on the grounds that it assisted the auditor's memory. However, he claims, this is simply not the case. Given what we know of how the memory works, he explains, abstract or complicated lists of headings are not what people remember about a message; "Concrete things with some practical application are what they retain best" (p. 114).

Neither is an artificial partition useful to the source; it is just another thing to be memorized. What is most useful to the source, Fenelon says, is "a division that is found ready-made in the very subject itself; a division that clarifies, that puts the material into classes, that is easily remembered, and that helps one to retain everything else" (p. 61). This natural approach allows one to "grow" a message organically in light of the subject, occasion, and audience. It requires careful study prior to the communication event and usually includes "parts," such as introduction, proof, statement or proposition, narration, motivation, and conclusion. However these are not prescribed or artificially segmented. Fenelon describes the "natural" approach:

The speaker must have throughout a sequence of proofs. The first must prepare for the second, and the second strengthen the first. He must display his whole subject in the round, and favorably predispose the listener by a modest and suggestive introduction, by an air of honesty and frankness. Then he lays down his premises. Next he sets forth the facts in a simple, clear, and concrete way, emphasizing the circumstances which he will have to make sense of soon after. From premises and from facts he draws his conclusions, and he must arrange the reasoning in such a way that all the proofs help one another to be easily remembered. He ought to proceed so that the discourse may always go on growing, and so that the listener feels more and more the weight of truth. Then he must march out lively images and the movements adapted to arousing passion (pp. 112–113).

Fenelon's summary of natural organization sets the tone for the modern period. The focus is on natural processes of ordering in terms of definition of the subject, audience, and purpose, division of the subject into parts, and proportioning of the materials in terms of situational constraints. As with the other parts of the paradigm, adherence to the principles of human nature and flexibility in adjusting to particular circumstances are the guiding considerations.

Definition

Modern theorists agree that there are two basic approaches to the initial ordering of information: analysis and synthesis. These had been viewed as the fundamental processes of scientific inquiry, and, for the most part, modern theorists view them as *the* basis for division and proportion. Although the terms are used somewhat loosely, the basic distinction is Newtonian. Analysis proceeds from the particular to the general. From the observation of specific effects, one infers specific causes, and from these, more and more general causes. Synthesis proceeds from the general to the particular. Once the most general causes of things are known, one takes them as established principles and attempts to account for all the consequences that result from them. Analysis, then, precedes synthesis.

Priestley calls organization "method" and explains that analysis and synthesis are the two basic "methods of argumentation." He says, "In all science, we either proceed from particular observations to more general conclusions, which is *analysis*; or, beginning with more general and comprehensive propositions, we descend to the particular propositions which are contained in them, which is *synthesis*" (p. 42). Analysis, Priestley says, is essentially a method for the *"investigation of truth,"* for it proceeds from self-evident particulars to discovery of "analogy in effects" to "uniformity in cause." Synthesis is a method for explaining a "system of science to others." The first organization "is more tedious, but perhaps more sure"; however, it is suitable only for audiences who have been prepared by previous study and are interested in "new speculations" (pp. 43–44). The second organization is more appropriate for general audiences, for it begins with a larger proposition or theorem, which is then demonstrated through particulars that are generally well-known (p. 45).

Blair says that the analytic method "leads" auditors "step by step, from one truth to another, till the conclusion be stolen upon them, as the natural consequence of a chain of propositions" (II., p. 373). This method, however, is best for discovery of new truth. Thus, it is used only for "learned" audiences and even then only on rare occasions. The synthetic method, "when the point to be proved is fairly laid down, and one argument after another is made to bear upon it, till the hearers be fully convinced," is the more common and more effective organization for presentation of truth to "popular" audiences (II., p. 374). Whately likewise points out that the analytic method is philosophical and used to discover truth. However, he says, when a philosopher sets out to prove a truth, he will not often strictly "adhere to the same course of reasoning by which his own discoveries were originally made" (p. 5). Priestley explains that it is only when ideas arouse strong feeling that we should prefer to present them "in the very *order* and *connexion* in which they actually presented themselves to us at that time." Because of the natural and universal operations of the human mind, others are likely to be struck with them in much the same way we were. Also, the discourse will seem natural and therefore form will reinforce content in affecting conviction. Of course, when the process by which we arrived at ideas was tedious and frustrating, this principle would lead us to choose a more synthetic method of presentation (p. 31).

Thus, in practice, the discovery/presentation distinction tends to break down. Most commonly, Priestley explains, analysis and synthesis are mixed because both work on the same basic principles and one leads to the other. As he says: "Truth, whether geometrical, metaphysical, moral, or theological, is of the same nature, and the evidence of it is perceived in a similar manner by the same human minds" (p. 45). In terms of communicating to others, he continues, the basic appeal is always to "self-evident truths." In moral matters, these are internal feelings shared by all human beings; in religious matters, they are the scriptures; and in scientific matters, they are axioms. Thus, to prove any proposition, we may use either synthesis or analysis (p. 46). The result of our argument will be conclusive if the statement and proof are internally consistent (p. 47).

Whether or not the organization of the arguments will be effective, however, depends, Priestley says, on the nature of the audience. In some cases, we may need to reinforce the conclusions with culturally accepted maxims, to engage the imagination and passions with a vivid style, to refute objections to the proposition that may occur to the audience in order to allay possible prejudice, etc. (pp. 46–49).

Whately also points out that choice of organization depends on the audience. In "popular" discourse, he says, it is usually not a good idea to build analytically to a global truth because "the generality of men [are] better qualified for understanding (to use Lord Bacon's words) 'particulars, one by one,' than for taking a comprehensive view of a whole" (p. 75). In a "Galaxy of evidence," where every point builds in a chain to every other, and the ultimate goal is appreciation of the "lustre of the combination," the auditors' abilities are heavily taxed. Popular audiences usually are not able or willing to follow such arguments (p. 76). On the other hand, he says, often "the combined force of the series of Arguments results from the *order* in which they are considered"; in such cases the "*progressive* tendency" is so strong that almost anyone can follow and will be convinced (p. 82).

Clearly, then, audience is not the only pertinent variable; the nature of the arguments and of the subjects must also be taken into account. Blair says that the division must be organic to the subject: "We must divide the subject into those parts into which most easily and naturally it is resolved, that it may seem to split itself, and not to be violently torn asunder" (II., p. 360). A further consideration, Whately says, is the purpose. In fact, he points out that it is the interaction of subject, audience, and purpose that is primary: "The first rule to be observed is, that it should be considered whether the principal object of the discourse be, to give *satisfaction to a candid mind*, and convey *instruction* to those who are ready to receive it, or to *compel* the assent, or silence the objections of an opponent" (p. 108). A *priori*, synthetic arguments from cause to effect are better for instruction. Analytic arguments from effect to cause are better for refuting error because they tend to be almost unanswerable. Analogy, for instance, is especially good for this purpose. Such a *posteriori* arguments are not as good for instruction because they require more effort and do not please and console the auditor (p. 109). This, however, is not a hard and fast rule. Kames, for instance, points out that in some cases the analytic movement from particular to more and more comprehensive views can be pleasurable, for it "expands" the mind (I., p. 22).

Division

When it comes to actually ordering a message for presentation to others, neither pure synthesis nor pure analysis is likely to be effective. As we have seen, modern theorists agree that few human concerns are susceptible to demonstration. In moral reasoning, we must take into account the "natural" processes of intuition and deduction, of beliefs arrived at through experience, testimony, etc., as well as the nature of the faculties of the mind.

Natural Principles   Kames says that a sense of order is inherent in human beings: "There is implanted in the breast of every man a principle of order, which governs the arrangement of his perceptions, of his ideas, and of his action" (I., p. 20). This natural principle is exemplified in our tendency to view history chronologically, to speak of a family in terms of founders and descendants, to conceive of a tree as a trunk with branches. Also, our emotional responses are natural, e.g., "the mind falls with a heavy body, descends with a river, and ascends with flame and smoke" (I., p. 21).

Priestley says that it is the operation of the laws of association which indicate "method" is natural to humans. The basic principle of organization is that "by means of their *natural relations* . . . ideas introduce one another, and *cohere*, as it were, in the mind" (p. 34). The strongest "order of nature," Priestley says, is time and place, for it is the one to which our minds are most accustomed and it is therefore most easily recognized and remembered (p. 34). The ordering of proofs, he says, should be in terms of such natural classes. In addition to time and place, he lists cause and effect, worth, dignity, importance, principal influence.

These are so basic, he says, "so habitually do we attend to them, that a considerable offense against them, even in common conversation, would be instantly perceived and give a sensible disgust" (p. 277). On a more general level, Priestley recommends that in moral and/or theological questions arguments may be grouped in terms of their common characteristics, e.g., in terms of arguments from observation or experience, from authority, from reason or common sense, and so on (p. 51). Kames makes a similar observation and provides a progressive listing of kinds of natural order:

> Order regards various particulars. First, in tracing or surveying objects, we are directed by a sense of order: we conceive it to be more orderly, that we should pass from a principal to its accessories, and from a whole to its parts, than in the contrary direction. Next, with respect to the position of things, a sense of order directs us to place together things intimately connected. Thirdly, in placing things that have no natural connection, that order appears the most perfect, where the particulars are made to bear the strongest relation to each other that position can give them (II., p. 516).

Examples of the principle of order by position are parallelism (first, second, third, or balanced sentence structure) and proportion (large, small, smaller). Also, says Kames, the overall structure of a message can be viewed as an instance of order by position reinforced by natural properties of the mind. The notion that a message should have a beginning, a middle, and an end is based on the "propensity" of the mind "to go forward in the chain of history." The natural structure is that the introduction takes the auditor "into the heat of action," the body involves him in the occurence of events, and the end satisfies him through the resolution of the events or the accomplishment of the plan. This structure appeals to us because the human mind "keeps always in view the expected event; and when the incidents or under-parts are connected together by their relation to the event, the mind runs sweetly and easily along them" (II., pp. 400–401).

Campbell points out that in the body of a discourse, the narration of events, the "first requisite" is that "the order in which they are exhibited be what is commonly called natural, that is, congruent to common experience" (p. 84). Priestley makes a similar point, explaining that narration is commonly required whenever our arguments are drawn from "cases of fact," and often our conclusions depend on the clarity and plausibility of the narration (p. 50). Whately reinforces the importance of natural and plausible narration. People, he says, "are apt to listen with prejudice to the Arguments adduced to prove anything which appears *abstractly* improbable" (p. 137).

Campbell expands on the requirement for natural order. He says,

"The credibility of the fact [a moral proposition] is the sum of the evidence of all the arguments, often independent of one another, brought to support it" (p. 75). Natural connections serve to help the auditor remember the evidence and prevent the possibility that information will efface the memory, and therefore impact, of earlier information. Also, natural connections contribute to ideal presence, a key source of evidence based on experience.

Artificial Structure   Priestley points out that the general rule for organizing is to dispose materials by "attention to the strongest and most usual *association of ideas* in the human mind" (p. 35). However, sometimes it is a good idea to digress, "to relieve the attention, please the imagination, refresh and assist the memory" (p. 35). Such digression, or "scholia," may serve not only for relief, but may in fact reinforce the central train of argument. For instance, scholia may "illustrate the nature and force of the evidence, or point out similar processes in other subjects."[17] Also, for strength as well as variety, we might want to insert some discussion of "corollaries," other truths which be deduced from our arguments, but which are not central to the case. For instance, we might mention the comparative advantages of our proposal over other possibilities (p. 51).

Such diversion from the natural order of reason is necessary because the division of a message must be in accord with not only the understanding, memory, and imagination, but with the passions. Whately points out, for example, that the natural order is to state the proposition, then give the reasons. This approach, however, can sometimes seem dogmatic. To avoid such an appearance, we may want to reverse the order and prove the proposition "in installments" (p. 142). Also, when our proposition is unfamiliar or potentially unacceptable to the audience, it should be stated after the arguments and proofs as a conclusion. The source thus conciliates the audience by "assuming in some degree the character of an *investigator*" (p. 141). Although this order is the opposite of nature, it is in many cases "better adapted to engage and keep attention" (p. 144). For similar reasons, Whately recommends placing refutation in the middle of the arguments, "but nearer the beginning than the end." Mentioning the objections too early gives the impression that the source accepts them as presumptive; leaving them until last is risky, for the audience's knowledge of them may prejudice their perception of the arguments. If the objections are generally well-known, they should be mentioned early in conjunction with a promise to treat them in more detail later (p. 146).

Along these same lines, the functioning of ethos dictates that when we have a number of arguments from authority, we should select those

---

[17] In writing, Priestley says, we may save scholia for footnotes, though in oral discourse we must insert them within the text.

from the best known sources. In terms of sermons, Whately says, the order of preference would be well-known scriptures, eminent Fathers, and Biblical scholars. The principle is to select arguments of which the most unlearned audience member is more likely to be "by his own knowledge, a competent judge" (p. 165). Likewise, in ordering arguments, we should follow the principle of placing first the most obvious ones and/or those which are naturally pre-eminent. The strongest argument should be placed last. However, Whately says, if it should happen that the strongest is also the most natural, then we should place it first but, to prevent anticlimax, we should recapitulate in reverse order in the conclusion (p. 168). As Blair says, we should always take advantage of the effects of recency and of the natural principle of climax and "place that last on which we choose that the strength of our cause should rest" (II., p. 394).

Spencer points out that the formal characteristics of messages can engage the passions. Emotional responses are "partially aroused by the forms themselves." Formal elements create a certain degree of animation. They induce a preparatory sympathy, and when the striking ideas looked for are reached, they are more vividly realized" (p. 15). Kames likewise points out that the passions are, in part, engaged simply by the perception of natural order: "We are framed by nature to relish order and connection, we are conscious of a certain pleasure arising from that circumstance" (I., p. 23). In terms of specific address to the passions, however, we may sometimes need to spend more time and give more detail than would normally be "reasonable," in order to allow for the natural development of a particular motive. Emotions, Kames says, "have different periods of birth and increment: and to give opportunity for these different periods, it is necessary that the cause of every emotion be present to the mind a due time; for an emotion is not brought to its height but by reiterated impressions" (I., p. 86). Also, he points out, strong emotions which are quickly raised are equally quick to dissipate; therefore they ought to be saved until the end of the message (I., p. 389). Fenelon reminds us of the association of passions when he says that we should use appeals to emotion progressively, so that one builds on the other, saving the most striking for last (p. 113). He explains that a communicator "must understand the connexions which the passions have among themselves: those which he can most easily arouse at first and then employ to arouse others; those next which can produce the greatest effects" (p. 114).

Message Parts   The only "parts" of a message that most modern theorists discuss explicity are introductions and conclusions. Blair cites the three traditional Ciceronian functions of the introduction, to lead the receiver to be benevolent, attentive, and receptive. He also includes the usual distinction between direct and indirect introductions, discussing them in terms of friendly, neutral, and hostile audiences. Like the classical theorists, he points out that the primary function of the introduction is establishment of ethos (II., pp. 344–356). Whately cites Aristotle in observing that introductions are not really necessary. However, he says, they do serve "to avoid an appearance of abruptness and to facilitate . . . the object proposed [by showing that the subject is] *important, curious,* or otherwise *interesting* and worthy of attention [perhaps because it has been] *neglected, misunderstood,* or *misrepresented"* (pp. 169–170).

The introduction, Whately says, may also be used to prepare the audience to avoid mistaking your purpose. A short narration that outlines the message "in miniature" can sometimes serve this function (p. 170). More importantly, however, the introduction establishes ethos, "a feeling of approbation towards the speaker, or a prejudice against an opponent," and can be used to stimulate pathos, "appeals to various passions and feelings in the hearers" (p. 172). The introduction can thus be very important. For instance, Whately says, book titles are introductions, and titles are often instrumental in attracting or repelling an audience. Like Blair (II., p. 345), Whately concludes his discussion by recommending that the communicator write the introduction last, after he has a complete idea of the message (p. 169)

The ending of a message may be of equal or more importance than the beginning. Conclusions, Blair says, should contain the "final" appeal to the auditors. This may be pathos, a summary of key arguments, or inferences growing out of the body (II., p. 394). The important thing is, he says, to signal the ending, close quickly but not abruptly, and leave the hearers with a favorable impression of both ourselves and our subject (II., pp. 394–396). Fenelon says that the conclusion should probably aim primarily at pathos, although sometimes a communicator may want to end with a summary of the "most persuasive things he has said" (p. 113).

Whately says that the conclusion should be a "compressed repetition" or recapitulation of the main points (p. 173). This should be as brief as possible but needs to be more detailed "the more uncultivated the audience" (p. 193). The important thing about conclusions is that they be neither too abrupt nor too long. To err on the side of length, however, is the worse fault. The audience, expecting the end to be imminent (from verbal and nonverbal clues) is likely to become impatient and even angry "because the disappointment caused is not . . . *single,* but repeated and prolonged" (p. 172). Such frustration, of course, tends to weaken the overall impact of the message. Finally, Whately says, the length and content of the conclusion is most important in oral communication. A reader can usually anticipate the length, can skim the content, and can return to it for future reference. In oral situations, the hearer is captive; he cannot manipulate the time that will be devoted to the conclusion, and he has only one chance to absorb the information (p. 172). Thus,

Whately says that one of the most important rules in preparing to speak is to outline the conclusion fully and "*never* depart from your design" (p. 174).

Word Order   Modern theorists extend the principles of natural order and structure in division beyond arguments, facts, and message parts to include the ordering of words in sentences. Campbell explains that the arrangement of words ought to contribute to perspicuity and vivacity:

> The placing of the words in a sentence resembles, in some degree, the disposition of figures in a history piece [a painting]. As the principal figure ought to have that situation in the picture which will, at the first glance, fix the eye of the spectator, so the emphatical word ought to have that place in the sentence which will give it the greatest advantage for fixing the attention of the hearer (p. 353).

Of course, Campbell points out, it is often more difficult in discursive than in presentational modes to determine which is the principal symbol or what is the principal position. Also, in English, word order is often not a matter of choice, for to a large extent order determines meaning. For the most part, he says, we should follow common usage except when we want to express passion or create special liveliness. Priestley makes similar observations, pointing out that "unnatural" word order is "natural" only in cases of strong emotion: "In all strong passions, some one idea being present to the mind more immenently than others, persons under the influence of them naturally express that idea first, even though it obliges them to throw the sentence in which it is introduced into disorder" (p. 102). "Disorder" resulting from passion, he says, is consistent with our habitual association. Disorder resulting from grammatical or syntactic error, however, is repellent for it "*baulks*, as it were, *our expectations*" (p. 277).

Spencer also uses the principle of association in his account of word order. The arrangement of words into sentences, he says, is based on "the mental act by which the meaning of a series of words is apprehended" (p. 5). When the order does not correspond to natural processes of apprehension, a "check is given in the process of thought," and/or a misconception is formed.[18] The best way to form a conception, he explains,

---

[18] Spencer gives a highly enthnocentric, but entertaining, argument for the superiority of English over French word order. He claims that the natural workings of the mind make the phrase "a black horse" easier to comprehend than "a horse black." This, he explains, is because if we hear the word "horse" first, we form a mental image of a horse, probably a brown one since that color is more common. If we then hear the word "black," we have to go back and erase the original image in order to replace it with a new one. This wastes

is one piece at a time, adding particulars to "build" a thought. This method works not only because it is consistent with the natural process of perception, but because of "our ability to anticipate the words yet unspoken" (p. 5). The principle behind the ordering of words is "economy" of mental energy and attention. As Spencer explains:

> A reader or hearer has at each moment but a limited amount of mental power available. To recognize and interpret the symbols presented to him, requires part of this power; to arrange and combine the images suggested, requires a further part; and only that part which remains can be used for realizing the thought conveyed (p. 2).

Thus, says Spencer, in general we should try to arrange words so that they are most easily interpreted. This means "placing first all words indicating the quality, conduct or condition of the subject," placing subordinate propositions before principal ones, and keeping similar ideas in close proximity. All of these lead to fewer "checks" or "suspensions" in the receiver's mind and therefore to smoother, easier, and more accurate conception (pp. 6–8).

This kind of order is synthetic. Spencer calls it the natural or "indirect" method. Sometimes, however, we may want to use the "direct" method traditionally known as the "periodic sentence." In the direct order, the principle words and phrases are suspended until the end of the sentence. As Campbell explains it, in periodic structure, "you defer the blow a little, but it is solely that you may bring it down with greater weight" (p. 372). Which of these methods we use, Spencer says, is "decided by considering the capacity of the persons addressed" (p. 9). The direct method is essentially analytic and thus requires a highly developed mind: "To recollect a number of preliminaries stated in elucidation of a coming idea, and to apply them all to the formation of it when suggested, demands a good memory and considerable power of concentration" (p. 9). The indirect method is thus best for the "uncultivated" because it is simpler and the more common. Finally, Spencer says that with most audiences it is best to mix the two, especially if the discourse is long. With intricate ideas and very subtle arguments, we will want to use

---

mental energy and is frustrating. On the other hand, if we hear the word "black" first, we form only a general conception of darkness, which is immediately connected with whatever word follows. This activity requires little energy and is intellectually pleasurable because of its naturalness (p. 5). Spencer never notes, in this argument, the possibility of culturally learned language patterns. In typical nineteenth-century style, he assumes that what is true for an educated Englishman like himself is true for all human beings. Still, the notion that people have normal expectations in terms of word order cannot be denied, and the concept of violation of expectations or drain on mental energies has appealing explanatory power.

the indirect method, saving the direct for more easily comprehended portions (p. 10).

Thus, modern theories of division, whether the focus is on the whole message, the arguments, the specific parts, or the words, stress naturalness and flexibility in adapting to the constraints of the subject and situation. Priestley gives an excellent summary of the nature of division in modern organizational theory:

> The meaning of the terms of the proposition should be accurately fixed, principles made use of in the demonstration [central argument] distinctly noted, and, if there be occasion, proved; the question stated in the most intelligible manner, with a circumstantial relation of every fact that may contribute to set it in the clearest point of light, and the subject divided into the distinct parts of which it consists. The order of nature must chiefly be consulted in arranging the arguments brought to support each of them, and slight probabilities should be introduced in an indirect manner. Observations relating to the nature of the proof that is made use of, with the connexion and mutual influence of the several arguments, and other miscellaneous remarks that may naturally occur, come next; and the whole discourse closes with a view of the extent of the doctrine, in all the valuable inferences and uses that may be drawn from it (p. 52).

Proportion

As we have seen, most of the modern lore of definition and division is based on proportioning, or adjusting, the organization to the subject, audience, occasion, and purpose. Blair gives the traditional precept behind proportion: "No one should ever rise to speak in public, without forming to himself a just and strict idea of what suits his own age and character; what suits the subject, the hearers, the place, the occasion; and adjusting the whole train and manner of his speaking on this" (II., p. 226). This principle, he says, can be summarized in terms of the three "decorums of time, place, and character" which must be attended to in all communication (II., p. 226).

Whately says that proportion depends greatly on ethos, the relationship between the source and the receiver. Some people, he explains, give deference "to a vigorous *claim*—to an authoritative and overbearing demeanor." Others will yield to influence only from those who have "a soothing, insinuating, flattering, and seemingly submissive demeanour" (p. 120). The first type, "those of arrogant disposition," are particularly influenced by authority. This is especially true, Whately says, if the authority is ancient (p. 120). The second type are more likely to be influenced by affection, by attraction to "the person's looks—tones of voice—gestures—choice of expressions" (p. 111). Authority, with this type, "seems to act according to the law of Gravitation; inversely as the squares of the *distances*"; they take the opinion of whoever is "nearest," or most attractive (p. 121).

In his discussion of audiences as people "in particular," Campbell analyzes a number of the social contingencies to which a communicator must adapt. He says that there are three basic genres of discourse: communication at the bar (forensic), in the senate (deliberative), and from the pulpit (epideictic). This listing, he says, is traditional and may seem constricted. However, it includes the major professional communication careers and allows for the illustration of general principles which apply to all communicative products or events (p. 99). Having established a taxonomy of situations, Campbell proceeds to discuss the comparative constraints within each of them in regard to the subject, the referent, the occasion, and the effect intended.[19]

Analysis of the *subject*, he says, should be carried out in terms of "the topics of argument, motives, and principles" which are suitable to the occasion and the effect desired, and in terms of "the persons or things in whose favour" the source wants to influence the audience's decision (p. 104). The lawyer is at a disadvantage in this area, Campbell says, because most of his subjects are boring, technical analyses of precedents and statutes. His three topics are law, fact, and justice, and only the last is likely to give rise to any "great principles" (p. 104). The senator's topics are the advantages and disadvantages of a course of action in terms of its utility. Though these sometimes lead to involved and complex arguments, they are "in the main more favorable to the display of pathos, vehemence, and sublimity than the much greater part of the forensic cause can be said to be" (p. 105). The preacher, however, is the most well off in this area, for his topics are the origin of man, his dignity and degeneracy, salvation, misery, and immortal happiness. These give "scope for the exertion of all the highest powers of rhetoric" (p. 105).

In terms of the *referent* of their subjects, the lawyer and senator are better off than the preacher. Their subject is persons; the preacher's subject is things. For example, Campbell says: "The preacher's business is solely to excite your detestation of the crime; the pleader's business is principally to make you detest the criminal." The "degree of abstraction" inherent in the subjects of preaching make it more difficult to engage the understanding. Also, they have a weaker "hold of the imagination" (p. 105).

The lawyer and senator likewise have an advantage in terms of the *occasions* of their communication. Their audiences come with basic

---

[19] Campbell's observations are repeated, with little or no modification, by a number of theorists (see Blair, II., pp. 213–296 and Whately, pp. 230–256). Thus, his treatment is characteristic of the general modern theory of communication situations and is a slight modification of classical theory.

knowledge of the specific subject to be discussed, a belief in its importance, and a "curiosity which sharpens their attention, and assists both their understanding and their memory." This results from the fact that "the point to be discussed hath generally for some time before been a topic of conversation in most companies, perhaps throughout the kingdom, (which of itself is sufficient to give consequence to any thing,) people are apprized beforehand of the particular day fixed for the discussion" (p. 105). The preacher's situation is very different. The congregation usually does not know the specific subject until he begins. Although the topic is more important in abstract terms, people's curiosity cannot be aroused "in an instant." Even on those occasions when the audience does know the specific subject, as on special holidays, the frequent recurrence of these and their predictability destroys any novelty; they know they will hear it all again next year (p. 106). Also, Campbell points out, the preacher suffers from the lack of "opposition and contradiction" common in the senate and courtroom: "Opponents sharpen one another, as iron sharpeneth iron. There is not the same spur either to exertion in the speaker, or to attention in the hearer, where there is no conflict" (p. 107).

The *effect* intended in the situation is the final constraint. Campbell says that the preacher's job is by far the most difficult, for he wants to bring about behavioral change: "Reformation of life and manners—of all things which is the most difficult by any means whatever to effectuate." This is, he adds, "of all the tasks ever attempted by persuasion, that which has the most frequently baffled its power" (p. 107). The senator and the lawyer need only to bring about a temporary conviction, one that lasts long enough for them to collect their votes. The preacher, however, wants "not a momentary, but a permanent effect" on hearts and dispositions. Only in the case of some occasional sermons, such as a plea for a special charity, is the preacher's task comparable to the lawyer's or senator's (pp. 110–111).

In terms of achieving his desired effects, the preacher also has to face constraints imposed by the mixed nature of a church congregation. He must be "analytic" for the educated and "synthetic" for the uneducated. He must discover ways to stir the passions and elicit motives from a group with widely varying predispositions. Lawyers and senators, on the other hand, usually have a homogeneous audience of highly educated people. Also, moving the passions is a special problem. Contrary to popular opinion, Campbell says, it requires more skill to move the more educated than to move the less educated. Appeals to the emotions must be more covert for the educated and based on more careful argument. Thus, the lawyer and senator may be thought to have a slightly more difficult task in this regard. However, Campbell says, the preacher should be addressing most of his effort toward the "learned" members of the congregation, for they set the example of behavior for the rest (p. 104).

His particular problem is to do so without alienating those who are "unlearned."

As we have said, Campbell did not intend that this analysis of situational constraints be interpreted as exhaustive. Rather it is intended to be indicative of the *kinds* of circumstances one should take into account in organizing a message. The principles of definition and division must be interpreted in terms of the principles of proportion.

The modern theorists, as we will see, were agreed in their preference for "unprepared," or extemporaneous address. Whether the end product was oral or written, they recommended much general preparation supplemented with, perhaps, a rough outline as a guide to actual operationalization. Whately says that an outline of the content and order should serve as a "track," not as a "groove." Its function is to give coherence and "due proportion" to the final composition (p. 25). Thus, Fenelon claims that Cicero's approach, although it is couched in terms of oral communication, is probably a good general guide to organizing a message:

> [Cicero] appears to limit himself to the wish that the speaker arrange carefully all parts of his speech in his mind and prearrange figures and central terms to be used, reserving to himself the opportunity to throw in on the spur of the moment whatever necessity and design of things would inspire (p. 109).[20]

Operationalization

Operationalization is the process of implementing messages. In practice, it is the process by which the message is embodied in some physical form for delivery to others. In theory, it is the study of the use of media, the nature of information transmission, and the processes of symbolic interaction.

Classical theorists focused on the use of voice and body in operationalizing oral messages. Although they unanimously emphasized the importance of "delivery," for the most part they had little to say about it. Aristotle claimed that it was not susceptible to theorizing but rather a skill to be developed through imitation and practice. Cicero made numerous observations about the natural expressive power of the voice and body and decried the lack of systematic study in the area. He especially emphasized the role of oral delivery in establishing ethos and eliciting pathos. The few other classical attempts to investigate "body language" tended to be technical and prescriptive, and their authors

---

[20] Cicero, of course, is also a primary source of the prescriptive six-part taxonomy. Fenelon, however, refers primarily to Cicero's more theoretic treatment of communication in *De Oratore*, rejecting, as Cicero himself did, the prescriptive *De Inventione* favored by medieval and early Renaissance scholars.

seemed to have little faith in their enterprise (see "Operationalization" in Chap. 2).

Medieval and Renaissance scholars maintained the customary classical emphasis, although they tended to ignore the more theoretic approach in favor of rehashing the prescriptive content of Roman rhetorics such as the *Rhetorica ad Herrenium*. A number of later Renaissance theorists complained about the poor oral delivery of their contemporaries, especially that of preachers. Both Bacon and Augustine made some preliminary observations on the more theoretic aspects of nonverbal communication, but neither elaborated.

What distinguishes modern scholars' approaches to operationalization is not only their emphasis on its extreme importance to all communication, but their development of a major body of literature devoted exclusively to oral delivery. The major theorists are Ciceronian in their handling of the subject, emphasizing general theoretic principles. As we have seen, the "elocutionists" tended to be prescriptive, emphasizing mechanical rules such as those found in the minor Roman rhetorics. The development, content, and nature of elocution was discussed in Chap. 4. Here we will refer to elocutionary doctrine only in terms of the major theorists' rejection of it.

Modern theorists agree that extemporaneous, oral communication is superior to all other modes of communication. They thus use it as the prototypical source of principles and standards in discussing operationalization. Although theirs is the age of print, reading and writing are discussed primarily in terms of their differences from, and "inferiority" to, speaking and listening. Modern operationalization theory focuses on the organic unity of medium and message. From an anlysis of the senses employed in perceiving messages, modern theorists conclude that oral communication is the most involving mode. From theories of the operation of the faculties and of the sympathetic nature of logos, ethos, and pathos, they conclude that extemporaneous communication is the most natural and persuasive form. Their criteria for effective operationalization grow out of these pragmatic concerns and are conceptually parallel to the criteria of symbolization (see Fig. 5.6).

Organic Operationalization

As we have seen, modern theorists emphasize the instrumental impact of form in conjunction with content. Kames, for instance, points out a variety of ways in which the form of literature is in itself persuasive. The chain of events in a narrative, from onset to resolution, reinforces our belief in cause and effect relationships. The rewarding of good and punishment of evil tends to reinforce "a habit of virtue, by exciting us to do what is right, and restraining us from what is wrong" (II., pp. 368–369). Furthermore, he says, each of the modes of communication has peculiar strengths that arise from its method of operationalization. Thus,

---

Fig. 5.6   Modern Taxonomy of Operationalization

I. Organic Operationalization—Unity of form and content
   A. Unity of sense and sound—Use of voice to reinforce meaning
   B. Unity of sound and sight—Use of gestures to reinforce verbalization
II. Extemporaneous Operationalization
   A. Logos—Reinforcement of the understanding and basis of conviction
   B. Ethos—Personal credibility; reinforcement of conviction
   C. Pathos—Engagement of the passions; instrumental to persuasion
III. Criteria of Operationalization—Natural and conversational standards
   A. Perspicuity—Clear or transparent manner
   B. Energy—Forcible expression
   C. Propriety—Appropriateness to subject, place, occasion, purpose, source, receiver

---

"dialogue is the best qualified for expressing sentiment" because of the exchange and clarification of thoughts. Narrative, because of its cause and effect structure, is best for "displaying fact." The "tender passions are more peculiarly the province of tragedy," because of its structure of hopes dashed, whereas the hopes-realized structure of epic poetry makes it more suitable for "grand and heoic actions" (II., p. 27). Furthermore, he points out, because music is uplifting, disagreeable passions should not be expressed in vocal arrangements, nor should villains express their evil sentiments in song (II., p. 131).

The strengths of the various communication arts, Kames says, also vary according to the media they employ. He explains that the "pleasure" we feel in responding to messages is stronger if we experience a mix of emotions. Also, the strength of mixed emotions is "inversely in proportion to the degree of connection between the causes." Thus, the strength of our response is increased to the degree that perception requires a combination of different senses (II., p. 119). Painting, for instance, can only command emotions "produced by sight." Gardening, on the other hand, engages the senses of touch and smell as well as sight. Thus, painting is especially effective in arousing painful emotions, but gardening can raise these and a variety of others: grandeur, sweetness, gaiety, wildness, surprise, and wonder. Architecture also engages a variety of senses and therefore a mix of emotions, although it especially evokes grandeur and utility (II., p. 426–427).

In terms of the more traditional media of communication, Kames says that theatre is one of the most powerful. Because of the combination of sight and sound, it most easily creates ideal presence. Print has less impact, for it is limited in terms of the senses engaged, primarily sight and touch. However, it can make the "succession of impressions" that are necessary to raise passion. Painting, of course, is limited to dealing with a single instant in time, engages only one primary sense, and is therefore more limited in its potentiality for raising emotional responses (I., p. 88).

The most engaging, powerful, and potentially pleasurable mode of operationalization, most modern theorists agree, is extemporaneous oral communication. Like theatre, public speaking involves both sight and hearing. Like gardening and architecture, it is an eventful art; people must become engaged in order to experience it. It takes place in time and thus can create ideal presence and strong emotional responses. Because it is "real" rather than mediated by the fiction of costumes, sets, and drama, it engages sympathy naturally. Priestley emphasizes the "personalness" of public speaking, using the pulpit and the theatre as examples: "It is really much more difficult to *preach* well, than to *act* well." This, he says, is because in acting we expect to see "art," but in preaching, art interferes with "earnestness." An actor speaks as a character; he is not personally responsible for his behavior. A preacher, like all public speakers, must speak as himself. In a very real sense, selfhood is always at risk in such a situation (p. 266). Campbell refers to the same characteristics, emphasizing their ability to arouse sympathetic emotional responses:

> A person present with us, whom we see and hear, and who, by words, and looks, and gestures, gives the liveliest sense of his feelings, has the surest and most immediate claim on our sympathy. We become infected with his passions. We are hurried along with them, and not allowed leisure to distinguish between his relation and our relation, his interest and our interest (p. 90).

Unity of Sound and Sense   Orality, in itself, is one source of the power of extemporaneous public speaking. Although modern theorists agree that language is arbitrary and words have no inherent connection with "things," they point out that some sounds (syllables, words, and combinations of words) seem to carry meaning above and beyond their assigned meaning. When the "meaning" of a sound is made to echo the sense of a word, the impression created is strengthened. For instance, Campbell explains that sound can reinforce sense in terms of time and motion, in terms of size, and in terms of difficulty and ease. Thus, rapid events can be narrated through a quick succession of short words; "things grand may be imitated by long and well-sounding words, things little by short words," and "what is performed with facility can be uttered with ease." A sense of difficulty can be conveyed by an aspirate placed between two vowels, e.g., "up the high hill he heaved a huge round stone" (pp. 32–325).

Also, Campbell says, rhythm may convey meaning: "When the cadences happen mostly after long syllables, the verse will naturally have an air of greater gravity" (p. 328). However, he goes on to point out that the imitation of sense with sound is rare and is appropriately used only in the pathetic and descriptive parts of poetry or in the most persuasive parts of prose. It would usually be incongruous in argumentation. Furthermore, he says, the absence of sound/sense unity is never a defect, although if used to excess its presence may be. The effectiveness of it depends on its "being placed with judgment" (pp. 331–332).

Kames' analysis of the resemblance of sound and sense is somewhat more technical and prescriptive than Campbell's. He points out that "sound itself cannot have a resemblance to anything but sound"; however, sounds can have a "resemblance of effects" with other phenomena. Thus rapid pronunciation can resemble motion in its effect (II., pp. 87–88). Roughness, interruptedness, ease, and labor can also be imitated (II., pp. 89–91). This resemblance, Kames says, is natural, for "in language, sound and sense are so intimately connected, as that the properties of one are readily communicated to the other" (II., p. 84).

This natural congruence can, of course, be heightened by art. For instance, Kames says that the harshness or smoothness of a sound or syllable and its length are dictated by customary rules of pronunciation. The tone in which it is pronounced, high or low, its volume, and the speed of delivery are all matters of art. Thus pronunciation, in these last three aspects, resembles music. The speaker can vary tone, volume, and speed to create mood: "In pronouncing words signifying what is elevated, the voice ought to be raised above its ordinary pitch; and words signifying dejection of mind ought to be pronounced in a low tone, etc." (II., p. 94).

Spencer says that the formal effects of the sounds of words are traceable to the laws of association. Saxon words, for instance, are more forcible than others because they are learned first and therefore have the strongest and most immediate associations. Since they are also the shortest words, the receiver expends less mental energy interpreting them. However, he says, the speaker should use long words when he or she wants the receiver's mind to linger on an idea and should use unusual words to express unusual ideas. Thus "vast" does not fill the mouth, or the mind, in the same way "stupendous" does (p. 4).

Both Fenelon and Priestley reinforce these basic ideas. Fenelon says that pronunciation ought to be organic to sense. Pronunciation is, he says, "a kind of music: all its beauty consists in the variety of its tones as they rise or fall according to the things which they have to express" (p. 102). Priestley adds that not only is pronunciation similar to music in its ability to create mood, but moods can determine pronunciation. Thus our state of mind may lead us to pause frequently or to speak quickly or slowly. In a sense, then, the meaning of sounds is not all that arbitrary. It is natural and inherent (pp. 289–293). Blair agrees that sounds have natural meanings. So also, he says, does absence of sound. The natural meanings of sounds or silences can be used artistically, e.g., pauses can be used to "fix the hearer's attention," or to "mark the distinctions of sense" as well as to convey or set a mood (II., p. 408).

Unity of Sound and Sight   Unmediated oral communication acquires additional power from the fact that it appeals not only to the sense of hearing but to the sense of sight. Fenelon writes that much of the impact of an oral message grows out of the organic unity of visual and oral expression with the purpose and meaning. For instance, he says: "The more the action and the voice appear simple and familiar in the places where you are only seeking to instruct, to report, and to suggest, the better do they prepare for surprise and emotion in those places where they are elevated by sudden enthusiasm" (p. 102). In the use of the body, he continues, the important thing is that "everything in it represent vividly and naturally the sentiments of him who is speaking and the nature of the things he speaks of" (p. 99). Similarly, Spencer says that, "in one possessed by a fully developed power of speech," voice, body, and sentiment naturally work together: "the play of the features, the tones of the voice and its cadences, vary in harmony with every thought uttered" (p. 19).

A number of theorists point out that nonverbal communication is the most impactful and natural. As Spencer explains: "To say 'leave the room' is less expressive than to point to the door. Placing a finger on the lips is more forcible than whispering 'Do not speak' " (p. 2). Priestley says that "attitudes, gestures, and looks" are more expressive of feelings than words (p. 77). Fenelon calls nonverbal communication the "painting of the thoughts of the soul" (p. 99). He cites Cicero's observation that the human face and eyes are the most expressive media: "Nothing speaks so fully as the face. It expresses everything. But of the whole face, the eyes make the chief effect. A single glance thrown to good purpose will strike the depths of the heart" (p. 105). Blair writes: "The tone of our voice, our looks, and gestures interpret out ideas and emotions no less than words do; nay, the impression they make on others, is frequently much stronger than any words can make" (II., p. 398).

The strength of nonverbal behaviors, Blair says, grows out of their naturalness. They are the "language of nature," and are universally understood, whereas words are merely "arbitrary conventional symbols." Our most immediate associations are to body language, gestures, postures, tones, etc., for we "learn" them long before we learn words. Also, Blair says, words communicate ideas—inventions of human beings—but gestures and paralanguage communicate emotions—realities of nature (II., p. 414). Kames makes the same points, saying that "the external expressions of passion form a language understood by all, by the young as well as the old, by the ignorant as well as the learned" (I., p. 411).

The conception of the use of body and voice as a universal language, of course, was basic to the elocutionists' attempts to develop a system of notation for nonverbal "talk." The conception of nonverbal behaviors as primarily expressive of emotions, led, as we will see shortly, to a theory of pathos based primarily on operationalization.

Extemporaneous Operationalization   The emphasis on orality in modern theory grows out of a general belief in the "persuasive" power of form and in the primacy of the senses of sight and hearing. The emphasis on extemporaneousness grows out of a general commitment to "natural" processes. In our discussion of every part of the paradigm, we have seen that "what is natural is better," or at least more "effective." This principle is equally fundamental to modern approaches to operationalization. Natural use of media as epitomized in extemporaneous oral communication is viewed as a key factor in achieving the ultimate goal of persuasion.

Speaking specifically of the nature of preaching, Fenelon provides a typically pragmatic justification for extemporaneous address. Like Augustine, Fenelon says that a great preacher first instructs, second pleases, and third persuades. All three, he says, depend on the preacher's ability to reach his audience, and the best way for him to do so is to speak extemporaneously. The primary concern of a preacher should be the reactions of his audience: "Since custom and propriety do not permit them [preachers] to be interrogated, it is their obligation to fear that they are not adjusting themselves enough to their listeners" (p. 140). Continuing to cite Augustine, Fenelon explains that the truly skillful communicator learns to observe and react to the responses of his audience:

> [He] adjusts subject matter to the effect that he sees it making upon the listener, for he notices very well what enters into the mind and what does not do these things. He repeats the same things in another way, he clothes them in more striking images and analogies; or perhaps he goes back to the principles from which are derived the truths that he wishes to persuade men of; or perhaps he seeks to allay the passions which prevent these truths from making an impression (p. 108).

A communicator who is tied to a text, whether written out or memorized by rote, is, of course, unable to adjust, "to repeat and clarify a truth" until he sees that it has been understood and accepted (p. 140). Of course, Fenelon says, the language of a written and/or memorized speech may be more exact and graceful than that of an extemporaneous one and therefore may "please" its hearers. However, the reader's or "declaimer's" inability to adjust will make it difficult for him to instruct the auditors, and the artificiality of his manner will make it almost impossible to persuade them. The "few little repetitions [and] inexact constructions" characteristic of extemporaneous address, Fenelon says, tend to make speakers seem more "real" (p. 107). Consequently the audience is likely to believe that "their mouths . . . speak from the abundance of their hearts" (p. 139), as well as to take "pleasure in recognizing nature at work" (p. 107). Nothing is more instructive, pleasing, and persuasive, says Fenelon, than well-informed, natural, spontaneous, and personal communication. This requires preparation, but not a fully written out and memorized speech. Rather it requires:

> The man who thinks deeply upon all the principles of the subject that he must handle and upon all the ramifications, who puts them in order in his mind, who devises the strongest utterances to make his subject visible, who arranges all his arguments, who prepares a certain number of striking figures . . . (p. 106).

Once this preparation is complete, the speaker needs only to embody his thoughts in "ordinary diction." The result will be that "he speaks naturally, he does not talk in the manner of a declaimer." The "warmth" of natural interaction in the actual delivery "converts itself into terms and figures that he will not be able to prepare in his study" (p. 108). Thus Fenelon concludes that naturalness is best:

> The entire art of the good orator consists only in observing what nature does when she is not hampered. Do not do what bad speakers do in striving always to declaim and never to talk to their listeners. On the contrary, each one of your listeners must suppose that you are speaking particularly to him. There you have what produces natural, familiar, and suggestive tones (p. 104).

Priestley likewise notes that memorized address tends to seem artificial. It detracts from both logos and ethos. In extemporaneous speaking, on the other hand, the speaker is free to adjust to his audience, to answer objections "just when it may be supposed they may have occurred to his hearers." This contributes to the understanding of the auditors and also builds ethos: "By this means an orator seems to read the very thoughts of his audience; and this cannot fail to operate powerfully in his favor" (p. 117). Also, says Priestley, we are more likely to believe a person who seems convinced of his own cause, and "the appearance of *present thought* and *extempore* unprepared address, contributes not a little to make a person seem to be in earnest" (p. 111). Furthermore, Priestley points out, extemporaneous address arouses "wonder" in the auditors, for everyone knows it is difficult (p. 112).

Whately also emphasizes the contribution of extemporaneousness to building belief, credibility, and sympathy:

> Besides that the audience are more sure that the thoughts they hear expressed, are the genuine emanation of the *speaker's* mind at the moment, their attention and interest are the more excited by their

sympathy with one whom they perceive to be carried forward solely by his own unaided and unremitting efforts . . . they view him as a swimmer supported by his own constant exertions; . . . the *surmounting of the difficulty* affords great gratification; especially to those who are conscious that they could not do the same (pp. 375–376).

Whately reinforces the point that persuasive power stems in great part from extemporaneous operationalization when he claims that all of their feelings would be significantly altered if the hearers "should perceive, or even suspect, that the orator had it written down before him" (p. 376). A message that is memorized or read from a text, Whately says, may be more "finished" but is likely to be less effective. The central criterion for operationalization, he says, should be the "*impression* made on the hearers' minds. It is not the polish of the blade that is to be considered, or the grace with which it is brandished, but the keenness of the edge and the weight of the stroke" (p. 362). Of course, on some occasions, it is necessary to read from a text, speak from detailed notes, or even to recite memorized lines. The key thing in such situations is for the speaker to come as close as possible to the appearance of extemporaneousness, "to strive to adopt as his *own*, and as his *own at the moment of utterance*, every sentiment he delivers" (p. 361). However, says Whately, even the most skillful communicator cannot make reading or reciting sound exactly like extemporaneous speaking. The difference will be apparent and will make a difference. Even if it is your own composition, he says, it will still not sound totally spontaneous. The result will be at least some loss of the "personal sympathy" naturally evoked by a speaker expressing his own immediate thoughts (pp. 342–343).

Though the primary focus in modern discussions of extemporaneous operationalization is on speaking, Priestley extends the notion to writing as well. He says that it is always best to write from inspiration, to write "freely" and revise later. Otherwise, he says, we tend to lose valuable "trains" of thought and our composition tends to seem labored and artificial (p. 30). He also takes exception to the idea that written discourse is necessarily more "polished" than oral. It may be true in fact, he says, but pragmatically it probably is not. That is, a good extemporaneous speaker can *sound* as polished as a good writer reads: "the want of close connexion, small improprieties, or even inconsistencies, pass unnoticed with most persons when they hear a discourse." These minor flaws are exposed only "when a good judge of composition hath the whole discourse before him in *writing*" (p. 30).

Ethos, Logos, and Pathos   A primary focus in modern theory is the efficacy of operationalization in terms of the classical modes of persuasion. As we have seen, in order for a person to be persuaded, he must first be convinced, and in order for him to believe in the cause, he must believe in the source. Thus ethos is instrumental to logos. In order to lead a person beyond belief, however, he must be moved. His passions must be engaged in order for him to develop a willingness to act. Sympathy with the source, or ethos, is the basis of emotional response and therefore of action. In short, logos, ethos, and pathos are all necessary ingredients, and ethos is basic, or instrumental, to the others. All three, as we have seen, can be enhanced by argumentation, ideal presence, natural order, etc. Operationalization, however, is equally important.

Priestley says that logos grows naturally out of ethos, and that ethos can, in part, be established by one's method and manner of operationalizing a message. He explains that "nothing more effectually conduces to gain belief, than the appearance of *candour* and *impartiality*" (p. 123). This appearance can be created by showing a willingness to listen to the other side of the argument, expressing personal doubt about some of one's own arguments, and admitting the strength of some of the counter arguments. All these contribute to sympathy, and the eventual conclusion takes on "the appearance of being a unanimous determination of all parties" (pp. 123–124). Also, says Priestley, anything we can do to indicate regard for the auditor adds to our case. For instance, abbreviating our mention of arguments known to be strong and indicating that we will omit a long list of particulars give "the appearance of *modesty*, and on that account contributes not a little to recommend the speaker to the favorable opinion of his audience" (p. 121).

Priestley explains that a natural manner is the surest source of conviction and persuasion: "Every art of persuasion founded upon nature, and really tending to engage belief, must consist of such forms of address as are natural to a person who is himself strongly convinced of the truth and importance of what he contends for" (p. 108). Thus, the more closely the operationalization resembles "umpremediated discourse," the more effective it will be. He points out that we all recognize the nonverbal signs of spontaneity. When a speaker or writer stops, retracts a statement, cites and answers objections, uses parentheses in sentences, digresses and returns to his subject, we tend to believe that the expression comes "directly from the heart" (p. 111).

The strongest ethos and logos, Priestley says, grow out of true feelings: "No form of expression can appear natural, unless it corresponds to the feelings of the person who uses it" (p. 83). Thus, a source who is convinced of the truth of his cause and knows his subject is more likely to influence others. He accounts for this observation in terms of sympathy:

> From the principle of *sympathy*, which is natural to the human mind, we universally feel ourselves disposed to conform to the feelings, the sentiment, and everything belonging to the situation of those we converse with, and particularly of all those persons who

engage much of our attention . . . Thus, in general we always feel ourselves more or less disposed to adopt the opinions of those persons with whom we have frequent intercourse. Consequently, we are, in all cases, more disposed to give our assent to any proposition, if we perceive that the person who contends for it is really in earnest, and believes it himself (p. 109).

Thus the "association of passions" makes it difficult for us to believe that a person who appears to have "studied the question" in depth, who seems "to have perfect knowledge of the subject," and who seems to believe strongly in it, is lying. There is, Priestley says, an intimate association between "strong persuasion" and "truth." Our own experience tells us that what we believe in most strongly is "truth" (pp. 111–116).

Kames also views ethos as a sympathetic emotion and says that it can grow out of the source's ability to make himself attractive to the audience. As he explains, the fact that "an agreeable object makes everything connected with it appear agreeable" accounts for the impact of a speaker's character as revealed through his manner. People, he says, naturally have affection for good character. The affection we feel for a good person extends to that person's opinions. And affection often turns into desire; we want to believe in the same things as attractive people believe in. The emotions which result from sympathy, Kames says, are "secondary," but nonetheless strong: "A secondary emotion may readily swell into a passion for the accessory object provided the accessory be a proper object for desire" (pp. 58–62). The strongly held opinions of a good person are, of course, "proper" objects.

Sympathy, Kames points out, works not only in affection but aversion; thus, "We never regard the opinion even of the wisest man, when we discover prejudice or passion [self-interest] behind the curtain" (p. 143). In short, says Kames, when it comes to contingent matters, "Our opinions, the result frequently of various and complicated views, are generally so slight and wavering, as readily to be susceptible of a bias" based on reputation, personal attraction, etc. (p. 143–144).

Campbell likewise explains that it is due to "the communicative principle" that "whatever lessens sympathy, must also impair belief." Thus the "speaker's apparent conviction of the truth of what he advanceth" and his reputation as "a good man" serve as proof in support of his statements (p. 97). Fenelon says, "Moralistic portraitures have no power to convert when they are supported neither by principles nor good practices"; thus, "The first and most essential attribute of the speaker is virtue" (pp. 76–77). Blair says that "good sense and knowledge are the foundation" of all effective communication. The first requirement is "moral qualities," and the second is "a fund of knowledge" (pp. 431–432). What, he asks, "contributes more to persuasion, than the opinion which we entertain of the probity, disinterestedness, candour, and other good moral qualities of the person who endeavours to persuade?" (p. 427). These qualities add weight and beauty; "They dispose us to listen with attention and pleasure; and create a secret partiality." This is most important in unmediated communication, but works even with books. A low credibility author might entertain us, he says, but will never persuade us (p. 427).

Although a number of modern theorists take the position that a "good man" has a better chance of affecting belief, the establishment of ethos is artistic; it depends upon the skill of the source in presenting himself to the audience. De Quincey says, "Any arts which conciliate regard to the speaker indirectly promote the effect of his argument" (*Rhetoric*, p. 92). Whately cites Aristotle as support for saying that ethos depends on good principle, good sense, and good will or a friendly disposition toward the audience. The goal, he says, is that the audience have esteem, regard, and admiration for the source's character, "not his *real* character (according to the fanciful notion of Quinctilian [sic]), but the impression produced on the minds of the hearers, by the speaker, respecting himself" (p. 188).

This "character," Whately says, can be, must be, created by the source's operationalization. Direct "self-commendation," he explains, is usually disgusting to auditors. However, we can demonstrate our inclination and power to do good through examples of our past activities. By our manner of relating these examples and of relating to the audience, we can demonstrate our moral character, our control of our own passions, our ability to postpone gratification and to overcome temptations, as well as the sincerity of our convictions (pp. 217–218).

Disadvantageous circumstances, like a "bad" reputation, can also be managed through operationalization. For instance, a reputation for eloquence may arouse distrust and envy and may detract from the source's influence: "Whatever is atrributed to the Eloquence of the speaker, is so much deducted from the strength of his cause." Thus it may be necessary for the speaker to play down his polished skills, to "*transfer* the admiration from his eloquence to his supposed political wisdom" (pp. 210–212). This can have further effect of highlighting the speaker's "virtuousness": "There certainly is a kind of moral excellence implied in that renunciation of all effort at display,—in that forgetfulness of self,—which is absolutely necessary, both in the manner of writing and in the delivery, to give full force to what is said" (p. 367).

Modern theorists tend to disagree as to whether one must *be* good in order to *appear* good. When it comes to pathos, however, they are united in claiming that emotions are almost impossible to simulate. The source must feel the emotions that he is trying to elicit. Preistley says: "Strong natural emotions are not to be counterfeited" (p. 113). The behaviors that grow out of these, he says, "have a quickness and vigour which are lost when they become voluntary; witness *fighting, laughing,* the gestures peculiar to *anger*, etc. and the same when imitated. The difference is too apparent to escape any person's observation" (p. 115).

Like Priestley, Kames distinguishes between voluntary and involuntary nonverbal signs. The first are conventional behaviors, such as kneeling to express veneration. The second are natural, temporary reactions to stimuli, such as an elevation of the posture in response to joy or pride (II., p. 412). Like Priestley, he says that the involuntary tones of voice and body movements cannot be fully simulated. Neither can they lie; they "are incapable of deceit" (I., p. 428). He points out that this results from "each class of emotion and passion, being invariably attended with an•external appearance peculiar to itself." Thus, he says: "Hope, fear, joy, and grief are displayed externally; the character of a man can be read in his face" (I., p. 410).

Blair likewise says: "To every emotion or passion, nature has adapted a set of corresponding objects; and, without setting these before the mind, it is not in the power of any orator to raise that emotion" (II., pp. 384–385). He explains that because of this natural correspondence between internal feeling and external expression and because of sympathy "only a native and unaffected glow of feeling" can be transmitted to others (II., p. 430):

> Sympathy is one of the most powerful principles by which persuasive discourse works its effect. The speaker endeavours to transfer into his hearers his own sentiments and emotions; which he can never be successful in doing, unless he utters them in such a manner as to convince the hearers that he feels them (II., p. 414).

The rationale behind this is the natural link between nonverbal signs and feelings and the principle of association of passions:

> There is obviously a contagion among the passions. . . . The internal emotion of the speaker adds a pathos to his words, his looks, his gestures, and his whole manner, which exerts a power almost irresistible over those who hear him (II., p. 386).

De Quincey reinforces the natural and inevitable character of the influence of feeling on expression: "The modes of human feeling are inexhaustible; the forms by which feeling connects itself with thought are indefeasibly natural; the channels through which both impress themselves upon language are infinite" (*Rhetoric*, p. 193). Fenelon points out that Cicero was the first to observe that one must "feel passion in order to paint it well." He adds: "Art, however great it be, does not speak as does actual passion. Hence, you will always be a very imperfect orator if you are not affected by the feelings which you wish to inspire in others" (p. 105). Like Blair, Whately, and others, Fenelon says that it may be necessary to use "art" to stimulate the feeling (p. 104). Blair cites Quintilian's recommendation that the speaker be a "method actor," that is, form a vivid mental picture of something, e.g., a personal experience, that will elicit the feeling he needs. Whately (p. 399) and Fenelon (p. 104) say that the best technique is to concentrate on visualizing the subject you are discussing, to forget about manner and concentrate on matter.

Criteria of Operationalization

Naturalness　Not surprisingly, the primary modern criterion for operationalization is naturalness. Modern theorists recommend that we study the natural correspondence between sounds and sense, sound and sight, emotion and expression, etc., in order to form a standard for judging operationalization. Kames says that we should especially study the correspondence between gestures and passions:

> Humility, for example, is expressed naturally by hanging the head; arrogance, by its elevation; and langour or despondence, by reclining it to one side. The expressions of the hands are manifold: by different attitudes and motions, they express desire, hope, fear; they assist us in promising, in inviting, in keeping one at a distance; they are made instruments of threatening, of supplication, of praise, and of horror; they are employ'd in approving, in refusing, in questioning; in showing our joy, our sorrow, our doubts, our regret, our admiration. These gestures, so obedient to passion are extremely difficult to be imitated in a calm state (I., p. 414).

These are the sort of observations that elocutionists use as a basis for prescription, but Kames says that they are not really susceptible to formula. Real feeling is the key, and instruction by rule necessarily inhibits true feeling.

Whately also rejects artificial systems for operationalization. He says that elocutionary teachings derived from analytic study of "emphases, tones, pauses, degrees of loudness," etc., are more appropriate to what he has called a "poetic" than to a "rhetoric" (p. 344). Good poetry, he says, focuses on expression; the thought is secondary. Good rhetoric, instrumental communication, however, focuses on the thought and the method of expression is secondary (p. 335). The principle upon which he rejects elocutionary approaches, then, is that "*everyone is expected to attend exclusively to the proper object of the action* he is engaged in." In the case of instrumental discourse, the proper object "is the expression of the thoughts—not the sound of the expression." If a communicator is preoccupied with how he is doing, rather than with what he is doing, this will be obvious to the receivers. They may be amused with him, but they will not be convinced or persuaded (pp. 344–345). The systems of Sheridan, Walker, et. al., are, he says, not only unnatural, but unnecessary and circuitous. If we concentrate on the sense, we will not need such rules and notations. If we do not concentrate on the sense, we cannot make them in the first place. Ultimately, Whately says: "Impress but the mind fully with sentiments, etc., to be uttered, withdraw the attention from the sound, and fix it on the sense; and nature, or habit, will spontaneously suggest the proper delivery" (p. 350). Through this natural approach, not only will the communicator withdraw his attention from his manner, but so will his receivers. Thus, "When the delivery is *really* good, the hearers (except any one who may deliberately set himself to observe and criticise) *never think about it*, but are exclusively occupied with the sense it conveys and the feelings it excites" (pp. 354–355).

Conversation   The standard for natural operationalization, most theorists agree, is conversation. Blair says that the basics of public operationalization "must be formed upon the manner in which we utter ourselves in ordinary, sensible conversation (II., p. 410). The artificial voice and cadence common "in the pulpit," he says, could be rectified by attention to the tones of conversation (II., p. 416). In terms of gesture, also, the model should be "common intercourse" (II., p. 419). Some occasions, he says, may call for a more solemn or dignified manner, but the basis is still ordinary conversation. This, of course, does not mean that everyone's conversational style is "good." Some people, Blair says, are inarticulate or naturally awkward. Thus we should study the best examples we can find, and we should practice before a mirror and with friends in order to learn what is "natural" and most appropriate to us (II., p. 420).

Fenelon says that for a standard of operationalization we should "study the movements" of natural expression: "For example, observe what the eyes do, what the hands do, what the whole body does, and what its posture is; what the voice does in a man wounded by grief or struck with surprise at the sight of a wondrous thing" (p. 104). Of course, he says, public speaking in a mass context is not exactly like conversation:

> The sight of a large audience and the importance of the subject which he is handling ought surely to stir a man much more than if he were engaged in an ordinary conversation. But in public as in private he must always act naturally. His body must have movement when his words have movement, and his body must stand moveless when his words are calm and simple (p. 100).

Whately also says that conversation is the best mode for operationalization. Earnest speakers, he says, manage to get their point across even if they are embarrassed, hesitant, temporarily inarticulate, etc. (p. 362). On the other hand, "natural" does not equal "familiar":

"He who should preach exactly as if he were speaking in private, though with the utmost earnesness, on the same subject, would, so far, be departing from the genuine Natural manner" (p. 365). For one thing, we must speak more loudly in public in order to be heard. He advises the speaker to select an auditor at the farthest point in the room and "talk to" him (p. 305). Also, though there is currently, and justifiably, much disgust with the system of "artificial gesturing" taught by the elocutionists, movements naturally are larger in front of a mass audience. Along these same lines, we must not allow our disgust with these systems to lead us into repressing all movement. Gestures are natural in emotional situations, and they always precede words: "An emotion, struggling for utterance, produces a tendency to a bodily gesture, to express that emotion more *quickly* than *words* can be framed; the words follow as soon as they *can* be spoken" (p. 390).

Kames also points out that movement is natural: "The total suppression of the voluntary signs during any vivid passion, begets the utmost uneasiness, which cannot be endured for any considerable time." Furthermore, he points out, "The involuntary signs cannot, by any effort be suppressed, nor even dissembled" (I., p. 434). Fenelon says that both movement and lack of movement are natural, but at different times: "It is not natural to be forever moving the arms in speaking. It is necessary to move the arms when one is really excited; but it should not be necessary to move the arms in order to put on the outward show of excitement. There are some things indeed which would have to be spoken quietly without stirring" (p. 97). For instance, he says, a person "filled with powerful feeling stands motionless a moment" (p. 100). Like Whately and others, he says movement grows out of real feeling. "Declaimers" who try to operationalize by rule accomplish exactly the opposite of what they intend: "Their voice has a continuous monotony, and their gestures a uniformity which is not less boring, nor less remote from nature, nor less contrary to the effect which one would expect action to have" (p. 101).

The natural conversational manner, Whately points out, can lead to stage fright because it puts the speaker's self at risk (p. 368). In oral situations, this results from "reflex sympathy." The auditors know that you are nervous; you know that they know; each auditor knows that everyone else knows; thus sympathetic association increases the anxiety of everyone involved (pp. 372–373). Recourse to artificial formulas will not, however, alleviate fear (or it will alleviate it at the expense of the desired effect on the auditors). The best thing to do, Whately says, is to use the emotion. The personal nature of the situation heightens the interest and attention of the audience and stimulates the speaker to better effort and thus to greater success (p. 369). The best way to prevent paralyzing fear and yet take advantage of spontaneity is to be adequately prepared through knowledge of the subject and occasion and through rehearsal before critical friends (p. 355). Blair says that a natural manner, even with stylistic defects, is better than a studied artificial manner, "because it shows us a man." Defects, he says, can be corrected in private conversation and the learning then transferred to public situations. The habits we form, plus earnestness and attention to the subject, are all that we need in order to feel confident (II., p. 423). The key thing, he says, is to not try to please. Stage fright, "flutter of spirits," will usually disappear if we attend to the subject, and we find that a person "will generally please most, when pleasing is not his sole nor chief aim" (II., p. 421).

Perspicuity, Energy, and Propriety   Beyond the general standards of a natural and conversational manner, modern theorists say that operationalization should be perspicuous, energetic, and appropriate.

Whately describes perspicuity in manner as Campbell describes it in style—the most perspicuous operationalization is "transparent." It does not call attention to itself and serves primarily to open a view to the subject matter (pp. 354–355). In reading a message to others, Whately says that what is important is for the reader to show that he understands the message "so that the hearers can also" (p. 347). The primary function of media, he says, is "to render compositions intelligible" (p. 337). Blair says perspicuity depends on appropriate volume, speech, articulation, pronunciation, pausing, and emphasis. These are generally matters of common sense and/or everyday usage though the inexperienced communicator needs to take them into account consciously (II., p. 397–407).

Energy, Whately says, comes from the source's feeling and being impressed with "what he utters" (p. 347). Even a speaker who is presenting someone else's work must be like the actor; he should study it until he can "make it his own" (p. 377). Kames says that noverbal behaviors are the primary source of forcibleness or energy: "Where the countenance, the tones, the gestures, the action, join with the words in communicating emotions, these united have a force irresistible" (I., p. 428). In his comparison of writing and speaking, Blair says that each have strengths, but speaking is superior in force: "The voice of the living speaker, makes an impression on the mind, much stronger than can be made by the perusal of any Writing." The tones of voice, the looks and gestures allow us to make things more clear and expressive; through them we create sympathy and communicate feelings (II., p. 157). Writing, he says, is "more extensive and a more permanent method of communication." It reaches more people and communicates across time and space. It preserves cultural memory as well as individual knowledge (for instance, we can take notes to help us recall specific information) (II., p. 156). Speaking, on the other hand, is what makes the history that books record. In short, he says, writing instructs well, but speaking persuades (II., p. 157).

In terms of propriety or appropriateness, as we have seen, every major theorist notes that the use of general principles depends upon the situation. In terms of operationalization, Kames says that a communicator must "know the nature of each passion in general," but more important, he must "know the various appearances of the same passion in different persons." Thus, he says, it is a general rule that "a passion be adjusted to the character, the sentiments to the passion, and the language to the sentiments. If nature be not faithfully copied in each of these, a defect in execution is perceived" (I., p. 435). Impropriety in these, he says, is like discord in music. Not knowing and adjusting to the constraints of the particular situation in oral communication is parallel to trying to paint portraits without knowing anatomy in general and in particular or trying to write a novel without knowing emotions and characters (I., p. 436). In all of the communicative arts, Kames says, we must operationalize in accord with the demands of coherence, simplicity, regularity, order, symmetry, and utility. The decisions we make in reference to each of these affect the decisions we must make in reference to the others. It also affects the eventual perception. Thus, in architecture, the size of stair steps, the progression from the entrance to the main room, the lighting, and the height of ceilings should all contribute to create a single impression, though each may have been dictated by different concerns. In gardening, coherence may suggest a fountain, but simplicity and utility both argue against it, and where the trees are planted is a function of the placement of the flowers (II., pp. 428–477).

Spencer says that "constant variety" is the rule in operationalization and it results primarily from "skillful adaptation of the form to the matter" (p. 19). Whately says that operationalization must be suited "not only to the *matter* of what is said, but also, of course, to the place and occasion" (p. 355). Campbell reminds us that reading differs from listening, and therefore writing requires different operational strategies from speaking:

> A reader has the command of his time: he may read fast or slow, as he finds convenient: he can peruse a sentence a second time when necesssary or lay down the book and think. But if, in haranguing the people, you comprise a great deal in a few words, the hearer must have uncommon quickness of apprehension to catch your meaning, before you have put it out of his power, by engaging his attention to something else (p. 338).

In a sense, everything modern theorists have to say about operationalization is based on propriety. The appropriateness of sound to sense, of voice and gestures to thought, the natural relationship between the manner of embodying a message and the functioning of ethos, logos, and pathos, the demand for clarity and energy, all are rooted in a concern for suiting means to ends. Whately's distinction between poetic and rhetoric, cited above, is probably the best way of characterizing the difference between the theoretic approach and the elocutionary approach. The theorists were primarily interested in how information is transmitted in symbolic interactions. Their concern was for the thing contained. The elocutionists were primarily interested in the aesthetics of the container.

Conclusion

In looking back over the modern period, we get a sense of progressive theory building. In contrast to the medieval and Renaissance periods, the modern period is characterized by vitality in the "secular" sciences. A number of theorists, working on the basis of classical thought and modern developments in psychology and epistemology, contribute to the progressive reconstruction of a discipline. The central question of the age seemed to be: "How do human beings come to know, to believe, and to act?" The answer, ultimately, is: "through communication."

In categorization theory, modern theorists focus on the processes by which human beings perceive, order, and verify "reality." The focus is on people as active "receivers," or processors of information. For the most part, what we "know" of the world comes to us through symbolic processing of perceptual data. In conceptualization theory, modern theorists focus on the "social construction of reality." The "sense" we make of data, our beliefs, opinions, attitudes, and ideologies, are symbolic universes composed of ideas and feelings about those ideas.

Action, modern theorists say, is to be accounted for in terms of the interaction between categorizational and conceptual processes and the symbolization, organization, and operationalization of messages. This interaction is fundamental to the decisions a communicator makes in attempting to guide his own or others' behavior. Action, modern theorists agree, grows out of belief plus feeling.

In symbolizing, vivid portaiture is the key to creating verisimilitude (ideal presence), which is the prerequisite for involvement of the feelings. Even in intrapersonal communication, vivid representation is requisite to realistic decision-making. As we have said, modern theorists claim that "to see is to feel, and to feel is to act." The organization of messages must take this process into account on a larger scale. The connections between the visualized object, the feelings, and the action urged must be built or "grown" through the ordering of ideas and sentiments. As message receivers, we all inherently appreciate order. We impose order on all of our perceptions. The more closely a purposive message fits our internal ordering processes, the more likely we are to be "positively" affected by it. If the order does not fit with our conceptual processes, we are likely to "distort" it and to be "negatively" affected.

Finally, the operationalization of ideas and sentiments is key to their efficacy. The nonverbal aspects of form are only theoretically separable from content. It is through the form that we perceive and conceive the content. Thus, our initial reaction to messages are reactions to media. Form may work to reinforce and/or assist our purposes or to inhibit them. In short, form has its own meanings; whether or not we consciously attend to it, it will influence our behavior.

A number of these observations anticipate contemporary thought. They also echo classical and, to some extent, medieval and Renaissance thought. In a very real sense, modern theory is the culmination of twenty-five centuries of theory and research. In the concluding chapter, which follows, we will identify some of the concepts that emerge as central or dominant throughout these centuries of thought, and we will make some observations on their "fate" in contemporary theory.

Chapter 6

Concluding Observations

One might expect this chapter to close the door on the past and open the door on the future. It would be more accurate, however, to say that it props open the door on the past in order to better glimpse the present and future. Thus this chapter is not a systematic analysis of contemporary theory. It is not a prognostication of the future. Nor does it repeat the summaries of theory development presented in the preceding chapter. It is a collection of observations. It highlights some of the concerns and concepts that have claimed the attention of communication scholars throughout history. Contemporary trends and concerns are referred to where they seem appropriate, but no claim is made to comprehensiveness.

Definitions of Communication

Although one- or two-sentence definitions of human communication are necessarily inadequate to encompass the complexity of the subject (as evidence by the literally hundreds of thousands of pages written on it), they can give us an idea of central characteristics. Definitions of human communication throughout history exhibit a striking consistency. Most major theorists agree that communication (1) is a natural ability that can be improved by study, (2) is a process that may be intrapersonal but that ultimately involves interaction between two or more persons, (3) may occur through both verbal and nonverbal symbols, but that "discourse" is the primary object of theorizing, (4) usually aims at influencing others' beliefs and/or behavior, and (5) has at least two basic aspects, discovery of ideas (categorization and conceptualization) and transmission of ideas (operationalization through symbolization and organization), or "sense" and "expression."

Natural Ability Improved by Study

Aristotle says that all human beings communicate their ideas to others. Some do it well. Some are more effective than others because of "spontaneous" skill, whereas others become effective through "acquired

262

habit." Given these observations, he concludes that communication must be susceptible to inquiry. It can be viewed as a science; the reasons for "success" can be discovered and taught (1354a 3–11). Priestley says that oratory, effective communication, is the "natural faculty of speech improved by art" (p. 1). Whately says that communication is a "natural gift" which can be improved by practice and study (pp. 13–14). Therefore, he explains, it is an important science (p. 16). This point of view is expressed in nearly every treatise on communication from Plato to Spencer, for it provides a justification for theorizing. Contemporary theorists tend to accept the naturalness of communication as a given and to use it as traditional theorists did, as a justification for their study. Thus Burgoon opens his 1974 textbook by explaining that although all of us communicate, few of us claim to be good at it. One way to become "better," he says, is to study it: "Examining the communication process carefully can help to make a person a more effective communicator."[1]

Interactional Process

Most major theorists have recognized that people may "communicate" with themselves. Isocrates says, "The same arguments which we use in persuading others when we speak in public, we employ also when we deliberate in our own thoughts" (*Antid.*, 255). Augustine says that a person may change an opinion because of internal "argument." In weighing alternative beliefs, one may discover that certain ones conflict with others and that it is necessary to give up some in order to retain the others without feeling cognitive discomfort (II. 31).[2] Kames says that one of the strongest motives is self-justification and that we all "talk" to ourselves in order to justify our own behavior (I. p. 144).[3] Campbell says that "thinking" is a communicational activity (p. 139). Whately says that self-persuasion is the strongest, and often most dangerous, kind, for we can more easily be misled by our own minds than by others' words (pp. 374–375).[4]

[1] Michael Burgoon, *Approaching Speech/Communication* (Holt, Rinehart and Winston, Inc., 1974), p. 2.

[2] What Augustine is describing is known as "dissonance" or "cognitive imbalance" in contemporary scholarship. See Leon Festinger, *A Theory of Cognitive Dissonance* (Stanford: Stanford University Press, 1957), and F. Heider, *The Psychology of Interpersonal Relations* (New York: Wiley, 1958).

[3] See Eliot Aronson, *The Social Animal* (San Francisco: W. H. Freeman and Co., 1960). Like Kames, Aronson claims that internal talk goes on constantly and that self-justification is one of the key topics of this monologue.

[4] The power of self-persuasion is the basis of our current notion of "counter-attitudinal advocacy," a technique based on dissonance theory. Research shows that a person who can be led to encode a message counter to his or her beliefs tends to change those beliefs in the direction of the message. See Gerald R. Miller and Michael Burgoon, *New Techniques of Persuasion* (New York: Harper & Row, 1973).

For the most part, however, communication theory has focused on interaction. Plato explains that the study of communication is the study of how people "enchant" each other's minds (*Phaedrus*, 261). Wilson defines communication as a "declaration of the mind" to another (p. 1). John of Salisbury defines it as the "science of verbal expression and reasoning" (I. 10). Augustine describes it as the process of "conveying to another the contents of one's mind" and says it functions to show our feelings, perceptions, and thoughts to others (II. 2). Blair calls eloquence the "power of communicating thoughts" (I., pp. 1–2). Campbell says eloquence functions to communicate ideas, sentiments, passions, dispositions, and purposes from one person to another (Intro., xlix).[5]

A number of theorists point out that intrapersonal communication is important, but it is the "sharing" of information that makes society function and that should be the focus of study. Isocrates says that "wisdom" is a fine thing, but it is the dissemination of knowledge, the instruction of others, and interpersonal accommodation that makes society possible (*Antid.*, 274–280). Cicero claims that all the knowledge of "philosophy" is "nothing at all" without effective communication (*De Or.*, I. xii. 53–54). The subject matter of human communication, he says, includes "all things relating to the intercourse of fellow-citizens, and the ways of mankind, or . . . everyday life" (II. xvi. 68). It is communication, he says, which determines our customs, laws, and rights, and which makes social government possible (III. xx. 76). Alcuin explains that it is the sharing of information that makes civilization out of chaos (pp. 68–69). John of Salisbury says that communication makes social organization possible through the dissemination of "wisdom" (I. 1). Both Campbell (Preface, xlix) and Whately (p. 10) point out that knowledge which is not shared might as well never have been discovered, and that communication increases knowledge. Kames says that communication creates society and maintains social coherence (II., p. 357; p. 490) and that the study of communication products improves reasoning, creates topics for conversation, improves morals and ethics, and moderates tendencies toward bad habits (I., pp. 8–11).[6]

The interactional nature of communication leads theorists to add another justification for its study. Not only is it important to be able to *communicate to* others in order to maintain society, but it is important to

---

[5] The interactional or "transactional" nature of communication is fundamental to contemporary theory. Definitions in our textbooks stress this characteristic. See Linda Costigan Lederman, *New Dimensions: An Introduction to Human Communication* (Dubuque, Iowa: Wm. C. Brown Co., 1977), pp. 1–9.

[6] This social justification for the study of human communication has appeared in nearly every treatise and textbook on the subject since the discipline began. Contemporary texts frequently include some version of it in the first few pages. Thus Burgoon says communication makes "living and working together possible." It allows us to "cope with the forces of nature" and "to establish and maintain social relationships" (*Approaching Speech/Communication*, p. 1).

be *communicated with*. It is through our ability to receive messages, Isocrates points out, that we learn "love of wisdom and love of honor" (*Antid.*, 280). Blair says that the study of "rhetoric and belles lettres" is the study of "taste" in receiving and of "style" in sending (Preface, iii-iv). Plato (*Phaedrus* 260C), Aristotle (1355a 21–23), and Whately (p. 12) all point out that the only defense against "evil" use of communication is equal skill on the part of "good." Augustine makes the same point and therefore devotes three-fourths of *On Christian Doctrine* to the subject of "ascertaining," or interpreting other's messages. The modern theorists, especially, point out that the principles of message-construction are equally applicable to message-interpretation. The same knowledge that makes us better speakers or writers also makes us better critics. This, of course, is the same reasoning that contemporary educators use in justifying the requirement of composition courses. It is also the basis of writing workshops that require extensive reading of literature. The view that study of communication products "expands the mind" through vicarious experience is fundamental to the concept of liberal education. Survey courses in literature and mass media are frequently justified as developing "educated consumers."

Focus on Discourse

Throughout its history, human communication theory has consistently focused on discourse, verbal symbols. Cicero was one of the first to attend to nonverbal communication. He points out that "the body talks" (*De Or.*, III. lix. 223). "Nature," he says, "has assigned to every emotion a particular look and tone of voice and bearing of its own," and every movement of the body or modulation of the voice reflects our feelings (III. lvii. 216). The most important part of the body, he explains, is the face, especially the eyes. The eyes are the most dominant feature and also the most reflective of feelings, and feelings are the special province of nonverbal communication (III. lix. 221). Nonverbal communication, he says *may* be susceptible to theory construction; however, efforts to systematize it have usually led to artificiality in performance, the "stagy" mimicry of theatre.

Later theorists add little to Cicero's observations. Fenelon (pp. 99–105), Blair (II., p. 398, 414, 428), Kames (I., p. 411ff), and Spencer (p. 2) echo Cicero in claiming that "body talk," voice and gesture, is a universal language, that emotion is its special province, that it is the most powerful mode of expression, and that the face, particularly the eyes, are the most expressive media. All major theorists, from Aristotle on, agree that nonverbal communication is a dominant mode and therefore ought to be studied, but that no "language" exists for a science of voice tone and body movement. In this sense, the modern elocutionists were pioneers. Their descriptions of nonverbal exprssion eventually made speech sciences possible (e.g., phonetics, speech pathology and audiology, speech therapy). They were also the forerunners of contemporary studies of the interaction between verbal and nonverbal behavior, e.g., the "rhetoric" of leave-taking and "communicative competence."[7] Elocutionary focus on the use of gestures and voice in public speaking, however, initially led only to increasing prescriptivism and artificiality, a focus on form at the expense of content.

Primary theoretic emphasis, on the other hand, has traditionally been placed on the *interaction* of verbal and nonverbal symbols. Augustine distinguishes between natural and conventional "signs." Conventional signs, like uniforms or perfumes, can be used to reinforce a verbal message. Natural signs, like damp ground after a rain or the expression on a person's face, tell something about a past event or an internal reaction and may thus influence perceptions and/or behavior, but cannot be used consciously by a source (IV., 1–3). On the other hand, he points out, as do Fenelon (p. 140) and others, that the "natural signs" of restlessness and confusion in a receiver can tell a sender how well his or her message is communicating; therefore such signs are important to communication theory (IV., 10). Bacon says that conventional symbols can be iconic or arbitrary. They may so closely resemble the thing symbolized that any human being would recognize the meaning (e.g., a cave drawing), or they may be understood through social "contract" (e.g., the use of the middle finger as a sign of contempt or anger) (*Adv. Learn.*, II. xvi. 1–2). Like Augustine, he says that arbitrary conventional signs are the more pervasive and more central to the study of communication because of the way they interact with verbal messages. De Quincey (*Rhetoric*, p. 92), along with Augustine (IV. 10), points out that "manner," the sender's nonverbal operationalization, can make "old" information seem new and exciting. The modern theorists, in general, claim that the nonverbal accompaniments of verbal messages can significantly contribute to, or detract from, ethos, logos, and pathos.

As this discussion shows, verbal communication is the central, preeminent concern of theory. The classical theorists focused on oral discourse. Quintilian's definition of human communication as the study of "the good man speaking well" is probably the most quoted definition in the history of the discipline. Plato affirms that writing is "rhetoric" but claims that it is inferior to speaking in both informative and persuasive power (*Phaedrus*, 275). The medieval and Renaissance and modern theorists include both speaking and writing. Agricola, for instance, says that "logic" is the study of communication in all its form; that is, it studies "all discourse" (p. 75). John of Salisbury includes dialectic, rhetoric, and grammar in "logic" and limits it exclusively to "verbal"

---

[7] For a "state of the art" review of nonverbal research and theory, see Mark L. Knapp, John M. Wiemann, and John A. Daly, "Nonverbal Communication: Issues and Appraisal," *Human Communication Research* (Spring 1978), pp. 271–280.

communication (I. 10). The belletristic modern theorists included presentational arts such as painting within the realm of communication criticism but focused on language as the central object of study. Campbell says that "rhetoric" studies the ways in which "discourse" is used to accomplish particular goals (p. 1). Whately says that "rhetoric" is primarily a theory of speaking, but "most of the rules for Speaking are, of course, equally applicable to Writing" (Intro., p. 2). He limits his study not only to discourse but to prose discourse. The Ramists viewed logic as verbal reasoning, grammar as written composition, and rhetoric as oral composition.

Influence in Contingent Matters

Aristotle says that the purpose of communication theory is to discover the "means" by which people are influenced (1354a 3–4). The ultimate use of communication, he says, is "to lead to decisions" in areas of thought and conduct where there is no obvious right or wrong. This is true, he points out, not only in public communication, in the senate, in court, or in ceremonial meetings, but also in private conversation, "even if one is addressing a single person and urging him to do or not to do something" (1391b 7–13). Plato makes similar observations, saying that communication is the "art" of influencing through arguments; it takes place "in private houses" as well as in public gatherings, and its subjects include "all matters" affecting everyday life (Phaedrus 261). The "ability to persuade with speech," he explains, gives people power over others. Thus, skilled communicators can make servants of their "doctor," "trainer," and "money-getter" (Gorgias 450A). Cicero says that "human life and conduct" is the province of "oratory" (De Or., I. xv. 68). As a science, he explains, human communication "embraces the origin and operation and development of all things . . . governing the morals and minds and life of mankind, and also determines their customs and laws and rights" (De Or., III. xx. 76). Isocrates says that the "faculty" of communication allows us to "both contend against others on matters which are open to dispute and seek light for ourselves on things which are unknown" (Antid., 255).

From the classical through the modern period, theorists agree that communication is ultimately a means of influencing others' beliefs and/or behaviors in "contingent" affairs.[8] Thus, in their definitions, most theorists emphasize conviction, or instruction, and persuasion. Augustine says that the basic function of communication is instruction, but

---

[8] One manifestation of continuing interst in influence and decision-making is the increasing number of interpersonal compliance studies in contemporary research. See, for instance, Arnie Cann, Steven J. Sherman, and Roy Elkes, "Effects of Initial Request Size and Timing of a Second Request on Compliance: The Foot in the Door and the Door in the Face," Journal of Pesonality and Social Psychology (1969), pp. 232–330.

information alone is not likely to have much impact on people (IV. 12). In order to affect belief and/or behavior, the communicator must also conciliate hostility and alleviate apathy (IV. 4). Agricola says that the whole object of communication theory is to help us "discover what will produce belief" and arrange it in accord with that knowledge (p. 65). Bacon says that in order to influence people we have to do more than inform them (*Adv. Learn.*, II xviii, 1). What is required, he says is "to apply reason to the imagination for the better moving of the will" (*Adv. Learn.*, II xviii. 2). Thus, the science of human communication focuses on the processes by which we can make future consequences present to the mind, or the process by which "lively representation" can be used to "second reason," to provide motives for believing or acting (*Adv. Learn.*, II. xviii. 2–4). This basic definition is repeated by nearly every major modern theorist (e.g., Fenelon, p. 125; Campbell, p. 1; Blair, II., pp. 424–425; Priestley, pp. 68–69).

The emphasis on influence grows out of the contingent subject matter of human communication. Blair (II., p. 375), Campbell (pp. 44-46), De Quincey (*Rhet.*, p. 90), and Whately (pp. 80–81) all agree with Aristotle, Isocrates, *et al.*, that what people "talk" about are their beliefs, values, attitudes, and actions in the areas of life where there is no determinate standard of "right" and "wrong." Given, as Whately explains, that most people cannot tolerate indecision over long periods of time, any information which is communicated to us is potentially influential (pp. 80–81).[9]

The general focus on influence, of course, does not rule out other functions. Cicero lists, for instance, warning, teaching, comforting, and encouraging (*De Or.*, II. xv. 68). Medieval letter writing theory focused on requesting and dispensing political favors, establishing legal and personal relationships, and making and recording agreements. John of Salisbury says that communication is fundamental to social contracts and business (IV. 13). Alcuin says that it is the central activity of administration (p. 68). Kames says that communication diverts us from our sorrows and allows us to share our joys and disclose our "secrets," to seek and to give advice, and to make contracts and agreements (II., p. 18).[10]

The traditional "ends" of communication, of course, are three—informing, pleasing, and persuading. Pleasing, however, has generally been subjugated to the other two. Plato attacks Gorgias' approach to communication on the grounds that it emphasizes "beauty" over substance. Augustine argues that the Christian communicator who is look-

[9] For a contemporary study of these notions, see D. E. Berlyne, "Uncertainty and Conflict: A Point of Contact Between Information-Theory and Behavior-Theory Concepts," *Psychological Review* (1957) pp. 329–339.

[10] For a comtemporary analysis of functions, see John R. Searle, *Speech Acts: An Essay in the Philosophy of Language* (Cambridge: Cambridge University Press, 1969).

ing for "applause" may achieve this goal but at the expense of any long term effects on belief or practice (IV. 24). Speaking for the modern theorists, Campbell says that to make pleasing the primary goals is to trivialize the functions of communication (pp. 108–111). On the other hand, pleasing has consistently been viewed as instrumental to both instrumentality and expressiveness. Thus, Watzlawick, et al., say that any "piece" of communication behavior has two functions, report and command, or any piece of behavior expresses both content and a relationship that effective communication is "the art of instructing and persuading men *by moving them*" (p. 125). The modern theorists went further in subjugating "pleasure" to the other ends than theorists in any other period. They defined even the fine arts, literature, poetry, painting, etc., as "rhetorical" (e.g., Kames, II., pp. 368–369).[11]

Today, communication textbooks tend to maintain the traditional view of function. The ends of communcative acts are generally defined as informing, entertaining, and persuading, with emphasis placed on the first and third.[12] In terms of theory, the usual distinction is between instrumental and consummatory, that is, communication which is goal-oriented and that which is "art for art's sake," or which achieves its goal simply with its existence.[13] Whether any communicative act or product can be purely consummatory is still a matter of debate, although scholars seem to agree that, for the most part, any message has elements of both instrumentality and expressiveness. Thus, Watzlawick, et al., say that any "piece" of communication behavior has two functions, report and command, or any piece of behavior expresses both content and a relationship between the communicators.[14] Thus, the statement, "my tooth hurts," tells you something about my internal feelings and also expresses my desire for sympathy or understanding, etc., and my belief that our relationship is such that you will not reject my claim. In mass communication theory, scholars are more likely to distinguish between the "primarily" entertaining and the "primarily" informative or persuasive. Thus, documentaries may be "popular" films or propaganda or "message" films.

---

[11] A number of contemporary scholars emphasize the persuasiveness of literature. See, for instance, Wayne C. Booth, *The Rhetoric of Fiction* (Chicago: The University of Chicago Press, 1961), and Edwin Black, *Rhetorical Criticism: A Study in Method* (New York: The Macmillan Co., 1965).

[12] For instance, in Alan H. Monroe and Douglas Ehninger, *Principles and Types of Speech*, 6th ed. (Glenview, Illinois: Scott, Foresman, and Co., 1967), the authors identify five "ends": to entertain, to inform, to convince, to stimulate, and to actuate. Two of the five are "informative"; two are "persuasive."

[13] For a discussion of this distinction, see John Waite Bowers and Donovan Ochs, *The Rhetoric of Agitation and Control* (Reading, Massachusetts: Addison-Wesley, 1971), pp. 1–2.

[14] See Paul Watzlawick, Janet Helmick Beavin, and Don D. Jackson, *Pragmatics of Human Communication* (New York: W. W. Norton and Co., Inc., 1967).

More generally, mass media practitioners agree that a "good" film, whatever its ultimate goal, must have some elements of entertainment. Often it is said that though the content of a film may be "boring," its form can be involving.[15] Thus, Flaherty's celebrated "propaganda-documentary" on Louisiana, produced for Standard Oil, is generally regarded as "art" and is still viewed for its aesthetic value long after its instrumental function ceased to be relevant.

Two Aspects: Discovery and Transmission

When forced by the demands of economy to epitomize the nature of communication, theorists throughout history have focused on two fundamental aspects—discovery (of content, or sense, or meaning) and transmission (expression or form or delivery). Augustine says that communication consists of two basic acts, the ascertainment of "truth" and the interpretation of it for the benefit of others (I. 1). Agricola says that it consists of the discovery of meaning and the arrangement of it so that others can see it for themselves (p. 65). Campbell says that there are two basic parts to any message, the sense and the expression (p. 32). Whately says that finding and arranging arguments is what communication theory is really all about (p. 39) and that interpreting messages and composing messages are the two basic processes (xxxiv). The belletristic theorists view "criticism," or the development of taste, and "composition," or the development of style, as the joint objectives of communication theory. From Aristotle to the present, theorists have generally agreed that analysis (dialectic or logic) precedes synthesis (oratory or eloquence).[16] A number of theorists, following the lead of Cicero, make this distinction in terms of the paradigm. For instance, Austin says that categorization, conceptualization, symbolization, and organization are the "internal" part of communication while operationalization is the "external" part (p. 1).

The most common forms of this distinction are between words (cognitive representations) and things (physical realities) and between verbal cognitions and physical operationalizations. The former is discussed under symbolization below; the latter has been discussed under "discourse" above.

---

[15] See, for instance, John L. Fell, An Introduction to Film (New York: Praeger Publishers, 1975).

[16] That "dialectic precedes rhetoric" is the thesis of Richard Weaver, The Ethics of Rhetoric (Chicago: Henry Regnery Co., 1953). Edward P. J. Corbett analyzes this traditional distinction in contemporary social movements in "The Rhetoric of the Open Hand and the Rhetoric of the Closed Fist," College Composition and Communication (October 1963), pp. 139–145. Henry W. Johnstone, Jr., explores the relationship between logic and rhetoric in more detail in "The Relevance of Rhetoric to Philosophy and of Philosophy to Rhetoric," Quarterly Journal of Speech (February 1966), pp. 41–46.

Treatments of the Paradigm

The differences and similarities between and among the treatments of the paradigm within the three historical periods have been summarized in the preceding chapter. There is no need to repeat them here. However, a number of issues emerge from those summaries that may be especially relevant to contemporary research and theory. Thus, we will briefly examine some of the invariant concerns that emerge for each part of the paradigm and highlight those that may be more fruitful for the continuing development of the discipline.

Categorization

In categorization theory, two basic questions have engaged the attention of theorists. First, what is memorable? Second (a related question), how can we account for the data human beings notice and the ways in which they order that data?

What Is Memorable?   Historically, theorists have agreed that people remember information that is exceptional, that seems to fulfill a need, and that is presented vividly and in accordance with "natural" order. Cicero says that we remember what is "exceptionally base, dishonorable, extraordinary, great, unbelievable, or laughable" (*De Or.*, III. xxii. 35). Fenelon points out that people remember whatever enages their passions (pp. 103–104). Kames (II. p. 89), Priestley (p. 84), and a number of others make similar observations. Belletristic theorists emphasize Aristotle's view that metaphor and other figures of speech are memorable because they "surprise" the mind through the assertion of unexpected resemblances between normally unrelated objects and events (1410b 10–25).

Augustine claims that people remember when they are exposed to data that they have a desire to learn and that authority says is valuable (II. 7–9). Fenelon says that "concrete things with some practical application" are what people remember (p. 114). Like other modern theorists, he rejects the medieval notion that people remember information in terms of the headings and subheadings of the message in which it is presented. Campbell explains that what we remember is information that affects ourselves or people close to us in time or space (pp. 87–88).

From the oral world of the classical period through the print world of the modern period, theorists have maintained that what people remember best is information that elicits vivid visual images. The artificial memory system (visual images in "backgrounds") of the Romans was based on this premise. Cicero says that memorable ideas are those that are "imprinted" upon our minds through our senses, especially our sense of sight (*De Or.*, II. lxxxvii. 357). Classical theorists emphasize the visual impact of figurative language. Aristotle says that metaphor is memorable because it is graphic; it sets the "scene before the eyes"; it is a form of "scene-painting" (1414a 7). The author of *On the Sublime* claims that figures create a strong and indelible memory (II). Quintilian says that schemes and tropes create credibility and stimulate the memory through the variety of images they elicit (IX. il. 25). Medieval and Renaissance theorists likewise focus on "sight" as the key to memory. Erasmus says that figures are impactful because they are essentially visual (p. 16). Bacon says that what is basic to perception, storage, and recall is the ability to form visual images in the memory (*Adv. Learn.*, II. xv. 3). Modern theorists claim that what is memorable is what impresses the mind in the same manner as original sense perception (Campbell, p. 81). Thus they say that a message that creates "ideal presence" is the most memorable. Hearing and sight, they explain, are the "highest" senses, but sight is the most impactful (Kames, I., pp. 80–85; Campbell, p. 75; Blair, II., p. 385; Fenelon, p. 90). Therefore, in order to create a strong and lasting impression on the memory, language must have "vivacity." Fenelon (pp. 93–94), Priestley, (pp. 79–89), Whately (p. 275), and De Quincey (pp. 138–139) emphasize the importance of "painting" a picture for the receiver, thus creating an impression similar to an unmediated sense perception (Campbell, p. 304; Spencer, pp. 3–4).

Finally, many theorists points out that what is memorable is information that is presented in conformity to "natural" order. What is natural is what fits with the way human beings perceive and classify data.

What Is Natural?   Classical theorists did not deal with this question explicitly. They seemed to assume that their empirical observation of "what works" was based on inherent characteristics of human beings, but they were not particularly concerned with specifying the details of the relationship. Augustine makes some comments on the kind of data people need to "learn" in order to become sophisticated receivers. He cites the laws of nature (II. 16), the liberal arts (II. 16–30), and knowledge of signs, both natural and conventional, and their cultural meanings and significances (II. 3). John of Salisbury is one of the first to attempt to account for the process by which human beings notice and order data. Basically, he says, people sense data, store it in their minds, imagine connections between the data, discriminate among possible relationships and meanings, and, finally, arrive at a comprehension or opinions about the implications of the data (IV. 9). Bacon expands upon this basic outline. He says that what we sense depends upon what we have been taught is worth noticing (*Nov. Org.*, I. 39). The time-binding processes of the human "tribe," he explains, build preconceptions, "prenotions" about what to look for. On the basis of these, we sense "reality," form images in our memory, and develop hypotheses about their meaning (*Adv. Learn.*, II. xv. 3).[17]

Modern theorists accept these basic ideas but investigate further the process by which one moves from initial perception to final conception. Campbell says that we sense, store, associate, generalize, and test data (pp. 47–48). The key process is association. Certain natural principles dictate the way in which we combine data to create information. These principles are strikingly similar to the classical "topics" of conceptualization, i.e., cause/effect, contiguity, resemblance, contrast, and antecedents and consequents (Campbell, p. 15; Kames, I., pp. 15–17; Priestley, pp. 129–132; De Quincey, *Rhetoric*, p. 103). Classical theorists view these as "places" to investigate in gathering information to be used in a message. The topics were an analytical tool. Medieval and Renaissance scholars view them as classifications for information, as a storage system. With the advent of associational psychology and common sense philosophy, they come to be viewed as the basic principles of perception. Throughout history, they have been regarded as inherent and natural abilities. The classical theorists focus on them as recall categories, the medieval and Renaissance theorists as storage categories, and the modern theorists as perceptual categories. What has not been questioned is the extent to which they are, in fact, "natural" categories possessed by all "normal" human beings. If they are inherent, then they certainly could be the key to understanding human categorization.

The topics or principles of association (or common sense notions possessed by everyone) may also account for a phenomenon noted by a variety of communication scholars—selectivity. Throughout history, theorists have pointed out that human beings selectively perceive, attend to, and retain certain kinds of data and information. In discussing "what is memorable," we have observed that unexpectedness, utility, and vividness may account for what people notice. We have hypothesized that the classical topics may also have some effect; that is, people may notice data that are contiguous in time and that seem to have a cause/effect relationship but not data that are contiguous but apparently unrelated. Bacon has suggested that what we notice depends upon our socialization. A number of modern theorists reinforce this idea, pointing out that education, life-style, career, etc., influence our receptivity to data and information (Campbell, p. 95ff). Others point out that initial perception can be accounted for in terms of "passion." What we "see" depends upon our motives and desires (Kames, I, p. 142ff). Contemporary research on "attitude change," "selectivity," "diffusion," and "uses and gratifications," to name a few of the relevant areas, seems to support these ideas.[18] Much of this research, however, has been carried out discretely,

[17] This, of course, is the central idea behind Whorf's assertion that language, the words we have available to us, structures our perceptions of reality. See Benjamin Lee Whorf, *Language, Thought, and Reality: Selected Writings* (Cambridge: Massachusetts Institute of Technology Press, 1956).

[18] For a comprehensive review of attitude-change research and theory, see Philip Zimbardo and Ebbe B. Ebbesen, *Influencing Attitudes and Changing Behaviors* (Reading, Mas-

that is, without benefit of a general theory of categorization. The long "forgotten" topics, or principles of association, may provide an entry to such an enterprise.

Conceptualization

Historically, conceptualization theory has focused on methods for analyzing the subject, audience, and occasion in order to gather material for messages. This concern has been dealt with in the context of a basic question, "What 'moves' people to belief and action?"

Throughout the three periods there is uniform agreement that the first step in constructing a message is thorough analysis of the subject. Cicero, Augustine, Fenelon, Campbell, et al., claim that a broad general education supplemented by specialized study is a prerequisite to informed discussion. Research, however, is not the whole of the conceptualization process. The communicator must "artistically" create many of the materials to be used in a particular message. These materials, the arguments, Aristotle says, are created out of "topical" analysis. He posits four "common" modes of argument that are relevant to all subjects and situations. We see instances of these daily in television commercials and use them constantly in conversation. For instance, the argument that Company X makes fittings for space ships and *therefore* makes durable tennis shoes is an argument from the *possible and impossible* common. This common posits that if one can do the harder task, then one can certainly do the easier. *Past fact* is an argument such as, if the least likely consequence has occurred (Susan has left Harry), then the most likely has occurred (Harry and Susan have had a fight). An instance of a *future fact* argument is that if the means exist and no circumstance intervenes (if I have written this book and the publishing company does not go bankrupt), then the end will occur (the book will be published). *Greatness and smallness* arguments grow out of concepts such as classes and norms. Thus the "bell-shaped curve" posits that most people will be similar on certain characteristics (e.g., achievement on a test) but that some will be very different (get very high or very low scores).[19] Any subject, Aristotle claims, can be analyzed in terms of these basic arguments (1393a 12–15). The formal

sachusetts: Addison-Wesley Publishing Co., 1970). For a slightly dated, but superior review of selectivity, see David O. Sears and Jonathan L. Freeman, "Selective Exposure to Information: A Critical Review," *Public Opinion Quarterly* (Summer 1967), pp. 194–213. For diffusion research and theory see Everett M. Rogers and F. Floyd Shoemaker, *Communication of Innovations* (New York: The Free Press, 1971). Uses and gratifications research is succinctly analyzed in Elihu Katz, Jay G. Blumler, and Michael Gurevitch, "Uses of Mass Communication by the Individual," in W. Phillips Davison and Frederick T. C. Yu, eds. *Mass Communication Research: Major Issues and Future Directions* (New York: Praeger Publisher, 1974), pp. 11–35.

[19] These kinds of arguments are obviously pervasive in daily life. What has not been investigated is the extent to which the four commons are exhaustive. Have we, for instance, invented new commons since the fourth century B.C.?

topics, antecedents and consequents, etc., can also be used to analyze any subject, for they represent the various relationships that can exist among pieces of data.

Medieval and Renaissance scholars preserved this system of analysis but thought of conceptualization primarily in terms of dialectical analysis of *theses*—general questions such as "Is war profitable?" and rhetorical *hypotheses* such as "Would it be more profitable for the economy to go to war in the present situation or to remain at peace?" A communicator who had researched the general question (or read the "commonplaces" formulated by previous researchers) had only to apply the general arguments to the specific situation. [20]

Modern theorists tended to reject the medieval doctrine of topics and commonplaces. Instead, they focused on "principles of human nature" as guides to artistic conceptualization. As we have seen, they reconceived the topics as "principles of association" and used them as the classical theorists did, as guidelines for combining pieces of information into arguments. Knowledge of theses they saw as growing out of a broad liberal education. More specifically, they focused on "natural" categorization processes. Thus a communicator might analyze a subject in terms of beliefs based on intellection, consciousness, and common sense and then formulate arguments based on demonstrative reasoning, e.g., mathematical demonstration, and/or arguments based on moral reasoning, i.e., experience, analogy, testimony, and calculation of chances (Campbell, pp. 35–60). In explaining the use of these arguments, modern theorists turn to the three classical modes of proof and the functions of the faculties of the human mind.

Audience analysis thus becomes a prime concern in modern human communication theory. Cicero had said that a communicator must know the "characters" of human beings and the "whole range of human nature," especially the motives that "spur" our actions (*De Or.*, I. xii. 53–54). More specifically, he claimed that one must know audience predispositions, their "thoughts, judgments, anticipations, wishes" (*De Or.*, II. xli, 186). Plato had explained that the central question is why some people can be persuaded to certain beliefs and actions while others cannot (*Phaedrus*, 269C). Aristotle had analyzed audiences in terms of age (youth, prime, old age) and status (birth, wealth, power) and in terms of the nature of common human emotions (1389a 2–10; 1378a 24–26). The classical theorists specified three general methods by which one might influence an audience once it had been analyzed: ethos, logos, and pathos.

---

[20] An interesting question: To what extent do contemporary composition and public speaking textbooks use this approach? In the examples they provide, are they not sources of commonplace arguments and directions for tailoring general arguments to specific cases?

Modern theorists accept all these concepts but proceed to specify why and how audience analysis is important to conceptualization. Logos, they say, works because the human understanding demands that arguments seem probable, or at least plausible (Campbell, p. 82). People like to believe that they are acting "reasonably" (Kames, II, p. 41). Because most of the subjects about which we communicate are contingent, truth cannot be established (Campbell, pp. 43–46). The next best thing, then, is validity or verisimilitude (De Quincey, p. 90). Pathos—creation of empathy (sympathy)—influences people because their memory allows them to make connections between the concerns of self and others, and because their imagination allows them to visualize events and conceive of themselves as being "present" in them (Campbell, pp. 82–93). Ethos functions as a kind of testimony. If we believe that a communicator has good sense, no hidden motives, and our best interests in mind, we are more likely to believe his or her assertion of fact and/or opinion (Whately, pp. 69–76). The association of passions increases the impact of ethos as we identify more closely with the source (Priestley, p. 109). Modern theorists explain that our chances of influencing increase significantly with this general knowledge of the principles of human nature, especially when it is "managed" in light of specific analysis of the particular auditor(s).[21]

In terms of occasions, theorists of all three periods agree on three basic genres—deliberative, or political; forensic, or legal; and epideictic, or ceremonial (preaching, letter writing, conversation, and poetry). [22] Classical theorists focused on analysis of the occasion in terms of "special topics," e.g., analysis of the financial and material resources of the nation, analysis of the letter and spirit of laws, etc. Medieval and Renaissance scholars focused on the special conventions attendant on occasions, e.g., the proper forms of address and the "moods" of the syllogism.

[21] This approach to conceptualization through audience analysis and the modes of proof is familiar to any reader of contemporary textbooks. For instance, see Douglas Ehninger and Wayne Brockriede, Decision by Debate (New York: Dodd, Mead, & Co., 1963).

[22] The usual contemporary classifications are information, persuasion, and entertainment. Preaching is seldom discussed. It has been replaced by a new subgenre, mass media. Television, radio, newspapers, magazines fulfill something of the same function in contemporary life as preaching did in modern life. That is, "everyone" attends to the media (but not everyone goes to a church). Everyone knows the subject matter of media, the names of popular television shows and of popular anchorpersons and rock groups, the central characters of prime time fare, etc. Media programming thus provides a wealth of illustrative examples that was once provided by religion. Letter writing has also tended to disappear from communication theory. The medieval and Renaissance lore, however, is retained in theories of etiquette. In Amy Vanderbilt's Everyday Etiquette (New York: Bantam Books, 1952), the rules for correspondence are given equal weight to the rules for behavior at funerals and in entertaining at home. In other words, much of the traditional lore of epideictic discourse is now classified as matter for polite manners rather than communication theory. Mass media and interpersonal conversation are the two main topics in contemporary discussions of "ceremonial" communication.

Modern theorists focused on the constraints of situations in terms of audience expectations, e.g., role expectations in regard to the source, acceptability of kinds of evidence, and the location of presumptions.

Current theory and research tends to include most of traditional conceptualization theory. The topical approach is taught in public speaking and composition textbooks under "patterns of development." Theorists like Wallace discuss many of them under the heading of types of evidence, that is, as a typology of "good reasons" for belief.[23] Toulmin includes many of the same ideas as "warrants for belief," or the kinds of relationships people view as reasonable justifications for linking a particular premise to a particular conclusion.[24] Ethos has been one of the most researched concepts in contemporary scholarship.[25] The distinction between "logical" and "emotional" proof is everywhere in the literature and has likewise been subject to extensive research.[26]

What has not been adequately explored are some of the assumptions behind these concepts. Modern theorists view logos as an outgrowth of pathos (sympathy). Is it possible that "reason and "emotion" are not separable? If, as some research indicates, auditors cannot identify the difference between "appeals" to logic and emotion,[27] is it at all useful to maintain the distinction? Both ethos and pathos, a number of theorists observe, may be elicited through identification with the source. Burke claims that identification is a central strategy or persuasion.[28] Social comparison theory, however, says that identification is unlikely to occur in those situations where we view the source as extremely superior to us in ability, power, knowledge, etc.[29] What, exactly, are the variables

---

[23] Karl Wallace, "The Substance of Rhetoric: Good Reasons," *Quarterly Journal of Speech* (Oct. 1963), pp. 239–249.

[24] Stephen Toulmin, *The Uses of Argument* (Cambridge: Cambridge University Press, 1969).

[25] For an example of the numerous studies of ethos, its dimensions, and methods of measuring it, see James C. McCrosky, "Special Report: Scales for Measurement of Ethos," *Speech Monographs* (March 1966), pp. 65–72. For an earlier review of research, see Kenneth Anderson and Theodore Clevenger, Jr., "A Summary of Experimental Research in Ethos," *Speech Monographs* (June 1963), pp. 59–78.

[26] For an analysis of this research, see Samuel L. Becker, "Research on Emotional and Logical Proofs," *Southern Speech Journal* (Spring 1963), pp. 198–207. Becker suggests that the distinction between pathos and logos is invalid. In "The Logical Fallacy, Cognitive Theory, and the Enthymeme: A Search for the Foundations of Reasoned Discourse" (*Quarterly Journal of Speech*, April 1970, pp. 140–148), Jesse Delia supports Becker's point of view and reconceptualizes logos.

[27] See, for instance, J. Morgan and J. Morgan, "The Distortion of Syllogistic Reasoning Produced by Personal Connections," *Journal of Social Psychology* (1944), pp. 39–59, and B. Thomas Florence, "An Empirical Test of the Relationship of Evidence to Belief Systems and Attitude Change," *Human Communication Research* (1975), pp. 145–158.

[28] Kenneth Burke, *A Rhetoric of Motives* (New York: George Braziller, 1955).

[29] For an explication of "social comparison theory," see J. Thibaut and H. H. Kelley, *The Social Psychology of Groups* (New York: Wiley, 1959).

upon which people compare themselves and what is the basis of identification?

In terms of persuasion, is it necessary to engage passion in order to
prompt action? Do people believe more "strongly" when a message elicits
a vivid visual image? In terms of genres, theorists have generally viewed
epideictic discourse as essentially entertaining. Modern theorists, however, argue that "entertainment" persuades in less obvious, but perhaps
more significant, ways then do overt attempts to influence. To what
extent are our perceptions of the importance of social issues, and our
opinions on them, formed by televised situation comedies? Do we know
what love "is" because of our experience of it or because of the novels we
have read and the films we have seen? Does advertising sell products
(e.g., soap) or does it sell behavior (daily showers)?

Finally, is the current emphasis on "inartistic" conceptualization
(i.e., researching the subject and polling the audience) productive of
useful theory? We have extensive research that could provide a basis for
an "artistic" approach (i.e., creation of arguments based on a theory of
source/receiver/situation interaction). Rokeach's analysis of beliefs, values, and attitudes[30] seems to be an extension of Campbell's analysis of
the intuitive and deductive "sources of belief" and their comparative
centrality. Subjective-expected-utility theory[31] seems to be an elaboration of the modern "wish-fulfillment" theory of persuasion (Whately, pp.
175–176; Campbell, p. 274). Cognitive complexity research may be an
extension of associational psychology.[32] Berger and Luckman's analysis
of the dialectical nature of inartistic (objective) and artistic (subjective)
conceptualization of social reality[33] provides a contemporary framework
for an elaborated theory that is consistent with traditional approaches.
Given such theory and research, an integrated theory of conceptualization comparable in complexity and scope to that of the classical and
modern periods is possible.

Symbolization

Traditional approaches to symbolization have focused on style, the
selection and arrangement of words in a message. The emphasis has
tended to be on pragmatics, the function of style in instructing, pleasing,

[30] Milton Rokeach, *Beliefs, Values, and Attitudes: A Theory of Organization and Change*
(San Francisco: Jossey-Bass, 1968).
[31] See James T. Tedeschi, Barry S. Schlenker, and Thomas V. Bonoma, *Conflict, Power,
and Games: The Experimental Study of Interpersonal Relations* (Chicago: Aldine Publishing
Co., 1973).
[32] See Jesse G. Delia, Ruth Ann Clark, and David E. Switzer, "Cognitive Complexity
and Impression Formation in Informal Social Interaction," *Speech Monographs*
(November 1974), pp. 299–308.
[33] Peter L. Berger and Thomas Luckmann. *The Social Construction of Reality: A Treatise in
the Sociology of Knowledge* (Garden City: Doubleday and Co., 1966).

and persuading and in creating logos, ethos, and pathos. Occasionally, as in the medieval and early Renaissance period, scholars have concentrated on syntactics (the technical analysis of language structure, especially the figures of speech) and semantics (the analysis of what words "mean"). For the most part, however, these concerns have been peripheral to symbolization theory. The central issues in symbolization have been the functions of style, or criteria for effective use of language, and the relationship between words and things.

Functions The pragmatics of symbolization led classical theorists to develop three criteria: vividness (liveliness), beauty, and propriety (appropriateness or decorum). These continued to be central to communication theory through the modern period and remain common topics in contemporary composition textbooks.

Accuracy or perspicuity is usually viewed as a prerequisite. A communicator who violates the grammar and syntax of a language is likely to suffer loss of credibility at least and to be misunderstood at best (Aristotle 1404b 1, 1407a 18; Quintilian, VIII; Augustine, IV. 7; Campbell, pp. 140, 216–221; Whately, p. 287; De Quincey, *Style*, p. 163). The aesthetics of symbolization are usually considered more important because accuracy merely informs, but pleasing holds attention and moves passions. Aristotle says metaphor, for example, pleases both cognitively and emotionally: "Liveliness is specially conveyed by metaphor, and by the further power of surprising the hearer; because the hearer expected something different, his acquisition of the new idea impresses him all the more. His mind seems to say 'Yes, to be sure; I never thought of that' " (1412a 17–21). Even theorists who devote attention to the more technical aspects of figurative language tend to justify their concern in terms of the functions of figures in adding diversity to style and thus increasing ethos[34] (the perception of the speaker as exceptionally competent) (On the Sublime, I; Quintilian, IX. il. 25; Erasmus, pp. 15–16). Belletristic modern theorists especially emphasize the "beauty" of figurative language and, concurrently, its effectiveness in promoting pathos and ethos; they add that it also increases logos by building plausibility (through "ideal presence" and "immediacy" of conception) (Blair, I., pp. 331–420; Kames, I., p. 182 and II., pp. 86–94; Spencer, pp. 2–4).

Propriety—appropriateness to source, receiver, subject, occasion —has consistently been viewed as the ultimate criterion. Cicero says, "The universal rule, in oratory, as in life, is to consider propriety" (*Orator*, XX. 69). Aristotle devotes seven chapters to analysis of the

---

[34] Contemporary research indicates that linguistic diversity does enhance ethos. See James J. Bradac, J. A Courtright, Gregson Schmidt, and Robert A. Davies, "The Effects of Perceived Status and Linguistic Diversity upon Judgments of Speaker Attributes and Message Effectiveness," *Journal of Psychology* (1976), pp. 213–220.

conditions, ranks, and positions in society that must be taken into account in symbolizing messages (1388b 30–1391b 5). Augustine (IV. 7, 23–24), Alcuin (p. 137), and Wilson (pp. 2–4) similarly emphasize the necessity to adjust style to the decorums of self, subject, audience, place, and time. A number of modern theorists make similar observations (e.g., Kames, I., pp. 428–477). They note especially the nature of symbolization in the various media, e.g., the differences between writing and speaking (Campbell, p. 338).[35]

Contemporary research and theory is rich in respect to functions of style. Research seems to indicate that the source's dialect, sex, age, choice, and placement of figures, etc., do affect receiver comprehension and judgment of the source's ethos.[36] Readability studies indicate that certain levels of style can be distinguished and are variously appropriate to particular audiences.[37] Source, subject, receiver, and style apparently do interact and the combination can either facilitiate or retard the effectiveness of the message.[38]

Words and Things   The distinction between sense and expression in definitions of human communication has most often been epitomized as the difference between "words" and "things." The nature of the relationship between words and things has traditionally been a central issue in symbolization theory. Both Aristotle (1403b 8-12) and Cicero (*Or.,* XX 69) observe that the word is not the thing, or that *what* we are saying cannot be viewed as equivalent to *how* we are saying it. In practice, however, they note that how something is said often determines whether it is understood and/or acted upon. Augustine makes this distinction the

[35] For a contemporary analysis of these differences, see Carroll C. Arnold, "Oral Rhetoric, Rhetoric, and Literature," *Philosophy and Rhetoric* (Fall 1968), pp. 191–210.

[36] Ethos and dialect are shown to be interrelated in John Waite Bowers and Charles Houk, "Dialect and Identification," *Language and Speech* (1969), pp. 180–186. Some of the effects of sex on perception of the source are discussed in Gerald R. Miller and Michael McReynolds, "Male Chauvinism and Source Competence: A Research Note," *Speech Monographs* (1973), pp. 154–155. "Vivid" language and its effects is studied in John Waite Bowers, "Language Intensity, Social Introversion and Attitude Change," *Speech Monographs* (1963), pp. 345–352. The use and placement of figures is investigated in John Waite Bowers and Michael Osborn, "Attitudinal Effects of Selected Types of Concluding Metaphors in Persuasive Speeches," *Speech Monographs* (June 1966), pp. 147–155.

[37] Rudolph Flesch's index of readability is the classic instrument and has led to more research then can be reviewed here. See Flesch, *The Art of Plain Talk* (New York: Harper, 1946). On a related concept, "closure" and the "cloze procedure," see W. L. Taylor, "Inferences about Language Communality: Cloze Procedure," in *Trends in Content Analysis,* ed. by I. D. Pool (Urbana: University of Illinois Press, 1959), pp. 78–85.

[38] The complexity of these interactions is documented in James J. Bradac, John Waite Bowers, and John A. Courtright, "Lexical Variations in Intensity, Immediacy, and Diversity: An Axiomatic theory and Causal Model," *Human Communication Research* (Winter 1980), forthcoming.

central organizing concept of *On Christian Doctrine*, devoting the first three books to analysis of "things" and "signs of things." For some theorists, this distinction has been viewed as the central "problem" in communication theory. Medieval and Renaissance scholars, for instance, viewed language as the "dress" of thought and therefore as a potential obstacle to effective communication. Bacon makes the tension between words and things his third "idol," or source of inaccurate perceptions of reality. The "idols of the market," he says, result from the abstractive, static, and socially constructed nature of language. The names we have for things "force" our understanding of them and prevent us from accurately perceiving and/or conceiving them. Thus, we operate as if we were dealing directly with physical reality, though we actually deal with it through the mediation of the "market," the socially constructed reality.

Modern theorists tend to reject the notion of language as an obstacle to communication. De Quincey notes that everyone "who has studied and meditated the difficulties of style must have had a subconscious sense of a bar in his way"; however, he says, language is the "embodiment" of thought and the only means we have of representing most of our ideas (*Style*, p. 191). A number of other modern theorists make this same observation. Language, they say, has no natural connection to reality; it is learned and imposed on reality, but it remains the primary vehicle of learning about, and interacting with, reality (Campbell, pp. 257–261, 215, 139; Priestley, p. 72; Whately, p. 310).

De Quincey's emphasis on language as the "incarnation" of thought (*Style*, pp. 138–141; *Rhetoric*, p. 110; *Language*, p. 262) is more representative of dominant traditional views as well as of contemporary theory. Early in the twentieth century the "General Semantics" movement focused on the separation of sense and expression. General Semanticists developed slogans such as "the map is not the territory" to emphasize the difference between "words" and "things."[39] Other theorists, such as Richard Weaver and Kenneth Burke, however, reacted against this dichotomy.[40] Like the classical and modern theorists, they basically ar-

[39] For a summary of the General Semantics movement, see Richard W. Budd, "General Semantics: An Approach to Human Communication," in Richard W. Budd and Brent D. Ruben, eds., *Approaches to Human Communication* (Rochelle Park, New Jersey: Hayden, 1972), pp. 97–119. For representative works in this area, see Wendell Johnson, *People in Quandaries: The Semantics of Personal Adjustment* (New York: Harper and Row, 1946), and I. A. Richards, *The Philosophy of Rhetoric* (Oxford: Oxford University Press, 1936).

[40] Richard M. Weaver, "Language is Sermonic" in Roger E. Nebergall, ed., *Dimensions of Rhetorical Scholarship* (Normal, Oklahoma: University of Oklahoma Press, 1963), pp. 49–63; Kenneth Burke, "Container and Thing Contained," in *A Grammar of Motives* (New York: Prentice-Hall, 1952), and "Semantic and Poetic Meaning," in *Philosophy of Literary Form* (New York: Vintage Books, 1957), pp. 164–189. For a more general analysis of the relationship between verbal and physical reality, see Roger Brown, *Words and Things: An Introduction to Language* (New York: The Free Press, 1958).

gued that the "territory" is not available to us, for the most part, except through the "map." People do not discuss what is "given" or "real." Normally we do not deliberate about whether or not to eat. Sometimes, however, we may discuss what to eat or where or when. These contingent or socially created matters can only be approached through language. Language, says Weaver, is "sermonic." In Watzlawick's terms, it not only *reports* a perception of reality, it *commands* an attitude toward it. In Burke's terminology, what is contained can be known, for the most part, only through the container. Thus, in terms of the relationship between words and things, the authority of history comes down on the side of organic unity rather than discrete segmentation.

Contemporary studies of symbolization have tended to go beyond concern for language into the symbolic nature of such nonverbal items as hairstyle and clothing. The interrelationships between words and things have taken on new dimensions in studies of the "rhetoric" of social movements.[41] Speech is often used to justify and explain such events as sit-ins while these events are characteristically used to reinforce and further operationalize verbal statements. Along these same lines, contemporary studies of the constraints on a communicator who must speak to a variety of audiences increases the complexity of propriety in symbolic strategies. Simons points out some of these complexities in his analysis of the leader who must maintain a relatively consistent stance with movement members while adjusting his strategies to recruit potential members and arouse apathetic or move hostile nonmembers.[42] Such studies have tended to reinforce Augustine's point that "pleasing" is often not the preferable effect of symbolization. In fact, angering and frustrating and the use of "ugly" language may sometimes be the most efficient and effective strategy.

For symbolization, as for categorization and conceptualization, a number of contemporary scholars have contributed research and theory, but much of what we know remains fragmented. A "complete" contemporary theory of symbolization could undoubtedly be built on the foundation of traditional approaches and would probably add new insights into the significance of the findings of the last half century.

Organization

Organizational theory has traditionally paid attention to the arrangement of message parts, including the distinction between introduction, body, and conclusion and various permutations on the number and nature of optional message parts. Contemporary theory and research

---

[41] For example, see Bowers and Ochs, *The Rhetoric of Agitation and Control* (Addison-Wesley, 1971), and Ted Robert Gurr, *Why Men Rebel* (Princeton: Princeton University Press, 1970).

[42] Herbert W. Simons, "Requirements, Problems, and Strategies: A Theory of Persuasion for Social Movements," *Quarterly Journal of Speech* (Feb. 1970), pp. 1–11.

reinforces the assumptions that people expect a message to establish its ground first and then to build to some central idea, usually through a series of oppositions (comparison and contrast of ideas, conflict between characters, etc.), and finally to conclude with a resolution.[43] Theories of composition, literary criticism, and public speaking and writing textbooks continue to teach these basic concepts. The central issue in organization of messages has been the relative merits of organic and prescriptive approaches. Both claim to teach an organization based on principles of human nature. The weight of history, however, is generally in favor of prescriptive approaches for initial instruction and organic approaches for more general use.[44]

The primary concern in human communication theory has traditionally been the situational constraints on message organization. From the classical through the modern periods, theorists have assumed two basic situations, those presented by "learned" and "popular" audiences. Classical, medieval, and Renaissance theorists conceive of dialectic as the proper organization for learned audiences. Dialectical organization is essentially syllogistic, that is, it proceeds by laying down premises from which conclusions may be logically drawn. It assumes previous knowledge of the general principles of a subject and aims at developing more and more refined concepts (Aristotle, 1354a 1; Plato, *Phaedrus*, 262C; Augustine, IV. 9; John of Salisbury, III. 10; Bacon, II. xvii. 3). In classical terminology, dialectical organization uses a division based upon the process of definition.[45] Rhetorical organization, for popular audiences, is organization based upon prior conceptualization of subject, audience, and occasion and adapted to the ends, the relative strength of arguments, and the modes of proof, ethos, logos, and pathos. The prescriptive approach to message parts is the traditional taxonomy.

Modern theorists employ the same basic concepts but discuss them in terms of analysis and synthesis. Analysis is the method of organization for learned audiences and corresponds in its procedures and aims to dialectic. Synthesis, like rhetorical organization, is for popular audiences and must be organic to subject, source, receiver, purpose, and occasion (Priestly, pp. 31, 42–49; Blair, II., pp. 373–374; Whately, pp. 5, 46, 75–82, 108–109; Campbell, p. 84; Kames, II., pp. 400–401, 516). Traditionally, organization for communicating to popular audiences is viewed as a division of the subject (synethesis) based upon prior dialectic or analysis and adjusted to the constraints of "propriety."

---

[43] See Kenneth Burke, *Counter-Statement* (Los Altos, California: Hermes Publications, 1931).

[44] For a summary of the organic/prescriptive "debate," see Louis T. Milic, "Theories of Style and Their Implications for the Teaching of Composition," *College Composition and Communication* (May 1965), pp. 66–69.

[45] See the discussion of "definition" and "division" in the preceding chapter under "Organization."

Within this overall framework, there are a number of testable hypotheses. For instance, Fenelon says that an organic organization is more effective in terms of the receiver's recall than an organization based on prescriptive approaches to message parts (pp. 66, 114). Kames (I., p. 20) and Priestley (pp. 34, 277) claim that order is inherent in human perceptions of messages. Therefore, one might speculate that receivers impute order to "disorganized" messages.[46] Priestley says that digressions "refresh" the receiver (pp. 35, 51).[47] Whately claims that deductive organization seems dogmatic but works well with authoritarian auditors (p. 142),[48] that inductive strategies are more effective with hostile audiences (p. 141), and that inductive strategies are also more effective in maintaining attention (p. 144). Whately (pp. 165–168), Blair (II., p. 394), and others say that the strongest arguments should be placed last unless they are also the most obvious arguments.[49] Kames asserts that reiteration is necessary in order to arouse emotion (I., p. 86).

From Aristotle to Whately, theorists have claimed that ethos is established in the introduction and that the conclusion must include the central points one wishes the auditors to remember. Campbell (p. 355), Priestley (p. 102, 277), and Spencer (p. 5) all point out that word order must follow common usage except when one wants to signal strong emotion or highlight a particular idea. Spencer claims that periodic sentence structure should be used only with the highly intelligent auditor. (p. 9).

[46] Some studies indicate that randomly "disordering" parts of a message may have little effect on receiver retention, attention, or attitude change. See, for instance, R. G. Smith, "An Experimental Study of the Effects of Speech Organization upon Attitudes of College Students," *Speech Monographs* (Nov. 1951), pp. 292–301. Others tend to indicate that receivers with high ability organize, retain, and comprehend "disordered" messages better than those with lower abilities. For instance, see E. Thompson, "An Experimental Investigation of the Relative Effectiveness of Organization Structure in Oral Communications," *Southern Speech Journal* (Fall 1960), pp. 59–69.

[47] Contemporary research is somewhat inconclusive but seems to support Priestley's general theory of the "beneficial" effects of distractive elements. See Leon Festinger, "On Resistance to Persuasive Communications," *Journal of Abnormal and Social Psychology* (1964), pp. 359–366. See also Jonathan Freedman and David Sears, "Warning, Distraction, and Resistance to Influence," *Journal of Personality and Social Psychology* (1965), pp. 262–266. In terms of distraction in informal social communication, see Robert R. Smith and Robert W. Hawkes, "The Fiddle Factor: Social Binding Functions of Distractions," *Journal of Communication* (Mar. 1972), pp. 26–38.

[48] Whately's assertion that audience personality characteristics affect susceptibility to certain persuasive strategies seems to be supported in contemporary research. See, for instance, W. Clifton Adams and Michael J. Beatty, "Dogmatism, Need for Social Approval, and the Resistance to Persuasion," *Communication Monographs* (November 1977), pp. 321–325. See also Gary Chronkite and Emily Goetz, "Dogmatism, Persuasibility and Attitude Instability," *Speech Monographs* (Dec. 1971), pp. 342–352.

[49] A classic study of primacy-recency is Percy H. Tannenbaum, "Effect of Serial Position on Recall of Radio News Stories," *Journalism Quarterly* (Summer 1954), pp. 319–323. Aronson summarizes much of this research in *The Social Animal*.

Many of these hypotheses (or assertions) have been partially tested in contemporary research; others have simply been repeated or, in some cases, ignored. Recently, attention in contemporary scholarship has tended to focus on the concerns embodied in the traditional concept of propriety. Upward and downard communication or information flow has become a primary concept in the study of complex formal organizations.[50] On the interpersonal level, scholars have categorized situations as symmetrical, equal-to-equal, or asymmetrical, superior-inferior and have studied the differences in communication strategies in terms of the relationships among the individuals involved.[51] Symbolization strategies, such as touching, seem to differ in one-up or one-down interactions.[52] Content of interactions also varies with comparative power relationships.

Traditional organizational theory was almost exclusively elaborated in terms of mass communication. Thus we see more isomorphy between "old" and "new" theory in this area. De Quincey's analysis of conversation is one of the few instances of historical concern with the organization of informal social communication, the more vital and pervasive concern of contemporary theory. The traditional concepts of perspicuity, forcefulness, and propriety, and the distinction between learned (usually rather informal and intimate) and popular (usually formal and public) situations may be a useful means of bridging the historical gap between formal/mass and informal/interpersonal communication. Communication on both levels is organized. What, exactly, the differences between the organization may be remains unclear, but only through some synthesis of research and theory can these differences be placed in perspective.

Operationalization

Traditionally, operationalization theory has focused on nonverbal communication as an organic accompaniment to verbal messages. Cicero points out that gesture and paralanguage are universally understood modes of communicating (*De Or.*, III. lxi. 223). The tones and movements that accompany verbal expression, he claims, are "natural" correspondences and inherent in human communicatin (*De Or.*, III. lvii. 216). As we have seen, the major theorists throughout history repeat Cicero's basic analysis (e.g., Kames, I., p. 411). Several theorists note that certain nonverbal symbols are used conventionally as words are, but no one notes the possibility, really the strong probability, that much of our "natural" nonverbal behavior (such as nodding to signal "yes") is

---

[50] For analysis of research in communication networks, see Richard V. Farace, Peter R. Monge, and Hamish M. Russell, *Communicating and Organizing* (Reading, Mass.: Addison-Wesley, 1977).

[51] See Watzlawick, et al., *Pragmatics of Human Communication.*

[52] For instance, see S. M. Jourard and J. Rubin, "Self-Disclosure and Touching: A Study of Two Modes of Interpersonal Encounter and Their Inter-relation," *Journal of Humanistic Psychology* (1968), pp. 39–48.

culturally learned.[53] However, most theorists do discuss the propriety of the use of voice and body, claiming that an effective communicator suits his or her nonverbal behavior to the place, subject, persons involved, occasion, and purpose (Aristotle 1404a 1–10; Cicero, *De Or.*, III. lvi. 214–220; Wilson, p. 71; Alcuin, p. 139; Kames, I., pp. 435–436; Whately, p. 355). Thus there is an assumption that although to some extent gestures and voice tone are natural and cross-cultural, they are also learned and specific to certain situations. Modern theorists point out that the unity of sound and sense is one aspect in which paralanguage can be purposively used to reinforce verbal meaning. For instance, they say that words can be selected in terms of their sounds and used to create or reinforce a sense of motion, time, size, or difficulty (Kames, II., pp. 84–91; Campbell, pp. 319–332; Priestley, pp. 289–293; Spencer, p. 4). Contemporary poetic theory makes much the same kinds of assertions.

A number of specific observations about operationalization have implications for contemporary scholarship. Aristotle's assertion that nonverbal communication (gesture and voice manipulation) is merely a skill that can be described and/or learned from practice and observation but is not susceptible to theory (1404a 1–10) seems to have some merit in light of the outcome of the elocutionary movement. Contemporary research into nonverbal behavior, which emphasizes form at the expense of content, may be similarly atheoretic in its tendencies. On the other hand, the insistence of traditional theory on the comparative strength of nonverbal over verbal communication (Cicero, *De Or.*, III. lix. 221; Fenelon, pp. 99–105; Spencer, p. 2; Blair, II., pp. 398–428) supports the current trend toward more research in this area. Contemporary diffusion research, in its comparison of mass and interpersonal means of informing and persuading, is supported by the traditional emphasis on the superior power of face-to-face, extemporaneous communication (Priestley, pp. 111–117, 226; Campbell, p. 90; Whately, pp. 368–376; Fenelon, pp. 104–108; Blair, II., pp. 156–157). Logos, ethos, and pathos, modern theorists claim, are more easily established in unmediated address. The risk of self is stronger, also, but the perception of risk increases the auditors' identification with the source[54] (Priestley, pp. 1–9, 116; Kames, I., pp. 143–144; Whately, pp. 342–362).

Other testable hypotheses grow out of traditional approaches to operationalization. For instance, Kames says that the strongest impact is

---

[53] Contemporary theorists seem to agree that nonverbal behavior that is controlled by the central autonomic nervous system can be manipulated. Only such facial expressions as blushing are truly "natural." They also tend to agree that the *interpretation* of nonverbal behavior is actually learned, although the action itself may be involuntary. See Knapp, Wiemann, and Daly.

[54] Douglas Ehninger discusses "risk of self" as a primary characteristic of argument in "Argument as Method: Its Nature, Its Limitations and Its Uses," *Speech Monographs* (June 1970), pp. 101–110.

created by messages that activate a mix of emotions and that are perceived through a mix of different senses (II., p. 119). De Quincey (*Language*, p. 261) and Augustine (IV. 10) both claim that when the subject is well-known to the auditor, it is the operationalization that catches and holds attention and leads to conviction and/or persuasion. Studies of the similarities of plot among "great" literary works tends to support this observation. Whately (and a number of others before him) asserts that the "best" operationalization is one that is not noticed (pp. 354–355). The modern theorists claim that in oral situations operationalization should be "conversational," but Whately (p. 365) and Fenelon (p. 100) point out that it should not be "familiar." No one specifies exactly what the difference is, although contemporary textbooks often include a number of examples to illustrate it. Finally, both classical and modern theorists claim that nonconventional gestures and paralanguage cannot "lie" (e. g., Kames I., p. 410, 428); thus we can speak of a "fake smile" or use expressions such as "I don't care what you say, the truth is written all over your face." Contemporary research supports this basic idea but implies that it may not be completely accurate; sometimes actions can lie, and perhaps more convincingly than words.[55]

Conclusion

A final hypothesis grows out of this study. In those periods (e.g., the early classical and the mid-modern) when all five parts of the paradigm were throughly integrated and also elaborated in the context of a commitment to scholarship on an interdisciplinary level, theory building was at its peak. Expressed negatively, in those periods (e.g., the Second Sophistic and the medieval) when certain parts of the paradigm were neglected and others elevated, when scholars became wedded to a single disciplinary point of view, theory building declined and prescriptivism abounded. Contemporary concerns over the fragmentation of human communication theory may well be a reflection of the lack of substantive understanding between and among academic fields and the lack of continuing paradigmatic synthesis. Hope for human communication as a discipline lies in research that takes into account the need for continuing elaboration of theoretic concepts such as those developed by Aristotle, Cicero, Augustine, John of Salisbury, Bacon, Kames, Campbell, Whately, and De Quincey.

[55] Nonverbal indicators of lying are the subject of Mark L. Knapp, Roderick P. Hart, and Harry S. Dennis, "An Exploration of Deception as a Communicative Construct," *Human Communication Research* (1974), pp. 15–29.

Bibliography

I. CLASSICAL PERIOD

A. *Primary Sources*

Anaximenes. *Rhetorica ad Alexandrum*. Translated by E. S. Forster, *Aristotle*. Oxford, Clarendon Press, 1908–31.

Aristotle. *Poetics*. Translated by I. Bywater, *Aristotle*. Oxford, Clarendon Press, 1962.

_____. *Poetics*. Translated by Lane Cooper. Rev. ed. Ethica: Cornell University Press, 1962.

_____. *Rhetoric*. Translated by John Henry Freese. Loeb Classical Library. Cambridge: Harvard University Press, 1967.

_____. *Rhetoric*. Translated by R. C. Jebb. Cambridge: The University Press, 1909.

Cicero. *Brutus*. Translated by G. L. Hendrickson. Loeb Classical Library. Cambridge: Harvard University Press, 1962.

_____. *De Inventione*. Translated by H. M. Hubbell. Loeb Classical Library. Cambridge: Harvard University Press, 1949.

_____. *De Oratore*. Translated by H. Rackham. Loeb Classical Library. Cambridge: Harvard University Press, 1942.

_____. *The Orations of Marcus Tullius Cicero*. Translated by Charles Duke Younge. [Containing the fourteen orations against Marcus Antonius, to which are appended the "Treatise on Rhetorical Invention," etc.]. London: G. Bell & Son, 1852.

_____. *Orator*. Translated by H. M. Hubbell. Loeb Classical Library. Cambridge: Harvard University Press, 1939.

Demetrius. *On Style*. Translated by W. Rhys Roberts. Loeb Classical Library. Cambridge: Harvard University Press, 1965.

Dionysius of Halicarnassus. *On Literary Composition*. Translated by W. Rhys Roberts. London: MacMillan and Company, Ltd., 1910.

_____. *The Three Literary Letters*. Translated by W. Rhys Roberts. Cambridge: Harvard University Press, 1901.

Herodotus: *The Histories*. Translated by A. de Selincourt. Roslyn, New York: Penguin Books, 1972.

Isocrates. *Antidosis*. Translated by Larue Van Hook. Cambridge: Harvard University Press, 1944.

_____. *Works.* Translated by George Norling. Loeb Classical Library. London: W. Heinmann, Ltd., 1928–45.

Longinus. *On the Sublime.* Translated by G. M. A. Grube. Library of Liberal Arts. New York: Liberal Arts Press, 1957.

_____. *On the Sublime.* Translated by W. Rhys Roberts. Cambridge: University Press, 1899.

Plato. *Gorgias.* Translated by W. C. Helmhold. Library of Liberal Arts. New York: Liberal Arts Press, 1952.

_____. *Phaedrus.* Translated by W. C. Helmhold and W. G. Rabinwitz. Library of Liberal Arts. New York: Liberal Arts Press, 1956.

_____. *Phaedrus and Gorgias.* Translated by Lane Cooper. New York: Oxford University Press, 1955.

_____. *Phaedrus Gorgias.* Translated by Benjamin Jowett. Oxford: Calrendon Press, 1952.

_____. *The Republic.* Translated by H. D. P. Lee. Baltimore: Penguin Books, 1955.

Quintilian. *Institutes of Oratory.* Translated by J. S. Watson. Bohn Library. London: G. Bell and Sons, 1888.

_____. *Institutionis Oratoriae.* Translated by H. E. Butler. Loeb Classical Library. Cambridge: Harvard University Press, 1922.

Rhetorica ad Herrenium. Translated by Harry Caplan. Loeb Classical Library. Cambridge: Harvard University Press, 1939.

Seneca the Elder. *Controverses et Suasoires.* Translated by Henri Bornecque. Classiques Garnier. Rev. ed. Paris: Garnier, 1932.

_____. *Suasoirae.* Translated by W. A. Edward. Cambridge: The University Press, 1928.

Tacitus. *Dialogues on Oratory: The Complete Works of Tacitus.* Translated by A. J. Church and W. J. Brodribb. New York: The Modern Library, 1942.

Tacitus. *Tacitus: Historical Works.* Translated by Arthur Murphy. Everyman's Library. New York: E. P. Dutton and Company, 1932.

Tacitus, Publius Cornelius. *Dialogus De Oratoribus.* Translated by Sir William Peterson. Loeb Classical Library. Cambridge: Harvard University Press, 1914.

B. Secondary Sources

1. Books

Atkins, J. W. H. *Literary Criticism in Antiquity.* Gloucester, Massachusetts: Peter Smith, 1961.

Baldwin, Charles Sears. *Ancient Rhetoric and Poetic.* New York: The MacMillan Co., 1924.

Benson, Thomas W. and Prosser, Michael H., eds. *Readings in Classical Rhetoric.* Boston: Allyn and Bacon, Inc., 1969.

Boak, Arthur. *A History of Rome to 565 A.D.* 4th ed. New York: Macmillan Company, 1955.

Bolgar, R. *The Classical Heritage and Its Beneficiaries.* Cambridge (Eng.): University Press, 1954.

Bowra, C. M. *Ancient Greek Literature.* Galaxy paperback. New York: Oxford University Press, 1969.

Cary, M. J. and Haarhoff, J. J. *Life and Thought in the Greek and Roman World.* London: Methuen and Company, Ltd., 1940.

Clark, Donald Lemen. *Rhetoric in Greco-Roman Education.* New York: Columbia University Press, 1966.

Clarke, M. L. *Rhetoric at Rome.* London: Cohen and West, Ltd., 1953.

Cooper, Lane, ed. *The Greek Genius and Its Influence.* Ithaca: Cornell University Press, 1952.

Cope, E. M. *An Introduction to Aristotle's Rhetoric.* London: Macmillan and Company, 1867.

_____. *The Rhetoric of Aristotle with a Commentary.* Rev. ed., J. E. Sandys, ed. Hildesheim, New York: George Olms, 1970.

Copleston, Frederick. *A History of Philosophy: Greece and Rome.* Garden City: Doubleday and Co., Inc., 1962.

Croker, L. and Carmack, P., eds. *Readings in Rhetoric.* Springfield, Ill.: C. C. Thomas, 1965.

D'Alton, J. F. *Roman Literary Theory and Criticism.* New York: Russell and Russell, 1962.

Drake, Henry L., ed. *Plato's Complete Works.* Patterson, N.J.: Littlefield, Adams, and Company, 1959.

Duff, J. Wright. *A Literary History of Rome in the Silver Age.* New York: Barnes and Noble, 1962.

Freeman, Kathleen. *The Murder of Herocles and Other Trials from the Athenian Law Courts.* New York: W. W. Norton and Company, Inc., 1963.

Grant, Michael. *Myths of the Greeks and Romans.* New York: New American Library, 1962.

Gilbert, A. H. *Literary Criticism: Plato to Dryden.* New York: American Book Company, 1940.

Grimaldi, W. *Studies in the Philosophy of Aristotle's Rhetoric.* Wiesbaden: F. Steiner, 1972.

Grube, G. M. A. *A Greek Critic: Demetrius on Style.* Toronto: University of Toronto Press, 1961.

_____. *The Greek and Roman Critics.* Toronto: University of Toronto Press, 1965.

_____. *Plato's Thought.* Boston: Beacon Press, 1960.

Gwynn, Aubrey and Osborn, S. J. *Roman Education from Cicero to Quintilian.* Oxford: Clarendon Press, 1926.

Hadas, Moses, ed. *Basic Work of Cicero*. New York: Modern Library, 1951.

Hamilton, Edith. *The Greek Way to Western Civilization*. New York: American Library, 1948.

Jaeger, Werner. *Aristotle: The Fundamentals of the History of His Development*. Translated by R. Robinson. 2nd ed. Oxford: Clarendon Press, 1968.

_____. *Paideia: The Ideals of Greek Culture*. Translated by Gilbert Highet. New York: Oxford University Press, 1962–63.

Jebb, R. C. *The Attic Orators from Antiphon to Isaeos*. London: Macmillan and Company, 1976.

Kennedy, George. *The Art of Persuasion in Greece*. Princeton: Princeton University Press, 1963.

_____. *The Art of Rhetoric in the Roman World*. Princeton: Princeton University Press, 1972.

Kennedy, George. *Quintilian*. New York: Twayne Publishers, 1969.

Kitto, H. D. F. *The Greeks*. Baltimore: Penguin Books, 1952.

Marrou, H. I. *A History of Education in Antiquity*. New York: New American Library, 1956.

McKeon, R. *Introduction to Aristotle*. New York: Random House, 1947.

Moravcsik, J. M. E., ed. *Aristotle*. Garden City: Doubleday and Company, Inc. 1957.

Murphy, James S., ed. *A Synoptic History of Classical Rhetoric*. New York: Random House, 1972.

Ong, Walter J., S. J. *Rhetoric, Romance, and Technology*. Ithaca, New York: Cornell University Press, 1971.

Peterson, Torsten. *Cicero: A Biography*. Berekeley, California: University of California Press, 1920.

Randall, John Herman. *Aristotle*. Columbia University Press, 1960.

Roberts, W. Rhys. *Greek Rhetoric and Literary Criticism*. New York: Longmans, Greek and Company, 1928.

Robinson, C. A., ed. *Selections from Greek and Roman Historians*. New York: Holt, Rinehart. and Winston, 1957.

Rolfe, John Carew. *Cicero and His Influence*. New York: Cooper Square Publisher, 1963.

Ross, W. D. *Aristotle: A Complete Exposition of His Works and Thought*. 2nd ed. Cleveland: The World Publishing Company, 1959.

Starr, C. *A History of the Ancient World*. New York: Oxford University Press, 1974.

Tarn, W. *Hellenistic Civilization*. 3rd ed. [Revised with G. Griffith]. Cleveland: New American Library, 1965.

Taylor, A. E. *Plato: The Man and His Work*. 7th ed. London: Methuen and Company Ltd., 1969.

_____. *Socrates*. Garden City, N.Y.: Doubleday and Company, 1953.

Walz, Christianus. *Rhetores Graece.* Stuttgart-Tubingen, London, Paris, 1832–6.

Warmington, E. H. *Remains of Old Latin.* Loeb Classical Library. Cambridge: Harvard University Press, 1935–9.

Zimmern, A. E. *The Greek Commonwealth.* 5th ed. [Revised]. New York: Oxford University Press, 1961.

2. Articles

Baldwin, Charles Sears. "Rhetoric." *Monroe's Encyclopedia of Education.* New York: The Macmillan Company, 1911–12.

Bevilacqua, Vincent. "Rhetoric and the Circle of Moral Studies: An Historiographic View." *Quarterly Journal of Speech.* 66 (1962), 99–155.

Bitzer, Lloyd. "Aristotle's Enthymene Revisisted." *Quarterly Journal of Speech.* (1959), 399–408.

Black, Edwin. "Plato's View of Rhetoric." *Quarterly Journal of Speech.* (1958), 361–374.

Brandes, P. "The Composition and Preservation of Aristotle's Rhetoric." *Speech Monographs.* 35 (1968), 482–91.

Brownstein, Oscar L. "Plato's *Phaedrus:* Dialectic as the Genuine Art of Speaking." *Quarterly Journal of Speech.* (1965), 392–398.

Cooper, Lane. "The Rhetoric of Aristotle and Its Relation to Poetics." *Aristotelian Papers.* Ithaca: Cornell University Press, 1939.

Harper, Nancy L. "An Analytical Description of Aristotle's Enthymene." *Central States Speech Journal.* (1973), 304–9.

Hendrickson, G. "Cicero's Correspondence with Brutus and Calvus on Oratorical Style." *American Journal of Philology.* 47 (1926), 234–58.

Hinks, D. A. G. "Tisias and Corax and the Invention of Rhetoric," *Classical Quarterly.* (1940), 59–69.

Hubbell, H. "Cicero on Styles of Oratory." *Yale Classical Studies.* 19 (1966), 171–186.

Jebb, R. C. "Rhetoric." *Encyclopaedia Britannica.* 11th ed. Cambridge: University Press, 1910–11.

Kennedy, George A. "The Earliest Rhetorical Handbooks." *American Journal of Philology.* (1959), 169–78.

McBurney, James H. "The Place of the Enthymene in Rhetorical Theory." *Speech Monographs.* (1936), 72.

Segal, C. "Gorgias and the Psychology of the *Logos.*" *Harvard Studies in Classical Philology.* 66 (1962), 99–155.

Smethurst, S. "Cicero's Rhetorical and Philosophical Works: A Bibliographical Survey." *Classical World.* 51 (1957), 1–41; 58 (1964), 36–45; 61 (1967), 125–33.

Solmsen, Friedrich. "The Aristotelian Tradition in Ancient Rhetoric." *American Journal of Philology.* (1941). 35–50 and 168–190.

Wagner, Russell, H. "The Rhetorical Theory of Isocrates." *Quarterly Journal of Speech.* (1922), 323–337.

Wilcox, Stanley. "The Scope of Early Rhetorical Instruction." *Harvard Studies in Classical Philology.* (1942), 121–155.

II. MEDIEVAL AND RENAISSANCE PERIODS

A. Primary Sources

Agricola, Rudolph. *De Inventione Dialectica Libri Tres.* Argentinae: Joannis Knoblouchi, 1521.

Alcuin. *The Rhetoric of Alcuin and Charlemagne.* Edited and translated by Wilbur S. Howell. Princeton: Princeton Univesrity Press, 1941.

Aphthonioud of Antioch. "Progymnasmata." Translated by Ray Nadeau. *Speech Monographs.* (1952), 264–285.

Ascham, Robert. *The Schoolmaster.* Edited by Donald C. Whimster. London: Methuen and Company Ltd., 1934.

Augustine. *De Doctrine Christiana.* A Select Library of Nicene and Post-Nicene Fathers of the Christian Church. Edited by Phillip Schaff. New York: Christian Literature Company, 1887.

_____. *De Doctrine Christiana.* Translated by Durant W. Robertson, Jr. New York: Library of Liberal Arts 80, 1958.

_____. *On Christian Doctrine.* Translated by J. F. Shaw. *Great Books of the Western World,* Vol. 18. Chicago: Encyclopaedia Britannica, Inc., 1952.

Bacon, Francis. *The Advancement of Learning.* Edited by Spedding, Ellis, and Heath. Boston: Brown and Taggard, 1961–63.

_____. *The Advancement of Learning and Novum Organum. Great Books of the Western World,* Vol. 30. Chicago: Encyclopaedia Britannica, Inc., 1952.

Bede (The Venerable). "Bede's Schmatibus et Tropis—A Translation." Translated by Gussie Hecht Tanenhaus. *Quarterly Journal of Speech.* (Oct. 1962), 237–253.

Boethius, Anicius Manlius Severinus. *An Overview of the Structure of Rhetoric and An Examination of the Rhetorical Places.* Migne, *Patrologia Latina,* Vol. 64.

Buffon, Comte de. *Discours sur le Style.* Paris: Hachette, 1931.

Butler, Charles. *Oratoriae Libri Duo.* Translation and commentary by Donovan Ochs. M. A. thesis, University of Iowa, 1963.

Butler, Charles. *Rhetoricae Libri Duo.* London: G. Turner, 1629.

Cassiodorus. *An Introduction to Divine and Human Readings.* Translation and introduction by Leslie Weber Jones. New York: Columbia University Press, 1946.

Cox, Leonard. *The Arte or Crafte of Rhetoricae*. Edited by Frederick I. Carpenter. New York: AMS Press, 1971.

Elyot, Sir Thomas. *The Book of the Governor*. London: J. M. Dent and Company, 1907.

Erasmus. *On Copia of Words and Ideas*. Translated by Donald B. King and H. David Rix. Milwaukee: Marquette University Press, 1963.

——————. *The Praise of Folly*. Translated by Hoyt H. Hudson. Princeton: Princeton University Press, 1941.

——————. *Apoptheqmes*. Translated by Nicholas Udall. Boston and Lincolnshire: Robert Roberts, 1877.

——————. *Ciceronianus*. Translated by Izora Scott. New York: Teachers College, Columbia University, 1908.

Farnaby, Thomas. *Index Rhetoricus*. Menston, England: Scholar Press, 1970.

Fenner, Dudley. *The Artes of Logike and Rhetorike*. Edited by Robert D. Pepper. Gainesville, Fla.: Scholar's Facsimiles and Reprints, 1966.

Fraunce, Abrahan. *Arcadian Rhetorike*. Edited by Ethel Seaton. Menston, England: Scholar Press, 1969.

——————. *The Lawyers Logike*. Menston, England: W. Haw, 1588.

Geoffrey of Vinsauf. *Poetria Nova*. Translated by Margaret F. Nims. Toronto: Pontifical Institute of Medieval Studies, 1967.

Guibert. *A Book About the Way a Sermon Ought to be Given*. Translated by Joseph Miller. *Communication Quarterly*. (1969), 45–47.

Hobbes, Thomas. *A Brief of the Art of Rhetorique*. London: Bohn, 1853.

Hoskins, John. *Directions for Speech and Style*. Edited by Hoyt H. Hudson. Princeton: Princeton University Press, 1935.

Isidore of Seville. *Etymologiarium sive originum libri, XX*. 2 Vols. Edited by Wallace M. Lindsay. Oxford: Oxford University Press, 1911.

John of Salisbury, *Metalogicon*. Translated by Daniel McGarry. Berkeley: University of California Press, 1955.

Lamy, Bernard. *La Rhetorique, ou L'Arte de Parler*. University of Sussex Library for the Committee for Research for French Studies, 1969.

Melanchthon, Philipp. *Elementorum Rhetorics*. Ann Arbor: University Microfilms, 1953.

Peacham, Henry. *The Garden of Eloquence Containing the Figures of Grammar and Rhetoric*. Gainesville, Florida: Scholar's Facsimiles and Reprints, 1954.

Petrarch. *Letters*. Translated by H. Nachod. *The Renaissance Philosophy of Man*. Edited by Cassirer, Kristeller, and Randall. Chicago: University of Chicago Press, 1948.

Puttenham, George. *The Arte of English Poesie*. Edited by Gladys D. Willcock and Alice Walker. Cambridge: The University Press, 1936.

Rainholde, Richard. *The Foundation of Rhetorike*. Edited by Francis R. Johnson. Menston, England: Scholar Press, 1972.

Ramus, Peter. *The Art of Logike.* London, 1626. Ann Arbor: University Microfilms.
_____. *Dialecticae Libri Duo.* Paris, 1560. Ann Arbor: University Microfilms.
Rollin, Charles. *Traite des Etudes.* Ann Arbor: University Microfilms, 1963.
Sherry, Richard. *Treatise of the Figures of Grammar and Rhetorike.* Ann Arbor Microfilms. British and Continental Rhetoric and Elocution, #7, 1953.
_____. *A Treatise of Schemes and Tropes.* Gainesville, Florida: Scholar's Facsimiles and Reprints, 1961.
Soarez, Cyprian. *De Arte Rhetorica.* Translated by Lawrence J. Flynn. Ann Arbor: University Microfilms, 1956.
Sprat, Thomas. *The History of the Royal Society of London.* St. Louis: Washington University, 1960.
Valla. *Dialecticae Disputationes.* Vol. 1, Series 1:5–6. Opera Omnia. Monumento Politica et Philosphica Rariora. Edited by Garin. Turin, 1962.
Vicars, Thomas. *Manduction to the Rhetorical Art.* Ann Arbor: University Microfilms, 1953.
Vives, Juan Luis. *De Consultatione.* Ann Arbor: University Microfilms, 1953.
_____. *On Education.* Translated by Foster Watsob. London: J. M. Dent and Company, 1908.
Wilson, Thomas. *Arte of Rhetorique.* Edited by G. W. Mair. Oxford: Clarendon Press, 1909.

B. Secondary Sources

1. Books

Abelson, Paul. *The Seven Liberal Arts.* Thesis, Columbia University, 1906.
Anstey, Henry. *Munimenta Academia Oxoniensis.* London: Longmans, Green, Reader & Dyer, 1868.
Artz, F. *Renaissance Humanism: 1300–1500.* Kent, Ohio: Kent State University Press, 1966.
Atkins, J. W. H. *English Literary Criticism: The Renaissance.* New York: Barnes and Noble, 1947.
_____. *English Literary Criticism: The Medieval Phase.* Cambridge: Oxford University Press, 1943.
Baldwin, C. S. *Medieval Rhetoric and Poetic.* New York: The Macmillan Company, 1928.

_____. *Renaissance Literary Theory and Practice*. New York: Columbia University Press.

Baldwin, T. W. *Shakespeare's Small Latine and Lesse Greeke*. Urbana: University of Illinois Press, 1944.

Bolgar, R. R. *The Classical Heritage and Its Beneficiaries: From the Carolingian Age to the Renaissance*. New York: Harper and Row, 1964.

Bochenski, I. M. *A History of Formal Logic*. Translated by Ivo Thomas. South Bend, Indiana: University of Notre Dame Press, 1961.

Bormann, Dennis. "Gottsched's Enlightened Rhetoric: The Influence of Christian Wolff's Philosophy on J. Gottsched's *Ausfurliche Redekunst*." Ph. D. dissertation, University of Iowa, 1968.

Cassirer, E., Kristeller, P., and Randall, J., Jr., eds. *The Renaissance Philosophy of Man*. Chicago: Univesrity of Chicago Press, 1948.

Caplan, Harry. *Of Eloquence: Studies in Ancient and Medieval Rhetoric*. Edited by Helen North and Anne King. Ithaca and London: Cornell University Press, 1970.

_____. *Medieval Artes Praedicandi: A Handlist*. Ithaca: Cornell University Press, 1936.

_____. *Medieval Artes Praedicandi: Supplement*. Ithaca and London: Cornell University Press, 1936.

Crane, William G. *Wit and Rhetoric in the Renaissance. The Formal Basis of Elizabethan Prose Style*. New York: Columbia University Press, 1937; Gloucester, Mass: Peter Smith, 1964.

Curtius, Ernst. Robert. *European Literature and the Latin Middle Ages*. Translated by Willard R. Trask. Bollingen Series, No. 36. New York: Pantheon Books, 1953.

Faulhaber, Charles. *Latin Rhetorical Theory in Thirteenth and Fourteenth Century Castile*. Berkeley: University of California Press, 1972.

Ferguson, W. *The Renaissance*. New York: Harper & Row, 1962.

Gilbert, Neal W. *Renaissance Concepts of Method*. New York: Columbia University Press, 1960.

Gordon, George N. *The Communications Revolution: A History of Mass Media in the United States*. New York: Hastings House, 1977.

Haskins, Charles Homer. *The Renaissance of the Twelfth Century*. New York: World Publishing Co., 1968.

Howell, Wilbur S. *Logic and Rhetoric in England, 1500–1700*. New York: Russell and Russell, 1961.

Howes, R. F. *Historical Studies of Rhetoric and Rhetoricians*. Ithaca: Cornell University Press, 1961.

Jones, L. W. *Divine and Human Readings*. New York: Columbia University Press, 1946.

Jones, Richard Foster. *The Triumph of the English Language*. Stanford: Stanford University Press, 1953.

Joseph, Sister Miriam. *Shakespeare's Use of the Arts of Language*. New York: Columbia University Press, 1947.

Kirsteller, P. *Renaissance Thought: The Classic, Scholastic, and Humanist Strains.* New York: Harper, 1961.

Larkin, James F., ed. and trans. *"De Ratione Studii:* Its Relationship to 16th Century English Literature." Ph. D. dissertation, University of Illinois, Urbana, 1966.

Lastner, M. *Thought and Letters in Western Europe:* A.D. *500–900.* Ithaca, New York: Cornell University Press, 1966.

Lechner, Sister Joan Marie. *Renaissance Concepts of the Commonplaces.* New York: Pagent Press, 1962.

Manitus, Max. *Geschichte der Lateininschen Literatur des Mittlealters.* Munich: C. H. Beck, 1923, p. 713.

McNally, Richard J. "An Appraisal of Rudolph Agricola's *De Inventione Dialectica Libri Tres* as a Philosophy of Artistic Discourse." Ph. D. dissertation, University of Iowa, Iowa City, 1966.

Miller, Joseph M.; Prosser, Michael H.; and Benson, Thomas W. *Readings in Medieval Rhetoric.* Indiana University Press, 1973.

Murphy, James. *Medieval Rhetoric: A Select Bibliography.* Toronto: University of Toronto Press, 1971.

_____. *Three Medieval Rhetorical Arts.* Berkeley: University of California Press, 1971.

_____. *Rhetoric in the Middle Ages: A History of Rhetorical Theory from Saint Augustine to the Renaissance.* Berkeley: University of California Press, 1974.

Mosher, Joseph A. *The Exemplum in the Early Religious and Didactic Literature of England.* New York: Columbia University Press, 1911.

Ong, Walter, J., S. J. *The Presence of the Word.* New Haven: Yale University Press, 1967.

_____. *Ramus and the Decay of Dialogue.* Cambridge: Harvard University Press, 1958.

Owst, Gerald R. *Preaching in Medieval England: An Introduction to Sermon Manuscripts of the Period, c. 1350–1450.* Cambridge, England, 1926; Reprint edition, New York: Russell & Russell 1965.

Paetow, Louis J. *The Arts Course at Medieval Universities with Special Reference to Grammar and Rhetoric.* Champagne, Ill.: University of Illinois Press, 1910.

Patch, Louis J. *The Tradition of Boethius: A Study of His Importance in Medieval Culture.* New York: Oxford University Press, 1935.

Patrick, J. Max, Evans, Robert O., et al., eds. *Style, Rhetoric, and Rhythm.* Princeton: Princeton University Press, 1966.

Power, Eileen. *Medieval People.* London: Metheun and Company Ltd., 1963.

Rand, E. K. *Founders of the Middle Ages.* New York: Dover, 1957.

Rashdall, Hastings. *The Universities of Europe in the Middle Ages.* Edited by F. M. Powicke and A. B. Emden. Three volumes. Oxford: The Clarendon Press, 1936.

Robins, Robert H. *Ancient and Medieval Grammatical Theory in Europe.* London: G. Bell, 1951.

Sandford, William E. *English Theories of Public Address, 1530–1828.* Columbus, Ohio: H. L. Hedrick, 1931.

Sandys, John E. *A History of Classical Scholarship.* 3rd ed. New York: Hafner Pub. Co., 1964. Vol. 1: *From the Sixth Century* B.C. *to the End of the Middle Ages.*

——————. *A History of Classical Scholarship.* 3rd ed. New York: Hafner Publishing Co., 1964. Vol. 2: *From the Revival of Learning to the End of the Eighteenth Century.*

Schwartz, J. and Rycenga, J. A., eds. *The Province of Rhetoric.* New York: Ronald Press Company, 1965.

Sonnino, Lee Ann. *A Handbook of Sixteenth Century Rhetoric.* London: Routledge and Kegan Paul, 1968.

Southern, R. W. *The Making of the Middle Ages.* London: Hutchinson, 1967.

Stahl, William Harris; Johnson, Richard; and Burge, E. L. *Martianus Capella and the Seven Liberal Arts.* New York and London: Columbia University Press, 1971.

Strayer, J., and Munro, D. *The Middle Ages: 1350–1500.* New York: Appleton-Century-Crofts, Inc., 1959.

Sweeting, E. J. *Early Tudor Criticism Linguistic and Literary.* New York: Russell and Russell, 1964.

Thorndyke, Lynn. *University Records and Life in the Middle Ages.* New York: Columbia University Press, 1944.

Wallace, Karl W., ed. *History of Speech Education in America.* New York: Appleton-Century-Crofts, Inc., 1954.

Wallach, Luitpold. *Alcuin and Charlemagne: Studies in Carolingian History.* Ithaca: Cornell University Press, 1959.

Wimsatt, William, and Brooks, Cleanth. *Literary Criticism: A Short History.* New York: Knopf, 1957.

2. Articles

Bird, Otto. "The Formalizing of Topics in Medieval Logic." *Notre Dame Journal of Formal Logic.* (1960). 138–141.

——————. "The Tradition of Logical Topics." *Journal of the History of Ideas.* (1962), 308.

Bliese, John. "The Study of Rhetoric in the Twelfth Century." *Quarterly Journal of Speech.* (1977), 364–383.

Caplan, H. "Classical Rhetoric and the Medieval Theory of Preaching." *Classical Philology.* (1933), 73–96.

Clark, D. L. "Rhetoric and the Literature of the English Middle Ages." *Quarterly Journal of Speech.* (1959), 19–28.

_____. "The Rise and Fall of Progymnasmata in Sixteenth and Seventeenth Century Grammar Schools." *Speech Monographs.* (1952), 259–263.

Cleary, James W. "John Bulwer: Renaissance Communicationist." *Quarterly Journal of Speech.* (1954), 391–398.

Dieter, Otto. "The Rhetoric of Notker Labeo." *Papers in Rhetoric.* Edited by Donald C. Bryant. Iowa City, Iowa: University of Iowa, 1940.

DeRijk, L. M. "On the Chronology of Boethius' Works on Logic II." *Vivarium.* (1964), 154.

Ehninger, Douglas. "Bernard Lamy's Arte de Parler." *Quarterly Journal of Speech.* (1946), 429–434.

Flynn, Lawrence J. "The *De Arte Rhetorica* of Cyprian Soarez." *Quarterly Journal of Speech.* (1956), 257–265.

_____. "Sources of Soarez's *Rhetorica.*" *Quarterly Journal of Speech.* (1957), 257–265.

Gilson, Etienne. "Michel Menot et la Technique de Sermon Medievale." *Revue d'Histoire Franciscaine.* (1925), 307.

Herrick, Marvin T. "The Early History of Aristotle's *Rhetoric* in England." *Philological Quarterly.* (1926), 240–248.

Howell, W. S. "Nathaniel Carpenter's Place in the Argument Between Rhetoric and Dialectic." *Speech Monographs.* (1934), 20–41.

_____. "Ramus and English Rhetoric." *Quarterly Journal of Speech.* (1951), 299–310.

Hudson, Hoyt H. "Jewel's Oration Against Rhetoric." *Quarterly Journal of Speech.* (1928), 374–392.

Knaub, David. "George Puttenham's Theory of Natural and Artificial Discourse." *Speech Monographs.* (1967), 35–42.

Lang, Robert A. "Rhetoric in the French Jesuit Colleges, 1556–1762." *Speech Monographs.* (1952), 286–298.

Nadeau, Ray. "A Renaissance Schoolmaster on Practice." *Speech Monographs.* (1959), 179–179.

_____. "Talaeus Versus Farnaby on Style." *Speech Monographs.* (1954), 59–63.

_____. "Thomas Farnaby: Schoolmaster and Rhetorician of the English Renaissance." *Quarterly Journal of Speech.* (1950), 340–344.

McNally, Richard J. "*Dux Illa Directrixque Artium*: Rudolph Agricola's Dialectical System." *Quarterly Journal of Speech.* (1966), 337–347.

Murphy, James J. "The Medieval Arts of Discourse: An Introductory Bibliography." *Speech Monographs.* (1962), 71–78.

_____. "Aristotle's *Rhetoric* in the Middle Ages." *Quarterly Journal of Speech.* (1966), 109–115.

_____. "Alberic of Monte Cassino: Father of the Medieval Ars Dictaminus." *American Benedictine Review.* (1971), 139.

_____. "The Earliest Teaching of Rhetoric at Oxford." *Speech Monographs.* (1960), 345–347.

_____. "Saint Augustine and Rabanus Maurus: The Genesis of Medieval Rhetoric." *Western Speech.* (1967), 88–96.

Reinsma, Luke M. "Rhetoric in England: The Age of Aelfric, 970–1020." *Communication Monographs.* (1977), 390–403.

Smith, Bromley and Ehninger, Douglas. "The Terrafilial Disputations at Oxford." *Quarterly Journal of Speech.* (1950), 333–339.

Wagner, Russell. "Thomas Wilson's *Arte of Rhetorique.*" *Speech Monographs.* (1960), 1–32.

_____. "Thomas Wilson's Speech Against usury." *Quarterly Journal of Speech.* (1952), 13–22.

_____. "Wilson and His Sources." *Quarterly Journal of Speech.* (1929), 525–536.

Wallace, Karl R. "Aspects of Modern Rhetoric in Francis Bacon." *Quarterly Journal of Speech.* (1956), 398–400.

_____. "Bacon's Conception of Rhetoric." *Speech Monographs.* (1936), 21–48.

III. THE MODERN PERIOD

A. Primary Sources

Adams, John Q. *Lectures on Rhetoric and Oratory.* New York: Russell and Russell, 1962.

Alison, Archibald. *Essays on the Nature and Principles of Taste.* London: S. S. G. and G. Robinson, 1790.

Arnaulf, Antoine. *La Logique.* Paris, 1662.

Austin, Gilbert. *Chironamia: or a Treatise on Rhetorical Delivery.* Edited by Mary Margaret Robb and Lester Thonssen. Carbondale: Southern Illinois University Press, 1966.

Blair, Hugh. *Lectures on Rhetoric and Belles Lettres.* Edited by Harold Harding. Three volumes. New York: Garland Press, 1970.

_____. *Lectures on Rhetoric and Belles Lettres.* Three volumes. London, 1818.

Blount, Theodore. *The Academy of Eloquence.* London, 1656.

Brightland, John. *A Grammer of the English Tongue.* 2nd ed. London, 1712.

Bulwer, John. *Chirologia: or the Natural Language of the Hand, and Chironomia: or the Art of Manual Rhetoric,* ed. By James W. Cleary. Carbondale: Southern Illinois University Press, 1974.

Burgh, James. *The Art of Speaking.* London, 1761.

Burke, Edmund. "A Philosophical Inquiry into the Origin of our Ideas of the Sublime and Beautiful; with an Introductory Essay on Taste" *Works of the Right Honorable Edmund Burke.* London, 1826.

Campbell, George. *Lectures on Systematic Theology and Pulpit Eloquence.* Boston: Lincoln and Edmonds, 1832.

_____. *Philosophy of Rhetoric.* Edited by Lloyd F. Bitzer. Carbondale: Southern Illinois University Press, 1963.

Constable, John. *Reflections Upon Accuracy of Style.* London, 1734.

Cull, Richard. *Garrick's Mode of Reading the Liturgy of the Church of England.* London, 1840.

DeQuincey, Thomas. *DeQuincey: Autobiographical Sketches.* Boston: Tickner and Fields, 1856.

DeQuincey, Thomas. *Selected Essays on Rhetoric.* Edited by Frederick Burwick. Carbondale: Southern Illinois University Press, 1967.

Dodsley, Robert. *The Art of Preaching.* London, 1735.

Engel, Johann Jacob. *Practical Illustrations of Rhetorical Gesture and Action Adapted of the English Drama.* Translated by Henry Siddons. London, 1807.

Ewing, Thomus. *Principles of Elocution.* 2nd ed. Edinburgh, 1816.

Farnaby, Thomas. *Index Rhetoricus.* London, 1646.

Fenelon. *Dialogues on Eloquence.* Translated by Wilbur S. Howell. Princeton: Princeton University Press, 1951.

Gerard, Alexander. *An Essay on Genius.* London: W. Straham & T. Cadell, 1774.

Glanuel, Joseph. *An Essay Concerning Preaching.* 2nd ed. London: Printed for C. Brome, 1703.

Hartley, A.M. *The Academic Speaker: A System of Elocution Designed for Schools and Self-Instruction.* Glasgow. 1846.

Hartley, David. *Observations on Man, with Notes and Additions by Herman Andrew Pistorius.* 4th ed. London: J. Johnson, 1801.

Henley, John. *The Appeal of the Oratory to the First Ages of Christianity.* London, 1727.

_____. *The Art of Speaking in Public.* 2nd ed. London, 1727.

Holmes, John. *The Art of Rhetoric Made Easy.* London, 1739.

_____. *The Art of Rhetoric Made Easy.* Ann Arbor: University Microfilms, 1953.

Howlett, John Henry. *Instructions in Reading the Liturgy of the United Church of England and Ireland.* London, 1826.

Jamieson, Alexander. *Grammar of Rhetoric and Polite Literature.* London, 1818.

Kames, Henry Homes (Lord). *Elements of Criticism.* New York: Garland Publisher, 1971.

Lawson, John. *Lectures Concerning Oratory.* Menston, England: Scholar Press, 1969.

Langley, Larret. *Manual of the Figures of Rhetoric.* Doncaster, 1835.

Mill, John Stewart. *A System of Logic.* London: Longmans, Green, Reader, and Dyer, 1872.

Newton, John. *An Introduction to the Art of Logick.* London, 1671.

────────. *An Introduction to the Art of Rhetorick.* London, 1671.

Ogilvie, John. *Philosophical and Critical Observations on the Nature, Characters, and Various Species of Composition.* London: G. Robinson, 1774.

Pascal, Blaise. "The Art of Persuading." *Works.* New York: Macmillan, 1963.

Priestly, Joseph. *A Course of Lectures on Oratory and Criticism.* Edited by Vincent Bevilacqua and Richard Murphy. Carbondale: Southern Illinois University Press, 1965.

Rapin, Rene. *Reflections Upon the Eloquence of These Times.* London: Printed for Richard Preston, 1672.

Shappell, William. *The Art and Method of Preaching.* London, 1656.

Sharp, Ralph. *The Flowers of Rhetoric, The Graces of Eloquence and the Charms of Oratory.* London, 1819.

Sheridan, Thomas. *A Course of Lectures on Elocution.* Dublin, 1764.

Smith, Adam. *Lectures on Rhetoric and Belles Lettres.* Edited by John M. Lothian. London: T. Nelson, 1963.

Smith, John. *The Mysteries of Rhetorique Unveiled.* London, 1657.

Spencer, H. *The Philosophy of Style.* New York: Pagent Press, 1953

Steele, Joshua. *Prosodia Nationalis.* Menston, England: Scholar Press, 1969

Swift, Jonathan. *A Letter to a Young Clergyman.* London: J. Roberts, 1921.

Talaei, Audomari. *Institutions Oratoriae Valentiae.* Paris: Iacobus Bogardus, 1545.

Vossius, G. J. *Commentarium Rhetoricorum Since Institutionum.* Leyden, Holland: Lugduni Batavorum, 1630.

Walker, John. *Elements of Elocution.* Boston, 1810.

────────. *Exercises for Improvement in Elocution.* London, 1777.

────────. *Hints for Improvement in the Art of Reading.* London, 1783.

────────. *The Melody of Speaking Delineated.* London, 1787.

────────. *A Rhetorical Grammar.* 2nd ed. London, 1787.

────────. *The Teacher's Assistant.* Carlisle, 1808.

Whately, Richard. *Elements of Logic.* New York: William Jackson, 1832.

────────. *Elements of Rhetoric.* Edited by Douglas Ehninger. Carbondale, I..: Southern Illinois University Press, 1963.

B. Secondary Sources

1. Books

Abrams, M. *The Mirror and the Lamp.* New York: Oxford University Press, 1953.

Artz, F. *From the Renaissance to Romanticism.* Chicago: University of Chicago Press, 1962.

Atkin, J. W. H. *English Literary Criticism: Seventeenth and Eighteenth Centuries.* London: Methuen, 1951.

Bate, Watler Jackson. *From Classic to Romantic: Promises of Taste in Eighteenth Century England.* New York: Harper and Row, 1961.

Beardsley, Monroe C., ed. *The European Philosophers from Descartes to Nietzsche.* New York: Random House, 1960.

Becker, Carl L. *The Heavenly City of the Eighteenth Century Philosophers.* New Haven: Yale University Press, 1966.

Bolgar, R. *The Classical Heritage.* Cambridge, England: University Press, 1954.

Bosker, A. *Literary Criticism in the Age of Johnson.* 2nd ed. New York: Gordon Press, 1970.

Brinton, C. *The Shaping of Modern Thought.* Englewood Cliffs, New Jersey: Prentice Hall, 1963.

Bryant, Donald C. *Rhetorical Dimensions in Criticism.* Baton Rouge: Louisiana State University Press, 1973.

Burrell, Sidney A. *Handbook of European History Since 1500.* New York: John Wiley and Sons, Inc., 1965.

Cailiet, Emile and Blankenagel, John C., eds. *Great Shorter Works of Pascal.* Philadelphia: Westminster Press, 1948.

Cassirer, Ernst. *Philosophy of the Enlightenment.* Translated by Fritz C. A. Koelin and James P. Pettegrove. Boston: Beacon Press, 1951.

Castell, Albury. *Mill's Logic of the Moral Sciences: A Study of the Impact of Newtonism on Early Nineteenth Century Social Thought.* Chicago: University of Chicago Libraries, 1936.

Copleston, F. *A History of Philosophy.* New York: Doubleday, 1964.

Davidson, Hugh M. *Audience, Words, and Art: Studies in 17th Century French Rhetoric.* Columbus: Ohio State University Press, 1965.

Drummond, A. M., ed. *Studies in Rhetoric and Public Speaking in Honor of James Albert Winans.* New York: Russell and Russell, 1962.

Golden, James L. and Corbett, Edward P. J. *The Rhetoric of Blair, Campbell, and Whately.* New York: Holt, Rinehart, and Winston, Inc., 1968.

Harper, Nancy L. "The Role of Imagery in Edmund Burke's *Reflections on the Revolution in France*" (A Computer Assisted Analysis). Unpublished Ph.D. dissertation, University of Iowa, 1973.

Howell, Wilbur S. *Eighteenth Century British Logic and Rhetoric.* Princeton: Princeton University Press, 1971.

Humphreys, A. R. *The Augustan World: Society, Thought, and Letters in Eighteenth Century England.* 2nd edition. London: Methuen and Campany, Ltd., 1964.

Jones, W. *A History of Western Philosophy.* 2nd edition. Volume 3: Hobbes to Hume. New York: Harcourt, Brace & World, 1969.

Lamb, John Hall. "John Walker: Elocutionist and Student of the English Language." Unpublished Ph.D. dissertation, University of Iowa, 1964.

Lovejoy, Arthur O. *The Great Chain of Being.* Cambridge: Harvard University Press, 1970.

Maritain, Jacques. *The Dream of Descartes.* Translated by Mabelle L. Andison. New York: Philosophical Library, 1944.

Monk, Samuel H. *The Sublime, A Study of Critical Theory in Eighteenth Century England.* Ann Arbor: University of Michigan Press, 1960.

Ochs, Donovan. " 'Charles Butler on Methods of Persuasion,' A translation with Introduction and Notes." Unpublished Ph.D. dissertation, University of Iowa, 1963.

Randall, Helen Witcomb. *Critical Theory of Lord Kames.* Smith College Studies in Modern Language. Northhampton, Mass. Department of Modern Languages of Smith College, 1944.

Saintsbury, Hugh, *History of Criticism.* New York: Humanities Press, 1961.

Sanford, William Phillipps. *English Theories of Public Address.* Columbus: H. L. Hendrick, 1965.

Schmitz, Robert M. *Hugh Blair.* New york: King's Crown Press, 1948.

Spingarn, J. E. *Critical Essays of the Seventeenth Century.* Bloomington: Indiana University Press, 1968.

Stephen, Sir Leslie. *History of English Thought in the Eighteenth Century.* New York: Harcourt, Brace & World, 1963.

Thomson, David. *England in the Nineteenth Century.* Baltimore: Penguin Books, 1966.

Trevelyan, G. M. *History of England.* New York: Oxford University Press, 1961.

Wallace, Karl R. *Francis Bacon on Communication and Rhetoric.* Chapel Hill: The University of North Carolina Press, 1943.

_____. *A History of Speech Education in America.* New York: Appleton-Century-Crofts, Inc., 1954.

Whitehead, A. *Science and the Modern World.* The Lowell Lectures, 1925. Free Press Paperback Edition. New York: Free Press, 1967.

Willey, Basil. *The Eighteenth Century Background.* Reprint Edition. Boston: Beacon Press, 1940.

Wimsatt, W., Jr. and Brooks, C. *Literary Criticism: A Short History.* New York: Knopf, 1957.

2. Articles

Bacon, Wallace. "The Elocutionary Career of Thomas Sheridan." *Speech Monographs.* (1963), 1–53.

Bevilacqua, Vincent. "Alexander Gerard's Lectures on Rhetoric." *Speech Monographs.* (1967), 384–389.

_____. "Baconian Influences in the Development of Scottish Rhetorical Theory." *Proceedings of the American Philosophical Society.* (1967), 212–218.

_____. "Lord Kame's Theory of Rhetoric." *Speech Monographs.* (1963), 309–327.

Bitzer, Lloyd. "A Re-evaluation of Campbell's Doctrine of Evidence." *Quarterly Journal of Speech.* (1960), 135–140.

Bowers, John Waite. "A Comparative Criticism of Hugh Blair's Essay on Taste." *Quarterly Journal of Speech* (1961) 383–389.

Durham, Weldom. "The Elements of Thomas DeQuincey's Rhetoric." *Speech Monographs.* (1970), 240–248.

Edney, C. W. "Whately on Disposition." *Speech Monographs.* (1954), 227–234.

Ehninger, D. "Campbell, Blair, and Whately Revisited." *Southern Speech Communication Journal.* (1963), 169–182.

_____. "Dominant Trends in English Rhetorical Thought, 1500–1800." *Southern Speech Communication Journal.* (1952), 2–12.

_____. "George Campbell and the Rhetorical Tradition: A Reply to LaRusso." *Western Speech.* (1968), 275–279.

_____. "George Campbell and the Revolution in Inventional Theory." *Southern Speech Communication Journal.* (1950), 270–276.

_____. "John Ward and His Rhetoric." *Speech Monographs.* (1951), 1–16.

_____. "Old Friends in a New Light." *Western Speech.* (1955), 263–269.

Ehninger, Douglas and Golden, James. "The Extrinsic Sources of Blair's Popularity." *Southern Speech Journal.* (1956), 16–32.

_____. "The Intrinsic Sources of Blair's Popularity." *Southern Speech Journal.* (1955), 12–30.

Frandson, Kenneth. "Ward, Adams, and the Classical Rhetoric." *Southern Speech Communication Journal.* (1968), 108–115.

Hauser, Gerard. "Empiricism, Description, and the New Rhetoric." *Philosophy in Rhetoric.* (1972), 24–44.

Hultzen, Lee S. "Charles Butler on Memory." *Speech Monographs.* (1939), 44–65.

Hoshor, J. "Lectures on Rhetoric and Public Speaking by Chauncey Allen Goodrich." *Speech Monographs,* (1947) 1–47.

Howell, Wilbur S. "Adam Smith's Lectures on Rhetoric: An Historical Assessment." *Speech Monographs.* (1969), 393–418.

_____. "DeQuincey on Science, Rhetoric, and Poetry." *Speech Monographs.* (1946), 1–13.

_____. "John Locke and the New Rhetoric." *Quarterly Journal of Speech.* (1967), 319–333.

LaRusso, Dominic. "Root or Branch." *Western Speech.* (Fall, 1968), 86–92.

Leathers, Dale. "Whately's Logically Derived Rhetoric: A Stranger in Its Times." *Western Speech.* (1969), 48–58.

McDermott, Douglass. "George Campbell and the Classical Tradition." *Quarterly Journal of Speech.* (1963), 403–409.

Meersman, Roger, "Pere Rene Rapins' *Eloquence des Belles Lettres.*" *Speech Monographs.* (1971), 290–301.

Newman, John B. "The Phonetic Aspect of Joshua Steele's *System of Prosody.*" *Speech Monographs.* (1951), 279–287.

———. "Joshua Steele's Role in the Development of American Speech Education." *Speech Monographs.* (March, 1953), 65–73.

Parrish, W. M. "Whately and His Rhetoric." *Quarterly Journal of Speech.* (1929), 58–79.

Rahskipf, Horace. "John Quincey Adams: Speaker and Rhetorician." *Quarterly Journal of Speech.* (1946), 435–441.

Reid, Loren. "Gladstone's Essay on Public Speaking." *Quarterly Journal of Speech.* (1953), 265–272.

Reid, Paul. "Francis J. Child: The Fourth Boylston Professor of Rhetoric and Oratory." *Quarterly Journal of Speech.* (1969), 268–275.

Reid Ronald. "The Boyleston Professorship of Rhetoric and Oratory." *Quarterly Journal of Speech.* (1959), 239–257.

———. "John Ward's Influence in America." *Speech Monographs.* (1960), 340–344.

Rogers, Paul. "Alexander Bain and the Rise of the Organic Paragraph." *Quarterly Journal of Speech.* (1965), 399–409.

Wagner, R. H. "Thomas Wilson's Contributions to Rhetoric." *Papers in Rhetoric.* Edited by Donald C. Bryant, Iowa City, Iowa: University of Iowa, 1940.

Weedon, Jerry L. "Locke on Rhetoric and Rational Man." *Quarterly Journal of Speech.* (1970), 378–387.

Winans, James. "Whately on Elocution." *Quarterly Journal of Speech.* (1945), 1–8.

Appendix

A HISTORICAL CHRONOLOGY OF SELECTED AUTHORS AND WORKS

I. CLASSICAL PERIOD

Plato	Gorgias Phaedrus	427–347B.C.
Isocrates	Antidosis Against the Sophists	351 391
Aristotle	Rhetoric Poetics Topics	336(?)
Hermagoras	Art of Rhetoric	150(?)
Cicero	De Inventione De Oratore Topica Orator De Partitiones	87 55 44 46 54
(Anon.)	Rhetorica ad Herrenium	82
Seneca	Controversiae Suasoriae	34A.D.(?)
Tacitus	Dialogue on Oratory	81
Quintilian	Institutes of Oratory	93
Longinus (pseud.)	On the Sublime	100(?)
Hermogenes	Progymnasmata	100–200(?)
Victor, Julius	Ars Rhetorica	300–400(?)
Aphthonius	Progymnasmata	300–400(?)

II. MEDIEVAL AND RENAISSANCE PERIOD

Capella	The Book of Rhetoric	410–429(?)
Augustine	On Christian Doctrine	426
Fortunatianus	Three Books on the Art of Rhetoric	450(?)
Rufinus of Antioch	A Commentary on the Meters Used by the Comic Poets and the Rhythms Used by the Orators	400–500
Boethius	The Consolation of Philosophy An Overview of the Structure of Rhetoric An Examination of the Rhetorical Places	480–524
Priscian of Caesarea	Institutes of Grammar Progymnasmata	500(?)
Cassiodorus Senator	Introduction to Divine and Human Readings	551–560(?)
Isidore of Seville	Etymologies	560–636
The Venerable Bede	Of Schemes and Tropes	701
Al-Baquillani	Rhetorical Figures in Poetry and Qur'an	750(?)
Rabanus Maurus	On the Training of the Clergy	780–856
Alcuin	The Dialogue of Alcuin and Charlemagne Concerning Rhetoric and the Virtues	794
Ibn al-Mu'tazz	Book of Ornate Style	908
Qudama ibn Ja'far	Book of Criticism of Poetry	932
Guibert de Nogent	A Book about the Way a Sermon Ought to Be Given	1084(?)
Alberic of Monte Cassino	Flowers of Rhetoric	1087(?)
Hugh of St. Victor	The Matter of Teaching	1097–1141
Alan of the Isles	A Compendium on the Art of Preaching	1100–1200(?)
John of Salisbury	Metalogicon	1159
Alexander of Ashby	On the Mode of Preaching	1200–1250(?)

Thomas of Salisbury	Summa de arte praedicandi	1200–1250(?)
Geoffrey of Vinsauf	The New Poetics	1210
Thomas Aquinas (pseud.)	The Art of Preaching	1225–1274
Giles of Rome	On the Difference between Rhetoric, Ethics, and Politics	1243–1316
Brunetto Latini	Li Livres dou Tresor	1260(?)
Dante	De vulgari eloquentia	1300(?)
Thomas of Todi	The Art of Giving Sermons and of Preparing Conferences	1350–1400(?)
Valla	Dialactical Disputationes	
Agricola, Rudolph	De Inventione Dialectica Libri Tres	1443–1485
Hawes, Stephen	The Pastime of Pleasure	1509
Erasmus	De Duplici Copia Verborum ac Rerum	1512
	The Praise of Folly	1509
	Apothegms	1542
	Ciceronianus	1528
Melanchton, Phillip	Institutiones Rhetorica Elementorum Rhetorices	1521
Cox, Leonard	The Arte or Crafte of Rhetoryke	1531
Vives, Ludovicus	On Education	1531
Sherry, Richard	Treatise of Schemes & Tropes	1550
Wilson, Thomas	The Rule of Reason	1551
	Arte of Rhetorique	1553
Foclin, Antoine	Rhetorique Francoise	1555
Ramus, Peter	Dialectique	1555
	Dialecticae Libri Duo	1556
Soarez, Cypriano	De Arte Rhetorica	1560
Rainholde, Richard	Foundacion of Rhetorike	1563 (1577)
Ascham, Roger	Scholemaster	1570
Peacham, Henry	Garden of Eloquence (Conteyning the figures of Grammar and Rhetorick)	1577

Talon (Talaeus, Audomarus)	Rhetorica	1584
Fenner, Dudley	The Artes of Logike and Rhetorike	1584
Fraunce, Abraham	The Sheapheardes Logike	1588
	The Lawiers Logike	1588
	Aracadian Rhetorike	1588
Bacon, Francis	The Advancement of Learning	1605
	Novum Organum	1620

III. THE MODERN PERIOD

Cressolles, Louis de	Vacationes Automnales	1620
Vossius	Institutes of Oratory	1622
Farnaby, Thomas	Index Rhetoricus	1625
Butler, Charles	Oratoriae Libri Duo	1629
	Rhetoricae Libri Duo	1598
Descartes, René	Discourse de la Methode	1637
Hobbes, Thomas	A Brief of the Art of Rhetoric	1637
Bulwer, John	Chirologia and Chironomia	1644
Wilkins, John	A Discourse Concerning the Gift of Prayer	1651
	Ecclesiastes: A Discourse Concerning The Gift of Preaching	1646
Hoskins, John	Directions for Speech and Style	1654
Le Faucheur, Michel	Traitte de L'Action de L'Orateur (Essay on the Action of an Orator)	1657
Pascal	Art of Persuasion	1658
Walker, Obediah	Some Instructions Concerning the Art of Oratory	1659
Arnaud, Antoine	La Logique	1662
Sprat, Thomas	History of the Royal Society of London	1667
Lamy, Bernard	De l'Arte de Parler	1675

Glanville, Joseph	An Essay Concerning Preaching	1678
Fenelon	Dialogues on Eloquence	1679 (pub. 1717)
Rapin, Rene	Reflections upon the Eloquence of these Times	1684
Locke, John	An Essay on Human Understanding	1690
	Thoughts Concerning Education	1693
Spinoza	On the Improvement of the Understanding Tractatus Theologico–Politicus Tractatus de Intellectur Emendatione	
Brightland, John	A Grammar of the English Tongue	1712
Rollin, Charles	De la Maniere d'Enseigner et d'Etudier les Belles Lettres	1726–1728
Constable	Reflections on the Accuracy of Style	1734
Holmes, John	The Art of Rhetoric Made Easy	1739
Mason, John	An Essay on Elocution, Or, Pronunciation	1748
A. Smith, Adam	Lectures on Rhetoric and Belles Lettres	1748
Hartley, David	Observations on Man	1749
Lawson, John	Lectures Concerning Oratory	1752
Ward, John	A System of Oratory	1759
Burgh, James	The Art of Speaking	1761
Sheridan, Thomas	Lectures on Elocution	1762
	Lectures on Reading	1775
Lord Kames (Henry Homes)	Elements of Criticism	1762
Rice, John	An Introduction to the Art of Reading with Energy and Propriety	1765
Bayly, Anselm	The Alliance of Music and Poetry	1771

Ogilvie, Richard	Philosophical and Critical Observations on the Nature, Characters, and Various Species of Composition	1774
Gerard, Alexander	Essay on Genius	1774
	Essay on Taste	1759
Steele, Joshua	Prosodia Rationalis (An Essay Towards Establishing the Melody and Measure of Speech to Be Expressed and Perpetuated by Peculiar Symbols)	1775
Enfield, William	The Speaker	1775
Cockin, William	The Art of Delivering Written Language	1775
Campbell, George	The Philosophy of Rhetoric	1776
Hume, David	An Inquiry Concerning Human Understanding	1777
Priestly, Joseph	Lectures on Oratory and Criticism	1777
	Rudiments of English Grammar	1761
Scott, William	Lessons on Elocution	1779
Walker, Obediah	Elements of Elocution	1781
Blair, Hugh	Lectures on Rhetoric and Belles Lettres	1783
Austin, Gilbert	Chironomia, or a Treatise on Rhetorical Delivery	1806
Engel, Johann	Practical Illustrations of Rhetorical Gesture and Action Adapted to the English Drama	1807
Adams, John Quincy	Lectures on Rhetoric and Oratory	1810
Ewing, Thomas	Principles of Elocution	1816
Jamieson, Alexander	Grammar of Rhetoric and Polite Literature	1818
Sharp, Ralph	The Flowers of Rhetoric, the Graces of Eloquence, and the Charms of Oratory	1819
DeQuincey, Thomas	Essays: Style; Rhetoric; Conversation; Language	1823–1858

Howlett, John H.	Instructions in Reading the Liturgy of the United Church of England and Ireland	1826
Whately, Richards	Elements of Rhetoric	1828
Innes, Henry	The Rhetorical Class Book	1834
Langley, Larret	Manual of the Figures of Rhetoric	1835
Gladstone, William	Essay on Public Speaking	1838
Cull, Richard	Garrick's Mode of Reading the Liturgy of the Church of England	1840
Hartley, A. M.	The Academic Speaker	1846
Mill, John Stewart	On Liberty of Thought and Discussion	1859
Spencer, Herbert	Philosophy of Style	1871

Index

Index